The Diaries of
GEORGE WASHINGTON

Volume II

1766–70

ASSISTANT EDITORS

Beverly H. Runge, Frederick Hall Schmidt,
and Philander D. Chase

George H. Reese, CONSULTING EDITOR

Joan Paterson Kerr, PICTURE EDITOR

THE DIARIES OF
GEORGE
WASHINGTON

VOLUME II

1766–70

DONALD JACKSON, *EDITOR*

DOROTHY TWOHIG, *ASSOCIATE EDITOR*

UNIVERSITY PRESS OF VIRGINIA

CHARLOTTESVILLE

This edition has been prepared by the staff of
The Papers of George Washington,
sponsored by
The Mount Vernon Ladies' Association of the Union
and the University of Virginia.

THE UNIVERSITY PRESS OF VIRGINIA

Copyright © 1976 by the Rector and Visitors
of the University of Virginia

First published 1976

Frontispiece: Martha Washington, by John Woilaston.
(Washington and Lee University, Washington-Custis-
Lee Collection)

Library of Congress Cataloging in Publication Data

Washington, George, Pres. U.S., 1732–1799.
    The diaries of George Washington.

    Bibliography: p. 341
    Includes index.
    1. Washington, George, Pres. U.S., 1732–1799.
I. Jackson, Donald Dean, 1919–   II. Twohig, Dorothy. III. Title.

E312.8 1976   973.4'1'0924 [B]   75-41365   ISBN 0-8139-0688-1 (v. 2)

Printed in the United States of America

93071

Administrative Board

Contents

Illustrations

Illustrations

Acknowledgments

The editors' first obligation is to the sponsors and agencies whose financial support and enthusiastic backing made our work possible. The cosponsors of *The Papers of George Washington* are the Mount Vernon Ladies' Association of the Union and the University of Virginia. Our principal governmental support has come from the National Endowment for the Humanities, with strong additional funding from the National Historical Publications and Records Commission. An annual grant from the William Stamps Farish Fund has been most appreciated.

Of the many colleagues at the University of Virginia who assisted in the formation and encouragement of *The Papers of George Washington,* the editors are particularly indebted to former president of the University, Edgar F. Shannon, Jr., and his special assistant Francis L. Berkeley, Jr. All the many others who gave us assistance with the countless details of planning, financing, and day-to-day operation are perhaps best represented by one person, Charles L. Flanders of the Office of the Associate Provost for Research at the University of Virginia.

We are grateful for the interest and encouragement of the Regent of the Mount Vernon Ladies' Association of the Union, and of her predecessor, the late Mrs. Francis F. Bierne. The editors also owe a debt of gratitude to the Mount Vernon staff, especially Charles C. Wall, resident director; John A. Castellani, librarian; Frank E. Morse, librarian emeritus; Robert B. Fisher, horticulturist, and Christine Meadows, curator.

For assistance in research on Washington's diaries, we would like to thank the staff of the Manuscript Division, Library of Congress, the research staff of the Colonial Williamsburg Foundation, and members of the Virginia Division of Parks. The Alderman Library at the University of Virginia has housed our editorial offices and its staff has graciously and efficiently performed all the library services essential to an editorial project.

The reproduction of Washington's diaries in these volumes has

Acknowledgments

been made possible by the cooperation of the following repositories and individuals who own the original manuscript material:
the Library of Congress, Columbia University Libraries, the Detroit Public Library, Mount Vernon, John K. Paulding, the Historical Society of Pennsylvania, the Virginia Historical Society,
and the Public Record Office, London.

Our typographic consultant for general design is P. J. Conk-
wright, of Princeton, N.J.

The editors acknowledge with appreciation the industry and
competence of the following members of the research and clerical
staff who over a period of several years were directly involved in
the laborious task of transcribing and checking the Washington
diaries: Lynne Crane, Dana K. Levy, Patricia Waddell, Corinne
Poole, Jessie Shelar, Kathleen Howard, Patricia De Berry, Roger
Lund, Barbara Morris, Cynthia S. Miller, Christine Hughes,
Nancy Morris, and Karen Whitehill.

Editorial Procedures and Symbols

Transcription of the diaries has remained as faithful as possible to the original manuscript. Because of the nature of GW's diary entries, absolute consistency in punctuation has been virtually impossible. Where feasible, the punctuation has generally been retained as written. However, in cases where sentences are separated by dashes, a common device in the eighteenth century, the dash has been changed to a period and the following word capitalized. Dashes which appear after periods have been dropped. Periods have been inserted at points which are clearly the ends of sentences. In many of the diaries, particularly those dealing with planting and the weather, entries consist of phrases separated by dashes rather than sentences. Generally if the phrase appears to stand alone, a period has been substituted for the dash.

Spelling of all words is retained as it appears in manuscript. Errors in spelling of geographic locations and proper names have been corrected in notes or in brackets only if the spelling in the text makes the word incomprehensible. Washington occasionally, especially in the diaries, placed above an incorrectly written word a symbol sometimes resembling a tilde, sometimes an infinity sign, to indicate an error in orthography. When this device is used the editors have silently corrected the word.

The ampersand has been retained. The thorn has been transcribed as "th." The symbol for per has been written out. When a tilde is used to indicate either a double letter or missing letters, the correction has been made silently or the word has been transcribed as an abbreviation. Capitalization is retained as it appears in the manuscript; if the writer's intention is not clear, modern usage is followed.

Contractions and abbreviations are retained as written; a period is inserted after abbreviations. When an apostrophe has been used in contractions it is retained. Superscripts have been lowered, and if the word is an abbreviation a period has been added. When the meaning of an abbreviation is not obvious, it has been expanded in square brackets: H[unting] C[reek]; so[uther]ly.

Other editorial insertions or corrections in the text also appear in square brackets. Missing dates are supplied in square brackets in diary entries. Angle brackets (< >) are used to indicate mutilated material. If it is clear from the context what word or words are missing, or missing material has been filled in from other sources, the words are inserted between the angle brackets.

A space left blank by Washington in the manuscript of the diaries is indicated by a bracketed gap in the text. In cases where Washington has crossed out words or phrases, the deletions have not been noted. If a deletion contains substantive material it appears in a footnote. Words inadvertently repeated or repeated at the bottom of a page of manuscript have been dropped.

If the intended location of marginal notations is clear, they have been inserted in the proper place without comment; otherwise, insertions appear in footnotes.

In cases where the date is repeated for several entries on the same day, the repetitive date has been omitted and the succeeding entries have been paragraphed.

Because Washington used the blank pages of the *Virginia Almanack* or occasionally small notebooks to keep his diaries, lack of space sometimes forced him to make entries and memoranda out of order in the volume. The correct position of such entries is often open to question, and the editors have not always agreed with earlier editors of the diaries on this matter. Such divergence of opinion, however, has not been annotated.

Bibliographical references are cited by one or two words, usually the author's last name, in small capitals. If two or more works by authors with the same surname have been used, numbers are assigned: HARRISON [2]. Full publication information is included in the bibliography for each volume. The symbols used to identify repositories in the footnotes precede the bibliography.

Surveying notes and dated memoranda kept in diary form have not been included in this edition of Washington's diaries, although the information contained in them has often been used in annotation.

The Diaries of
GEORGE WASHINGTON
Volume II
1766–70

Sowing and Harvesting

1766

January

14. Flax at the Mill put out to Rot.

18. Flax at Doeg Run put out to Rot.

March

21. Sowed Hemp about the old Tobo. House at Muddy hole.
Note, the latter part of Feby., & all Mar. till the 19th. was extreamely wet and disagreeable—scarce two fair days together & sometimes hard Frosts, insomuch that neither Hoe nor Plow coud be stuck into the Ground, which prevented my sowing Hemp till the 21st. as above.

22. Began to sow Hemp (adjoining the Lane going to Mrs. Wades) at the Mill. Sowed as far as a stick drove into the Ground.
Also sowed Ditto in the lower part of new Ground at Muddy hole—to a stake.
First part of this day warm Sun & southerly Wind. Latter part showery—high Wind at same place.

Mrs. Valinda Wade, widow of Zephaniah Wade (died c. 1746), lived with her three daughters, Valinda, Sarah, and Eleanor, on a 193-acre tract of land adjoining GW's mill plantation.

23. High wind at No. Wt.—cold & Cloudy.

24. Sowed Hemp at Muddy hole to the second stake.
Hard frost—clear, but very cold the first part of the day—the Wind being at No. West.

25. Hard frost—afterwards warm & hazy. Wind Southwardly.
Sowed Hemp at Muddy hole to the third Stake, and at the Mill to the Second stake.

26. Constant close Rain, from sometime in Night till 3 in the afternoon. Wind at North East—when it shifted to No. Wt. but did not blow hard.

[1]

27.   Cloudy, Wind at No. Wt. but not hard, nor very cold. Ground exceeding wet. No Hemp sowed this day.

28.   Sowed Hemp at Muddy hole to the 4th. stake. Ground too wet. No Hemp sowed elsewhere.
   Wind Westerly, with Clouds, & Raw.

29.   Sowed Hemp at Muddy hole to the 5th. Stake & at Doeg Run (in the Orchard round Gists House) to the first (beginng. at that end of it next the Gate). Hoeing in Farm Dung at the Mill.
   Wind at No. West, with some Clouds, & Cool.

30.   Cool, & Cloudy all the day. Wind Northwardly.

31.   Sometimes cloudy but warm and pleasant. Wind at South.

April

1st.   Sowed Hemp at Muddy hole to the Road—at the Mill to the 3d. Stake—and finished the Orchard at Doeg Run.
   Wind at up No. Et. & very cloudy the whole day. At one O'clock it sat in to Raining which at 6 turnd to Snow.

The April entries in this diary are missing from the diary at DLC. The entries of 1–8 April are taken from a facsimile in the Toner collection at DLC and those of 9–13 April from a transcript in the same collection.

2.   Day warm & fine. Wind Northwardly in the Morning—Southwardly afterwards. Ground too wet to prepare for or Sow in Hemp.

3.   Sowed Hemp at Muddy hole to the first Stake (beging. at the [   ]and next the woods) —at the Mill to The 4th. stake— and at Doeg Run (by the Lane) to 1st. stake beginng. at the great Mulberry.
   Clear & pleasant—but not warm—the Wind being Northwardly in the forenoon—calm in the Evening.

4.   Sowed Hemp at Muddy hole to the 2d. stake, at the Mill to the 5th. & at Doeg Run to the 2.
   Hazy—Wind Southwardly & Rain. At 6 in the afternoon began to Rain. Ground full Wet for sowing, or Working before.

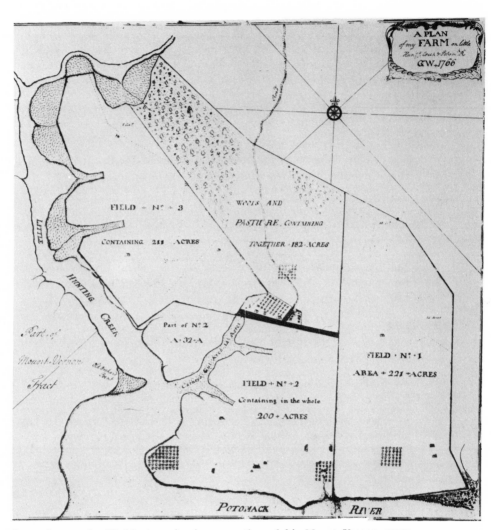

An early map by Washington, showing a portion of his Mount Vernon estate. From *George Washington Atlas,* Washington, D.C., 1932. (Rare Book Department, University of Virginia Library)

5.   Constant Rain all Night, and till 10 O'clock this day (Wind hard at No. Et.) & cloudy afterwards. At 6 in the Evening sat into close Raining again. No Hemp sowd to day.

6.   Wind at No. Et. & raining all day – Sunday.

7.   Raining till 10 Oclock – very cloudy afterwards till Night when it began to Rain again. Wind at No. East. Ground exceeding wet.

8.   Cloudy the first part of the day – wind westwardly. Ground very wet.

9.   Clear, wind hard at Northwest. Sowed Hemp at the mill to the 6th. stake. None sowed elsewhere – ground too wet.

10.   Fine clear day till late in the afternoon when it cleared. Being little wind Sowed Hemp at the mill in the 7th. stake at Muddy hole to the 3d stake. At dog Run none sowed.

11.   Cloudy, with light showers all day, wind briskly from the Southard. Sowed Hemp at the Mill to the 8th. stake – at Muddy hole to the 4th. & at Dog Run to the third.
   Sowed a little Flax by the Peach orchd. Ground very wet.

12.   Sowed Hemp at the Mill – none elsewhere ground being wet. Clear wind Northwardly.

13.   Sunday – clear & warm – wind South.

On this day GW set out for the lower Tidewater, stopping at Fredericksburg to pick up Fielding Lewis. After stopping at Eltham, they crossed the James River and visited the Dismal Swamp. They then returned to spend a week at Eltham and in Williamsburg, where GW settled some accounts, including the purchase of two indentured servants. GW was back at Mount Vernon by 10 May.

June

16.   Began to cut my Meadows at Home.

GW hired an extra hand, Thomas Plummit, who worked seven days on the mowing at 2s. 6d. per day (LEDGER A, 232).

25.   Finishd Do. & brought it into Barnes. Weather often Raining – Hay hurt.

26.   Began to Cut my Timothy Meadow at Doeg Run & did not finish it till the 8th. of July—the Weather being Rainy & bad—which almost spoil'd 30,000 weight of Hay.

July

3.   Cut my early Wheat behind Garden.

7.   Began to cut Wheat in the Neck with the hands there.

8.   Set into it with my whole force & two Cradlers hired. My Hay at D. Run finishd yesterday.

The two hired cradlers were James and Daniel Starke, who worked about 2½ weeks for 5s. per day each. GW also hired another helper, Amoriah Bonham, for a total of 23 days, which apparently was the duration of the harvesting. Bonham was also paid 5s. per day (LEDGER A, 232, 234).

9.   My Schooner arrivd at Colchester.

12.   Finished cuttg. binding & shocking Wheat in the Neck—152 Bushels sowing.

GW has added the following additional entries out of order in the diary. In the manuscript he placed them between 21 and 22 July.
"5. Pull'd my flax at home.
 7. Pulld two patches at Doeg Run.
 8. Put part of what I pulld at Home in Water.
12. Took it out, & spread it on the Green."

14.   Began Harvest at Muddy hole.

15.   Finished it—in Shocks 75 Bushels sowing.

16.   Began and finishd at the Mill, in shocks 52 bushels Sowing.

17.   Began Harvest at Doeg Run. My Schooner also came up with 10,031 feet of Plank from Occoquan Saw Mills.

Among the group of mills established on Occoquan Creek were two sawmills, which at this time were being operated by John Semple (see main entry for 23 Jan. 1770).

21.   Securd all my Harvest in shocks at D[ogue] R[un].

[5]

22 .   Put into the House.

23.   Sowed Turneps in the flax patch at Home. Also sowed Do. at Muddy hole and ditto at Morris's.

24.   Pulld a small patch of Flax at Doeg Run.

25.   Began to Sow Turneps in Drills behind Quarter.

26.   Sowed Do. in Do.—Do.

27.   Sowed a few Do. Do.—Do. Hard Rain 28 & 9.

30.   Sowed Do. in Neck.

31.   Finishd Sowing behind Quartr. in Drills.

August

1.   Began to Sow Wheat at the Mill.
Began to Sow Do. in the Neck in the upper part of the field.

6.   Began to Sow Do. at Muddy hole.
Finished Sowg. Do. in clovr. patch at the Mill—9 Bushels.

22.   Began to Sow Wheat at Doeg Run.
Finishd Sowing up Cut in the Neck.

25—26. 27. & 28.   Spreading flax at Home.

28.   Finishd sowing Wheat altogether at the Mill 46½ Bushls. the other side—in all 55½ Bl.

29.   Finishd Sowing the Field by the Meadow at Doeg Run—26 Bushels.
Stopd sowing Wheat at Muddy hole & Doeg Run. Sowed 108 at the first place 18 Bl. in little fd.
Began to pull Hemp at the Mill and at Muddy hole—too late for the blossom Hemp by three Weeks or a Month.

[September]

4. 5. & 6th.   Spreading flax at Doeg Run.
Do. Do. pulling Peas at Ho[me] House.

PULLING PEAS: *Lathyrus sativus*, field pea, of which GW tried many varieties. His diaries and other farm records refer to the crowder pea; early, or "forward," pea; red pea; small white pea; small round pea; small gray pea; Yateman pea; and the "Albany or field pea," which persisted through more than a decade of GW's crop experiments. His diary entry for 16 April 1785 indicates a planting of the Albany variety, and he wrote Thomas Jefferson 6 July 1796 that it grew well but was subject to the same insect pests as the garden pea. The field pea differs from the cowpea, *Vigna sinensis*, of which the best known is the black-eyed variety, which GW called the Indian pea.

8.   Began to Cut my Meadows a Second time.

10.   Began to get Fodder at Muddy hole Quarter & at the Mill.

12.   Began to get Fodder in the Neck.

15.   Do.–Do.–Do.–at Doeg Run. Turnd flax at Home House.

27.   Finishd getting & securing fodder at the Mill.

30.   Ditto–Ditto at Doeg Run–that is, exclusive of what belonged to that Plantation at the River Quarter.

October

1st. 2, 3, & 4.   Sowing Wheat Doeg Run.

2.   Finished getting & securing Fodder at Muddy hole.

3.   Getting Peas at Ditto–too late a good many of which being rotten on the Ground.

3 & 4.   Continued Sowing Wheat at Do.

4.   Finishd Sowing the little field at Doeg Run with 16 Bls.

6.   Put my English Ram Lamb to 65 Ewes. Sheep at home as follows viz.

Old Ewes	64
Ewe Lambs	1
Old Weathers	18
Young Do. this yrs. Lbs.	11
1 Ram Lamb Engh.	1
	95 in all

Sent 33 Ewe Lambs to Doeg Run &
   2 Rams, 1 of them this yrs. Lamb.
   ‾‾‾
   35 in all.

⟨8.⟩   Finishd getting & securing Fodder in the Neck also that which belongd to Doeg Run there.

9.   Sowed a piece of Hemp Gd. at the Mill in wheat 2½ Bls. which makes in all th⟨r.⟩ 58 B.

25.   Finishd Sowing large field with [   ] Bls.
   Finishd Sowing Wheat at Muddy hole – 170 Bushels in all – 18 of wch. white Wheat in the little field.

Mostly the Weather

1767

[February]

1. Cloudy & Cool in the forenoon & till towards night. Wind at No. West. Gd. not froze.

2. Frozen Morning, clear still & pleast. afterwards.

3. Frozen morning. Clear, pleast. & thawing afterwards. Wind risg. from So. Wt.

4. Frozen—clear & Windy abt. 10, from the Northwest but thawing.

5. Soft, calm, & pleasant. Wind rising from No. West abt. 10 & blew hard but not cold.

6. Frozen morning. Clear & cold Wind still at No. West & fresh.

7. Frozen Morng., brisk & cold Wind from the Southward. Clear till the Afternoon then cloudy. In the Evening clear again.

8. Soft, clear, & Warm. Wind Southwardly.

9. Soft, warm & Lowering, high Wind from the Southward. Hard rain in the Night.

10. Soft, cloudy & light showers of Hail Rain &ca. till ten Oclock—then excessive hard Wind from No. West. Cold.

11. Frozen & cloudy morning. Afterwards clear Wind Southwardly.

12. Soft & cloudy till Noon. Afterwards clear & still. Wind No[rth]wardly in Mg.

13. Soft Morning & snowing all day more or less from the Northward.

14. Hazy in the Morng. Clear afterwards; w. hard wind from the No. West. Snow abt. 3 or 4 Inches deep.

15. Hard frost. Wind Westwardly & then Southwardly & cloudy.

16. Grey & frosty Morning. Wind Southwardly & thawing. Also clear afterwd.

17. Clear & cool. Wind at No. West. Morng. frozen thawing afterwards.

18. Frozen Morning. Thawing afterwards & pleasant tho somewhat Cool. Wind No. & No. Et.

19. Soft Morng. Somewhat Cloudy & still.

20. Soft Morng. Brisk wind from So. Wt. with which the Ground much dried. Snow all gone two days ago.

21. Ground not froze. Wind came to No. Wt. early in the Morning & blew very hard & turnd very cold towards Evening.

22. Ground froze. Clear, wind Southward & Warm.

23. Cloudy with spits of Snow first part of the day. Raining afterwards with the Wind at No. Et. In the Night Snow again which covd. the ground abt. an Inch.

24. Cloudy & Cold Wind at No. West.

25. Hard frost. Clear & not very cold. Wind at No. West—not high.

26. Brisk wind from the Southward. Clear warm & pleasant. According to Colo. West the greatest part of the next Moon shoud be as this day—i.e. the same kind of weather that happens upon the thursday before the change will continue through the course of the next Moon at least the first & 2d. quarter of it. Quere is not this an old woman's story.

27. Soft clear, warm, & Still.

28. Soft, Mild & pleasant. Wind Southwardly. Somewhat hazy & smoky. A little rain in the Night.

[February]

13th.   Vestry to meet by 2d. appointmt.

Some of GW's diary entries, such as these three in February, are appointment reminders rather than a record of occurrences. The vestry of Truro Parish met on 23 Feb.

16th.   Vestry to meet at Pohick.

26.   Sale of Colo. Colvills Negroes.

Thomas Colvill had died in 1766, and these slaves apparently were sold to pay some of his debts. On his deathbed Colvill had persuaded GW to be one of his executors by assuring him that he would be expected only to give his good name to the administration of the will and to check occasionally on its progress, while the actual work was done by the other executors: Colvill's wife Frances (d. 1773) and John West, Jr., husband of Colvill's niece Catherine. As it happened, the estate was so troublesome and Mrs. Colvill and West proved to be so unequal to their task that GW had to take an active part in the matter, which was to plague him until 1797 (GW to Bushrod Washington, 10 Feb. 1796, DLC:GW). One difficulty was that Colvill had left legacies to English relatives who could not be easily identified and whose confusing claims were almost impossible to authenticate. A second problem was that in May 1765 Colvill, as executor for his brother John, had sold Merryland, a 6,300-acre tract in Frederick County, Md., to John Semple of Prince William County, Va., for £2,500 sterling. That sum was to have paid John's debts, including £742 owed to Thomas, but Semple gave a bond for the £2,500, which he was later unwilling or unable to honor. Thus, neither Colvill estate could be settled until some agreement could be reached with the contentious Semple (see main entry for 31 Dec. 1771; GW to William Peareth, 20 Sept. 1770, DLC:GW).

March

1st.   Soft mild, still, & pleasant. Somewhat cloudy.

2.   (No frost) Cloudy till abt. 11 Oclock then Rain & almost all Night very hard Wind at No. Et.

3.   Fine clear Morning & Warm Wind southwardly. Cloudy abt. 1 Oclock & at 3 began to Rain hard & constant.

4.   Soft morning. Clear day, & very high wind from No. West but not cold.

5.   Clear, warm & pleast. forenoon. Wind southwardly. Afterwards hazy & lowerg.

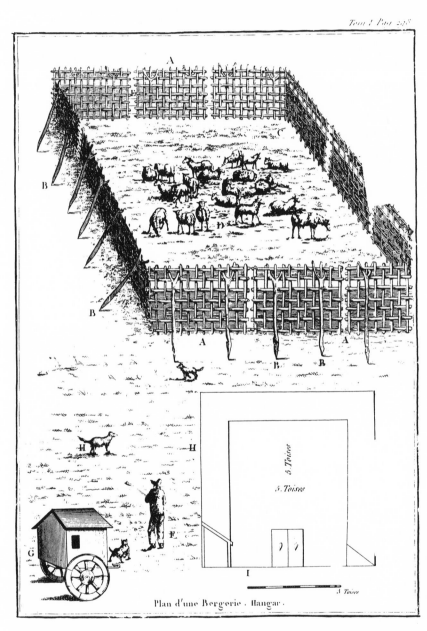

Plan d'une Bergerie . Hangar .

This typical sheepfold was designed to be moved easily to better grazing land. From *La Nouvelle Maison rustique,* Paris, 1798. (Mount Vernon Ladies' Association of the Union)

6. Raining constantly the whole day. Wind at No. Et. but not cold.

7. Wind in the same place & Raing. more or less all day.

8. Flying clouds in the forenoon. Wind brisk from the No[rth]-ward. Clear afternn.

9. Lowering Morning. Clear afternoon. Wind southwardly.

10. Fine, clear & mild day. Wind for the most part Westwardly & No. West.

11. Turnd cold abt. 10 oclock & after spittg. snow—wind hard at No. West.

12. Ground hard froze; wind high at No. West. Often spittg. snow in the forenoon & very cold.

13. Ground very hard froze & exceedg. Cold. Wind hard at No. West & clear.

14. Ground exceeding hard froze & cold in the Morning but pleasant afterwards, clear. Wind Westward.

15. Clear & tolerably pleasant. Wind westwardly. Little frost.

16. Little frost again but exceedg. pleast. Afterwards wind at south West.

17. Fine & Pleasant. Very warm wind at So. West.

18. Wind at No. Et. Somewhat cool in the Morning. Cloudy in the afternoon with Thunder Lightning—Hail Rain & Snow.

19. Cloudy & cold. Wind Northwardly.

20. Continual Rain. Wind at No. East.

21. Constant & hard Rain till 11 Oclock. Wind Southwardly. Afterwds. Westwd. & clear.

22. Clear. Wind westwardly & South[ward]ly.

23.   Clear Morning. Cloudy afterwds. Wind Southwardly, & eastwardly.

24.   Cloudy Morning. Abt. 11 Constant Rain & contind. till 5. Wind varying.

25.   Fine & clear. Wind Southw[ard]ly & brisk.

26.   Clear & pleasant tho cool.

27.   Clear pleast. & warm. Wind Southwardly & fresh.

28.   Clear but cool. Wind fresh from the No. Et.—exceeding hard in the Evening—with Rain all Night.

29.   Rain till 9 Oclock. Cloudy the remainder of the day with a brisk eastwardly Wind.

30.   Cloudy all day. Wind at No. East and cold.

31.   Cloudy, raw, & disagreeable Wind continuing at No. East.

April

16.   Sowed a little flax at Muddy hole.

18.   Sowed a little more of Do. by the Road at Ditto.

21.   Began to Plant Corn in the Neck & at the Mill.

27.   Began to Plant Ditto at Doeg Run & Muddy hole.
   Sowed behind the Quarter 1320 sqr. yds. of flax with a little more than a Peck of Seed.
   Sowed the same quantity of Ground along side of the flax with little more than 1/2 Bushel of Hemp Seed.

29.   Sowed more flax seed behind the quarter.

30.   Planted Irish Potatoes behind Do.

Solanum tuberosum, Irish potato. GW's plantings included red potatoes and white, with small and large varieties of each, grown both as a table product and a field crop. He instructed Anthony Whitting 4 Nov. 1792 to plant them early so they could be harvested before the planting of wheat on the same ground. More commonly he planted potatoes with corn. Thomas Jefferson described GW's method in this way: "He puts them in alternate drills, 4 f. apart, so that the rows of corn are 8 f. apart, & a single stalk every 18 i. or 2 f. in the row" (Jefferson to Thomas Mann Randolph, 11 Aug. 1793, DLC: Jefferson Papers).

April

1. Fine clear morning. Cloudy & cold afterwards. Wind at No. Et. all day.

2. Cloudy morng. Hard & violent Rain from 10 Oclock till 4. Wind Eastwardly.

3. Clear morning. Somewhat cloudy in the Afternoon. Wind at So. West.

4. Wind at So. West and pleasant tho sometimes lowering.

5. Weather lowering. Wind at No. Et. & Eastwardly all day. At Night Rain but not much.

6. Wind at No. East & very cloudy till abt. Noon—then constant Rain but not hard the remaindr. of the day & all Night.

7. Very cloudy & drizley all day. Wind still Eastwardly.

8. Cloudy & Misty till abt. Noon then clear, wind abt. So. West. In the Afternoon Cloudy & Rain again with Rain in the Night. Wind at East.

9. Clear middle day. Eveng. & morng. Cloudy with Rain & heavy Rain at Night. Wind So. West.

10. Clear and cloudy alternately with some Rain & variable wind. Rain.

11. Clear & pleasant tho somewhat cool. Winds Northwardly.

12. Morning clear. Wind very high from So. West. Afterwards cloudy with frequent showers of Rain & hail.

13. Clear & cool. Wind at No. West.

14. Clear Morning. Cloudy & threatng. Afternoon. Wind at So. West.

15. Clear Morng. Wind at No. West & afterwards Southwardly.

16. Grey Morning. Clear Noon. Lowering Afternoon. Wind varying—chiefly Northwardly.

17. Clear with the Wind Eastwardly & cool.

18. Lowering with intervening sunshine till 5 Oclock then very cloudy & hard shower of Rain for 10 or 15 Minutes & high gust of Wind from So. West where it was all day.

19. Wind at No. West & cool in the Morng. Afterwards still clear & very warm.

20. Wind Eastwardly & fresh all day with some Showers of Rain in the Afternoon.

21. Cloudy with some gleams of Sunshine & Showers in the Afternoon. Wind very high & boisterous the whole day from South Et.

22. Squaly kind of a day. Wind mostly at So. West & fresh with some showers of Rain & hail & cool their falling a good deal of Rain at Night.

23. Clear Morning & cool. Wind Westwardly. Rainy afternoon.

24. Wind for the most part of the day at No. Et. & cloudy. Afternoon clear the whole day cool.

25. Clear. Wind at No. West & moderate.

26. Clear. Wind Nor[th]wardly—moderate & pleasant.

27. Clear, still, warm & pleast. Wind what little there was Southwardly.

28. Very warm & pleast. Wind So. Westwardly with clouds & appearances of Rain in the Afternoon.

29.　Warm & pleasant. Wind Southwestwardly till abt. 7 Oclock then fresh from No. East & Wind cold.

30.　Cold Raw & cloudy. Wind Eastwardly. Rain in the Night.

[May]

8.　Sowed Flax at Muddy hole.

9.　My Schooner returnd.

11.　Finishd plantg. Corn in the Neck & began with 4 plows to break up the 5 foot cut.

12.　Finishd plantg. Corn at the Mill, & began to break up the field round the Overseers House.
　　Cut 22 old Rams in the Neck & began to shear my Sheep.

14.　Finishd plantg. Corn at Muddy Hole.

16.　Finishd plantg. at Doeg Run.
　　Sowed flax at Muddy Hole.
　　Finishd breakg. up the 5 foot cut in N. with 4 plows two days & 5 plows almost 3 days. Made in all abt. 20 days work.

18.　Sowed flax at Muddy hole by the Pond.
　　Also began to plow Corn at Doeg Run with 3 plows.
　　Set into plowing at Muddy hole w. 3 plows – 1 plow has been at work a day or two there.

22.　Sale of the Glebe 18 Months Credt.

The sale of the Truro Parish glebe (and church plate) was necessitated by the creation of Cameron Parish (1749) and Fairfax Parish (1765) out of Truro and was authorized by an act of the assembly passed in Nov. 1766 (HENING, 8:202), which provided for an equal division of the parish property among the three parishes. As a churchwarden GW was responsible for running the sale, and on this date he went to the glebe with the vestry and sold the glebe and plate to Daniel McCarty, who in turn donated the plate back to Truro Parish. The income from this sale was split among Truro, Cameron, and Fairfax parishes.

23.　Morris finishd plowing his first cut (Doeg Run) with 3 plows by 12 oclock.

Finishd plowg. the 5½ foot cut in the Neck with 4 plows, & replanted this & the 5 foot cut there.

25. Early Wheat at Muddy hole beginng. to head—that is the heads of some out some bursting the blade & others swelling Do.

26. Sowd. Hemp over again with near 5 pecks of Seed—the first comg. up much too thin.

28. Finishd plowing the 3–9 Inch cut in the Neck.

29. Finishd plowg. all the Mill Corn.

30. Finishd plowg. the other Cut in the Neck.

May

1. Cloudy & cool in the Morning. Wind Eastwardly. Clear & warm afterwards till 5. Wind Southwardly—then Eastwardly again.

2. Cool in the Morning. Wind Eastwardly. Clear & pleasant afterwards.

3. Cloudy. Wind at So. Et. & fresh. Rain in the Night but not much.

4. Hard Rain early in the morning. Wind abt. So. Et. & fresh with Clouds. Afternoon Rainy with hard wind & Hail from So. West.

5. Very cold & cloudy. Wind hard from No. West & West.

6. Clear and cool. Wind at No. West & hard.

7. Clear & warm. Wind southwardly till about Sunset—then No. East.

8. Still the first part of the day. Wind Eastwardly afterwards & cool—with flyg. Clouds.

9. Cloudy more or less all day. Wind at No. Et. & cool.

10. Wind at No. East. Cool & clear.

11. Clear. Wind Northwardly & cool.

12. Clear. Wind Do. & warmer.

13. Warm & still. Wind what little there is Southwardly.

14. Very warm clear & still. Wind what there was of it South-wardly.

15. Warm & clear. Wind brisk from abt. SS. Wt.

16. Brisk Wind from same place in the Morning. Cloudy & still afternoon.

17. Cloudy & lowering till the Afternoon. Wind southwardly then clear & cool wind Northwardly.

18. Clear. Wind Southwardly in the Morning. Afternoon cloudy & likely for Rain but went of with cold No[rthw]ardly Wind.

19. ⟨Wind⟩ Southwardly, clear & some⟨what⟩ cool.

20. Cloudy & sometimes dropping of Rain in the forenoon with the Wind Southwardly. Afterwards clear. Wd. at No. West & Cool.

21. Very cloudy all day. Wind at No. Et. and very cool.

22. Cloudy till Noon with the Wind at No. Et. then Sunshine & somewhat warmer, afterwards cloudy with Lightning & rumbling in the No. West.

23. A little Rain in the Night with lightning & pretty loud thunder. Morng. Cloudy, as it was all day. Abt. 10 Oclock a fine shower fell with thunder & lightning for an hour. Wind variable but not cold.

24. Good Rain in the Night. Cloudy & often drisling till the Afternoon when it cleard. Wind for the most part at No. Et. but not cold.

25.   Clear & pleast. Wind Southwdly. & warm.

26.   Lowering & warm, wind South.

27.   Clear – cool in the morning. Wind at No. West. Afterwards very warm & still.

28.   Wind Southwardly. Warm, & cloudy in the afternoon with lightning.

29.   Rain last night, but not much, then refreshing Shower. Calm & warm in the Morning. Clear & cool afterwards. Wind at No. Wt.

30.   Clear. Wind southwardly & warm.

31.   Clear. Wind abt. So. West & warm.

June

1st.   Wind abt. So. West & warm. Cloudy in the afternoon & some Rain (in Fredk.).

2.   Cloudy with Rain & thunder in the Morning. Afterwards clear – in Fred.

3.   Clear & warm – in Fredk.

4.   Do. & very warm – Do.

5.   Do. – Do. – travelling down.

6.   Do. & extreame Hot. Wind what little there was Southwardly.

7.   Very hot & Sultry. Wind Southwardly. Some Clouds & a little thunder in the Afternoon.

8.   Wind ⟨at No.⟩ West but warm in the Evening.

9.   Wind Northwardly with much appearances of Rain in the fore noon but none near home.

10.   Very warm & Sultry but no Rain. Wind for the most part Eastwardly but little of it.

11.   Exceeding warm & but little wind wch. blew from the So[uth]ward. In the Evening a refreshing shower from the Westward for abt. 15 Minutes with severe lightning & thunder none of wch. or very little reachd. either Doeg Run or the Mill.

12.   Exceeding Sultry. Little or no Wind.

13.   Very warm. In the Afternoon a fine Shower here & in the Neck but little at the Mill again, less at Doeg Run & not much at Muddy h[ole.]

14.   Very warm with some appearance of Rain but none fell hereabouts.

15.   Warm with Do. Do.

16.   Cooler wind at No. West & clear.

17.   Cool wind at No. West in the Morning. In the Afternoon at No. Et. & cloudy.

18.   Drisling till abt. 9 Oclock then constt. & close Rain for abt. an hour or two—this pretty genl. & wet the gd. very well. Wind abt. So. Wt. & warm.

19.   Wind Northwardly & warm.

20.   But little Wind & variable. Warm and grewing weather.

21.   Exceeding warm & still.

22.   Warm. Wind Southwardly.

23.   Wind Southwardly & not very warm.

24.   Wind Southwardly & hot. Morng. cloudy as was the Afternoon with some thunder. In the Night a fine shower of Rain. Less at Doeg Run than elsewhe.

25.   Warm wind Southwardly, with a good shower of Rain abt. 3 Oclock.

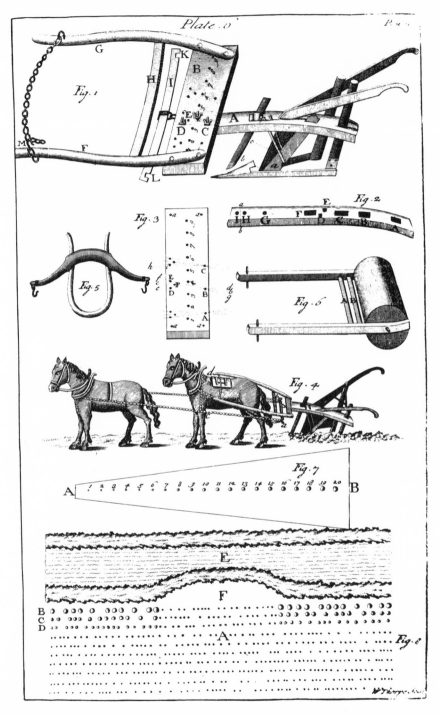

Washington copied material from Jethro Tull's *Horse-Hoeing Husbandry*, London, 1733, into his diaries for ready reference. (Beinecke Rare Book and Manuscript Library, Yale University)

26. Cool & pleast. morng. Wind Northwardly afterwards, still & warm.

27. Pleasant in the Morning, Wind Southwardly. Warm & still afterwards.

28. Clear. Wind Eastwardly & not very warm.

29. Clear & warm. Wind Southwardly.

30. Wind Southwardly & exceeding hot. Little rain in the Evening wth. some thunder and a good deal of Lightning.

[June]

22. Pulled some Flax & put it into the water at the Wharf at Night.

23. Finishd setting Corn at Muddy hole & Doeg Run.

24. Began to cut Wheat at Muddy hole. Note—the straw of a good deal of wch. was green.

27. Took out & spread the flax this Morng.

July

14. Finishd my Wheat Harvest.

16. Began to cut my Timothy Meadow which had stood too long.

25. Finishd Ditto.
   Sowed Turnep seed from Colo. Fairfax's in sheep pens at the House.
   Sowed Winter Do. from Colo. Lees in the Neck.

26. Waggon to be down.

27. Began to Sow Wheat at the Mill with the early White Wheat wch. grew at Muddy hole.

28.   Began to Sow Wheat at Muddy hole with the mixd Wheat that grew there.

Also began to Sow Wheat at Doeg Run of the red Chaff from Home.

Also sowed Summer Turnep behd. Garden.

29.   Sowed Colo. Fairfax's kind in Flax Gd. joing. sheep pens.

July

1st.   Clear and very Cool. Wind at No. West.

2.   Do. Do. Do.

3.   Do. Do. Do.

4.   Still & somewhat warmer.

5.   Winds varying. Cool & cloudy.

6.   Winds Southwardly. Cool & cloudy with a good shower of Rain in the Night.

7.   Cool & clear, wind No. West.

8.   Do. Do. Do.

9.   Clear & still but not hot.

10.   Brisk Southwest Wind with clouds & a small sprinkle of Rain in the Afternoon.

11.   Brisk southwest Wind in the forenoon. Very warm Afternoon with light Rain introduced with high Wind from No. West.

12.   Southwardly Wind & clear.

13.   Clear & pleasant. Wind northwardly in the morning.

14.   Clear and not very warm. Wind Southwardly.

15.   Clear with the Wind at South Wt.

16.   Warm & woud have been Sultry but for a pleasant breeze fm. S.W.

17.   Very warm with the Wind at So. West. In the Afternoon a fine Rain.

18.   Clear. Wind No[rth]wardly.

19.   Ditto—Do. Do. and Cool.

20.   Cloudy & Cool. Wind Eastwardly with a little light Rain.

21.   Rainy & Misty all day. Wind Eastwardly. Gd. very wet.

22.   Cloudy & warm first part of the day with Rain in the Aftern.

23.   Warm and pleasant, growg. Weathr.

24.   Very warm and still.

25.   Cloudy & warm the first of the day—with Rain for some hours in the Afternoon.

26.   Cloudy with Rain now & then but not hard. Wind Southwardly & warm.

27.   Warm & Clear. Also calm.

28.   Ditto—Ditto in the forenoon. Afterwards Rain.

29.   Clear Warm and still.

30.   Warm & clear. Wind Southwardly.

31.   Warm & clear in the forenoon. Afterwards slight Rain.

August

9.   Finishd sowing the cut of Corn on the other side at the Mill with 43 Bushels of Wheat.
   Finishd sowing the 4 foot cut in the Neck with Wheat viz. 45½ Bushl.

15.   Finishd sowing the 39 Inch Cut of Corn in the Neck with 44½ Bushl. Wheat.

Finishd sowing that half of Muddy hole Corn field with Wheat round the Barn [   ] Bushel.

22.   Finishd sowing Wheat on this side at the Mill viz. 28 Bushels which makes in all sewed there 71 Bushls.

25.   Also finishd the 18 Inch cut at Doeg run. Sowd therein 35 Bushels of Wh. The 6 by 3 foot cut was sowed with 40½ Bushels abt. the 13th.

26.   Finishd sowing the 5⟨ ⟩ Cut of Corn in the Neck with 53 Bushels Wheat.

August

1st.   Calm & still. Also warm.

2.   Cloudy for the most part & wind southwardly with some thunder & showers abt. 4 Oclock.

3.   Close and Cloudy the greatest part of the day. In the Afternoon Rain where I was (at Mr. Moodys).

Moody's is probably the home of Benjamin Moody (d. 1784), of Fairfax County. Moody, who was related by marriage to Thomas Colvill, was named a beneficiary in Colvill's will.

4.   Warm with some Clouds & sprinkles of Rain abt. the long Glade.

5.   Warm with Clouds—on the blue Ridge.

6.   Very Warm.

7.   Very warm. Arrivd at the Warm Springs.

8.   Very warm also with some Rain.

9.   Warm and Clear.

10.   Cool & pleasant.

11. Not very warm.

12. Tolerably pleasant but w.

13. Very warm, & Cloudy in the Afternoon.

14. Much Rain fell last Night & the forepart of this day—The Weather Warm.

15. Pleasant yet warm.

16. Cloudy & warm.

17. A good deal of Rain fell last Night. Pleast. today.

September

5. Finishd sowing the other half of Muddy hole field with Wheat viz. [   ] Bushl. wch. make in all there [   ] Bushels.
   Also finishd the two foot Cut at Doeg Run with 39 Bushels.

12. Finishd sowing the 5½ foot cut in the Neck with Wheat viz. 51 Bushels which make in all there 194.

18. Finishd Sowing the 6 by 4 feet Cut at Doeg Run with 36 Bushels. Sowed the simling Rows at Do. with 11½ Bushels which makes in all there 152.

SIMLING[?]: a conjectural reading. GW did include the cymling, or summer squash (*Cucurbita pepo* var. *condensa*), in his crop rotations. In his instructions for the operation of River Farm, 10 Dec. 1799 (DLC:GW), he directed that one quarter of field No. 2 be planted to pumpkins, "simlins," turnips, and Yeatman peas.
   The diary entries for August and early September can only be retrospective, perhaps compiled from reports submitted by GW's cousin Lund Washington. GW and Mrs. Washington set out with the George Fairfaxes for Warm Springs, now Berkeley Springs, W.Va., about 3 Aug. By the next day they were in Leesburg and by 8 Aug. were settled at the Springs in a house owned by George Mercer. The expenses for the trip are recorded in an account headed "Expences in going to, from, and at the Springs [10 Sept.] 1767" (DLC:GW). The family cook who accompanied the Washingtons had soon laid in a quarter each of veal and venison and such sundries as butter, eggs, squash, corn, cucumbers, watermelons, peaches, and apples. Mrs. Washington's two children, John Parke Custis and Martha Parke Custis, remained at Mount Vernon under the care of Lund, who reported in letters of 22 Aug. and 5 Sept. to GW (ViMtV) that they were well. In his letter of

5 Sept., Lund acknowledges GW's letter of 27 Aug., not found, and says he is glad to learn that the mineral waters have benefited Mrs. Washington. When GW and Fairfax split their expenses 10 Sept., the amount each owed was £7 8s. 7d. in Virginia currency. In a later letter to Rev. Jonathan Boucher, 9 July 1771, GW mentions having spent two seasons in the Mercer house at the Springs (DLC:GW).

[November]

Nov. 20.   Vestry in Truro Parish.

This entry is from DIARIES, 1:240; the manuscript containing the entry has been lost since Fitzpatrick used it.

At the vestry meeting it was resolved to replace the old frame Pohick Church in Mason's Neck. Because the church was so near the southern boundary of the parish, it was no longer in a central location convenient to all of the Pohick parishioners, many of whom by the 1760s were settled in the northern half of the area served by Pohick Church. After a warm debate over a more central location for the new Pohick building, the new majority was able, by a vote of seven to five, to locate the new church in Pohick Neck, two miles north of the old Pohick Church at a site called the Crossroads (MVAR, 1964, 22–25; SLAUGHTER [2], 64).

Publick Levy 1767   8 lbs. Tob[acco] pr. Poll – No.
No. of Tythables in   1762 – 121022
                      1764 – 128000
                      1766 – 131799
Depositum – in 1767

Brunswick	11983
Charles City	15184
Dinwiddie	896
Gloucester	17514
Henrico	5757
James City	5299
Isle of Wight	8522
Louisa	10182
Middlesex	5163
New Kent	7569
Southampton	13882
Surry	6663
Sussex	6250
	114864 total

Sold & applied to the fund for giving a Bounty on Hemp

PUBLICK LEVY: These notes appear on one of the last blank pages of the 1767 almanac. Except for GW's notation of the number of tithables for 1762,

1764, and 1766, the rest of this entry is an abstract of an act of the assembly passed in April 1767 entitled: "An act for raising a public levy" (HENING, 8:273–75; the 34 acts in this series are incorrectly dated by HENING as Nov. 1766). In the act, which set the new levy at 8 pounds of tobacco per tithable (or poll), the above-named counties are listed as being in arrears for the 1764–66 levy period, and the respective number given for each county is the amount of arrearage in pounds of tobacco. The act provided that the income from this arrearage tobacco would be set aside as a "depositum" to support the colony's bounty for growing hemp. From time to time the assembly would lay a "general" or "public" levy colonywide on a per capita basis, which in the eighteenth century ranged between 4½ and 12½ pounds of tobacco per tithable. In 1767 a tithable was any white male aged 16 or over and every black and mulatto aged 16 and over, which in essence defined tithables as all adult workers. Although there was a technical difference between the terms *poll* and *tithable*, the two were commonly used interchangeably. Of the three years for which GW here notes tithable totals, the figure for 1762 is exactly the same as that reported by Governor Fauquier (GREENE [2], 141).

Where & How My Time Is Spent

1768

[January]

Jany. 1st. Fox huntg. in my own Neck with Mr. Robt. Alexander and Mr. Colvill—catchd nothing. Captn. Posey with us.

Although John Posey joined in the chase today and on other occasions during the next few months, he was now, in GW's opinion, a man "reduced to the last Shifts," for he was being destroyed financially by enormous debts that he had acquired over the past several years (GW to Posey, 24 Sept. 1767, DLC:GW). GW was one of Posey's principal creditors, holding mortgages on his lands and slaves for a total of £820 Virginia currency conveyed since 1763. With interest accumulating at the rate of £41 a year and miscellaneous charges against him, Posey now owed GW nearly £1,000 (LEDGER A, 168, 256). But Posey was strongly opposed to selling his property to clear his books and had begged GW several times to lend him more money in order to avoid that end. GW had agreed not to press Posey for repayment of his previous loans and was willing to act as his security for a £200 sterling loan from George Mason, but he refused to advance Posey any more cash (GW to Posey, 24 June and 24 Sept. 1767, DLC:GW).

2. Surveying some Lines of my Mt. Vernon Tract of Land.

The Mount Vernon tract was the original Washington family land on Little Hunting Creek, being part of a grant for 5,000 acres between Little Hunting and Dogue creeks that the proprietors of the Northern Neck had made 1 Mar. 1674 to Col. Nicholas Spencer (d. 1689) of Albany, Westmoreland County, and GW's great-grandfather, Lt. Col. John Washington (1632–1677) of Bridges Creek, Westmoreland County (Northern Neck Deeds and Grants, Book 5, 207–8, Vi Microfilm). The Spencer-Washington grant was divided in 1690 between Colonel Spencer's widow, Frances Mottram Spencer (died c.1727), and John Washington's son Lawrence Washington (1659–1697/98). Mrs. Spencer chose the western half of the grant which bordered on Dogue Creek, or Epsewasson Creek as the Indians had called it, and Lawrence Washington took the eastern half on Little Hunting Creek (survey and division by George Brent, 18 Sept. and 23 Dec. 1690, ViMtV). The Little Hunting Creek tract was inherited by Lawrence's daughter Mildred Washington (1696–c.1745), who, after her marriage to Roger Gregory of King and Queen County, sold it for £180 to her brother Augustine Washington, GW's father (deed of Roger and Mildred Gregory to Augustine Washington, 19 Oct. 1726, ViMtV).

From Augustine the tract passed to GW's half brother Lawrence, who during the 1740s named it Mount Vernon (will of Augustine Washington, 11 April 1743, DLC:GW). After Lawrence's death in 1752, his widow Ann and her second husband, George Lee (1714–1761) of Westmoreland County, rented the tract and 18 slaves to GW for her lifetime at the rate of 15,000 pounds of tobacco or £93 15s. Virginia currency a year, and upon Ann's death in 1761, it became GW's outright by virtue of a provision in Lawrence's will (deed of George and Ann Lee to GW, 17 Dec. 1754, KETCHUM, 25; LEDGER A, 47; will of Lawrence Washington, 20 June 1752, ViMtV). Although the tract was originally supposed to contain about 2,500 acres, it now contained only about 2,126 acres because of a change in the northern boundary that had been made about 1741 (survey by R. O. Brooke, c.1741, CALLAHAN, facing p. 3; GW's quitrent lists 1760–73, DLC:GW).

3. At Home with Doctr. Rumney.

Dr. William Rumney (d. 1783), who was born and trained in England, served as a surgeon with the British army in the French and Indian War and settled in Alexandria in 1763.

4. Rid to Muddy hole, D. Run, & Mill Plantns.

5. Went into the Neck.

6. Rid to Doeg Run and the Mill before Dinner. Mr. B. Fairfax and Mr. Robt. Alexander here.

7. Fox hunting with the above two Gentn. and Captn. Posey. Started but catchd nothing.

8. Hunting again in the same Compy. Started a Fox and run him 4 hours. Took the Hounds off at Night.

9. At Home with Mr. B. Fairfax.

10. At Home alone.

11. Running some Lines between me and Mr. Willm. Triplet.

Triplett's land bordered on part of GW's Dogue Run farm (see main entry for 17 Mar. 1770).

12. Attempted to go into the Neck on the Ice but it wd. not bear. In the Evening Mr. Chs. Dick Mr. Muse & my Brother Charles came here.

Charles Dick (b. 1715), of Caroline and Spotsylvania counties, supplied GW's troops in 1754–55 as a Virginia commissary for the British forces. By 1768 Dick's mercantile business was centered in Fredericksburg. George Muse of Caroline County, married Elizabeth Battaile (d. 1786) in 1749 and had a son, Battaile Muse (1751–1803), who also appears in the diaries.

13. At Home with them—Col. Fairfax, Lady, &[ca.]

14.   Ditto—Do. Colo. Fx. & famy. went home in the Evening.

15.   At Home with the above Gentlemen and Shooting together.

16.   At home all day at Cards—it snowing.

GW lost 3s. 6d. in playing cards with his friends (LEDGER A, 269).

17.   At Home with Mr. Dick &ca.

18.   Went to Court & sold Colo. Colvils Ld. Returnd again at Night.

As an executor for Thomas Colvill's estate, GW signed an advertisement in Rind's *Virginia Gazette* (24 Dec. 1767) announcing that "upwards of six hundred acres of valuable LAND . . . will be sold to the highest bidder, at the court-house of *Fairfax* county, on the 3d *Monday* in next month (being court day)." The high bidder was Benjamin Moody.
   GW today recorded losing 11s. 3d. at cards (LEDGER A, 269).

19.   Went to Belvoir with Mr. Dick, my Bror. &ca.

20.   Returnd from Do. by the Mill Doeg Run and Muddy hole.

21.   Surveyd the Water courses of my Mt. Vernon Tract of Land—taking advant. of the Ice.

The freezing over of the Potomac River and Little Hunting Creek enabled GW to survey their shorelines on this day more easily than he usually could, "the ice permitting him to work from the water at will, which greatly simplified the calculating" (DIARIES, 1:247 n.1).

22.   Fox hunting with Captn. Posey, started but catchd nothing.

23.   Rid to Muddy hole & directed paths to be cut for Fox hunting.

24.   Rid up to Toulston in order to Fox hunt it.

TOULSTON: Towlston Grange on Difficult Run, home of Bryan Fairfax.

25.   Confind by Rain with Mr. Fairfax & Mr. Alexander.

26.   Went out with the Hounds but started no Fox. Some of the Hounds run of upon a Deer.

27.   Went out again—started a Fox abt. 10. Run him till 3 and lost him.

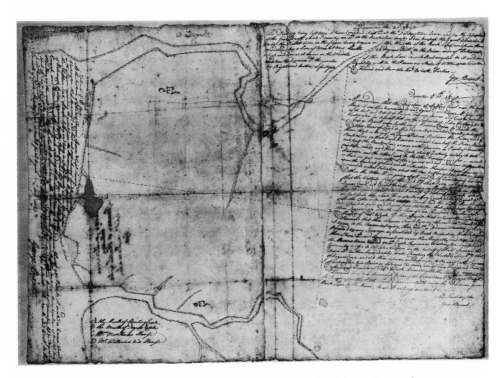

The Spencer-Washington grant, as divided in 1690, gave Washington's grand-father Lawrence about half the tract shown here. (Mount Vernon Ladies' Association of the Union)

28.   Returnd Home. Found Mr. Tomi Elsey there.

Thomasin (many spellings) Ellzey (Elzey) was a vestryman of Truro Parish from the 1765 election to the dissolution of the Virginia vestries in 1785. He was a son of Lewis Ellzey (d. 1786) and Mary Thomasin Ellzey (d. 1791). Thomasin married Alice, daughter of Col. Thomas Blackburn (d. 1807) and Christian Scott Blackburn, of Rippon Lodge.

29.   Went to Belvoir with Mrs. W——n &ca. after Dinnr. Left Mr. Ellzey at home.

30.   Dined at Belvoir and returnd in the Afternoon. Borrowd a hound from Mr. Whiting—as I did 2 from Mr. Alexr. the 28th.

GW was connected with the Whiting family of Gloucester County through his Uncle John Washington (1692–1743), who had married Catherine Whiting (1694–1734), daughter of Henry and Elizabeth Whiting of Gloucester County. The Mr. Whiting who loaned GW the dog today may be Catherine's nephew Francis Whiting (d. 1775), who was born in Gloucester County and moved to the Shenandoah Valley later in his life. Francis's older brother Beverley Whiting (c. 1707–1755), burgess of Gloucester County, may have been the Beverley Whiting who was one of GW's godfathers (*Va. Mag.*, 32:130; LEDGER A, 126; FREEMAN, 1:47n).

31.   At Home alone all day.

Remarks of the Weather

Jany. 1st. Ground exceedg. hard froze, but this day calm & moderate.

2.   Moderate. Wind Southwardly. Thawing a little.

3.   Rain, with the Wind at So. West. Gd. still hard froze, except the Top of it.

4.   Foggy & Warm. Mid day clear. Frost still in the Earth. Calm.

5.   Very thick & Foggy in the Morning. Wind afterwards at No. Et. and Rain all day the Wind shifting southwardly.

6.   Warm, clear, & pleasant, in the Morng. Wind high from No. Wt. & cool afterwards.

7.   Clear and frosty. Wind brisk from No. W.

8.   Clear, frost, & still.

9.   Cloudy, with Misty forenoon & constt. Rain afterwards. Wind Southwardly.

10.   Weather clear. Wind Southwardly, yet raw and Cold. Hard frost.

11.   Clear with the Wind at West. Evening very cold & Wind Northwardly. Severe Frost. River froze across.

12.   Wind at No. West and exceeding cold and frosty.

13.   More moderate, and yet very cold, with a little Snow in the Morng. and Eveng. clear.

14.   Clear and pleast. Wind at South River still froze.

15.   Clear and pleasant. Wind Southwardly. Thawd a good deal.

16.   Constant Snow the whole day from the Northward.

17.   Clear and pleasant. Wind So. West and West. Hard frost.

18.   Still & cloudy. Very like to Snow but broke away abt. Sun Set. Cold.

19.   Clear and pleast. Morning. Afternoon Raw & cold.

20.   Clear, still, & warm. Thawd a great deal.

21.   Very warm and Still. Snow dissolving fast.

22.   Warm, still, and clear again. Snow almost gone.

23.   No Frost last Night. Warm, & clear in the forenoon. Cloudy with some Rain in the Afternoon—afterwards clear again. Ice broke in the River.

24.   Lowering Morning, but very fine & Warm till 7 in the Afternoon, when the Wind shifted to No. East from So.

25.   Drizling & Raing. all day. Wind—No. Et.

26.   Wind at No. West. Cloudy & cold, with Spits of Snow.

27.   Cold—cloudy—& still morng. Clear & pleast. afterwards. Wind Southwardly.

28.   Wind at No. West & very cold.

29.   Do. at Do. & Do. River froze up again last Night.

30.   Very hard frost last Night. Morng. cold but more moderate afterwards. Wind gettg. Southwardly.

31.   Lowering. Wind Southwardly & moderate. Ice breaking and dispersing.

Observations

Jany. 1st.   Neck People clearing a piece of ground which was begun the 23d. of Decr.

Doeg Run People working in the Swamp which they began to clear this Fall.

Muddy hole People (except two threshing) clearing the Skirt of woods within the fence 4 Men & 2 Women from Doeg Run assisting.

Mill People also clearing.

6.   Doeg Run People finishd grubbing the Swamp they were in and proceeded to another adjacent.

12.   Threshing Wheat at all Plantations Ground being too hard froze to Grub to any advantage.

16.   Finishd my Smiths Shop—that is the Carpenters work of it.

18.   Carpenters went to Saw Plank at Doeg Run for finishing the Barn there.

Will put new girders into my Mill where they had Sunk.

19.   Mike, Tom, & Sam went abt. the Overseers House at Muddy hole.

20.   Plantations chiefly employd in getting out Wheat.

22.   Davy, George, Jupiter and Ned, finishd Sawing at Doeg Run & Joind Mike &ca. abt. Overseers House at Muddy hole.

[February]

Where & how—my time is Spent.

1st.   Rid round into the Neck and directed the running of a Fence there.

2.   Rid to Muddy hole—Doeg Run & Mill.

3.   Fox hunting with Captn. Posey & Ld. Washington. Started but catchd nothg.

Lund Washington (1737–1796), a distant cousin of GW, was the son of Townshend and Elizabeth Lund Washington, of the Chotank area, where GW spent part of his youth. Lund had managed the Ravensworth estates of Henry Fitzhugh (1723–1783) during the early 1760s, and in 1765 GW hired him as manager for his Mount Vernon plantations.

4. Snowing all day—but not very fast—at home.

5. At home alone till Mr. Robt. Alexander came in the Evening.

6. Fox hunting with Mr. Alexander & Captn. Posey. Started but catchd nothing.

7. At Home alone.

8. Rid to Muddy hole—Doeg Run & Mill and in returng. met Mr. Alexander Mr. Stoddard and Captn. Posey, who had just catchd 2 foxes. Returnd w. them to Dinner.

Stoddard is possibly a member of the Stoddert family of Prince George's and Charles counties, Md. Thomas Stoddert, who served with the Maryland troops in the French and Indian War, was the father of Benjamin Stoddert (1751–1813) by his wife Sarah Marshall Stoddert, daughter of Thomas Marshall of Marshall Hall.

9. Went out Hunting again. Started a fox. Run him four hours & then lost him. Mr. Stoddard went home. Alexr. stayd.

10. Rid to Muddy hole, Doeg Run, and Mill, Mr. Alexander going in the Morng. as Mr. Magowan did to Williamsburg.

Walter Magowan (d. 1784), an immigrant from Scotland, was hired by GW in the fall of 1761 to tutor the two Custis children at a wage of £35 a year. Magowan left the position in the late fall of 1767 and applied for the rectorship of Frederick Parish in Frederick County. The parish promised to hold the position open until Dec. 1768, and Magowan was now preparing to go to England for ordination. For this trip GW gave him a letter of introduction to Robert Cary & Co., dated 10 Mar. 1768 (DLC:GW).

11. Went into the Neck and returnd to Dinner.

12. Fox hunting with Colo. Fairfax, Captn. McCarty, Mr. Chichester, Posey, Ellzey & Manley who dind here with Mrs. Fairfax & Miss Nicholas. Catchd two foxes.

Richard Chichester (c. 1736–1796), son of Richard Chichester (d. 1743) and Ellen Ball Chichester of Lancaster County, was, through his mother, a distant relation of GW. He inherited his father's plantation, Fairweathers, and in 1759 married Ann Gordon (1743–1765) of Lancaster County. Shortly after Ann's death he moved from Lancaster to Fauquier County and married Sarah McCarty (d. 1826), daughter of his cousin Capt. Daniel McCarty of Mount Air, here mentioned. In 1774 Chichester bought land on Accotink Creek in Fairfax County, near McCarty's home and settled there with his family for the rest of his life (HAYDEN, 106–7; deed of Richard Watts to Chichester, 6 Dec. 1774, Fairfax County Deeds, Book M-1, 28–32, Vi Microfilm).

Harrison Manley (d. 1773), the son of John Manley (d. 1751) and Sarah Harrison Manley, was one of GW's closest neighbors. Manley occasionally sold wheat to GW and used the services of GW's mill, blacksmith shop, and weaving shop as part payment in return (LEDGER B, 9).

Two daughters of Wilson and Sarah Cary—Sarah and Elizabeth—married the brothers George William and Bryan Fairfax. A third daughter, Anne Cary (b. 1733), married Robert Carter Nicholas (1728–1780) of James City County and had four daughters, one of whom, probably either Sarah Nicholas (b. 1752) or Elizabeth Nicholas (1753–1810), is the Miss Nicholas who appears here.

13. Hunting in the same Company. Catchd 2 More foxes. None dind at Mt. Vernon.

GW today lent Ellzey £10 (LEDGER A, 269).

14. At home alone.

15. Ditto–Ditto.

16. Went up to Alexa. and returnd in the Eveng.

While GW was in town today he received £75 cash as part payment for wheat sold to the Alexandria firm of John Carlyle & Robert Adam. This partnership, which was separate from the one Carlyle had with John Dalton (see entry for 17 April 1760), had been formed in 1764 to deal in wheat and flour and lasted until about 1770. During that period GW sold most of his wheat to the firm and regularly drew on his account with it for his cash needs (LEDGER A, 180, 271, 280, 310, 326).

17. Rid to Muddy hole, Doeg Run, & the Mill. Returnd to Dinner and alone.

18. Went a ducking between breakfast & dinner. In the Afternoon Mr. Thruston Mr. Alexander, & Mr. Carter from Gloster came in.

Charles Mynn Thruston (1738–1812), originally of Gloucester County, raised a body of volunteers in 1758 and joined William Byrd's Virginia Regiment as a lieutenant (WRITINGS, 3:2; HAMILTON [1], 2:292). In 1760 he married Mary Buckner, daughter of Col. Samuel Buckner of Gloucester County; she bore him three sons and died in 1765. In the fall of 1764 Thruston, having been chosen minister of Petsworth Parish, Gloucester County, went to England to take orders, and was licensed for Virginia in Aug. 1765 (PETSWORTH, 323–24; GOODWIN, 312). The Alexander family of Gloucester County had been headed by David Alexander (d. 1750), who emigrated to Virginia from England. This Mr. Alexander may have been David's son Morgan Alexander (b. 1746), who, like Thruston, was now looking for land, in either Loudoun or Frederick County, where he could settle. There were several Carter families in Gloucester County at this time.

19. After dinner the above Gentlemen went to Belvoier.

20. Fox hunting with Captn. Posey. Catchd a Fox.

21. At home all day. Mr. Wm. Gardner dind here. A Gentleman from York River came to buy Wheat.

22. Rid to Muddy hole, Doeg Run and the Mill before Dinner and went out with my Gun after it.

23. Fox hunting with Captn. Posey. Catchd a Fox we suppose, but being dark coud not find it.

On this day, while ordering a butt of Madeira wine from a dealer in the Madeira Islands, GW asked for some cuttings of the grape. As if suspecting that the request would run counter to the policy of the vintners, he wrote, "but if in requiring this last Article there be any sort of Impropriety I beg that no notice may be taken of it" (GW to Scott, Pringle, Cheape & Co., 23 Feb. 1768, DLC:GW).

24. Went a ducking between breakfast & dinner & killd 2 Mallards & 5 bald faces. Found Doctr. Rumney here at Dinner who staid all Night. Mr. Magowan returnd.

Rumney had come to see GW's stepdaughter, Martha Parke Custis, who was known as Patsy (Patcy) to her family and friends. Now 11 or 12 years old, Patsy had suffered from epilepsy at least since the age of 6, and with the beginning of her adolescence, the malady showed no signs of abating (receipt from James Carter, 12 April 1762, ViHi: Custis Papers). On this occasion Rumney prescribed 12 powders of unidentified composition, "a vial of Nervous Drops," and a package of valerian, a drug that was thought to be useful in controlling epileptic spasms (receipt from William Rumney, 18 Feb. 1769, ViHi: Custis Papers; HOOPER, 981). But these medicines, and the many others that would be tried in the future, could not relieve Patsy's condition. She was beyond the help of eighteenth-century physicians, and much to the dismay of her family, epileptic attacks would plague her at frequent intervals until one caused her death in July 1773.

25. Doctr. Rumney went away. I went to the Creek but not cross it. Killd 2 Ducks—viz. a sprig tail and Teal.

Until he became too old for the chase, Washington hunted foxes at every opportunity. This print still hangs in the library at Mount Vernon. (Mount Vernon Ladies' Association of the Union)

26.   Laid of a Road from Mt. Vernon to the Lain by Mr. Manleys.

27.   Went on the Road, clearing between Mt. Vernon, and the Mill. In the Evening Mr. Stedlar came.

In 1765 GW hired John Stedlar, a local music teacher, for the purpose of "teaching Mrs. Washington & two Childn Musick" (LEDGER A, 231). During the next six years Stedlar frequently visited Mount Vernon to give lessons, mostly to the children. Patsy was learning to play the spinet, and her brother, John Parke Custis, the fiddle (GW to Robert Cary & Co., 12 Oct. 1761 and 20 July 1767, DLC:GW).

28.   In the Afternoon went up to Mr. Robt. Alexanders in order to meet Mr. B. Fairfax & others a fox Huntg. None came this day but Captn. Posey.

Robert Alexander lived just north of Four Mile Run. He had inherited the house and 904 acres of land from his father, Gerard Alexander (will of Gerard Alexander, 9 Aug. 1760, Fairfax County Wills, Book B-1, 327–29, Vi Microfilm).

29.   At Mr. Alexanders all day with his Phil & Captn. Posey—it raining.

PHIL: probably Robert Alexander's younger brother Philip Alexander (d. 1790), whose home was just north of Alexandria.

Remarks of the Weather

Feby. 1st.   Mild, Still, & Warm.

2.   Lowering Morning—but Wind Westwardly & clear afterwards.

3.   Clear, & somewhat cool in the Morning. Cloudy afterwards.

4.   Snowing all day; but not very fast. Towards Night it turnd to hail and then to Rain. Very little Wind.

5.   Raining more or less till the Afternoon when it ceasd & became foggy & remaind Cloudy.

6.   Cloudy & dull Morng. Clear Afterwds.

7.   Gloomy Morning. Cloudy afternoon—and rainy Evening and Night.

8.   Calm and Misty Morning & dull day.

9.   Clear—calm—& warm Morning. Windy afternoon—from the westward.

10.   Clear & fine day. Little wind.

11.   Still and Lowering kind of a day wt. drops of Rain every now and then.

12.   Dull Morning, & lowering Day but no Rain & very little Wind.

13. Cloudy Morning–but very pleasant Mid day & afternoon being clear with very little wind.

14. Raining more or less till the Afternoon when turnd to a kind of Mist. Winds changeable.

15. Heavy Morng. Rain abt. 8 Oclock & till 2 then Snow. Variable Winds.

16. Clear and pleasant with little Wind and that variable.

17. Very white Frost; Morning clear, & Still. Afternoon muddy with the Wind at So.

18. Lowering day with drops of Rain every now and then. Afternoon Misty with the Wind at No. Et.

19. Thick mist the whole day with very little wind.

20. Foggy & Misty Morng. Cloudy all day. Wind Southwardly in the Afternoon.

21. Quite warm–still–and tolerably clear.

22. Warm and Cloudy–with Showers of Rain and some Thunder. Wind fresh from the So. West &ca.

23. Rainy morning & Misty day, with but little wind.

24. Clear, & cool. Wind brisk from the North West.

25. Hard frost. Clear & cool, Wind at No. West in the Morning but calm & pleasant in the Afternoon.

26. Dull morng. Wind at So. Wt. and cool. Clear Noon & Muddy Sky in the Afternn.

27. Showery all day (misty Showers) & still.

28. Misty Showers with intervening Sun. Wind Southwardly & fresh.

29. Constant Rain from abt. 7 Oclock till three–then Snow with variable Wind from So. Wt. to No. Et. Westwardly.

Observations

Feby. 1st.   Carpenters all (except Will) Went to Sawing Pailing for a Goose yard.

13.   Finishd the Goose Pen at Home. Also finishd clearing the Point of Woods between where Carney & Rollins & Crump livd in the Neck abt. 30 Acres.

Richard Rollins and William Crump apparently moved out of Clifton's Neck soon after GW purchased it in April 1760 (LEDGER A, 74, 80). John Carney remained as a tenant, paying GW the standard annual rental of 730 pounds of tobacco until 1765, when GW bought out his lease (LEDGER A, 82, 136, 218).

18.   Rais'd Overseers House at Muddy hole.
   Finishd Threshing & cleaning my Wheat at Doeg Run Plantn.
[   ] Bushl.

23.   Stopd clearing the Field on the Ck. in the Neck, and began upon those pieces of Woods in the other field by Mr. Sheridines.

John Sheridine of Charles County, Md., had rented land in Clifton's Neck from William Clifton in 1741. After GW bought the land in 1760, Sheridine continued to rent until GW bought out the remainder of the lease in 1773. Sheridine's son, John Sheridine (d. 1768), seems to have lived on the land until his death. After this, his widow Barberry (Barbara?) remained there for several years (deed of Sheridine to GW, 9 Aug. 1773, MWA; LEDGER A, 75, 134, 227, 351; LEDGER B, 39).

26.   Began to deliver my Wheat to Mr. Kirk.
   Carpenters not having quite finishd the Overseers Ho[use] at Muddy hole for want of some Plank went abt. a Corn Ho. there.
   Much abt. this time a Hound Bitch Mopsey of Mr. R. Alexanders (now with me) was proud, & shut up chiefly with a black dog Taster who lind her several times as did Tipler once, that is known of. The little Bitch Cloe in the House was also proud at the same time—but whether lined or not cannot be known. See how long they go with Pup—and whether both the sametime—being very difft. in size.

James Kirk, an immigrant from England, established himself as a wheat merchant and also invested heavily in western lands. He kept a store and office in Alexandria and maintained a country residence across the Potomac in Maryland (LEDGER A, 270–71; CRESSWELL, 4, 27, 52). GW's wheat is today being loaded on a ship owned by Kirk for Carlyle & Adam, the purchasers.

26 & 27. Transplanted trees of differt. kinds into the Lucern Patch.

[March]

Where & how my time is Spent.

Mar. 1st. Went a fox hunting with the two Alexrs. and Posey. Was during the chase (in which nothing was catchd) joind by Mr. Fairfax, Jno. Alexander & Muir.

John Alexander (1735–1775), of King George and Stafford counties, was in this period the eldest of three brothers in the "Philip" branch of the Alexander family. John, who had inherited a portion of the 1669 Howsing Patent from his father, Philip Alexander (1704–1754), was a burgess from Stafford County 1765–75. He married Lucy Thornton (d. 1781). John Muir (c. 1731–1791), of Dumfries, Scot., settled as a merchant in Alexandria; in 1758 he was chosen a town trustee.

2. Hunting again, & catchd a fox with a bobd Tail & cut Ears, after 7 hours chase in wch. most of the Dogs were worsted.

3. Returnd home much disorderd by a Lax, Griping and violent straining.

4. At Home, worse with the above complaints. Sent for Doctr. Rumney, who came in the Afternn.

5. Very bad the Doctr. staying with me.

6. Something better – Doctr. still here – & Mr. Ramsay came down to see me.

7. Rather better. Doctr. went home after breakfast. Mr. Ramsay staid to Dinner.

8. Mending fast. Colo. Thos. Moore calld here on his way from Alexa. Home, but made no stay. Colo. Fairfax, & Mr. Gilbt. Campbell (Comptroller) Dined here.

Moore, who was heavily indebted to the estate of the late Speaker of the House of Burgesses, John Robinson (d. 1766) of King and Queen County, was now trying to renew his bond to GW for his debt to the Custis estate, which GW had been carrying, with interest, for eight years (LEDGER A, 204; see main entry for 4 Nov. 1768).

Gilbert Campbell, of Westmoreland County, was comptroller of the South Potomac Naval District. He was a signer of the Westmoreland County association to prevent the execution of the Stamp Act in the colony, 27 Feb. 1766, and was still serving as comptroller in 1776.

9.   Still mending. At home alone.

10.   Mending still. Rid out. Mr. Peake & Auge. Darrel dind here.

Humphrey Peake (1733–1785), who inherited Willow Spring from his father, William Peake (d. 1761), was a neighbor and fox-hunting companion of GW and a frequent visitor to Mount Vernon.

    Augustus Darrell (d. 1777) of Fairfax County, a son of Sampson Darrell, married about 1771 Sarah McCarty Johnston, widow of George Johnston of Belvale and sister of Daniel McCarty of Mount Air (LEDGER A, 300).

11.   At home alone all day.

12.   Rid to the new Road—Mill, Doeg Run & Muddy hole Plantns. & found Doctr. Rumney upon my return, who dind & stayd all Night.

During this visit Rumney treated Patsy Custis with valerian and powders and applied some type of plaster (receipt from William Rumney, 18 Feb. 1769, ViHi: Custis Papers). GW today paid him £5 in cash (LEDGER A, 269).

13.   At Home alone all day.

14.   With the people working upon the New Road between breakfast and Dinner.

15.   At home alone all day.

16.   Hunting with Captn. Posey & L[un]d W. Started and catchd a fox in abt. three hours.

17.   Rid into the Neck—to Muddy hole and upon the New Road. When I came home found Colo. Carlyle & his Wife & Children there.

Col. John Carlyle's first wife, Sarah Fairfax Carlyle, bore him two children: Sarah, who appears in the diaries as "Sally," and Anne (1761–1778), who appears as "Nancy." After the death of Sarah Fairfax Carlyle in 1761, Colonel Carlyle married Sybil West, daughter of Hugh West (d. 1764) and Sybil Harrison West (d. 1787). They had one child, George William Carlyle (d. 1781).

18.   Went with Colo. Carlyle & our Families to Belvoir. Myself & Mrs. W——n returnd leaving the others there. Found Mr. Stedlar at Mt. Vernon.

19.   At home all day. Mr. Stedlar here.

20.   At home all day. Mr. Stedlar still here. In the Afternoon Mr. Carlyle & Family returnd from Belvoir.

21.   Went to Court. Colo. Carlyle & Family also went up. Mr. Stedlar stay'd – & Sally Carlyle.

22.   Rid to the Mill, Doeg Run and Muddy hole Plantation.

23.   Rid out to see, & examine whether a Road coud not be discovd. & opend from Posey's ferry back of Muddy hole Plantn. thereby avoidg. the Gumspring, which I think may be done to advantage.

24.   Rid out again with Mr. Peake on the above Acct. and observd that a good Road might be had along H[untin]g C[ree]k upon Colo. Masons Land.

25.   Went into the Neck. Grafted some Cherries & began to manure the ground for my Grapevines.

26.   Went Fox huntg. – but started nothing. Mr. Lawe. Washington came here & Miss Ramsay in the Afternoon.

MR. LAWE. WASHINGTON: probably Lawrence Washington (1728–c.1809), usually called "of Chotank," the son of John and Mary Massey Washington and first cousin to Lund Washington. His home was on a bluff of the Potomac River near Chotank Creek. This Lawrence was one of the two Chotank cousins remembered in GW's will as "acquaintances and friends of my Juvenile years" (WRITINGS, 37:286; EUBANK, 18–20). Lund Washington also had a brother named Lawrence (1740–1799), who may be the one referred to here.

William Ramsay (1716–1785) and his wife Ann McCarty Ramsay (c. 1730–1785) had two sons and five daughters. "Miss Ramsay" is probably the eldest daughter, Elizabeth, who appears in the diaries variously as "Betsy," "Betcy," and "Betty."

27.   At home. Lawe. Washington went away.

28.   At home.

29.   Fox hunting—with Jacky Custis & Ld. Washington. Catchd a fox after 3 hrs. chase.

JACKY: GW's stepson, John Parke Custis. He was described by GW in May of this year as "a boy of good genius, about 14 yrs. of age, untainted in his Morals, & of innocent Manners. Two yrs. and upwards he has been reading of Virgil, and was (at the time Mr. Magowan left him) entered upon the Greek Testament" (GW to Jonathan Boucher, 30 May 1768, PHi: Dreer Collection).

30.   Rid to Muddy hole—Doeg Run & Mill Plantation's.

31.   Went into the Neck. At my return found Doctr. Rumney & Mr. Wm. Crawford at the House. Dr. Rumney went away in the Afternoon.

On the following day Rumney charged twelve "Nervous Powders" and ingredients for a medicinal brew to Patsy Custis's account (receipt from William Rumney, 18 Feb. 1769, ViHi: Custis Papers).

Remarks—of the—Weather

Mar. 1st.   Cool & clear. Wind fresh from the No. West. Ground froze.

2.   Cool morning but clear, still, and pleasant afterwards. Frost again.

3.   Lowering with some sprinkles of Rain.

4.   Cool, Wind at No. West, & frosty.

The Custis family coat of arms. (Mount Vernon Ladies' Association of the Union)

5. Cool, & Cloudy. Ground froze. Towards Night Snow—just to whiten the Ground.

6. Ground & snow hard froze. Clear, Wind Northwardly.

7. Clear & cool, wind still Northwardly.

8. Frosty Morning—but clear & pleast. day. Wind Southwardly.

9. No frost. Clear & pleast. forenoon & Mid day—but hazy afternoon. Wind fresh from South.

10. Lowering Morning. Rainy, & Windy afternoon from the So[uth]ward.

11. Clear with high Wind from the So. Wt.

12. Cloudy for the Most Part. Wind Southwardly. In the Evening Rain.

13. Wind at No. West and Cool—with a lowering Sun—& sometimes Cloudy.

14. Wind Southwardly till the Afternn. then Northwardly with first Rain then Snow, being cloudy & raw all day.

15. Snow abt. half an Inch thick. Morng. cold & clear. Wind at No. West till the Afternoon, then North with a thick Muddy Sky. Ground froze.

16. Ground froze. Morning thick and threatening—but clear afterwards with the Wind Southwardly.

17. Morning frozen and cold, wind Raw from the Northward. Afterwards something warmer but still cold & clear.

18. Hard frost. Clear and cool. Wind at Northwest.

19. Ground froze. Morning threatng. & cold. Abt. 8 Oclock began Snowg. which it did constantly the whole day from the No. Et. & was one of the most disagreeable day of the whole Winter. Snow abt. 6 Inchs. deep.

20. Cold and boisterous. Wind at No. West and Snow drifting. Afternoon somewhat more moderate.

21. Moderately warm. Wind Southwestwardly & sometimes lowering but clear Aftn.

22. Calm, clear, & pleasant. Snow melting fast.

23. Calm, & cloudy, with a little Rain in the Morning—so likewise in the Evening.
    Note. This Moon, wch. changd the 18th. appeard with the points directly upwards exactly of a height.

24. Clear & cool. Wind at No. West.

25. Clear. Morning Cool, & wind at No. West. Evening Mild & calm. Ground froze.

26. Morning still, clear, & warm. Afternoon clear & cool. Wind at No. West.

27. Cloudy & lowering till abt. 3 Oclock then Snowing more or less till Night when it raind a good deal but little Wd.

28. Cloudy & sometimes drizling with but little Wind. After Sunsetting clear.

29. Raw, cold, & cloudy forenoon. Clear & more moderate Afternoon, Wind being pretty fresh from No. Wt. all day.

30. Calm, clear & pleast. Morng. Afternoon also clear, but more cool—Wind being brisk from southward.

31. Grey Morng. Clear Afterwards & raw. Wind fresh from the Southward.

Observations

Mar. 3d. Deliverd a Load of 508 Bushels of Muddy hole Wheat to Mr. Kirks Ship and my Schooner returnd.

5. Deliverd another Load of 517½ Bushls. of the Neck Wheat to the above ship and returnd the same day.
    Finishd cutting down Corn Stocks at all my Plantations.

12.   Large parts of my Wheat Field at Doeg Run—the same I believe at the Mill—were found to be exceedingly Injurd by the Frost (and I apprehend by the last frost abt. the 7 & 8th. Instt.). Upon examining the Wheat which appeard to be so much hurt, I found the Roots for the most part were entirely out of the ground. Some indeed had a small fibre or so left in, & here perhaps a green blade might be found in a bunch, but where the Root was quite Out the whole bunch seemd perishd & Perishing.

Note. Watch the Progress of this Wheat, & see if there be any possibility of its taking Root again (as it lyes thick on the gd.). Near a stake in the 18 Inch Cut and abt. 100 yds. from the Barracks is a spot of an Acre or so of this kind. Observe this place—being poor gd. also.

Carpenters returnd from the Road abt. Muddy hole Corn House.

15.   Deliverd the last load of my Wheat to Mr. Kirks Ship which makes 1921 Bushls. delivd. him in all. Reckg. in 15 Bushls. to be deliv'd him by Mr. Digges.

GW had previously lent 15 bushels of wheat to William Digges of Warburton, the equivalent of which was now earmarked for delivery by Digges to Kirk as part of GW's total delivery (LEDGER A, 156). The total included 475 bushels delivered 11 Mar. but not mentioned in the diary (LEDGER A, 271).

16.   Began to list Corn Ground at Muddy hole.
Recd. my Goods from Mr. Cary by Captn. Johnston.
Sent my Vessel abt. 4 Oclock in the Afternoon to Mr. Kirk agreeable to his Letter.

John Johnstoun, captain of the *Lord Cambden,* was delivering GW's major spring shipment of supplies from England; the shipment comprised a great variety of goods collected from 39 different London shops, including a set of surveyor's instruments for John Parke Custis and some harpsichord music for Patsy. These were all gathered together and shipped by Robert Cary & Co., which was the major London merchant house for the Custis estates and was subsequently retained by GW after his marriage to Martha Dandridge Custis.

18.   Began to lay of my Corn ground in the Neck.

19.   Sent Chaunter (a Hound Bitch) up to Toulston; to go to Mr. Fairfax's Dog Forester—or Rockwood—She appearg. to be going Proud. Forrester not beg. at Home she went to Rockwood.

25.   Observ'd a Lamb in my Pasture being the first fallen from Ewes put to my Ram the [   ].

26.   My Vessel returnd from Mr. Kirks employ abt. sundown—
being 10 days gone.

29.   Began to Cork & pay the bottom of my schooner.

30.   Finishd my Fencing & began to Enlist my Corn Ground at
the Mill.
   Looked again at the Wheat at Doeg Run (particularly abt. the
Stake near the Barracks) and found no alteration for the better—
it appearing to have no root in the Ground.

31.   Finishd Corking my Vessel & weeding out my Lucern.

Memms.

If Ewes & Lambs are restraind from Wheat Fields, & no green
food sowd to support them in the Spring—contrive that no more
fall after this year till the last of March.

[April]

Where & how—my time is Spent.

April 1st.   At home with Mr. Crawford.

William Crawford's visit was not purely social. By the fall of 1767 GW had
concluded that because the Pennsylvania-Maryland boundary line (Mason
and Dixon's Line) would soon be completed, and because western expansion
(temporarily barred by the Royal Proclamation of Oct. 1763) would soon
be at least partially opened up by a treaty with the Indians, the time was
ripe for acquiring some parcels of choice land in western Pennsylvania and
the Ohio Valley. GW wrote to Crawford (21 Sept. 1767, DLC:GW), who
had settled the year before at Stewart's Crossing on the Youghiogheny River
(BUTTERFIELD [1], vii), and proposed a partnership for taking up land.
Crawford quickly replied that he would "heartly imbrass your Offer upon
the Terms you proposed," and went on to sketch out the prospects, necessary
procedures, and possible problems that the two land hunters might encounter
(29 Sept. 1767, DLC:GW). Crawford's appearance at Mount Vernon, allowing land discussions which were spread over a six-day period, was GW's first
opportunity to confer personally with his man in the field.

2.   Rid to Muddy hole—Doeg Run & the Mill. Mr. Crawford
went to Alexandria.

3.   Went to Pohick Church & returnd to Dinner. Mr. Crawford
returnd in the Afternoon.

4.   Fox hunting with Messrs. Chichester, the Triplets, Manley, Posey, Peake & Adams. Never started a Fox–but did a Deer.

Abednego Adams (1721–1809), originally of Charles County, Md., married Mary Peake, a sister of Humphrey Peake. They appear to have settled for a time on land in the fork of Little Hunting Creek which Adams's wife inherited from her father in 1761.

5.   At home with Mr. Crawford. Mr. Campbell came here & dined, Mrs. Washington, Miss B. Ramsey & Patcy Custis went to Belvoir & returnd.

As an agent for the Alexandria partnership of Carlyle & Adam, Matthew Campbell (d. 1782) had come to Mount Vernon to pay GW £121 11s. 9½d. for wheat purchased from him during the past six months (LEDGER A, 271).

6.   Mr. Crawford set of home, and we (together w. Miss Betcy Ramsay) went up to Alexa. to a Ball.

GW had given Crawford £20 on the previous day (LEDGER A, 269).

7.   We returnd from Alexandria thro Snow.

8.   At home alone. Except with Price the Bricklayer who has been here since Tuesday.

In 1767 Thomas Price was asked by the Truro vestry to inspect the work at the still unfinished Falls Church building, around which the town of Falls Church later developed (Truro Vestry Book, 116, DLC). Several years later GW bought "a Bricklayer named Isaac Web" from Thomas Price for £30 Maryland currency (LEDGER B, 106).

9.   Fox hunting with the two Triplets Mr. Peake & Mr. Manley. Started, but catchd nothing.

10.   At home alone.

11.   Planting out Grape Vines according to M[e]m[orandum]. Mrs. Posey dined here and Mr. Alexander & Mr. Edwd. Payne Supd. & lodgd.

Edward Payne served with GW as a vestryman of Truro Parish 1765–74. When Payne contracted with the parish in 1766 to build a chapel of ease (later called Payne's Church) for the parishioners in the northwest corner of the parish, GW was appointed to the building committee (SLAUGHTER [1], 22, 50).

12.   Payne and Alexander went away after Breakfast. And Miss Tracy Digges & her sister Betty came in the Aftern. Rid to Muddy hole Doeg R. & Mill.

Theresa Digges (b. 1744) and Elizabeth Digges (1743–1845) were the two eldest daughters of William and Ann Digges of Warburton Manor.

13. At home. The Miss Digges here. In the Afternoon Mr. Chichester came.

14. Fox hunting with Mr. Chichester Captn. Posey Messrs. Triplet Peake & Adams. Startd but catchd nothing. Posey & Adams dind here as did Mr. Digges.

15. At home. Mr. Digges & his daughters went away after breakfast.

16. At home alone. In the Evening went into the Neck.

17. Went to a Church & returnd to Dinner.

18. Went to Court and returnd in the Evening.

19. Measurd the Field designd for Corn at the Mill, and Doeg Run this year.

20. At home alone all day.

21. Rode to Muddy hole Doeg Run and Mill Plantns.—at the first & last of wch. just began to check Corn Gd. Mr. Stedlar came here.

22. At home all day. Mr. Stedlar here.

23. At home all day again. Mr. Stedlar still here.

24. Mr. & Mrs. Peake & their daughter dined here as also did Mr. Stedlar.

Humphrey Peake of Willow Spring married Mary Stonestreet, daughter of Butler Stonestreet (d. 1755) of Prince George's County, Md. The Stonestreet home, Exeter, was on Piscataway Creek, which emptied into the Potomac almost directly across from Mount Vernon. Of the two daughters of Humphrey and Mary Peake, this is probably the elder, Ann Peake (d. 1827), often referred to in the diaries as "Nancy."

25. Went to Muddy hole, Doeg Run & Mill before Dinner, & into the Neck afterwards.

26.   Set of for Williamsburg with Mrs. Washington, Jacky & Patcy Custis & Billy Bassett. Lodgd. at Mr. Lawsons.

GW may have originally planned to combine this visit to Eltham and Williamsburg with attendance at a session of the House of Burgesses which, although scheduled to open on 1 May, had met from 31 Mar. to 16 April (H.B.J., 1766–69, 138, 140, 175–77). Billy is William Bassett (1760–1775), eldest son of Mrs. Washington's sister Anna Maria Dandridge Bassett and Col. Burwell Bassett of Eltham. The Washingtons probably stayed at the home of Thomas Lawson, who ran John Tayloe's ironworks on Neabsco Creek, Prince William County, from which GW bought some bar iron in 1761 (ViHi: Tayloe Papers; Lawson to GW, 28 June 1761, ICHi).

27.   Reachd Fredericksburg.

28.   Stayed there all day at Colo. Lewis.

29.   Proceeded on our Journey and reached Hubbards Ordy. in Comy. with Colo. Lewis & Mr. Dick.

Benjamin Hubbard, who died about 1780, was one of a group of Quakers who moved from Pennsylvania to settle in Caroline County in the 1730s. Hubbard later embraced the established church and served as a Caroline County justice 1754–60. Hubbard's ordinary, located about 37 miles southeast of Fredericksburg in lower Drysdale Parish, was his base of operations for an extensive mercantile business in the Mattaponi River valley from 1756 to 1780. GW had stayed at Hubbard's as early as 1759, when he and his new bride apparently made a trip from the White House to Fredericksburg, possibly to visit the mother of the bridegroom (LEDGER A, 52, 55; CAMPBELL [1], 175–76, 347, 392, 412).

30.   Breakfasted at Todds Bridge—dind at Claibornes & came to Colo. Bassetts.

From Todd's Bridge on the Mattaponi River, GW's party followed his regular route through King William County to a fork in the road just beyond King William Court House. Although on previous trips GW chose the south fork, which crossed the Pamunkey River at Williams' ferry near the White House, the party now took the east fork, remaining on the main road to arrive at Sweet Hall, the home of William Claiborne, which lay on the Pamunkey River opposite New Kent County. About nine miles beyond Sweet Hall was Col. Burwell Bassett's home, Eltham, which he inherited as the eldest surviving son of his father, William Bassett (1709–c.1743).

GW today paid a Dr. Lee, possibly Arthur Lee, £2 3s. 9d. for Patsy Custis (LEDGER A, 269; see main entry for 6 July 1768).

Remarks—of the—Weather

April 1st.   Ground a little froze. Day very cold, with flying Clouds & Wind high from No. Wt.

2.   Ground hard froze. Morning very keen & sharp, wind being at No. Wt. Afterwards more moderate winds varying—with Clouds.

3.   Wind fresh from the Westward & very cold with Snow at times & Clouds.

4.   Ground very hard froze (as it was yesterday). Day clear. Morning calm—but Wind from the Southward afterwards & Cold.

5.   Ground very hard froze. Wind high from No. West. Very cold & Clear.

6.   Ground hard froze. Morng. Calm—clear & pleast. Afternoon Muddy & cold. Wind at So. West. Abt. 10 Oclock at Night it began Snowg.

7.   Snowed all Night, and all this day without Intermission from the No. and No. East. Ground coverd six or 8 Inches.

8.   Clear and cold. Wind fresh from the No. West. Snow melting fast notwithstandg.

9.   Clear & cool in the Morng. Wind at No. Wt. & ground hard froze. Still & pleast. in the Aftern.

10.   White frost, & ground a little crusted over. Moderate but lowering. Wind at So. Et.

11.   Clear—calm, and springing.

12.   Clear—Warm & still till abt. three Oclock. Then fresh Wind from E.S.E.

13.   Clear and rather Cool. Wind fresh from S.W. to N.W.

14.   Lowering day. In the Afternoon a little Rain—with the Wind at So. Et.

15.   Now and then slow Rain. Very cloudy till abt. 4 Oclock when it cleard—but little Wind, and that abt. So. Et.

16.   Lowering most of the day, with the Wind Southwardly & cool till the afternoon when it was still, clear & warm.

17.   Clear & cool wind at No. West.
   Note—the horns of this Moon (wch. changd yesterday) were directly up as the last.

18.   Clear & Cool. Wind Northwardly.

19.   Rather Cool for the Season. Wind variable. & in the Evening low.

20.   Clear and Cool. Wind brisk from the East.

21.   Cool—Cloudy & Raing. more or less all day. Wind at East.

22.   Constant Rain all last Night, and all this day, with the Wind at East.

23.   Constant Rain again all last night & all this day. Wind still at No. Et.

24.   Raining in the Night and till after Sunrise. Wind at No. West & cloudy, that is flyg. clouds, in the Morng. but clear still & warm in the Afternoon.

25.   Still, clear, warm, & pleasant.

26.   Warm, still, & very smoky. In the Evening the Wind very fresh from the Southward.

27.   Clear and Cool, wind fresh from the No. West.

28.   Clear, & rather Cool, wind variable and in the Evening at No. Wt.

29.   Lowering all day & sometimes sprinkling of Rain. Wind southwardly & pretty fresh.

30.   Clear and warm with but little Wind till Night when it blew very fresh from the Southward.

Observations

April 2d.   Sewed a patch of Flax in the Neck.
   Also sewed a patch at Doeg Run by the last yrs. Turneps.

6.   Sewed part of the Ground at home (the Cowpens) in Flax.

7.   Carpenters finishd the Corn Ho. at Muddy hole. And went to trimmg. fish Barrls.

11.   Planted out Grape Cuttings accordg. to Memm.

12.   Sewed remainder of Flax Ground at Home.
   Also sewed Flax Seed at Muddy hole.
   White fish began to Run. Catching 60 or 70 at a Haul with some Her[rin]g.

14.   Sowed Flax at Doeg Run at the head of the Meadow.
   Began plowing at Doeg for Corn—that is to list.
   Ditto Carpenters went to getting Staves for Cyder Casks.

18.   Began fishing for Herrings with Carpenter's &ca.

21.   Began to cross gd. at Muddy hole & the Mill—having Run only a single furrow for a list.

23.   The great abundance of Rain which fell within this 48 hours carrd. away my Dam by the Miss Wades & broke the back Dam by the Mill.

The land north of GW's mill plantation was now jointly owned by three daughters of Zephaniah and Valinda Wade, Mrs. Wade having apparently died sometime within the previous two years. The dam near the Wades' property was about 300 yards up Dogue Run from the mill and had probably been built a short time before in an attempt to store more water for use in the mill during droughts. Nevertheless, the run regularly went dry in the summer. THE BACK DAM: the lower dam.

[May]

Where & how—my time is Spent.

May 1.   Rid to a place calld Root's to see a Meadow of Colo. Bassetts. Returnd to Dinr.

ROOT'S: land owned by the Rootes family of Virginia. The first Rootes to appear in Virginia records was Maj. Philip Rootes (d. 1756), who lived at Rosewall, in King and Queen County, across the Mattaponi River from West Point; he also owned land in New Kent County. Rootes married Mildred Reade, who bore him four sons: Philip, of Rosewall; Thomas

Reade, of Gloucester County; Col. George, who settled on the Virginia frontier; and John, who served in the 2d (William Byrd's) Virginia Regiment.

2.   Went to Williamsburg with Colo. Bassett, Colo. Lewis & Mr. Dick. Dind with Mrs. Dawson & went to the Play.

Mrs. Dawson was born Elizabeth Churchill (c.1709–1779), daughter of Col. William and Elizabeth Churchill of Middlesex County. In 1729 she married Col. William Bassett (1709–c.1743) of Eltham, by whom she had at least five children, one of whom was Col. Burwell Bassett. After the death of her first husband, Elizabeth Churchill Bassett moved to the Bassett family town house in Williamsburg, two blocks south of the market square. In 1752 she married Rev. William Dawson, then commissary of the Church of England in Virginia, who died within a fortnight after the wedding. Although Mrs. Dawson continued to live in the Bassett town house, where GW dined on this date, she died at the Bassett country seat of Eltham.

The play was given in Williamsburg's second theater, built by local subscription in 1751 behind the Capitol on Waller Street. In 1768 a group of players—male and female—was formed by David Verling, their actor-manager, into the Virginia Company. After opening in Norfolk they moved to Williamsburg, where they opened their run on 31 March, coinciding with the meeting of the Burgesses. Which play GW saw is not known; the Virginia Company had a broad repertory, including Restoration comedy, eighteenth-century satire such as the popular *Beggar's Opera* by John Gay, and many of the plays of William Shakespeare, who was being "rediscovered" by the eighteenth-century English theater (see RANKIN).

3.   Dined with the Speaker.

THE SPEAKER: Peyton Randolph (c.1721–1775), son of Sir John and Susanna Beverly Randolph, was king's attorney and burgess for Williamsburg. From Nov. 1766 until the Revolution, Randolph served as Speaker of the House of Burgesses.

4.   Dined with Mrs. Dawson, & suppd at Charlton's.

Richard Charlton (d. 1779) had announced in June 1767 that he had opened "the Coffee-House" in Williamsburg "as a Tavern," and GW had supped there on a visit to the city the previous fall (*Va. Gaz.*, P&D, 25 June 1767; LEDGER A, 262). The exact location of the coffeehouse is not known, but it was "nigh the Capitol" (*Va. Gaz.*, R, 2 Feb. 1769). In 1775 Charlton was said to be living "in the back street," probably present-day Francis Street (*Va. Gaz.*, D, 7 Jan. 1775). In addition to being an innkeeper, Charlton was a barber and wigmaker, and he may have plied those trades at his tavern (*Va. Gaz.*, P, 14 June 1776, and D&N, 11 Dec. 1779).

5.   Dined at Mrs. Campbells.

Christiana Campbell's tavern was GW's habitual lodging place in Williamsburg from 1761 to 1771. On this visit to the city, he paid Mrs. Campbell £2 10s. "for Board," which included his lodgings as well as the daily break-

Peyton Randolph in a portrait by John Wollaston. (Virginia Historical Society)

Elizabeth Harrison Randolph, wife of Peyton Randolph, in a portrait attributed to John Wollaston. (Virginia Historical Society)

fasts and other occasional meals that he ate at the tavern (LEDGER A, 274). Mrs. Campbell (1722–1792) was playfully described by a young Scottish merchant in 1783 as "a little old Woman, about four feet high; & equally thick, a little turn up Pug nose, a mouth screw'd up to one side" (MACAULAY, 187–88). The daughter of a Williamsburg innkeeper named John Burdett (d. 1746), she had married Dr. Ebenezer Campbell, an apothecary in Blandford, and had lived there with him until his death about 1752 (JETT, 24–25). Returning to Williamsburg a short time later, she had by 1760 begun to operate her tavern on Duke of Gloucester Street in the second block from the Capitol (GIBBS, 152–54). She was assisted in her business by her unmarried daughter Molly.

6.   Rid to the Plantations near Williamsburg & dined at Mr. Valentines.

Joseph Valentine (d. 1771), who was in charge of all the Custis estates when GW married Martha Dandridge Custis in 1759, stayed on as the "Common Steward" for both John Parke Custis's inherited portion and GW's dower portion of the Custis plantations (GW to Robert Cary, 24 Oct. 1760, CSmH).

7.   Came up to Colo. Bassetts to Dinner.

8.   Went to Church & returnd to Dinner.

When in Williamsburg, Washington sometimes attended Bruton Parish Church. (College of William and Mary)

GW probably joined the Bassetts in worship at Warrenray Church, a few miles from Eltham. Warrenray was the upper church of Blisland Parish, serving the eastern part of New Kent County. Col. Burwell Bassett was for many years one of the most active vestrymen of the parish; in 1768 he was joined on the vestry by Bartholomew Dandridge, younger brother of Mrs. Bassett and Mrs. Washington (CHAMBERLAYNE, 179).

9. Went a Fox hunting and catched a Fox after 35 Minutes chace; returnd to Dinner & found the Attorney his Lady & daughter there.

John Randolph (c.1728–1784), of Williamsburg, succeeded his older brother Peyton Randolph as attorney general of Virginia in 1766. John married Ariana Jennings (1730–1801) of Maryland, who bore him a son, Edmund, and two daughters, Susanna and Ariana. Like GW, John Randolph was an avid gardener, and he wrote a book on vegetable gardening (probably during the 1760s) which became the first gardening book published in the American colonies (see RANDOLPH).

10. Rid to the Brick House & returnd to Dinner—after which went a dragging for Sturgeon.

The phrase "the Brick House" referred originally (in the seventeenth century) to a particular house built of brick, indicating how unusual such a building was in the early years of the colony. The original house lay about three miles east of Eltham on the south side of the York River across from West Point; after 1738 it was also the location of the Brick House tobacco warehouse (HENING, 5:15). By the mid-eighteenth century the Brick House lent its name to its immediate surrounding neighborhood, which is the sense in which GW refers to it here. In that neighborhood lay land that had been in the Bassett family for many years, as well as one of the larger quarters of the Custis estate, which GW was managing for Jacky (CHAMBERLAYNE, 335, 669–70; see also the Custis Papers in ViHi).

11.   Dined at the Glebe with Mr. Davis.

Rev. Price Davies, of County Montgomery, Wales, who was born about 1732, received his B.A. from Christ Church, Oxford, in 1754. He later migrated to Virginia, married Elizabeth Perry of Gloucester County, and in 1763 became rector of Blisland Parish, New Kent County (GOODWIN, 262).

12.   Went to New Kent Court with Colo. Bassett.

13.   Went after Sturgeon & a Gunning.

14.   Went to my Plantation in King William by Water, & dragd for Sturgeon & catchd one.

MY PLANTATION IN KING WILLIAM: Claiborne's (see entry for 24 April 1760).

15.   Rid to see Colo. Bassetts Meadow at Root's.

16.   Fishing for Sturgeon from Breakfast to Dinner but catchd none.

17.   Rid to the Brick House & returnd to Dinner.

18.   Did the same & got my Chariot & Horses over to Claibornes.

19.   Went a Shooting, & hair huntg. with the Hounds who started a Fox wch. we catched.

20.   Set of from Colo. Bassetts for Nomony. Crossd over to Claibornes—from thence by Frazers Ferry to Hobs hole dining at Webbs Ordinary.

Nomini was a Westmoreland County neighborhood clustered around Nomini Creek, which emptied into the Potomac River about 12 miles below GW's birthplace at Pope's Creek. From Claiborne's ferry, GW's party rode through King William County to cross the Mattaponi River at William Frazier's (many spellings) ferry (HENING, 7:402). They then proceeded al-

Hannah Bushrod Washington, wife of John Augustine Washington. (Dr. and Mrs. John A. Washington)

Washington's brother, John Augustine, often called "Jack." (Mount Vernon Ladies' Association of the Union)

most due north through King and Queen County, crossing into Essex County where they stopped in the afternoon for dinner at Webb's tavern (for the Webb family of Essex County, see WEBB [1], 270–77). After dinner they rode north to Hobbs Hole (now Tappahannock), a tobacco port on the south side of the Rappahannock River and the seat of Essex County, which was described by a visitor in 1774 as "a small Village, with only a few Stores, & Shops" (FITHIAN, 203). GW spent £2 1s. 6d. for overnight lodgings, ferriages, and other expenses there (LEDGER A, 274).

21.   Reachd my Brothr. John's who & his wife were up the Country. Crossd over to Mr. Booths.

Bushfield, where John Augustine Washington lived with his wife Hannah and their several children, was on the east bank of the Nomini near the mouth of the creek. "His House," said young Philip Vickers Fithian who saw it in 1774, "has the most agreeable Situation, of any I have yet seen in Maryland Or Virginia" (FITHIAN, 89). "Brother John" had succeeded his father-in-law, John Bushrod, as master of the Bushfield plantation upon the latter's death in 1760, and although the plantation contained only about 1,200 acres, he was now one of the ten leading landowners in Westmoreland County (MVAR, 1964, 18–21).

Col. William Booth lived almost directly across the Nomini from Bushfield at Nomini Plantation, which he, like John Augustine Washington, had taken over from his wife's father, in this case Col. William Aylett, who died in 1744. Aylett had married twice and had no sons, but four daughters. Elizabeth, who was probably the oldest, married Booth, and her sister Anne married GW's half brother Augustine Washington (EUBANK, 47–49).

22.   Went to Church (nomony) & returnd to Mr. Booths to Dinner who was also from home in Glousester. Mr. Smith the Parson dind with us.

Nomini Church was on the east bank of Nomini Creek about 3½ miles upstream from William Booth's home. Rev. Thomas Smith (1738–1789) was the rector of Cople Parish, which comprised the lower end of Westmoreland County, including both Nomini and Yeocomico churches. He had assumed that post soon after his graduation from Cambridge University in 1763 and retained it until his death 26 years later (EATON, 22–23). A highly respected minister, Smith was a prosperous planter also; in 1782 he was credited with having 42 slaves, a total that made him the twentieth largest slaveholder in Westmoreland County at that time (*Va. Mag.*, 10:234). His wife Mary Smith (1744–1791) was a daughter of John Smith of Northumberland County and was a distant relation of GW, her great-grandmother Mary Warner Smith having been a sister of GW's grandmother Mildred Warner Washington (EUBANK, 52).

23.   At Mr. Booths all day with Revd. Mr. Smith.

24.   Came up to Popes Creek & staid there all day.

Pope's Creek was an addition to the Bridges Creek plantation, the original seat of GW's family in Virginia. In the 1720s GW's father, Augustine, built a house on the site lying on the west side of Pope's Creek about three-quarters of a mile from the Potomac River, and it was there that GW was born. On the death of GW's father, the plantation was inherited by GW's half brother Augustine Washington. It was now the home of Augustine's widow, Anne Aylett Washington, and their four children, including their only son, William Augustine Washington (1757–1810), who inherited the plantation upon his mother's death in 1773 and renamed it Wakefield. The present house, constructed in the 1930s, is a memorial house near the site of the original one (see FREEMAN, 1:15–47).

25.   Got up to my Brother Sams. to Dinner. Found Mrs. Jno. Washington & ca. there.

GW lost 10s. playing cards today (LEDGER A, 274).

26.   Remaind at my Brother Sams where my Brother Jno. came as also Mr. Lawe. Washington &ca. to Dinner.

27.   Dined at Mr. J. Washingtons with the compy. at my Brs.

John Washington (1730–1782) of Hylton was, like GW, a great-grandson of John the Immigrant. He married Catherine Washington, a sister of Lawrence Washington of Chotank. His home, Hylton, was in the Chotank neighborhood.

28.   Went to Boyds hole & returnd to my Brother's to Dinr., where we found Colo. Lewis & my Br. Charles.

At Boyd's Hole on the Potomac River in Stafford (now King George) County was a small settlement of merchants clustered about one of the original tobacco warehouses established in 1730 (HENING, 4:268).

It was probably on this date, while at Boyd's Hole, that GW paid his share of a general levy on members of the Mississippi Company to the treasurer, William Lee (LEDGER A, 274). During the first four years of its existence the company had been making such a small impression in England that many contemporaries and most early authorities did not even know it had existed before 1767 (CARTER [1], 109 n.19). By Mar. 1767 the executive committee had decided that the time was ripe for another attempt at pressing their memorial. During the company meeting at Stafford Court House 16 Dec. 1767, which GW attended, a quota of £13 11s. sterling was approved for "employing an agent to proceed immediately to Britain, there to solicit the Company's Grant, as fully, speedily, and effectually as the nature of the Business will admit." GW recorded this payment as £16 18s. 9d. Virginia currency (CARTER [2], 16:316–19; LEDGER A, 169).

29.   Went to St. Paul's Church & Dined at my Brothers.

Few churches in eighteenth-century Virginia had official names. Rather, a church tended to take a name from its location in the parish (the "upper" or the "lower" church), from its builder (Payne's Church), from a nearby geographical location (Nomini Church, Pohick Church) or simply from the name of its parish. Thus GW here refers to attending the church of St. Paul's Parish in Stafford County, which was the one closest to the home of his brother Samuel, a vestryman for St. Paul's Parish until 1770. By a change in county boundaries in 1776 this parish and its church became part of King George County (MEADE [1], 2:192, 187–88).

30.   Went fishing & dined under Mr. L. Washingtons Shore.

GW today lost £1 8s. 9d. at cards (LEDGER A, 274).

31.   Returnd home crossing at Hooes Ferry through Port Tobacco.

Remarks–of the–Weather

May 1.   Cool. Wind Northwardly & fresh.

2.   Cold & chilly wind to the Northward.

Barnsfield, home of the Hooe family which ran Hooe's Ferry for many years. From Smoot, *Days in an Old Town,* Alexandria, Va., 1934. (Alexandria Library)

3. Warm, wind getting Southwardly and Cloudy.

4. Very Warm & Sultry, with flying Clouds & appearance of Rain.

5. Warm again. Wind Southwardly & fresh.

6. Rain in the Morning. Warm afterwards with Clouds.

7. Cool Wind Northwardly.

8. Less Cool than yesterday but not warm.

9. Very warm & Sultry. Wind Southwardly.

10. Wind Eastwardly & not so warm as yesterday—being Cloudy.

11.   Much Rain fell last Night and this Morning. Evening clear & warm.

12.   Cool Evening and Morning but warm midday.

13.   Wind Northwardly & rather Cool.

14.   Warm & sometimes Sultry, with but little wind. In the Afternoon thunder & clouds with Slight Showers.

15.   Not so warm as yesterday.

16.   Wind at South but not fresh & tolerable warm, & clear.

17.   Warm with but little Wind and that Southwardly.

18.   Ditto————Ditto————Ditto.
   Note the Horns of this Moon were also up as the two last were tho a little more declining.

19.   Warm and but little Wind which was Southwardly. The weather very hazy as it had been for several days with the Sun and Moon remarkably red.

20.   Clear, and but little Wind, & that Southwardly.

21.   Warm, & clear in the Morning. Afternoon lowering, Wind Southwardly.

22.   Showery all day. Wind pretty fresh from the Southward.

23.   Wind shifted in the Night to No. Et. Blew and Raind hard all Night & till One or two Oclock this day, when it ceasd. The Afternoon became pleasant.

24.   Morning clear but Cool. Afternoon lowering & very Cool wind No. East.

25.   Misty all day and Cold with but little Wind.

26.   Cloudy & very Cold Wind Northwardly. Sometimes Sun appearg.

27.   Clear and somewhat Cool tho' there was but little Wind.

28. Clear & Warm. Wind, tho' little of it Southwardly.

29. Clear with a small breeze from the Northward.

30. Clear & warm with little Wind & that Eastwardly.

31. Warm & flying Clouds. Wind abt. South.

Observations

May 2d. My Carpenters & House People went to Planting Corn at Doeg Run after they had finishd fishing.

3. The hound bitch Mopsey brought 8 Puppys, distinguishd by the following Names—viz.—Tarter—Jupiter—Trueman—& Tipler (being Dogs)—and Truelove, Juno, Dutchess, & Lady being the Bitches—in all eight.

23. My Carpenters & House People went to Work at my Mill repairing the Dams—hightening of them—& opening the Race.

29. The bitch Chanter brought five Dog Puppies & 3 Bitch Ditto which were named as follow—viz.—Forrester—Sancho—Ringwood—Drunkard—and Sentwell. And Chanter—Singer—& Busy.

[June]

Where & how my time is Spent.

June 1st. Rid to Muddy hole Doeg Run & the Mill.

2. Went into the Neck.

3. Rid to Muddy hole Doeg Run & Mill.

4. At Home all day writing.

5. Went to Church at Alexandria & dined at Colo. Carlyles.

6. Rid to Muddy hole and the Mill, & met with Doctr. Rumney upon my Return who dined here.

While Rumney was at Mount Vernon, he gave Patsy Custis "a large Julep," probably a syrupy, nonalcoholic drink intended to soothe her nerves (receipt from William Rumney, 18 Feb. 1769, ViHi: Custis Papers).

GW today paid £15 for a horse for Jacky Custis (LEDGER A, 274).

7. Went up to Alexandria to meet the Attorney Genl. & returnd with him, his Lady & Daughter, Miss Corbin and Majr. Jenifer.

The Major Jenifer mentioned frequently in the diaries is Daniel of St. Thomas Jenifer (1723–1790), who lived at Stepney, a large estate in Charles County, Md. He served in various public offices in Maryland before the Revolution and was at this time a member of the Maryland Provincial Court. From 1778 to 1782 he was a member of the Continental Congress. In 1785 he was made one of the commissioners to settle the navigation of the Potomac River, and later he was a member of the Constitutional Convention.

8. At Home with the above Company. Colo. Fairfax, his Lady & Miss Nicholas—Colo. West & his Wife—& Colo. Carlyle Captn. Dalton & Mr. Piper—the three last of whom stayd all Night.

9. The Attorney &ca. went away leavg. Miss Nicholas only here.

10. Rid to Muddy hole Doeg Run and the Mill.

11. Rid to Ditto—Ditto & Ditto.

12. Went to Pohick Church and returnd to Dinner.

13. Went to Belvoir where Mr. Seldon his Lady &ca. were.

Mary Cary (1704–1775), an aunt of Sarah Cary Fairfax, married Joseph Selden (d. 1727) of Elizabeth City County and had three sons: Col. Cary Selden of Buckroe, Elizabeth City County; Col. Samuel Selden of Selvington, Stafford County; and Rev. Miles Selden (d. 1785) of Henrico County (*Va. Mag.*, 9:109; MEADE [1], 2:205).

14. Returnd home again, & found Mr. B. Fairfax here. Sent for Doctr. Rumney to Patcy Custis who was seized with fitts. Mr. M. Campbell lodgd here.

Rumney treated this outbreak of epileptic convulsions by bleeding Patsy and prescribing some of the same medicines that he had given her earlier: valerian, "nervous drops," and ingredients for another medicinal brew (receipt from William Rumney, 18 Feb. 1769, ViHi: Custis Papers).

15. Colo. Fairfax & Family together with Mr. Seldon & his dind here as also Doctr. Rumney. Mr. B. Fairfax went in the Mg.

16. Rid to the Mill Doeg Run and M. Hole. Mr. Campbell came here in the Eveng.

17. Rid into the Neck and to Muddy hole.

18. At home all day prepg. Invoices and Letters for England.

The "Invoices and Letters" were all dated 20 June 1768, the "Invoices" listing personal and plantation items needed from England for Mount Vernon and the Custis estates. To Charles Lawrence of London, GW wrote for a "Suit of handsome Cloth Cloaths," reminding the tailor that his long-legged correspondent stood a "full Six feet high" and was "not at all inclind to be corpulent." GW also ordered new clothes, including a green riding outfit for "Mastr. Custis . . . now 15 Yrs. of age & growing fast" and "a Suit of blew Livery" for Jacky's body servant (DLC:GW). From John Didsbury of London, GW ordered 32 pairs of shoes and boots for the Washington family, including 2 pairs of satin pumps, one in black and one in white, for Patsy Custis; also ordered were 4 pairs of "strong, course" shoes for Jacky's body servant (DLC:GW). In his cover letter to Robert Cary & Co., GW complained that for "four years out of five" he had made less profit by consigning his tobacco to Cary to sell in England than he would have made if he had sold it in Virginia (DLC:GW).

19. At home. Do. Do.

20. Went to Court and returnd at Night.

21. Went up again and stayd all Night.

22. Returnd home in the afternoon.

23. At Home all day.

24. Rid to Muddy hole, Doeg Run, and the Mill before Dinner, & was sent for by express to come to Alexa. to settle and Arbitrate an Acct. between Mr. George West & Mr. Chs. Alexander wt. Mr. Thomson Mason & Mr. Ellzey.

George West (d. 1786), son of Hugh and Sybil West and brother of John West, Jr., was a Fairfax County surveyor. He married Ann Alexander, who was a first cousin of Charles Alexander (1737–1806) of Preston in Fairfax County. Charles Alexander married Frances Brown (d. 1823), daughter of Richard Brown of Maryland.

William Ellzey (d. 1796), a son of Lewis Ellzey by his first wife and thus a half brother to Thomasin Ellzey of Truro Parish, married Frances Westwood and lived in the neighborhood of Dumfries, where he practiced law until about 1773. By 1774 he was living on his father's land in Loudoun County. GW sought his legal help in several disputes in the late 1760s.

Jacky Custis rode up to Alexandria with GW this afternoon.

25.   Returnd Home & remained there all day. Doctr. Rumney came in the Afternoon & stayd all Night.

26.   At Home. Doctr. Rumney went away in the Afternoon.

27.   At home. Colo. Fairfax & his Lady dined here & returnd in the Aftern.

28.   Set of for, and Reachd Fredericksburg.

GW was taking Jacky Custis to a boarding school in St. Mary's Parish, Caroline County, which the parish rector, Rev. Jonathan Boucher, ran in his home on a small plantation about 11 miles from the parish church. Jacky had received no instruction since Christmas when Magowan had ceased tutoring him, and GW was now anxious to have the boy resume his education. To school Jacky took his luggage, a body servant, and two horses (GW to Boucher, 30 May 1768, PHi: Dreer Collection).

29.   Rid round and examind the Wheat Fields there. Which were fine.

30.   Went to Mr. Bouchers. Dined there and left Jackey Custis. Returnd to Fredericksburg in the Afternn.

Jonathan Boucher (1737/8–1804), son of a poor English schoolmaster, came to Port Royal in 1759 to earn his living by tutoring gentlemen's sons. He soon began incurring heavy debts, a habit that would plague him for most of his life, but his fortune took a turn for the better in 1761 when he was offered the rectorship of neighboring Hanover Parish in King George County.

Jonathan Boucher, schoolmaster and clergyman, ran a boarding school below Fredericksburg which Jacky Custis attended. (Yale University Art Gallery, Mabel Brady Garvan Collection)

During the following year he took holy orders in England and, returning to Virginia, was confirmed as Hanover's rector. He later moved to his present position as rector of St. Mary's Parish in Caroline County, where he had a busy bachelor existence, preaching, working his plantation, and running the school for boys that Jacky had come to attend. Boucher was a genial and often witty man, but he also had traits that frequently led him into difficulty, as he readily admitted in his *Reminiscences:* "There was nothing quite ordinary or indifferent about me; my faults and my good qualities were all striking. All my friends (and no man ever had more friends) really loved me; and all my enemies as cordially hated me. Women, in particular, were apt to be pleased with me, because I had a natural gallantry and attachment to the sex which made them secure of my good-will and friendship. . . . In most respects, when thwarted and opposed, I was obstinate and mulish; yet there was nothing which I might not be coaxed into. A woman might do anything with me. . . . As to my conduct in life, it was of a piece with the rest of me: no man took more pains, or laboured harder, to earn money, but I took no adequate care of it when I had earned it. I always intended well, but often acted ill" (BOUCHER [1], 80–81; see also CLARK [3], 19–32).

Remarks — of the — Weather

June 1st.   Warm & still forenoon. Pleast. Afternoon a breeze from So. West.

2.   Warm morning with Clouds & Thunder & Rain. Towards Night a good deal more Rain & Loud thunder.

3.   Very warm morning with Rain abt. One Clock & a little thunder.

4.   Cold and sometimes Raining. Wind Westwardly.

5.   Cool with clouds & sometimes a sprinkle of Rain. Wind Westwardly.

6.   Cool and Cloudy but no Rain the Wind Northwardly.

7.   Clear & Cool. Wind at No. West.

8.   Ditto — Do. — Wind Westwardly.

9.   Clear and Warm, Wind abt. So. West. In the Afternoon Cloudy with Rain, and high wind from W.S.W.

10.   Cloudy Morning but clear & cool afterwards with brisk Wind from No. Wt.

11. Midling warm—with the Wind at So. Wt.

12. Warm. Wind Southwardly & fresh.

13. Wind Southwardly till the Afternoon when it Shifted to the Westward & blew a mere hurricane attended with hard Rain.

14. Wind very hard from the No. West with thunder & sevl. Showers of Rain.

15. Blustering Wind & varying from So. West to No. West. Cool.

16. Still & Warm with Rain in the Night.

17. Still & hot till abt. 2 Oclock then thunder & Rain with some Wind which afterwards dyed away.

18. Calm & cloudy with some Rain in the forenoon & thunder & Showery in the Afternoon & Night.

19. Clear & cool. Wind at No. West.

20. Clear and Warm. Wind Southly.

21. Warm & in the Afternoon Cloudy with Rain at Night.

22. Cool. Wind fresh from the No. Wt.

23. Wind very fresh from the So. West, and in the Night it blew a mere Hurricane from the same point with a little, & but a little Rain.

24. Wind fresh from the Westward.

25. Calm and Still & yet Cool. In the forenoon Wind Eastwardly in the Afternoon & Cloudy.

26. Cloudy with appearances of Rain in the Afternoon.

27. Wind fresh from the So. West & Warm. In the Afternoon thundr., & Rain for half an hour or more.

28.   Showery till 11 Oclock with very high Wind from the So. West & West all day, & cool.

29.   Warm with but little Wind till the Evening then Cool with the Wind fresh from the No. West.

30.   Cool with the Wind though not much of it Westwardly.

Observations

June 1st.   Upon looking over my Wheat, I found all those places which had been injurd by the March frosts extreamely thin, low & backwards, having branchd but little, & looking puny—indeed in many places the Ground was entirely naked and where it was not, there was but too much cause to apprehend that the Wheat woud be choaked with Weeds.

It was also observable that all my early Wheat (generally speaking) was headed and heading. The common Wheat was but just putting out head; & the Red Straw Wheat had but very little or no appearance of head & was lower than any of the other, although first sown.

The heads of the whole appeard short & did not promise any great increase.

It was also remarkable that the Red Straw Wheat had a great number of Smutty or blasted heads in the same manner it had last year, when they did put out.

8th.   Carpenters went to getting the frame for my Barn at the House.

[1]5.   The Maryland hound Bitch Lady took Forrester & was also servd by Captn., & refusd the Dogs on the 11th.

Finishd breaking up Corn Ground at Doeg Run.

17.   Finishd breakg. up Corn Ground at Muddy hole.

18.   Finishd Do. Do. at the Mill.

22.   About this time Captn. Posey's Bitch Countess was discoverd Lind to Dabster & was immediately shut up & none but Sterling sufferd to go to her.

Musick was also in heat & servd promiscuously by all the Dogs, intending to drown her Puppy's.

25. The Carpenters finishd getting the Frame for the Barn at my Ho. House.

28. Began to cut the upper part of my Timothy Meadow.

[July]

Where & how—my time is Spent.

July 1st.   Went over to Stafford Court House to a meeting of the Missisipi. Dined and lodged there.

With another change of ministers in England, and because of the new Indian treaties in progress which opened large parts of trans-Appalachian land to white settlement, the Mississippi Company's hopes were quickening. Dr. Arthur Lee, brother of the company's treasurer, William Lee, was taken into the company and chosen as the agent to be sent to England. He probably received his instructions at this meeting (CARTER [2], 318; CARTER [1], 109). The new agent, however, had little luck in his petitioning and lobbying. Although the Lee family—the original movers for the company—maintained their hopes up to the outbreak of the Revolution, GW was not so sanguine. While transferring his accounts to a new ledger in Jan. 1772, GW wrote off his £27 13s. 5d. investment in the company as a total loss instead of carrying it over (Richard Henry Lee to William Lee, 15 April 1774, BALLAGH, 1:106; LEDGER A, 169).

Stafford County's courthouse at this time stood on the south side of Potomac Creek about four miles upstream from Marlborough. During the Revolution it was moved to a site near present Stafford, Va. (WATKINS, 115–18), the location shown on the map on p. 1:220–21.

2. Dined at Dumfries and reachd home.

3. At Home all day.

4. Rid to see my Wheat at differt. Places. Doctr. Rumney came here in the afternn.

5. Went to Muddy hole with Doctr. Rumney to see the Cradlers at work.

6. Rid to Muddy hole and Doeg Run after Doctr. Rumney went away. When I returnd found Mr. Wm. Lee & Doctr. Lee here.

Arthur Lee (1740–1792) was the youngest of the six surviving sons of Thomas Lee (1690–1750), builder of Stratford Hall, Westmoreland County, and his wife, Hannah Ludwell Lee (1701–1749/50). He attended Eton and the

George Digges lived at Warburton, Prince George's County, Md. (Mr. and Mrs. Walter A. Slowinski)

One of the many Lees in the Washington circle of friends, Dr. Arthur Lee had studied medicine in Edinburgh. (Independence National Historical Park Collection)

University of Edinburgh, where he took a medical degree in 1764, and then returned to Virginia to practice medicine in Williamsburg. Arthur and his elder brother William (1739–1795) were now preparing for a visit to England which would see Arthur take up the study of law and William enter the tobacco trade in London (LEE [1], 195). During this visit to Mount Vernon the brothers probably discussed with GW the prospects for the Mississippi Land Company, in which both were deeply involved.

7.   Mr. Lee went away. Mr. Darnel & Daughter – Mr. Geo. Digges & his two eldest Sisters came here & stayed all Night.

The Darnall (many spellings) family of Maryland descended from Col. Henry Darnall (d. 1711), who emigrated from England in 1672. This Mr. Darnall may be a great-grandson of Col. Henry, also named Henry, whose daughter Mary married Charles Carroll of Carrollton this same year (ROWLAND [1], 2:445–47).

   George Digges (1743–1792) was the eldest son of William Digges of Warburton Manor. George's two eldest sisters were Theresa (Tracy) and Elizabeth (Betty).

8.   Doctr. Lee & all the rest went away & I rid to the Cradlers (cutting my Wheat at the Mill).

9. Rid to Muddy hole, the Mill, and Doeg Run before Dinner & to the Mill afterwards—where my People was harvesting.

10. Went to Church and returnd to Dinner.

11. Rid to Muddy hole where three white men were Cradling —& then to the Mill where we were getting in Wheat. Mr. Chichester with his wife Miss S. McCarty, & Dr. Rumney came.

Sinah McCarty (died c.1809) was a daughter of Capt. Daniel McCarty of Mount Air and a sister of Mrs. Sarah McCarty Chichester, with whom she appears here.

Rumney continued his treatment of Patsy Custis by giving her two capsules of musk, which in the eighteenth century was thought to be a strong anti-spasmodic agent and was commonly used as a remedy for epilepsy. Four or five days later Rumney apparently sent a dose of valerian to Patsy (receipt of William Rumney, 18 Feb. 1769, ViHi: Custis Papers).

12. Rid to Muddy hole before breakfast where all hands were harvesting the Wheat. The Company went away.

13. Went in to the Neck where I this day began my Harvest. Colo. Fairfax & Doctr. Lee dind here and returnd.

14. Attended in the Neck Again.

15. Went over again & drove back by Rain about One Oclock, which continued all the Afternoon.

16. Went by Muddy hole & Doeg Run to the Vestry at Pohick Church. Stayd there till half after 3 Oclock & only 4 Members coming returned by Captn. McCartys & dined there.

By Virginia law, the presence of at least 7 of the 12 vestrymen was necessary to form a quorum (HENING, 7:303). The absence of so many members of the vestry on this occasion suggests the beginning of a new strategy by those vestrymen who disliked the location for the proposed new Pohick Church.

17. At home all day.

18. In the Neck with my People Harvesting.

19. In Ditto with Ditto. Mr. Richd. Graham came here in the afternoon.

Richard Graham (d. 1796) was a Scottish merchant of Dumfries, Prince William County, who was heavily involved in western lands. In 1757 he married Jane Brent (b. 1738), the youngest daughter of Col. George Brent (d. 1778).

20.   In Ditto with Do. in the Forenoon. In the Afternoon went with them to cut the Wheat at Doeg Run.

21.   Went to the Harvest Field at Ditto.

22.   Rid to Ditto in the forenoon with my Wife & Patcy Custis.

23.   Rid to Ditto in the forenoon—where I met with one Russel, a Tenant of mine upon the Land I bought of Carters Estate, coming down to see upon what terms he coud get the Land.

George Russell was a tenant on land in Fauquier County formerly owned by the late George Carter (see main entries for 10 and 17 March 1769).

24.   Went to Pohick Church.

25.   Went to Alexandria & bought a Bricklayer from Mr. Piper & returnd to Dinner. In the Afternoon Mr. R. Alexander came.

Michael Tracy (Treacy), probably an Irish indentured servant, was bought by GW for £18 4s., a good price if Tracy was an apt bricklayer (LEDGER A, 277). In July 1770 a Michael Tracey was advertised in the *Virginia Gazette* as a runaway from Andrew Wales, brewer, of Alexandria (R, 26 July 1770).

26.   Rid with Mr. Alexander to my Meadow & returnd with him to Dinner. Mr. Vale. Crawford here. They went away.

27.   Rid to the Meadow again. Vale. Crawford & his Br. Wm. both came this Afternoon.

28.   Went to the Meadow with the above two.

29.   But little Wind—that Southwardly—very Warm. Rid to the Meadow in the Afternn. Writg. in the Fore.

30.   Rid into the Neck and from thence to Doeg Run where we were Haymakg. Colo. Carlyle & Lady came last N. & went to Day.

31.   Went to Alexa. Church. Dind at Colo. Carlyles & returnd in the Afternoon.

The Fairfax vestry decided 27 Nov. 1766 to replace the parish's two church buildings with new brick structures, one near Four Mile Run called Falls Church, and one at Alexandria, later called Christ Church. The vestry advertised for bids and on 1 Jan. 1767 agreed with James Parsons (d. 1785) to build the church at Alexandria for £600. Because work on the new church was not yet finished, the worship services GW attended in town today must have been held in the old building (see entry for 3 Feb. 1760; POWELL, 85–87).

Remarks—of the—Weather

July 1st.   Cloudy & Cool in the Morning—but clear and very warm in the Afternoon and Night.

2.   Clear and exceeding Hot with but little Wind. Night also Warm.

3.   Clear and Warm but Windy from the So. West.

4.   Cool in the Morning, warm afterwards & Cool at Night again—but little Wind.

5.   Warm & Cloudy—with appearances of Rain. Wind Southwardly. The Afternoon, & Evening Cool.

6.   Drizling in the Morning, & very cloudy, all day—with the Wind Southwardly.

7.   Cool & clear—with the Wind at No. West & westwardly.

8.   Clear & tolerably cool. Wind at So. West.

9.   Clear, warm, & still abt. Noon. Afterwards cooler Wind being risen from the Southward.

10.   Very Sultry and hot—although the Wind blew fresh from So. & So. West. Clear.

11.   Wind Southwardly—Warm—& showery abt. 2 Oclock.

12.   Very warm and Sultry with appearances of Rain—but none fell. Wind Southwardly.

13.   Warm and but little Wind—& that Southwardly.

14.   Clear & Warm with a little Wind from the Southward.

15.   Cloudy Morning & drizling & rainy Afternoon—with wind westwardly. Note this Rain continued slow till some time in the Night and with but little Wind.

16.   Clear & cool in the forenoon with thunder abt. 11 Oclock. Abt. 2 Oclock a black Cloud with Wind and Rain from the No. West & at 5 a Secd. Cloud from the same Quarter.

17.   Wind Westwardly and little of it. Day moderate.

18.   Warm & but little Wind. Some appearance of Rain—but none fell.

19.   Clear and very warm with a small breeze from the Southward.

20.   Very warm with but little Wind and that Southwardly. Clear.

21.   Clear & Exceeding hot till abt. 10 Oclock—then a little cooler by the Wind Rising from the Southward.
    Note—last Night & the Night before makes but the 4 or 5th. warm Night we have had this year.

22d.   Clear & very warm—with the Wind Southwardly. Last Night warm.

23.   Clear & very warm, with but little Wind & that variable. Hot Night again.

24.   Very warm notwithstanding the Wind blew high from the So. W.
    In the Afternoon some Rain & Wind here but a good deal towards Alexa.

25.   Cool & showery in places. Very cool in the Eveng. Wind at No. West.

26.   Wind at No. West & cool & clear.

27.   Wind Westwardly, clear, & somethg. warmer.

28.   Clear & something warmer still. Wind Southerly.

29. But little wind & that Southwardly. Very warm.

30. Very little Wind but very hot with appearances of Rain tho none fell.

31. Very warm, with Rain flying abt. but none fell with us. Wind fresh from the southward in the Afternoon.

Observations

July 2d. Finishd going over my Corn ground in the Neck—both with the Plows & Hoes.

4. Began to cut my Wheat at the Mill—but upon examination, finding it too green desisted.

Note, upon looking into my Wheat the Rust was observd to be more or less in it all—but, except some at Doeg Run it was thought no great damage woud follow as the Wheat was rather too forward.

5. Jonathan Farmer coming down last Night, & examining my Wheat to day was of opinion that some of Muddy hole field was fit, at least might be cut with safety. Accordingly began it with himself 3 other White Men & 4 Negroe Cradlers letting the grain lye upon the stubble abt. 2 days to dry.

The three white cradlers were Eliab Roberts, Abner Roberts, and Andrew Jones. The text clearly reads Jonathan "Farmer," but GW meant to write Jonathan Palmer, who was hired as head harvester for 10s. per day (LEDGER A, 274, 277).

8. Began to cut the Wheat at the Mill in the field round the Overseers House which was cut, & abt. 4 Acres in the other this day by 10 and sometimes 11 Cradlers which were all that worked amounting in the whole to abt. 40 Acres.

9. Six and sometimes 7 Cradlers, cut the remainder of the field (abt. 28 Acres) on this side to day.

The Wheat at Muddy hole, was (that is all that was cut down) got into Shocks by 11 Oclock to day—and abt. 3/4 of the field round the Overseers House at the Mill.

Pulld the Flax at Muddy hole.

On this day GW paid off Abner Roberts and Andrew Jones, giving them a total of £3 1s. 6d. for their work (LEDGER A, 274).

11 & 12th.   Pulld the Flax at home.

Got in the most of the Mill Wheat but was prevented finishing by Rain.

Three white Men (Cradlers) cut down abt. 10 or 12 Acres of Muddy hole Wheat.

Hands Went to Muddy hole & finishd Harvesting the Wheat there—that is cutting & securing it in shocks.

The three white cradlers were Jonathan Palmer, Eliab Roberts, and Robert Langley.

13.   Some hands went & got the residue of the Mill Wheat into the House & all the Rest with the Cradlers went into the Neck & cut down & securd little more than 20 Acres of Wheat.

14.   The hands from the Mill joind the others, & altogether finishd the Cut of Wheat (containing 50 Acres) at the Orchard point great part of which was very thick, Rank, & heavy Cuttg.

15.   Began cuttg. the Wheat next to it on the Riverside. Abt. One Oclock was stopd by Rain which continued the whole afternoon.

16.   Finishd this cut, & began the one next to the House. This day it also Raind & stopd the Harvest abt. an hour or two.

17.   Dischargd three Cradlers keepg. only Jonathan Palmer & Eliab Roberts.

The three discharged cradlers, each of whom was paid 5s. per day, were David Kinsey, paid for 2 days of work; William Black, for 1¾ days; and Robert Langley, for 6 days (LEDGER A, 274).

18.   Nine Cradlers at work including the two white men.

20th.   About 11 Oclock finished Harvesting the Wheat in the Neck; that is cutting it down, & securing it shocks. In the whole, allowing for the time lost by Rain we were six days doing it.

About 2 Oclock in the Afternoon began to cut the Field at Doeg Run containing 150 Acres with 10 Cradlers—3 of them sorry hands.

21.   Finishd one quarter of the above field abt. 2 Oclock.

Note this cut was, in places, greatly injured by the Rust.

22. About 2 Oclock finishd another Cut in this field being of the same Size of the last. This was also injured by Rust—as well as by the frosts.

23. At 12 Oclock finishd the third cut of 37½ Acres at Doeg Run & clapd into the last one.

25. Finishd the last cut abt. One Oclock this day (Monday) part of wch. was much hurt by the Rust—& cut down the small piece at home & securd it.

Note—from the most accurate experiments I coud make this year, upon Wheat siezd with the Rust before it is fully formd & beginning to Harden, it appears to be a matter of very little consequence whether it is cut down so soon as it is siezd with this distemper (I mean the parts of the field that are so) —or sufferd to Stand—for in either case the grain perishes & has little or no flower in it. That indeed wch. is sufferd to stand may gain a little, & but a little in respect to the grain & the other in respect to the straw so that I think it is nearly equal wch. of the two methods is followed.

Note also—from this year's experiments, it appears certain that Wheat may be cut down (suffering it to take a day or two's Sun) much Sooner than it generally is. I took Wheat of three differt. degrees of Ripeness i.e., some whose Straw and head was green (but the grain of full size and Milky) —some whose Straw from the upper joint was colouring—and some that the Straw from the said joint was col[ore]d but the Knots (at the Joints) Green, & observd after they had lain 2 or 3 days in the sun that the grain of the first was but little shrunk—the 2d. scarce perceptable—& the last plump & full by wch. it evidently appear's that to cut Wheat Knot green is not only safe but the most desirable state it can be cut in—& that where there is a large qty. the question is, whether it may not be better to begin while the wheat is colouring from the upper joint as the grain will loose but little (if any) than to cut it in an overripe state when it may loose a good deal more by shattering. For my part I am clear it is better to cut it green & shall have no reluctance to practice where the whole cannot be cut at the exact period one woud choose it.

26. Began to cut my Timothy Meadow.

GW discharged Eliab Roberts today, paying him £5 13s. (LEDGER A, 277).

30. Finished Do. & got into Stacks without damage.

About the 27 and 28 Sowed some Turnep Seed in Corn Ground at Morris's—that is at Doeg Run Plann.

Memm. On the 30th. of this Month I agreed with Jonathan Palmer to come and Work with my Carpenters; either at their Trade—Cowpering—or, in short at any thing that he may be set about—In consideration of which, I am to pay him £40 pr. Ann. allow him 400 lbs. of Meat & 20 Bushels of Indian Corn. I am also to allow him to keep two Milch Cows (one half of whose Increase I am to have) and to have Wheat for which he is to pay. He is to be allowed a Garden & I am to get the old dwelling House at Muddy hole repaird for him. I am also to take his Waggon at £17, if he brings it free from damage and it is no older than he says— that is about a 12 Month. Note he is to be here as early as possible in April—if not in March.

On this day GW paid Edmund Palmer 17s. for 1 day of cradling and 4 days of mowing. He also settled accounts with his head harvester, Jonathan Palmer, who was paid £6 for 18 days of cradling and 4 days of mowing, plus a bonus of £1 4s. "in considn. of his g[oo]d. behaviour" (LEDGER A, 277). The contract with Palmer is typical of the time: while the form is standard, the content, being the product of bargaining by both sides, reflects the particular strengths and needs of each party. Such contracts were usually annual, and their renegotiation tended to reflect the changed circumstances of one or both parties.

COWPERING: an older spelling of coopering.

[August]

Where and how my time is Spent.

Aug. 1st.   Went to Belvoir & dined. Returnd in the Afternoon.

2.   Rid to the Mill, Doeg Run, and Muddy hole. Miss Manly dind here & Mr. Alexr. came in the Evening.

MISS MANLY: probably Mary (Molly) Manley, eldest daughter of Harrison and Margaret Manley.

3.   Mr. Alexander & Miss Manly went away. Rid to the Mill & Muddy hole.

4.   Went a fox hunting in the Neck with Lund Washington & Mr. Thos. Triplet. Started nothing.

5.   Went by Muddy hole—the Mill—& Doeg Run Plantations to a Race at Cameron. Returnd in the Evening.

Cameron was the name of the neighborhood which began at the junction
of several major roads leading into Alexandria, between one and two miles
west of town, and thence extending several miles west along Cameron Run,
the stream which fed into Hunting Creek. In GW's lifetime Cameron lent
its name to a proposed town, several family homes, a mill, and an ordinary.
In the sense that GW uses the name here, Cameron was probably the junction point itself, a convenient location for horse-racing fans who lived in
Alexandria or in the surrounding countryside (see HARRISON [1], 414–15;
RICE, 2:89).

6.   At home all day.

7.   Ditto – Ditto.

8.   Went a fox hunting but Started nothing. Visited Plantation's
in the Neck & Mill.

9.   At home all day.

10.   Rid to the Mill Doeg Run and Muddy hole and returnd to
Dinner.

11.   Rid to the same places as yesterday & returnd to Dinner.

12.   Rid to Muddy hole Doeg Run & Mill & returnd when I
found Doctr. Rumney.

13.   The hounds havg. started a Fox in self huntg. we followd
& run it after sevl. hours chase into a hold when digging it out it
escapd. The Doctr. went home.

14.   At home. Mrs. Fairfax & Miss Nicholas came in the Afternoon.

15.   Went to Court. Mr. Igns. Digges Mr. Lee and Mr. Hill
came here.

Ignatius Digges (1707–1785) of Melwood, Prince George's County, Md., was
the grandson of William Digges (d. 1698), who moved from Virginia to
Maryland in the late seventeenth century. Ignatius, a first cousin to William
Digges of Warburton, married Elizabeth Parnham, and after her death Mary
Carroll, daughter of Daniel Carroll of Duddington (1707–1734). His only
child, a daughter Mary Digges (1745–1805) by his first wife, married Thomas
Sim Lee (1745–1819), of Prince George's County, Md., who is probably the
Mr. Lee mentioned here. Lee was a grandson of Philip Lee (1678–1718),
who moved from Virginia to Maryland in 1700.

Washington owned many hunting prints such as this one, evidence of his deep interest in fox hunting. (Mount Vernon Ladies' Association of the Union)

In the mid-seventeenth century Clement Hill settled in Maryland, where he sat on the council. Since Hill had no issue, his nephew, also named Clement Hill (1670–1743), inherited his uncle's lands in Maryland, migrated from England to Maryland in 1696, and eventually settled at the Woodyard, Prince George's County. This Clement had three sons, John (d. 1800), Clement (1707–1782), and Henry (d. 1796), and two grandsons, Clement Jr. (1743–1807) and Henry Jr., all of whom were alive in 1768 (MACKENZIE [1], 2:310–17).

16.   At home with the above Gentlemen. Mrs. Fairfax & Miss Nicholas went home after Dinner.

Ignatius Digges of Melwood in Prince George's County, Md. (Mr. Outerbridge Horsey)

Mary Carroll Digges, second wife of Ignatius Digges. (Peter H. Davidson & Co., Inc.)

17.   Dined at Belvoir with the above Gentlemen & returnd in the afternoon.

18.   Rid round all my Plantations after the above gentlemen went away.

19.   At home—settled & paid the Sheriff.

Once a year the justices of each county would submit the names of three of their number to the governor and council, who would choose one of the three to be sheriff for the ensuing year. The Virginia county sheriff was more an administrator than a law officer, having the major responsibility for running elections, serving summonses, and collecting the annual levies in his county, which included those laid by the county and the parishes within the county as well as public levies set for the entire colony by the General Assembly. Much of this collecting was done by sub-sheriffs; in 1768 Sampson Darrell was sheriff of Fairfax County and Pierce Baily was the sub-sheriff who appears here to collect the balance owed by GW for this year, £1 15s. 3d. (LEDGER A, 277).

For the Fairfax County levy this year GW paid for 85 tithables at 14 pounds of tobacco each. Sixty-seven of these tithables lived in Truro Parish and thus came under that parish's levy of 41 pounds of tobacco per tithable. GW also paid the public tax of £1 10s. on his chariot and his chair as well as some minor fees he owed for government services. The total of the levies paid by GW in 1768 was 3,937 pounds of tobacco and £3 14s. 4d. cash. Because GW no longer grew tobacco at Mount Vernon, he paid his tobacco levies in local tobacco warehouse, or transfer, notes, mostly on tobacco paid him by his local Mount Vernon renters. With tobacco worth 2d. a pound, these notes were equivalent to £32 16s. 2d. in currency (LEDGER A, 236; Truro Vestry Book, 128, 130, DLC. See also FLIPPIN, 312–17; SYDNOR, 68–70, 78; HENING, 7:643–44).

20.   Set of for my Brother Sam's & Nomomy. Crossd at the Mouth of Nangamy & went to my Brothers.

Mrs. Washington and Patsy Custis accompanied GW on this trip, and Jacky Custis, taking a vacation from his studies, met them today at Samuel Washington's house (GW to Jonathan Boucher, 19 Aug. 1768, owned by Mr. Sol Feinstone, Washington Crossing, Pa.). During the family's stay in the Chotank area, GW loaned Samuel £1 and apparently played cards twice, losing £1 on one occasion and winning 3s. 9d. on the other (LEDGER A, 277).

21.   At my Brothers. Colo. Lewis & my Brothr. Charles came there.

22.   Still at my Brothers with other Company—his Child being Christned.

This child was one of several that did not live to maturity (DIARIES, 1:285n).

23.   Hauling the Sein under Mr. Lawrence Washington's shore.

24.   Imbarkd on board my Schooner for Nomomy. Lay of Captn. Laidler's.

John Laidler (d. 1773), of Laidler's ferry, just above lower Cedar Point in Charles County, Md. Laidler's was the major ferry crossing to the Virginia shore on that part of the Potomac River.

25.   Hauling the Sein upon the Bar of Cedar point for Sheeps heads but catchd none. Run down below the Mouth of Machodack & came to.

Upper Machodoc Creek, in Stafford (now in King George) County, flows into the Potomac about 14 miles above GW's birthplace at Pope's Creek, Westmoreland County.

26.   Reachd my Brother John's at Night.

While the Washingtons were in Westmoreland County, Jacky Custis became "much disorder'd by an intermitting fever, attended with billeous vomittings," and Dr. Charles Mortimer of Fredericksburg was called to treat him. Jacky was soon better, but he remained so "very weak & low," that "his Mamma" insisted on taking him to Mount Vernon until he was fully recovered (GW to Jonathan Boucher, 4 Sept. 1768, PU; BLANTON, 358–59).

27. Hauling the Sein upon Hollis's Marsh Bar & elsewhere for Sheeps heads but catchd none.

Hollis Marsh was at the upper cape of Nomini Bay.

28. Went to Nomony Church & returnd to my Brother's to Dinner.

29. Went into Machodack Ck. fishing and dind with the Revd. Mr. Smith.

Lower Machodoc Creek empties into the Potomac River about two miles below Nomini Bay in Westmoreland County, forming a bay about one mile wide at its mouth. This creek is not to be confused with Jackson's Creek, also in Westmoreland County, which empties into the Potomac six miles below Lower Machodoc Creek and was sometimes called "Lower Machodoc" (EATON, 71).

The Cople Parish glebe, where Thomas Smith lived, was near the mouth of the Lower Machodoc Creek about three miles east of Bushfield (FITHIAN, 190).

30. Hauling the Sein on the Bars near Hollis's Marsh & other places.

31. Dined with Mr. Jno. Smith who was marryed yesterday to the widow Lee.

John Smith (1715–1771) of Fleets Bay plantation on Indian Creek, Northumberland County, was a second cousin to GW. He had previously been married to Mary Jaquelin (1714–1764) of Jamestown and had lived for many years at Shooter's Hill plantation, Middlesex County. In 1767 he established a smallpox inoculation hospital at Fleets Bay, despite the fear of some Virginians that he was opening "a second Pandora's Box," spreading the disease instead of preventing it. In Feb. 1768 he was accused of causing two or three outbreaks of smallpox in the colony, including one in Williamsburg, by failing to quarantine his patients long enough after inoculation (William Nelson to John Norton, 14 Aug. 1767 and 27 Feb. 1768; MASON [1], 31–33, 38–40). But he persisted in offering his services as an inoculator until his death (*Va. Gaz.*, R, 9 June 1768 and 20 April 1769).

THE WIDOW LEE: Mary, daughter of J. Philip Smith and widow of both Jesse Ball (1716–1747) of Lancaster County and Col. John Lee (1724–1767) of Essex and Westmoreland counties. John Lee had left Mary the use, for her lifetime, of his land and slaves at Cabin Point in Westmoreland County, about 3½ miles east of Bushfield near the mouth of the Lower Machodoc Creek (indenture between John Smith and Mary Lee, 30 Aug. 1768, Westmoreland County Deeds and Wills, 1768–73, 13–15, Vi Microfilm). The newly married couple were now living at Cabin Point, and it was probably there that GW dined with Smith on this day.

Remarks – of the – Weather

Augt. 1.   But little Wind & yet not very warm.

2.   Clear & warm. Wind Eastwardly.

3.   Wind Eastwardly – with appearances of Rain but none fell.

4.   But little Wind with great appearance of a settled Rain after noon tho not enough fell to make the House eves run.

5.   Very warm with the wind Southwardly.

6.   Exceeding hot – & still till the Evening, then a slight breeze from the Southward.

7.   Very Warm, Wind Southwardly. Abt. 3 Oclock a slight Shower here & better at the Mill & Doeg Run – to the No. Wt. & Southward the appearance of a great deal of Rain.

8.   Cloudy Morning, with Showers in difft. places but none here. Wind Southwardly.

9.   Cloudy, with sometimes a mist till abt. One clock – after which two or three smart Showers for a few Minutes from the S.W.

10.   A fine Settled Rain from the Northward for two or three hours in the Morning – with slight Showers afterwards.

11.   Cool Wind being at No. West – with gt. appearances of Rain – but none fell.

12.   Clear and tolerably warm. Wind Southwardly.

13.   Warm with very little Wind. Clouds to the Westward – but no Rain here.

14.   Wind abt. Southwest & tolerably fresh, otherwise Warm. Clouds to the Westward & thunder with a great deal of Rain upwards – but none here.

15.   Great appearances of Rain but none fell with us. Warm.

16.   Clear and Warm with very little Wind.

17.   Clear and warm in the first part of the day–with a fine Rain tho rather heavy abt. 5 Oclock lasting 2 hours first from the So. West–then from the North.

18.   Clear and warm–also still.

19.   Clear with the Wind fresh from the No. West–& cool.

20.   Clear, & not warm–wind, what little there was, abt. So. West.

21.   Clear & cool. Wind So. West.

22.   Clear and Warm with very little Wind from the So. West. Abt. 11 Oclock at Night the Wind (witht. any Cloud or apparent cause) came out hard at No. West & blew so all Night.

23.   The Wind fresh from the No. West all day and very cold.

24.   Warmer, but still cool, with the Wind from the Eastward.

25.   Warm with very little Wind and that Southwardly.

26.   Exceeding Hot with very little or no Wind all day.

27.   Very warm also with very little wind. Abt. 1 Oclock Thunder, but no rain. At Nomony.

28.   Warm with but little wind and some Clouds, but no Rain.

29.   Brisk Eastwardly Wind in the Morning. Calm midday, & Westwardly Wind in the Evening.

30.   Very calm–& warm all day.

31.   Clear with the Wind Westwardly & not warm.

Observations–in–August

Augt. 1st.   Began to tread out Wheat at the Mill. Also began to draw it in, in the Neck.

An ox cart of Washington's day. From Arthur Young, *Annals of Agriculture,* London, 1792. (Mount Vernon Ladies' Association of the Union)

2.   Began to draw it in (that is to carry it from the field on this side the Run over to the Barn) with only my Ox Cart at Doeg R.

5.   Began to cut my Timothy Seed—there. Getting Wheat in at Muddy hole.

6.   The Hound Bitch Lady brought four Puppys that is 3 dogs and a bitch distinguished by the following Names—viz. that with the most black Spots Vulcan—the other black spotted Dog Searcher—the Red spotted Dog Rover—and the red spotted bitch Sweetlips.

8.   Sowed Turnep Seed at home—in the Neck and at Muddy hole Plann.
   Began to Sow Wheat at the Mill & at Doeg Run.

10.   Sowed Turneps at the Mill.

11.   Began to beat Cyder at Doeg Run Muddy hole, & in the Neck.

15.   Set in to Sowing Wheat at Muddy hole.

26.   Finishd drawing in & securing my Wheat in the Neck.

29.   Began to Sow Wheat at Ditto.

[September]

Where & how my time is spent.

Septr. 1.   Set out from Nomony in my return to Chotanck. Lodgd on board the Vessel between Swan Point & Cedr. P.

Here GW must mean Lower Cedar Point, in St. Mary's County, Md., only a few miles up the Potomac River from Swan Point and just across the river from the lower side of Chotank (now Mathias) Neck.

2,   Came up as high as Hoes ferry & Walk to my Brother Sams.

3.   Went to Mr. John Stiths & dined there. Returnd in the afternoon.

GW's host is probably John Stith (1724–1773), son of Drury and Elizabeth Buckner Stith; John married Elizabeth Wray (d. 1806) of Hampton and King George County.

4.   Went to Church. Dined at Colo. Harrison & returnd to my Brs. in the afternoon.

Nathaniel Harrison (1703–1791), of Brandon, Surry County, was the eldest son of Nathaniel Harrison (1677–1727) and Mary Cary Harrison of Wakefield, Surry County. After the death of his first wife, Mary Digges Harrison (1717–1743), he married Lucy Carter, daughter of Robert "King" Carter and widow of Henry Fitzhugh (d. 1742) of Eagle's Nest, where GW was visiting on this date.

5.   Crossd over to the lower point of Nangemoy where I met my Chariot & returnd home.

6.   Went in the Forenoon to the Mill–Doeg Run & Muddy hole. In the Afternoon paid a visit to Majr. Fairfax (Brother to Lord Fx.) at Belvoir.

Maj. Robert Fairfax (1707–1793), of Leeds Castle, Yorkshire, Eng., was the younger brother of Thomas Fairfax, sixth Baron Fairfax of Cameron. Robert had recently arrived from England to visit his relatives, dividing his time between Belvoir and Lord Fairfax's home, Greenway Court, in the Shenandoah Valley. Robert preferred Belvoir, finding that Valley living placed him "quite beyond the gentry . . . among the woods, with nothing but buckskins,

Maj. Robert Fairfax, later seventh Baron Fairfax of Cameron, had just arrived in Virginia when he visited Mount Vernon in 1768. (Virginia Historical Society)

viz., back-woodsmen and brutes . . . it is almost past description" (quoted in BROWN, 160).

7.   Dined at Belvoir with Mrs. W– –n &ca.

8.   Went to a Ball in Alexandria.

9.   Proceeded to the Meeting of our Vestry at the New Church and lodgd at Captn. Edwd. Paynes.

The "New Church," built for the vestry by Edward Payne to serve the upper part of Truro Parish, was about 12 miles north-northwest of Colchester. Although the building was not quite finished at the time of this meeting, the vestrymen, "understanding that it is the general Desire of the People in this part of the Parish to have the Church received," voted four to three to open it for use, GW voting with the majority (Truro Vestry Book, 131, DLC).

10.   Returnd home & dind at Belvoir with Lord Fairfax &ca.

11.   At Home all day.

12.   Lord Fairfax, & his Brother & Colo. Fairfax & Mr. B. Fairfax dind here. The latter stayd all Night.

13.   Went a fox huntg. with Lord Fairfax Colo. Fairfax & B. Fairfax. Catchd nothg.

14.   Mr. B. Fairfax & myself went a huntg. Started a Fox & run it into a hole but did not catch it.

15.   Dined at Belvoir with Colo. Robt. Burwell.

Robert Burwell (1720–1779), a planter from Isle of Wight County, was a member of the council 1764–76. Besides his home plantation in Isle of Wight, he owned land in Surry, Loudoun, Prince William, and Frederick counties (ISLE OF WIGHT, 311–13).

16.   Went into the Neck. Returnd to dinner.

17.   At home – Colo. Robt. Burwell, Mr. Grymes & Colo. Fairfax dind here. The latter went home in the Evening.

In GW's lifetime the Grymes family of most prominence in Virginia descended from John Grymes (1691–1748), grandson of Charles Grymes the immigrant. John, who was receiver general of Virginia, 1723–48, bought Brandon in Middlesex County, which became the Grymes family seat. At the time of this diary entry two of John's three sons were still living: Benjamin Grymes (1725–c.1776), of Smithfield, Spotsylvania County, which he represented in the House of Burgesses 1766–71; and Ludwell Grymes (b. 1733), of Gloucester County and by 1771 of Burlington, Orange County. John Grymes's eldest son, Philip, died in 1754; Philip's sons were Peyton, Benjamin, Charles, John (who was at Eton in 1760), and Philip Ludwell Grymes (1746–1805) of Brandon, a burgess for Middlesex County, 1769–70.

18.   Colo. & Mrs. Fairfax dind & lodgd here.

19.   Went to Court with Colo. Burwell &ca.

On this day the Fairfax County court formally received a new commission of the peace from the governor and the council. Dated 29 July 1768, it authorized 23 justices for the county, including all the current justices but one and adding three new members to the court: GW, Daniel French, and Edward Payne (VA. EXEC. JLS., 6:345). The total number of justices varied from time to time and from county to county. The law only required that a minimum of 8 justices be appointed for each county, and the number added above that limit depended primarily on the changing population and needs of the various counties (HENING, 5:489; SYDNOR, 79). In court today several of the old justices renewed their oaths of office according to law, but GW did not take his oaths until 21 Sept. (Fairfax County Order Book for 1768–70, 36–55, Vi Microfilm).

20.   Colo. Burwell &ca. went away to Belvoir – & Mrs. Washington & the two Childn. went up to Alexandria to see the Inconstant, or way to Win him Acted.

The Inconstant, or The Way to Win Him, by the Irish playwright George Farquhar (1677–1707), was first produced in London in 1702. Although not one of Farquhar's better farces, it became highly popular later in the century, enjoying long runs at Covent Garden and Drury Lane (FARQUHAR, 1:213–78). GW, who accompanied his family to town today, paid £3 12s. 6d. for tickets to this play and the one seen on the following day, both of which were performed by David Verling's Virginia Company (LEDGER A, 277; RANKIN, 145–46).

21.   Stayd in Town all day & saw the Tragedy of Douglas Playd.

Douglas, written by John Home (1722–1808), a Presbyterian clergyman of Edinburgh, was produced first in Edinburgh in Dec. 1756 and opened in London at Covent Garden the following year. The play was considered one of the finest British tragedies of the period and with its medieval Scottish setting, probably drew well in Alexandria, a town founded and still heavily populated by Scots (see TUNNEY).

22.   Came home in the forenoon.

23.   Went a fox hunting & catchd a Bitch Fox, after abt. 2 Hours Chase.

24.   At Home all day. Colo. Henry Lee & Lady, & Miss Ballendine came to dinner & stayd all Night.

Col. Henry Lee (1729–1787) of Leesylvania, Prince William County, was a younger son of Henry Lee (1691–1747) of Lee Hall, Westmoreland County, and a cousin of William and Arthur Lee. His wife was Lucy Grymes Lee,

Col. Henry Lee of Leesylvania, from an unlocated miniature. (The Society of the Lees of Virginia)

[95]

daughter of Charles Grymes of Moratico, Richmond County. Colonel Lee, like GW, was first elected to the House of Burgesses in 1758 and served until the Revolution.

Miss Ballendine is probably Frances Ballendine (d. 1793) of Dumfries, sister of John Ballendine.

25. At Home. The above Company went away after Breakfast.

26. Went Fox huntg. in the Neck. Started & run a Fox or Foxes 3 Hours & then lost.

27. Rid to Muddy hole, Doeg Run, & Mill.

28. Dined at Colo. Fairfax's and returnd in the Afternoon.

29. Went to a Purse Race at Accatinck & returnd with Messrs. Robt. and George Alexander.

GW spent 12s. 6d. at the race and also paid Robert Sanford 12s. "for Pacing my Horse" (LEDGER A, 277).

George Dent Alexander (d. 1780), of Fairfax County, was a younger brother of Robert Alexander.

30. At Home all day. After Dinner Mr. Geo. Alexander went away. The other (Robt.) stayd.

Remarks—of the—Weather

Septr. 1. Brisk Eastwardly Wind in the Morning. Northwardly afterwards & Cool.

2. Wind at No. West and very cool.

3. Cool wind, tho very little of it Eastwardly.

4. Warm. Wind rather Westwardly tho but little of it.

5. Tolerably pleast. Wind Eastwardly in the Morning & Evening but calm Midday.

6. Very little Wind and that Eastward and rather Cool.

7. Cloudy forenoon, with appearances of Rain; & Wind Southwardly.

8.   Heavy Cloud in the Night, with thunder & lightning, but not rain sufft. to lay dust.

9.   Very cool & clear, with the Wind at No. West.

10.   Cool & clear again, Wind Shifting to the Southward.

11.   Great appearances of Rain in the Morning, with thunder & Lightning but no Rain fell.

12.   Clear and Cool. Wind at No. West.

13.   Clear but not so cold as yesterday Wind being Southwardly.

14.   Wind Southwardly with a fog in the Morning & Clouds all day.

15.   But little Wind yet cool with some appearances of Rain.

16.   Wind Northwardly & cool — with great appearances of Rain — especially in the Afternoon.

17th.   But little Wind & that Westwardly. Cool — with appearances of Rain.

18.   Wind at No. West & very cool, with great appearances of Rain in the Forenoon, but clear afterwards.

19.   A Severe frost, wch. killd much Tobo. &ca. abt. Ravensworth & higher up. Wind Shifting Southwardly became warmer.

20.   Warm with the Wind at South.

21.   Very warm. Wind still Southwardly with appearances of Rain in the Morning and Evening but none fell.

22.   Thunder, with severe wind (from the Northwest) and some Rain in the Morning. In the afternn. & Night a gd. deal of Rain.

23.   Cloudy, and sometime misty all day; in the afternoon a good deal of Rain. NB. These are the only Rains to lay the dust since the 17th. of August, now 36 days.

[97]

24.   Cloudy & Misty forenoon. Clear Afternoon with but little Wind & that variable.

25.   Clear & pleasant with but little Wd.

26.   Flying Clouds with but little Wind & that Southwardly.

27.   Clear with the Wind Westwardly & sometimes blowing fresh.

28.   Clear, calm, & Warm, the fore part of the day, with a little wind from So. in the Aftern.

29.   Misty all day, with the Very little Wind from the Northward & warm.

30.   Heavy Rain for several hours in the forenoon, after which it now & then Misted. But little Wind and that variable & Warm.

Observations–in–Septembr.

6.   My Ox Cart finishd drawing in the Wheat at Doeg Run–but during this time it was employd in getting home the Cyder from all the Plantation's.

14.   Finishd Sowing the Second cut of Wheat in the Neck which compleated the half of the Corn Ground there.

16.   Anointed all my Hounds (as well old Dogs as Puppies) which appeard to have the Mange with Hogs Lard & Brimstone.

17.   Got done Sowing Wheat at Doeg Run. Sowed 92½ Bushels.
  The Hound Bitch Mopsey going proud, was lind by my Water dog Pilot before it was discoverd–after which she was shut up with a hound dog–Old Harry.

18.   My Schooner Saild for Suffolk for a load of Shingles.

22.   Spread my Flax for Rotting at the Home House.

23.   Finishd Sowing the third Cut of Wheat in the Neck.

27.   Spread Flax for Rotting at Doeg Run.
   Began to Cut Tops at Doeg Run.

28.   Finishd Sowing Wheat at Muddy hole. The field took 106 Bushls. to Sow.

[October]

Where & how—my time is—Spent.

Octr. 1.   Fox huntg. back of Mr. Barry's with Mr. Robt. Alexander Mr. Manley & Captn. Posey. Started & catchd a bitch Fox. Mr. Stedlar came here in the Afternoon.

2.   At home. Mr. Alexander went away before breakfast. Mr. Stedlar remd. all day.

3.   Clear & pleasant with very little Wind. Rid to Muddy hole & Doeg Run. Miss Sally Carlyle came here.

4.   Went into the Neck—& up the Creek after Blew Wings.

5.   Went to Alexandria, after an early dinner to see a Ship (the Jenny) Launched but was disappointed & came home.

6.   Went up again. Saw the Ship Launchd. Stayd all night to a Ball, & set up all Night.

On this date GW lost 19s. at cards and paid 5s. for a play ticket for Jacky Custis (LEDGER A, 277).

7.   Came home in the Morning & remaind. Mr. Townd. Dade (of Chotk.) came here.

Townsend Dade (d. 1781), originally of the Chotank area of Stafford County, had by his first wife, Elizabeth Alexander Dade, five children who lived to adulthood, including Elizabeth Dade (b. 1734), who in 1751 married GW's Chotank cousin Lawrence Washington (1728–c.1809). Dade next married Parthenia Alexander Massey, widow of Dade Massey, Jr. (died c.1734); she bore Dade at least three children, including a son named Townsend.

8.   Went Fox huntg. (in the Neck) in the forenoon. Started but catchd nothing & in the Afternoon went up the Ck. after Blew Wings—killd 7 or 8.

9.   At Home all day. Mr. Dade went away.

10.   Rid to Muddy hole, Doeg Run, & the Mill. Captn. McCabe dind here.

11.   At home all day alone.

12.   Rid to Muddy hole, Doeg Run, & Mill in the forenoon. In the Afternoon went into the Neck.

13.   Went a fox hunting and catchd a Bitch Fox after two hours chase.

14.   Went into the Neck in the forenoon.

15.   Went a hunting with Captn. Posey & Ld. Washington. Catchd a Bitch Fox after a chace of 1 Hour and 10 Minutes.

16.   Went to Pohick Church. Dind at Captn. McCartys & came home at Night. Doctr. Rumney who came here last Night went away this Morning & Mr. Ramsay & Mr. Adams came here at Night.

17.   At Home all day. Ramsay & Adams went home this Evening.

18.   Rid to Muddy hole Doeg Run, & the Mill.

19.   Set of on my Journey to Williamsburg & reachd Colo. Henry Lees to Dinner.

GW is beginning a multipurpose trip. Although the Assembly was not scheduled to meet, the General Court had begun its 24-day fall session, which would draw most of the merchants and many lawyers and planters to Williamsburg for both their public and private affairs. Virginia was also expecting the arrival in Williamsburg of a new governor; Norborne Berkeley, baron de Botetourt (c. 1718–1770), was appointed 12 Aug. 1768 to be the royal governor of Virginia. Rather than sending a deputy to the colony, Botetourt chose to reside in Virginia and govern directly, thus becoming the first peer in 80 years to reside as governor in Virginia.

Jacky Custis accompanied GW on this trip as far as Boucher's school where he resumed his studies.

Col. Henry Lee's home, Leesylvania, was on the south side of Neabsco Creek near the Potomac River. Henry and his wife Lucy had eight children who lived to maturity, all of whom appear in the diaries.

20.   Detaind there all day by Rain.

GW today gave Jacky 11s. (LEDGER A, 281).

21.   Reachd Fredericksburg, found Warner Washington &ca. there.

Warner Washington (1722–1790), of Gloucester County, was a son of John and Catherine Whiting Washington, and a first cousin to GW. Warner's first wife, Elizabeth Macon Washington (c.1729–1763), of New Kent County, bore him one child who lived to maturity, Warner Washington, Jr. (1751–1829). In May 1764 Warner married Hannah Fairfax (1742–1808), daughter of William Fairfax of Belvoir, and by this date they had two children, Mildred Washington (b. 1766) and Hannah Washington (1767–1828). Warner was now in the process of moving his family from Gloucester County to settle in the Shenandoah Valley.

While GW was in Fredericksburg, he paid 5s. to have his watch cleaned and 1s. 3d. for repair of his boots (LEDGER A, 281).

22.   Dined at Parkers Ordy. & lodgd at Mr. Benjn. Hubbards— Colo. Lewis also.

In the 1760s William Parker, a planter and justice of the peace, operated an ordinary in his home in Caroline County (CAMPBELL [1], 347, 413).

23.   Dined at the Causey & got to Colo. Bassetts.

Because the shores of the lower Pamunkey River were rather marshy, it was difficult to maintain convenient ferry landings. In 1749 Thomas Dansie, who had a wharf on the north, or King William, side of the Pamunkey, was authorized to build a "Causeway from the [south shore of the Pamunkey] River opposite to his said Wharf through the said Marsh to the High Land in the said County of New Kent" (WINFREE, 413). Five years later the General Assembly authorized Dansie to run a ferry between his wharf and the causeway landing at "the same rates as are by law now taken . . . at Claiborne's Ferry," and also directed New Kent County to build a road from the causeway to the main road leading to Claiborne's ferry landing (HENING, 6:427).

Dansie's ferry was not yet open in May 1755 when a northbound traveler recorded: "came to Claibornes about Twelve [o'clock]. Was an hour in passing here; by making a long slant up the River, upon the account of large marshes" (FISHER, 165). The two ferries were so close to one another that travelers did not always bother to differentiate one from the other. Thus, although GW here records his dining at the causeway, he noted in his ledger that his dinner expenses and ferriages today were at Claiborne's (*Va. Gaz.*, 24 July 1752; LEDGER A, 281).

24.   Dined at Josh. Valentine's sent Chair's & Horses over James River & lodgd in Wmsburg. ourselves.

Lower down the James River the 50-gun ship of the line of the Royal Navy, H.M.S. *Rippon,* was dropping anchor. On board was Virginia's new governor, whose pedigree had been printed earlier that month for the elucidation of all interested Virginians: "NORBORNE BERKELEY, Lord Botetourt, Lord Lieutenant and Custos Rotulorum of the county of Gloucester, Lord Lieutenant of the cities of Bristol and Gloucester, Constable of St. Briavel's castle, Colonel of the South battalion of the Gloucestershire militia, L.L.D. . . . His Lordship claiming the barony of Botetourt from the Lord Botetourt, High Admiral of England, and constable of St. Briavel's castle, in the time of Edward I, and III, after a solemn hearing of his claim in the House of Peers, had the title adjudged and confirmed to him in 1764, and accordingly took his seat in the House, next to Lord Dacre, being the 5th Baron of England. . . . His Majesty has since appointed him one of the Lords of the Bedchamber" (*Va. Gaz.*, P&D, 6 Oct. 1768).

25.   Crossd James River & by Rain was forcd to lodge at one Captn. Stowe's.

GW crossed at Hog Island, about six miles south of Williamsburg (LEDGER A, 281). Captain Stowe may have been Joseph Stowe, a ship captain who sailed out of Virginia in the wine trade (*Va. Gaz.*, 24–31 Aug. 1739, and P&D, 29 Sept. 1768).

26.   Breakfasted in Suffolk. Dined & lodgd in the Dismal Swamp at Jno. Washington's.

Suffolk, a small port town established on the east side of the Nansemond River in 1742, was the principal shipping outlet for products of the Dismal Swamp: rice, shingles, and naval stores. Although a large family of Washingtons of unknown origin had lived in the Suffolk area since the seventeenth century, this Washington was probably Lund Washington's brother John (1740–1777), who acted as manager of the Dismal Swamp Company before the Revolution (*Va. Mag.*, 26:419–20). On this trip GW opened an account with John Washington of Suffolk, buying 14,000 shingles, 4 pairs of shoes, and 2 barrels of crab-apple cider (LEDGER A, 281, 282).

For GW's interest in the Dismal Swamp, see the diary for 15 Oct. 1763.

27.   Went up to our Plantation at Norfleet's in Carolina & returnd in the Aftern.

28.   Went into the Pond with Colo. Lewis Majr. Riddick & Jno. Washington & at Night went to the Majrs.

THE POND: Lake Drummond.

29.   Got to Smithfield in return to Wmsburg.

30.   Set out early, breakfasted at Hog Island and dined in Wms.

GW returned to a capital in thrall over the presence of a peer of the realm: Lord Botetourt, who had arrived in the city four days before. Writing to Lord Hillsborough, Botetourt later described his reception: "Colonel Cary finding me eagerly bent upon being at Williamsburg that night, immediately order'd his Chariot and convey'd me within four miles of the City, where I was met by Mr. Secretary Nelson and his Brother; at the Capitol we found the Council and all the Gentlemen of Williamsburg assembled to receive us. I was immediately conducted to the Council Chamber; and after my Commissions were read took the oaths and swore in the Council" (1 Nov. 1768, P.R.O., C.O.5/1346, f. 103).

GW lodged at Mrs. Campbell's tavern.

31.   Dined at the Mayor's. Ent[ertaine]d at the Govr. in Ditto.

Colonial Virginia had a number of towns, such as Alexandria, that had a board of trustees with very limited powers. Two colonial towns, however, were incorporated in the eighteenth century: the Borough of Norfolk (1736) and the City of Williamsburg (1722). Under such a charter, the city gained governmental powers comparable to those of a county court, including a city hustings court and the right to one representative in the House of Burgesses. The city government consisted of a board of 6 aldermen, a 12-member common council, a recorder, and a mayor, the last of whom was elected from among the aldermen on 30 Nov. of each year. James Cocke, a prominent merchant, was mayor for 1767–68, and 1772–73. Cocke's home was about a block west of the Governor's Palace (WALKER, 36, 49).

In a session held the previous spring, which GW had not attended, the Virginia House of Burgesses had unanimously resolved to endorse a Massachusetts protest of the Townshend Acts by which Parliament, beginning late in 1767, imposed duties on certain British exports to the colonies: tea, glass, lead, paints, and some types of paper. Denying Parliament's right to levy such duties without consent of the colonists, the burgesses had petitioned both houses of Parliament and the king for repeal of the acts and had hinted that there would be a boycott of British goods into Virginia if their request was denied. The new governor was especially instructed by the king in Council to "converse with, the members of our . . . council [in Virginia], separately and personally, as also with the principal persons of influence . . . and endeavor to lead them . . . to disclaim the erroneous and dangerous principles which they appear to have adopted." The ship *Rippon* was to remain to assist Botetourt, including the ferrying from Boston of British troops, in case Botetourt encountered any "sudden commotion of the populace" (LABAREE [1], 1:364–65; Lord Hillsborough to the Lords of Admiralty, 28 July 1768, P.R.O., C.O.5/1346, f. 75).

Remarks—on the—Weather

Octr. 1.   Clear and pleasant. Still forenoon but brisk Southwestwardly Wind afterwds.

2.   Clear, Warm, & Still in the forenoon, a small Southwardly breeze in the Afternoon.

3.   Clear & pleasant, with but little Wind & that Southwardly,

4. Brisk Southwestwardly Wind & warm with flying Clouds.

5. Rain in the Night—& in the Morning—clear abt. 8 Oclock with showers afterwards with the Wind westwardly & cool.

6. Clear & cool. Wind brisk from West.

7. Clear with but little Wind—& that Southwardly.

8. Clear with a fresh No. West breeze in the morning, but still afterwards.

9. Cloudy with appearances of much Rain—but none fell. Wind Southwardly in the Morng. & westwardly & cool afterwds.

10. Cool in the Morng. Moderate Afterwds. with little Wind.

11. A Frost this Morning to bite Fodder. Calm & warm fore-noon. Brisk So. Westwardly wind & like for Rain in the Afternn.

12. Clear and cool morning. Wind fresh at No. West. Calm afternoon & warm.

13. Clear and cool. Wind still at No. West—in the Evening Eastwardly.

14. Calm and warm forenoon. Cloudy afternoon with appear-ances of Rain.

15. Foggy & Misty Morning. Warm, clear, & still afterwards.

16. Cloudy with the Wind Northwardly—then cold & Chilly—with appearances of Rain.

17. Cold Rain & disagreeable, with the Wind abt. No. East.

18. A severe frost this Morning—but Calm clear & warm day.

19. Calm, clear, & Warm forenoon, but lowering afternoon.

20. Moderate Rain till abt. 2 Oclock & Cloudy & misty after-wards. Wd. North.

21.　A good deal of Rain in the Night & more or less till 9 or 10 Oclock then clear with the Wind Westwardly.

22.　Clear and pleasant with a small Southwardly breeze.

23.　Ditto—Ditto—Ditto.

24.　Clear with the Wind Southwardly & Warm.

25.　Foggy Morng. & Clouds—with a good deal of Rain in the Afternoon & night from No. East.

26.　Clear & cool Wind brisk from the Westward.

27.　Cold & clear. Wind abt. No. West.

28.　Less cold Wind being at So. West & clear.

29.　Warmer still. Wind continuing Southwardly & the weather clear.

30.　Clear and very cool morning. Wind Westwardly. Afternoon Mild.

31.　Mild Wind Southwardly and Clear.

Observation's—in—October

Octr. 1st.　The hound Bitch Tipsey, was lind by the little Spaniel dog Pompey before she was shut up in the House with old Harry.

4.　Finishd Sowing Wheat at the Mill which field took 75 Bushels.

5.　Finishd Sowing in the Neck. This field took 216 Bushels. Which makes the quantities sowed as follow—Viz.—

At Doeg Run	92½ Bush.
Muddy hole	106½
Mill	75
Neck	216
	490

Began getting Fodder at the Mill.

6.   Began getting Ditto in the Neck.

11.   Sowed Apple Pummice in the New Garden–from Crab Apples.

SOWED APPLE PUMMICE: The pomace, a residue from cider making, contained apple seeds that would produce seedlings to use in grafting.

15.   Finishd pulling (but not securing) Fodder at Doeg Run Quarter.
    Did the same also at Muddy hole.

[November]

Where & how–my time is–Spent

Novr. 1.   In Williamsburg Dined at the Speakers–with many Gentlemen.

2.   In Ditto. Dined at the Attorney Genls. with Lord Botetourt (the Govr.) & many other Gentlemen.

Botetourt described to Lord Hillsborough his dining out during his first week in Williamsburg: "I have been asked every day to dinner by the principal Gentlemen and am at present upon the very best terms with all. I like their stile exceedingly" (1 Nov. 1768, P.R.O., C.O.5/1346, f. 104).

3.   In Ditto. Dined at Mrs. Dawson's.

4.   In Ditto. Dined with several Gentlemen at Ayscoughs. Colo. Byrds Lottery began drawing.

Christopher Ayscough and his wife Anne (both died c.1772) had recently opened a tavern on Francis Street about 100 yards south of the Capitol. Before Governor Fauquier died in March, Christopher had been a gardener at the palace, and Anne had cooked for the governor, performing her duties so well that she was rewarded with a bequest of £250 from Fauquier's estate. That sum was probably used to buy and stock the tavern, the chief attractions of which were Mrs. Ayscough's cooking skills and a supply of fine liquors (*Va. Gaz.*, P&D, 6 Oct. 1768; GIBBS, 147–48).
    Col. William Byrd III, in a desperate attempt to pay his debts, was raffling off much of his property, including "the intire TOWNS of ROCKY RIDGE and SHOCKOE, lying at the Falls of James river," valued at over £50,000, at £5 per ticket (*Va. Gaz.*, R, 23 July 1767). Besides owing gambling losses, Byrd was the largest single debtor to the estate of the late Speaker-Treasurer John Robinson. Upon Robinson's death it was discovered that he had loaned out personally over £100,000 worth of retired notes which had been issued

Christopher Ayscough

BEGS leave to acquaint the publick that he has opened TAVERN fronting the fouth fide of the *Capitol*, WILLIAMSBURG. As he is provided with the beft LIQUORS, and Mrs. *Ayfcough* very well underftands the COOKERY part, he flatters himfelf that thofe Gentlemen who may pleafe to favour him with their cuftom will find every thing to their fatisfaction, he being determined to do all in his power to oblige.

*** The greateft care will be taken of Gentlemens SERVANTS and HORSES.

Ayscough's was a tavern frequented by Washington during his trips to Williamsburg. From *Virginia Gazette*, P&D, 6 Oct. 1768. (Colonial Williamsburg Photograph)

by the Virginia government to finance the French and Indian War. The paper notes were supposed to be destroyed as they were collected by the treasurer in payment of taxes and fees to the government, but Robinson privately had made loans to dozens of large and important but financially pressed planters, many of whom were burgesses or council members. To settle Robinson's estate and satisfy his creditors (mainly the government), his administrators had to force the sale of the land and slaves of a number of Robinson's debtors. Some debtors, like William Byrd, turned to lotteries. Besides causing financial confusion, the "Robinson affair" created an unsettling effect on the political life and social fabric of Virginia in the late years of the colonial period (see MAYS, 1:174–208).

GW, who, unlike Byrd, did not gamble for high stakes, lost £1 at cards today (LEDGER A, 281).

5. Dined at Mrs. Campbells where I had spent all my Evenings, since I came to Town.

Today GW bought 100 forms for leasing land to tenants at John Dixon and Alexander Purdie's printing office on Duke of Gloucester Street. A few days earlier he had purchased 4 almanacs, probably at this same place (LEDGER A, 281).

6. Left Williamsburg – & Dined & lodgd at Colo. Bassetts.

John Robinson, late Speaker of
the House of Burgesses. (Colonial Williamsburg Photograph)

7.   Set out for home with Betcey Dandridge. Dined at King Wm.
Court Ho. & lodgd at Mr. Wm. Ayletts.

BETCEY: Elizabeth Dandridge (b. 1749), the younger of Mrs. Washington's
two sisters who reached adulthood. In 1773 she married William Aylett's
brother John.

The "publick house" at King William Court House was described in 1777
as being "72 feet by 20 with a portico the whole length, there are 4 rooms
below and 4 above, with 4 closets on a floor" (*Va. Gaz.*, D&H, 26 Dec. 1777).
The tavern was leased to various innkeepers by its owners, the Quarles
family of King William County.

William Aylett (1743–c.1781) of Fairfield, King William County, which
county he represented as a burgess 1772–75 and in all five of the Virginia
Conventions 1774–76, was appointed in 1776 deputy commissary for the
Continental Army, serving until his death.

8.   Dined at Parkers and lodgd at Fredericksburg.

9.   Reached home in about 7 Hours & an half. Found Doctr.
Rum[ne]y & Miss Ram[sa]y here.

Patsy Custis probably had another attack of epilepsy about this date, be-
cause during Rumney's visit he bled her and gave her another "vial of
Drops" and two more musk capsules (receipt from William Rumney, 18
Feb. 1769, ViHi: Custis Papers).

10.   At Home all day. The Doctr. & Miss Ramsay went home.

11.   Rid to Muddy hole Doeg run and the Mill. Mr. Magowan &
Mr. Stedlar came to Dinner as Mr. R. Alexr. did in the Aftern.

Walter Magowan was now the Rev. Mr. Magowan, having taken his Episcopal orders in England in the summer of 1768.

12.   Went Fox huntg. in the Neck. Started & was run out of hearg. of the Dogs—owing to the Wind. Whether they catchd or not is not known.

13.   Went to Pohick Church, & dined at Home with Mr. Ths. Triplet H. Manley & Mr. Peake.

14.   Rid to Muddy hole & all my Plantns.

15.   Went a Fox hunting in the Neck. Catchd a bitch fox—after an hour and 40 Minutes chace.

16.   Went to Colo. Fairfax's & Dind with Mrs. Wn. & Miss Dandridge. Returnd in the Afr.

17.   Went up to a Race by Mr. Beckwiths & lodgd at Mr. Edwd. Paynes.

Mr. Beckwith is possibly the Marmaduke Beckwith who appears on the tax lists of Fairfax County for 1782 and 1785 (HEADS OF FAMILIES, 18, 85).

18.   Returnd home. Breakfasted at Captn. McCartys—& came by the Mill & Muddy Ho.

19.   At home all day—alone.

20.   At home all day alone.

21.   Went up to Court and returnd in the Evening with my Brothr. John.

GW was attending the Fairfax County court as a justice for the first time since taking his oaths of office 21 Sept. The Fairfax court by law convened on the third Monday of every month except when there was no business to be considered, and it continued to meet, beginning daily about 9:00 A.M., until the docket for the month was finished, usually within six days (HENING, 5:489–91, 8:47). In November the court convened on this date and remained in session until 24 Nov., but GW was present only today (Fairfax County Order Book for 1768–70, 56–75, Vi Microfilm). Like most Virginia county justices of the time, GW attended court primarily at his convenience, coming when his affairs allowed or when a matter of special concern was to be heard. Irregular attendance, however, seldom caused any problems, because the law only required a quorum of 4 justices, a number that was relatively easy to obtain from the many available, especially in Fairfax County where several of the 23 justices lived in Alexandria near the courthouse (HENING, 5:489; SYDNOR, 79). County courts had powers and responsibilities in many areas as most criminal, civil, moral, administrative, and political matters in the counties came under their jurisdiction. They could try nearly all crimes committed by slaves and, for freemen, those crimes, such as minor theft and assault, that did not involve punishment by loss of life or limb. Civil cases heard by the monthly courts—usually suits for land, debts, or damages—had to be for at least 25s. or 200 pounds of tobacco. Suits of less value were decided out of court by individual justices. County courts also levied some taxes, registered most legal documents, judged cases of bastardy and public drunkenness, supervised the care of orphans by guardians or the parish vestry, issued ordinary licenses and set tavern prices, controlled the construction of roads and public buildings, and either recommended or appointed most county officials, including militia officers below the rank of brigadier. Justices as individuals, besides handling minor civil cases, had other duties and powers, such as the right to order attachments of property for debt and the right to issue warrants and peace bonds (HENING, 5:491–92, 6:105–11; SYDNOR, 76–83; CHITWOOD, 80–87).

22.   Went a fox huntg. with Lord Fairfax & Colo. Fairfax & my Br. catchd 2 Foxes.

23.   Went a huntg. again with Lord Fairfax & his Brother, & Colo. Fairfax. Catchd nothing that we knew of. A fox was startd.

24.   Mr. Robt. Alexander here. Went into the Neck.

25.   Mr. Bryan Fairfax as also Messrs. Grayson & Phil. Alexander came here by Sunrise. Hunted & catchd a fox with them & My Lord his Br. & Colo. Fairfax all of whom with Mrs. Fx. & Mr. Watson of Engd. dind here.

Benjamin Grayson (d. 1757) immigrated to Viriginia from Scotland and built Belle Air, two miles south of Occoquan Creek, Prince William County. He married twice-widowed Susannah Monroe (1695–1752). Of their four children this Mr. Grayson was probably William (c.1736–1790), the third son, who, after graduating from the College of Philadelphia (now University of Pennsylvania) in 1760, returned to practice law in Dumfries, which became the Prince William County seat in 1762 (W.P.A. [1], 91).

Mr. Watson of England is possibly Josiah Watson, who settled in Alexandria as a merchant before the Revolution. In answer to a query from the Whitehaven tobacco partnership of Dixon & Littledale, Harry Piper of Alexandria wrote on 14 July 1775: "Mr. [Josiah] Watson has been here and Trading Now about two or three Years, and is generally esteemed by all his acquaintances" (Piper Letterbook, ViU).

26.   Hunted again in the above Compa. but catchd nothing.

27.   Went to Church.

28.   Went to the Vestry at Pohick Church.

After settling on the tithes for the year and disposing of minor business, the vestry discussed the proposed new Pohick Church. Agreement was reached that "notice be given in the Virginia and Maryland Gazettes of the building of the said Church, and that the undertakers may attend at the Vestry House at Pohick on the first friday in March next with Plans and Estimates" (Truro Vestry Book, 136, DLC; see also *Va. Gaz.,* R, 2 Feb. 1769). No division among the vestrymen over this action was recorded.

29.   Went a Huntg. with Lord Fairfax & catchd a Fox.

30.   At home all day. Colo. Mason & Mr. Cockburne came in the Evening.

Martin Cockburn, son of Dr. James Cockburn, of Jamaica, settled in Virginia after marrying Ann Bronaugh, daughter of Jeremiah Bronaugh, of Fairfax, and cousin of George Mason. His estate was Springfield near Colchester. Cockburn served on the Truro Parish vestry 1770–79.

Remarks – on the – Weather

Novr. 1.   Clear, pleasant, & agreeable.

2.   Rainy Morning. Wind eastwardly. But clear & pleast. Afternoon.

3.   Clear & Pleasant. Wind Southwardly.

4.   Do.————Do.————Do.————Do.

5.   Do.————Do.————Do.————Do.

6.   Do.————Do.————Do.————Do.

7.   Do.————Do.————Do.————Do.

8.   Cool, the Wind shifting Northwardly.

9.   Very cool, & hard frosty Morng. In the Evening Rain (tho not much) & the Wind Eastwardly.

10.   Very Cool. Wind at No. West & blowg. hard. With flying Clouds.

11.   Moderate. Wind shifting Southwardly. The weather clear.

12.   High wind from the Southwest. And clear, till the Eveng. then Cloudy.

13.   Hazy, but otherwise clear and Mild. Wind Southwardly.

14.   Cloudy forenoon—but clear, & warm afterwards. Wind Southwardly.

15.   Rainy forenoon—that is slow moderate rain—& Wind Southwardly—but clear, cool & windy afternoon from the Northwest.

16.   Cold & Windy from the Northwest. Clear also.

17.   Lowering Morning, but clear & pleasant afterwards. Wind Southwardly.

18.   Clear Morning, but lowering Afternoon. Wind fresh from the Southwest and a good deal of Rain in the Night.

19.   Raining more or less all the forenoon. Wind fresh from the No. West with Spits of Snow and some Rain in the Afternoon. Cold.

20.   Very Cloudy with great appearances of Snow but none fell. Wind fresh from No. West & very cold.

21.   Clear & cool. Wind at No. West—yet pleasant and agreeable—being clear.

22.   Sometimes lowering but in genl. clear & pleast. with but little Wind.

23.   Clear & pleasant—also Warm—there being no Wind.

24.   Clear & pleasant, there being little or no Wind.

25.   Warm and lowering with but little Wind. In the Evening Rain as there was in the Night.

26.   Heavy & lowering day. Evening & Night Rain with some intermixture of Snow.

27.   Wind at No. West & cold, with flying Clouds.

28. Clear and cold Wind Northwardly till Night, then So. West. Hard frost.

29. Very hard frost, in the Morning but moderate & thawg. afterwd.

30. Pleast. forenoon with the Wind Southwardly but the Afternoon very cold & freezing.

Observations–in–November

Novr. Put up my Beeves & Weathers to Fatten–about the 25th.–of Octr.
    Put up Hogs to fatten.

14. Began to gather Corn at Muddy hole in the Neck.

21. Measurd the Cut of Corn in the Neck adjoing. to the Gate, the contents of which was [   ].

22. Began to gather Corn at the Mill.

[December]

Where & how–my time is–Spent.

Decr. 1. Went to the Election of Burgesses for this County, & was there, with Colo. West chosen. Stayd all Night to a Ball wch. I had given.

The election, held at the county courthouse in Alexandria, had been called by the new governor, Lord Botetourt. White adult males who owned a minimal amount of real property were allowed to vote. This property restriction satisfied two convictions long held in English tradition: only a man who owned property would be free from being influenced at the polls by an employer or landlord, and those who held property held the interests of the society at heart. Free Negroes and mulattoes, whether they owned property or not, lost their franchise in Virginia in 1723 (HENING, 4:133). Although many women in colonial Virginia owned real property in their own right (Martha Custis, for instance, while she was a widow), their sex barred them from the polls.

In accordance with the English belief that secrecy bred corruption, all voting was done in public. The election proceedings were the responsibility of the county sheriff. As the clerks (one provided by each candidate) sat together at a table, each voter would step forward and announce his two choices, which were then marked down by the clerks on their respective poll sheets. As each vote was given and recorded, the candidate chosen would often thank the voter, and toward the end of a close election, when every vote would elicit a round of cheering, the crowd sometimes got rather unruly. During the voting in the 1755 Fairfax County burgess poll, GW got into a violent argument over the candidacy of his friend George William Fairfax (FREEMAN, 2:146).

In this election GW and Col. John West were standing for reelection. A third candidate was GW's neighbor and fox-hunting companion Capt. John Posey, who was trying for the second time to unseat West, possibly because West's nephew, John West, Jr., was pressing Posey over an inheritance left to Posey's wife by her first husband, George Harrison, who was John West, Jr.'s uncle. The final poll this day was: GW, 205; John West, 175; John Posey, 132. GW spent about £25 on his election, including cakes and drink (unspecified) and £1 each for his clerk, John Orr, and his "fidler [at] the ball" (FREEMAN, 2:146, 3:141, 209; Posey to GW, 25 May 1771, DLC:GW; LEDGER A, 281, 287; HENING, 4:476, 7:518). For detailed descriptions of elections in colonial Virginia, see SYDNOR.

2.   Returnd home after dinner accompanied by Colo. Mason Mr. Cockburn & Messrs. Henderson Ross & Lawson.

Alexander Henderson (d. 1815) emigrated from Scotland in 1756 and settled as a merchant at Colchester. He was Fairfax County justice of the peace 1770–post 1785; Fairfax County representative in the House of Delegates 1781, 1783; Truro Parish vestryman 1765–85; and churchwarden 1769–70, 1779–80.

3.   Went a fox huntg. in Company with Lord & Colo. Fairfax Captn. McCarty & Messrs. Henderson & Ross. Started nothg. My Br. came in the Afternoon.

4.   At Home all day.

5.   Fox hunting with Lord Fairfax & his Brothr. & Colo. Fairfax. Started a Fox & lost it. Dind at Belvoir & came in the Evg.

6.   Rid to Muddy hole Doeg Run, & Mill.

7.   At home all day—alone.

8.   Fox huntg. with Lord Fairfax & Brothr. & Colo. Fairfax all of whom dind here. Started nothing.

9.   Rid to Muddy hole, Doeg run, & the Mill.

10.   Went a fox hunting in the Neck & catchd a fox. Afterwards went to the Plantatin. there. Doctr. Rumney came to Dr. & Mr. Alexr. in the Eg.

11.   They went away after breakfast—alone aftds.

12.   Rid to the Mill Doeg run & Muddy hole. Miss Carlyle & Miss Dalton came here.

Elizabeth Dalton was the daughter of John Dalton of Alexandria.

13.   Set of abt. 12 Oclock for Towlston to hunt with Mr. Bryan Fairfax. Got there in the Afternn.

14.   Stayd there all day. In the Evg. went to see his new Mill.

15.   Returnd home, by the way (that is near Muddy hole) started & catchd a Fox.

16.   At home all day. Jacky Custis came home from Mr. Boucher's.

17.   Rid out with my Gun but killd nothg. Mary Wilson came to live here as a Ho. keeper a[t] 15/. pr. Month.

Mrs. Mary Wilson was probably a widow. She left her position at Mount Vernon in June 1769 (LEDGER A, 288).

18.   At home all day. Miss Sally Carlyle & Miss Betcy Dalton went away & Mr. Stedlar came.

19.   Went up to Court & returnd at Night.

Although today was the third Monday in the month, the day on which the Fairfax County court normally began its monthly sessions, the court apparently did not meet today or any other day in December because of a lack of pressing business.

20.   At home all day.

21.   Ditto—Ditto.   } Snowing.

22.   Ditto—Ditto.

Today GW bought "Fish &ca. of the New Englandman," which apparently visited Mount Vernon several times (LEDGER A, 112, 286).

23.   Went a Pheasant Huntg. Carrd. hounds & they started & followd a Deer.

24.   Rid to the Mill & Doeg run.

25.   At home all day.

26.   Ditto – Do. – L. W——n. set of for Staffd.

27.   Ditto – Do. – except Shooting between breakfast & Dinner.

28.   At home all day alone.

29.   Went a fox hunting. Started one but did not catch it. In the Afternoon Messrs. Dalton, Piper & Riddell came here. Also Mr. Mag[owa]n.

Mr. Riddell is probably either John or Henry. John was a merchant in Dumfries. Henry, to whom GW later wrote concerning the seating of his western lands, was a merchant at Piscataway, Md., and the chief Maryland factor for Glassford & Co. of Glasgow, Scot. (GW to Henry Riddell, 22 Feb. 1774, DLC:GW; MACMASTER, 61:153 n. 32).

30.   At home with them all day.

31.   Went a hunting & catchd a bitch fox – the above Gentlemn. with me.

GW played cards on this date, losing an unspecified amount (LEDGER A, 286).

Remarks – on the – Weather

Decr. 1st.   Ground exceedg. hard froze. Weathr. very cold – & Snowing at times. The Eveng. of this day was remarkably cold.

2.   Weather clear & very cold. Wind at No. West. River half froze over.

3.   Night exceeding hard – but this day somewhat more moderate Wind Southwardly.

4.   Close Rain all day with the Wind chiefly at No. East – but afterwards shifting to No. West & clearing.

5.   Clear & tolerably pleast. Wind abt. West. Ground hard froze.

6.   Hard frost–& cool Morning–but mild afternoon. Wind Southwardly.

7.   Constant slow rain all day–with the Wind variable–but chiefly Eastwardly.

8.   Clear, & tolerably pleasant, although the Wind was fresh from the No. West.

9.   Very cloudy & like to rain but none fell.

10.   Also Cloudy, with sometimes Sunshine & Warm–being still. No frost.

11.   Again cloudy & like for rain but none fell. Wind shifting to the No. West but not cold. No frost.

12.   Lowering Morning, but clear & calm Noon. No Wind nor frost.

13.   Fine mild & warm forenoon, Wind Southwardly–but lowg. afternoon wind No. Et. & Cold.

14.   Snowd the best part of last Night and till 2 Oclock this day.

15.   Snowd again this Morng. & cold Wind Northwardly. Snow 8 or 10 Inches deep.

16.   Clear & cool tho the Wind was Southwardly.

17.   Wind Southwardly yet cold & raw with great appearances of Snow.

18.   A Little rain fell in the Night & this day lowering. But mild & thawg. Wind So.

19.   Clear & pleast. forenoon. Lowering Aftern. with a good deal of Snow in the Night.

20.   Snowing best part of the day–abt. 6 or 8 Inches deep.

21.   Snowing on and of all day. With but little Wind.

22. Snowing fast the forepart of the day with the Wind at No. West. Snow very deep; I suppose 15 or 18 Inches generally.

23. Clear & cold. Wind at No. West & fresh. Towards Evening it shifted Southwardly.

24. More moderate. Wind Southwardly. Clear Morng. & Eveng. — threatng. Noon.

25. Clear, with the Wind moderately from the No. West and not very cold.

26. Wind rather to the East of North and Cloudy, but not cold. Frost this Mg.

27. No frost. Foggy & misty all day and thawing fast.

28. Raining more or less all Night, Snow mostly gone—off the open ground entirely. Good deal of Rain this day also—no frt.

29. Cloudy—Misting—& sometimes rain with the wind southwardly. No frost.

30. Clear. Wind at No. West, & fresh in the Morning but incling. Southwardly in the afternoon. No frost.

31. No frost. Wind southwardly—& Cloudy—but no rain. Evening clear.

Observation's—in—Decr.

13th. Killd Hogs.

Vestryman, Fox Hunter, Country Squire

1769

[January]

Where & how—my time—is Spent

Jany. 1st. At home alone. Mr. Magowan returnd from Alexandria in the Evening.

2. Went to Colo. Fairfax's with the Family and stayd all Night.

3. Came home again. Colo. Carlyle & Mr. Ramsay returnd with us.

The visit may have been more than social. About three weeks later, on 29 Jan., GW wrote William Ramsay to say that it was "out of my power . . . to furnish you & Mr. Fairfax with the sum asked." Then shifting to a subject closer to his heart, GW continued: "Having once or twice of late heard you speak highly in praise of the [New] Jersey College as if you had a desire of sending your Son William there (who I am told is a youth fond of study & instruction, & disposed to a sedentary Studious Life; in following of which he may not only promote his own happiness, but the future welfare of others) I shou'd be glad, if you have no other objection to it than what may arise from the expence, if you wou'd send him there as soon as it is convenient & depend upon me for Twenty five pounds this [Virginia] Currency a year for his support so long as it may be necessary for the completion of his Education. . . . No other return is expected or wished for, for this offer, than that you will accept it with the same freedom & good will with which it is made, & that you may not even consider it in the light of an obligation, or mention it as such; for be assur'd that from me it never will be known" (DLC:GW).

4. Went a fox huntg. with the above Gentlemen, & were met by the two Colo. Fairfax's but found nothing. Messrs. C & R. went home.

5. Calm Morning with heavy Clouds & gr. appearance of Rain. Abt. 10 Oclock the Wind comg. to No. Wt. & blowg. fresh dispeld the Clouds toward the afternoon. Rid to Muddy hole Doeg Run and the Mill and in the Afternoon went into the Neck.

6. The two Colo. Fairfax's & Mrs. Fairfax & Dr. Rumney dind here & spent the Evening.

THE TWO COLO. FAIRFAX'S: Robert and George William Fairfax.

Rumney brought two musk capsules for Patsy Custis on this visit (receipt from William Rumney, 18 Feb. 1769, ViHi: Custis Papers).

7.   After Dinner the Compy. from Belvoir returnd home. Doctr. Rumney stayd.

8.   At home all day with Doctr. Rumney.

9.   At home all day. Opening the Avenue to the House—& for bringing the Road along.

10.   Went a Fox huntg. with L[und] W[ashington]—Jackey Custis, & Mr. Manley. Found nothing.

11.   Went a fox hunting in the Neck with Mr. Peake, but found nothing.

12.   Went out in the Morng. with the Hounds in order to meet Colo. Fairfax but did not. In Hell hole started a fox and after an hours chase run him into a hole, & left him. In the afternoon went to Alexa. to the Monthly Ball.

13.   Havg. lodgd at Captn. Daltons was confind there till the Afternoon by Rain & then came Ho[me].

John Dalton lived on the north side of Cameron Street between Water (now Lee) and Fairfax streets (MOORE [1], 71–72).

14.   At home all day. And alone.

15.   Ditto   Do.   Do.

16.   Went a ducking in the forenoon—otherwise at home all day. In the Afternoon Mr. B. Fairfax came here.

During this month Bryan Fairfax bought a hunting horn from GW for 6s. and paid him 2s. 3d. lost at cards (LEDGER A, 287).

17.   Fox huntg. in the Neck with Mr. Fairfax Triplet & Peake—started nothing.

18.   Fox huntg. again in the above Compa. and Harn. Manley—started a Fox and lost it. The above dind here as Mr. Wagener also did.

MR. WAGENER: Probably Peter Wagener (1742–1798), who was a member of the committee of associators of Fairfax County, served as county lieutenant of Fairfax during the Revolution, and married a daughter of Daniel McCarty. He is generally referred to in the diaries as "Mr. Wagener." His father, Peter Wagener (1717–1774), Occoquan Creek, came to America from England in 1738, served as vestryman in Truro Parish 1771–74, and was captain of a company of Virginia Rangers during Braddock's expedition. GW usually calls him "Major Wagener" in the diaries.

19. Fox hunting in the same Company—fd. nothing. Mr. Fairfax & Mr. Wagr. dind here.

20. Fox huntg. again with Mr. Wagener Mr. Fairfax and Mr. Clarke. The two last dind here. Mr. Wagener went home.

MR. CLARKE: perhaps a member of the Clarke family of Salem, Mass., and Barbados, who were related by marriage to the Fairfaxes and the Washingtons.

21. Fox huntg. again upon long Branch with Mr. Fairfax Mr. Clarke Mr. Mac[ar]ty & Mr. Chichester. All went home from the field. Found Doctr. Rumney here.

LONG BRANCH: a tributary of Accotink Creek near Capt. McCarty's home, Mount Air.

22. Went to Pohick Church. Doctr. Rumney stayd all day & Night.

23. At home. Captn. McCarty & Wife, Mr. Chichesr. & his dind and stayd all Night.

24. At home. The above Company dind here & went home in the afternoon.

25. Hunting below Accatinck with Captn. McCarty Mr. Chichester & Mr. Wagener with their dogs. Found a fox & killd it in abt. an hour and 35 Minutes.

26. At home all day. Jacky Custis set of for School & Mr. Robt. Alexr. came here in the Aft.

27. At home again all day—Mr. Alexander Staying.

28. Went a Huntg. with Mr. Alexander. Traild a fox for two hours & then lost it. Mr. Alexander went home from the field.

Dr. Hugh Mercer practiced medicine in Fredericksburg after serving in the French and Indian War. (Metropolitan Museum of Art, Gift of Robert W. de Forest, 1906)

29.   Ground froze. Weather clear. Wind tolerable fresh at No. West but not very Cold. At home all day—alone.

30.   At home all day, Mr. Campbell the Comptroller dind here & in the afternoon Doctr. Mercer came.

Hugh Mercer (c.1725–1777) was born in Aberdeenshire, Scot., and studied medicine at the University of Aberdeen from 1740 to 1744. In April 1746 Dr. Mercer served as a surgeon's mate with Prince Charles Stuart's forces at the bloody Battle of Culloden, where the prince's army was destroyed. Soon thereafter Mercer immigrated to America, settling on the Pennsylvania frontier. There he practiced medicine until the outbreak of the French and Indian War, when he joined the Pennsylvania forces as an officer. During this service he became acquainted with GW. After retiring from the military, he settled in Fredericksburg, where he opened an apothecary shop and practiced medicine. Dr. Mercer was not related to John Mercer of Marlborough.

31.   Doctr. Rumney dind and lodgd here and in the afternoon Mr. Addisons and Mr. Baynes Sons came and lodgd here.

Rumney and Mercer apparently consulted with one another today about Patsy Custis's case and decided on a new way of treating her epilepsy, because four days later Rumney recorded giving her mercurial pills, purging pills, and ingredients for a decoction (receipt from William Rumney, 18 Feb. 1769, ViHi: Custis Papers). Unfortunately, those medicines, like the others tried previously, would give Patsy no relief from her fits.

The youngest son of Thomas Addison (1679–1727) of Oxon Hill, Md., was Rev. Henry Addison (1717–1789), rector of St. John's Parish, Prince George's County, Md., from 1742 to 1775. At this time Addison, a friend of Jonathan Boucher, had placed his two sons in Boucher's school in Caroline County, Va.; the Addison boys appearing here are probably those sons. Col. John Baynes (born c.1726), a local Maryland merchant with Whitehaven connections who worked out of his store at Piscataway, Prince George's County, Md., had at least one son, Joseph Noble Baynes, who was about 18 years old in 1769 and, like the Addison boys, was probably a schoolmate of John Parke Custis (BOUCHER [1], 51; MACMASTER, 61:151, 309 n.107, 317 n.140).

An Acct. of the–Weather in Jan.

Jany. 1st. Ground but little froze, & soon thawed, day clear & pleasant–Wind Southwardly.

2.   Perfectly calm, clear, and warm–the Morning was a little frosty–but gd. soon thawd.

3.   A large white frost–the gd. a little froze, but soon thawd. Morng. calm & clear–afternoon lowering, & Wind Southwardly.

4.   Lowering Morning without frost, but clear afternoon. Wind Southwardly.

5.   Calm Morning with heavy Clouds & gt. appearances of Rain. Abt. 10 Oclock the wind comg. out fresh from the No. Wt. the Clouds were dispeld & the afternoon clear & cool.

6.   Ground hard froze–but soon thawd the Morning being clear & moderate–the Wind Still–afternoon a little Muddy.

7.   Wind at Southwest & moderate. Raing. slowly most part of the day.

8.   Rainy morning with little or no Wind. Abt. 10 Oclock the wind came out at No. Wt. but neither blew hard nor cold. In the Eveng. it cl[eared].

9.   Hard frost. Clear & cold wind comg. keen from the No. Wt. More moderate towards the Afternoon with less Wind—but gd. not much thawed.

10.   White Frost & Ground hard froze. A little thawd in the Afternoon. Cloudy & Still all day. In the Eveng. Wind at No. Et.

11.   Rain from about 9 Oclock in the Morng. with very little Wind.

12.   Clear & Calm morning but lowering Afternoon.

13.   Raining all the forenoon, & till three Oclock in the Afternoon with very little Intermisn. Much rain fell in this time.

14.   Cloudy & sometimes misty with little or no Wind as there was not yesterday.

15.   Cloudy, & sometimes dropping—quite Calm and Warm.

16.   Very cloudy and little Wind—sometimes droppg. of Rain & sometimes snow.

17.   Clear. Wind high from the No. West & cool. Towards the afternoon wind lowered.

18.   Ground froze. Wind fresh from the So. West & clear till the Afternoon then Muddy.

19.   Clear—the Ground froze—and Wind at No. West but not hard. Afternoon hazy.

20.   Clear and but little Wind—that variable. Ground froze.

21.   Very little or no Wind. Clear and very Warm. A large white frost but the ground very little froze.

22.   Clear, still & warm in the Morning. Wind brisk from the So. West in the Afternoon & in the Night very hard with a little Rain.

23.   Ground very slightly froze. Wind came out at No. Wt. this morning, & blew very hard, Day clear.

24.   Ground very hard froze. Day clear and very cold. Wind still at No. West but not so hard as yesterday.

25.   Forenoon cloudy & cold—afternoon clear & more moderate. Wind variable but chiefly Easterwardly. Grd. hard froze.

26.   Cloudy Morning. Wind Northwardly and Cold—with a mixture of hail & rain in the Afternoon. Ground hard froze.

27.   Raining moderately all day with little Wind & that chiefly Southwardly and warm.

28.   Clear & cool forenoon. Wind at No. West. Cloudy & threatning afternoon.

29.   Ground froze. Weathr. clear. Wind tolerable brisk at No. West—but not very cold.

30.   Clear and pleasant Wind Southwardly. Ground hard froze.

31.   Clear forenoon and ground froze; afternoon lowering & Raw wind Southwardly.

Remarks & Observations—in Jan.

Jany. 4.   Finishd measuring Corn in the Neck—total quantity 694 Barrels. About this time Muddy hole People began clearing Ground.

5.   Began clearing Ground in the Neck. Mill People getting Rails to fence Corn field by Mr. Manleys.

9.   Began to open the Avenue in front of the House in order to bring the Road along it.

10.   Finishd gathering Corn at Doeg run Quarter. 242 Barrels.
    A Very spewing frost among Wheat particularly in the little field at Doeg run. Note the consequence of this.

SPEWING FROST: Farmers now refer to this process, which lifts and injures the roots of plants, as "heaving."

16.   Began to open my New Road that is to cut the Bank down this side Hell hole.

18.   Another Spewing frost.

22.   The hound bitch Musick got out of her confinemt. & was lind by Pilot.

26.   She was lined by Mr. Fairfax's Hound Rockwood.

27.   The black hound bitch Countess was lined by the above Dog Rockwd.

28.   Countess was again lind by Rockwood.
   This day recd. 505 Bushels of Oats from the Eastn. Shore for 500 that was put on board.

The freight of the oats was £6 5s. (LEDGER A, 287).

[February]

Where & how—my time is—Spent

Feby. 1st. Doctrs. Mercer & Rumney went away as did Mr. Addison's sons &ca. I dind at Belvoir & returnd in the Evening.

Before Mercer left, GW paid him £6 for seeing Patsy (LEDGER A, 287).

2.   Rid to Muddy hole, Doeg Run, and the Mill.

3.   Went a Gunning up the Creek—killd 7 Ducks. In the Afternoon Colo. F. Lewis & son Fieldg. & Mr. Rozer came here.

Fielding Lewis, Jr. (1751–1803), was the eldest son of GW's sister Betty and Col. Fielding Lewis. In 1771 Fielding Jr. married Ann (Nancy) Alexander, daughter of Mary Dent and Gerard Alexander of Alexandria, and settled in Fairfax County (SORLEY, 142).
   MR. ROZER: probably Henry Rozer (Rozier) of Prince George's County, Md.

4.   Mr. Rozer went away after breakfast, the others stayd. At home all day.

GW today recorded losing 19s. at cards (LEDGER A, 287).

5.   At home all day with Colo. Lewis &ca.

Col. and Mrs. Fielding Lewis—she was Washington's sister, Betty—lived in Fredericksburg. (Kenmore Association, Inc.)

6.   At home all day with &ca.

7.   At home as above.

8.   Colo. Lewis and son set of to go home but being stopd at Colchester by Ice returnd in the afternoon. I rid as far as the Mill with them.

9.   Went a Ducking with Colo. Lewis. His son & Betcy Dandridge went to the Monthly Ball at Alexandria.

10.   Went a shooting again. In the Afternoon fieldg. Lewis returnd from Ball.

11.   Ducking till Dinner. Mr. Piper dind here. Betsy Dandridge came home in the Evening.

12.   Mr. Piper went away after Breakfast. At home all day with Colo. Lewis & Son.

13.   Colo. Lewis & Son set of for home. Rid into the Neck and to Muddy hole & Doeg Run.

14.   Went a fox hunting—but started nothing. The two Colo. Fairfax's dind here.

15.   Rid to the Mill Doeg run, & Muddy hole.

16.   At home all day, Joshua Evans who came here last Night put an Iron Ring upon Patcy (for Fits) and went away after Breakfast.

Joshua Evans is probably the blacksmith of that name who was living in Loudoun County at this time and died there in 1773 (Loudoun County Wills, Book B, 71–79, Vi Microfilm). According to an English folk tradition dating from the fourteenth century, certain rings called cramp rings could relieve or cure epileptic convulsions when worn on a finger. These rings varied in design and composition, depending on a particular blessing, inscription, or material for their supposed efficacy (JONES [2], 154–55, 162–65, 522–26). GW today paid Evans £1 10s. for his service (LEDGER A, 287).

17.   Rid out with my hounds. Started a fox and lost it, after an hours chase. Doctr. Rumney came in the Afternoon.

18.   Went a hunting with Doctr. Rumney. Started a fox or rather 2 or 3 & catchd none. Dogs mostly got after Deer & never joind.

On this date GW paid Rumney for his medicines and visits during the past 12 months: £4 18s. on his own account and £19 6s. 6d. for Patsy Custis (LEDGER A, 287).

19.   Went to Pohick Church & returnd to Dinner.

20.   Went up to Alexandria to Court. Returnd home in the Evening.

While GW was in town, he apparently visited Dr. Rumney, who today supplied more ingredients for decoctions and another box of pills for Patsy Custis (receipt from William Rumney, 21 Sept. 1770, ViHi: Custis Papers). The February court lasted three days (Fairfax County Order Book for 1768–70, 76–92, Vi Microfilm).

21.   Went to Court again and returnd home at Night.

The court today ordered GW and Col. John West to "settle & adjust accounts" in a dispute between William Payne and Francis Dade and to report at the next court, their decision to be the court's official judgment in the case. The report was not made until 18 April, when Dade was ordered to pay Payne 992 pounds of tobacco plus costs (Fairfax County Order Book for 1768–70, 85, 125, Vi Microfilm).

22.   At Court again & home in the Eveng.

23. Rid to Muddy hole Doeg run and the Mill.

24. At home all day without Company.

25. At home all day receiving my Goods from Captn. Johnstouns Craft.

Capt. John Johnstoun, master of the ship *Lord Camden,* brought goods from London shipped by Robert Cary & Co. for GW. The goods totaled £315 13s. 6d. (LEDGER A, 198).

26. At home all day alone.

27. Fox hunting with Colo. G. Fairfax & Mr. Warnr. Washington. Started & killd a Dog fox after havg. him on foot three hours & hard runng. an hour and a Qr. Dined at Colo. Fairfax's.

28. At home all day. Mr. Warnr. Washington & Lady & Miss Betcy Washington came here and staid all Night.

BETCY WASHINGTON: probably Warner Washington's niece Elizabeth, daughter of Henry Washington (c.1718–1763) of Middlesex County.

An Acct. of the Weather—in Feby.

Feby. 1st. Ground not froze. Day calm & warm & mostly clear— but sometimes lowering.

2. The Ground slightly froze, Wind fresh from the northwest. Cloudy and cold.

3. Hard frost. Wind sharp & fresh from the No. West. Moderate & very pleast. afternn.

4. Ground froze. Cloudy with great appearances of Rain. Calm & still forenoon. Wind Eastwardly afterwards.

5. A little Snow & Rain in the Night. Wind hard (& cold) from the No. West. All day.

6. Clear and very cold—Wind being hard from the No. West. Gd. very hd. Froze.

7. Ground very hard froze havg. thawd none yesterday. Weathr. exceeding cold wind being still hard from No. Wt.

8.   No thaw yet. Grd. close blockd up and very cold. Wind still at No. Wt. but not so hard. Afternoon somewhat more moderate — quite clear. On the 6th. at Night the River was almost froze across & on the 7th. & last Night quite.

9.   No thaw. Ground very hard froze. Weather clear with little Wind in the forenoon but No. Wt. in the Aftn.

10.   Wind at No. West & cold. Ground hard froze & no thaw, weathr. Clear.

11.   Ground hard froze in the Morning, & but little thawd afterwards. Wind at No. West in the Morng. & So. West in the aftern.

12.   Ground still froze hard & no thaw; Morning cloudy with the Wind at No. Wt. as it contind. to be all day. Afternoon clear.

13.   Clear & pleasant — with but little Wind and that Southwardly.

14.   Raw, cloudy, & still forenoon. Cold afternoon and wind at No. West.

15.   Cold Morning with Snow from 8 till one with the wind Northwardly — then clear with the wind Eastwardly & warmr.

16.   Very hard frost. The River which hath never been clear of Ice since the 6th. was quite shut up today. Morng. clear & cold, wind Northly. — afternn. wind Southly.

17.   Clear, still, warm, & pleasant. Ground still froze but from the continued frost not slopy.

18.   Again Calm clear warm, & pleasant being hazy.

19.   Warm. Wind at So. West — fresh in the forepart of the day — the latter part Cloudy with the Wind at No. Et. At Night Rain.

20.   Rain more or less all Night with the wind fresh at So. West which cleard the river for the first time (since the frost set in) of Ice. Morning lowering but clear, calm, & pleast. day — no frost.

21.   No frost. Fine clear Morng. Lowering day with the Wind fresh at South.

22.   No frost. Rain in the Night. Morng. exceedg. fine & calm. Day clear & pleast.

23.   No frost. Day clear & pleast. Wind southwardly. In the Eveng. a little lowering.

24.   Morning cloudy but not frozen. Aft[ernoon] clear & cooler than for some days past wind being at No. West.

25.   A large white frost & grd. a little froze but not very cold. Wind first Northwardly & then Eastwardly and lowering.

26.   A good deal of Rain fell last Night & some today. The Wind at So. West and fresh. No frost.

27.   Cloudy Morning, but clear day—the wind being No. West & westwardly but not cold nor hard.

28.   No frost. Lowering Morning with the wind at So. Et.— afterwards clearer, with the Wind at So. and warmer.

Remarks & Observations in Feby.

Killd a Wether which waid alive—
    being a middlesized one

		103 lbs. Gross
When dressd	60 lbs. nett a 3d.	0.15.0
	5½ Tallow 7½	3.5
	3 Wool 15	3.9
	Skin	1.3
		£1. 3.5

Note—the above at a low estimate, appears to be no more than the worth of a fat Wether—it being imagind, that they woud average the above weight and 3d. pr. lb. is a low price at this Season of the year.

25.   Finishd the New road leadg. across Hell hole, to the House.

[March]

Where & how—my time is Spent—

Mar. 1.   Rid to Muddy hole—Doeg Run & Mill Plantations with Mr. W[arne]r Washington, who with his Lady & Miss Betcy Washington that came yesterday also dind & lodgd here today &ca. Mr. Willm. Crawford came in the Afternoon.

2.   At home all day with the above Company.

3.   Went to the Vestry at Pohick Church and returnd abt. 11 Oclock at Night. Found Mr. Tibbles here.

GW was late in returning because the proposed location of the new Pohick Church was not wearing well with the minority of vestrymen who lived conveniently near the old church. After prolonged debate lasting well into the evening, the vestry finally accepted Daniel French's bid for building the new church, but "not having compleated their business," they adjourned till "Fryday the Seventh Day of April next" to sign the articles of agreement (Truro Vestry Book, 137, DLC). For the tradition that GW led the Crossroads majority and George Mason led the old-location minority, see SLAUGHTER [1], 63–64; MVAR, 1964, 22–25.

MR. TIBBLES: GW to Thomas Lewis, 5 May 1774, refers to "Mr. Theobald (or Tibbles, as he is commonly called)," who was a partner of Michael Cresap in a western land speculation scheme (DLC:GW).

4.   Warnr. Washington & Lady & Captn. Crawford & Mr. Tibbles went away after Brea[kfast]. Myself at home all day.

5.   Went up to Alexa. after fieldg. Lewis & brot. him down to Dinner where I found Mr. Wr. Washington—who returnd after Din[ner].

6.   Set out with Fieldg. Lewis for Fredg. where we reachd after dinner at Peyton's on Acquia—i.e. reachd my Mother's.

Peyton's ordinary, on Aquia Creek in Stafford County, was about 16 miles above Fredericksburg on the main road from Alexandria (see RICE, 2:93, 177). While GW was at Ferry Farm he gave his mother £3 cash (LEDGER A, 287).

7.   Went to Fredericksburg & remaind there all day—ding. at Colo. Lewis's.

8.   Still there, dind at the same place, spending the Evening at Weedon's at the Club.

George Weedon (c.1734–1793) kept a "large and commodious" tavern on the main street of Fredericksburg (now Caroline Street) "nearly opposite" the town hall and public market. Frequented "by the first gentlemen" of Virginia and "neighboring colonies," it contained "a well accustomed billiard room" and was the place where local horse races were arranged (*Va. Gaz.*, P&D, 12 Sept. 1766 and P, 15 Sept. 1775; Fredericksburg *Va. Herald*, 23 Oct. 1788). His fellow Freemasons sometimes adjourned there for food and entertainment after meeting at the town hall (GOOLRICK, 37). Born in Westmoreland County, Weedon served in the Virginia Regiment during the French and Indian War, being commissioned an ensign in 1755 and later rising to the rank of captain. Before April 1764 he married Catharine Gordon (d. 1797) of Fredericksburg, and by 1766 he was running the tavern on the main street, which her parents had previously owned and operated (KING [2]).

THE CLUB: It was a common practice among Virginia gentlemen of this time, when dining or supping at a tavern, to do so in groups either at a private table or, at a large tavern like Weedon's, in a private room. They would be served as a unit by the innkeeper and then would *club* for the cost of the food, drink, and room; that is, they would divide the total bill equally (GIBBS, 98–107). On this evening GW paid 2s. 6d. as his share of the club and lost 1s. 6d. at cards (LEDGER A, 287).

9.   Set of for Robt. Ashbys, and after dining by the way, reachd it a little after dark.

Capt. Robert Ashby (c.1707–1792) was the second son of Thomas Ashby (see entry for 12 Mar. 1748). Robert had worked as a marker for GW during the survey of the Fairfax lands in 1748 and was now living at Yew Hill, Fauquier County, about eight miles south of Ashby's Gap on the southern road to Winchester.

10.   Went out to run out the bounds of the Land I bot. of Carters Estate but the Weathr. being very cold & windy was obligd to return.

George Carter, the youngest son of Robert "King" Carter, died intestate in England c.1742. To settle his estate the Virginia Assembly passed an act (HENING, 5:300) in 1744 directing trustees to sell Carter's vast holdings of more than 20,000 acres of land in Prince William, Fairfax, and Frederick counties. Twenty years later less than half of the lands had been sold, and Carter's heirs petitioned the Assembly to name a new set of trustees to sell the remaining acreage. An act was passed in 1766 (HENING, 8:215) naming Robert Burwell, Fielding Lewis, and GW as the new trustees. In Nov. 1767 they met at Capt. Robert Ashby's home in Fauquier County to sell the remaining lands and GW bought 2,682 acres "of Geo Carter's Estate" for himself (*Va. Gaz.*, P&D, 19 Nov. 1767; LEDGER A, 257).

11.   Went out again on the same business & returnd at Night to Captn. Ashbys.

12.   At Captn. Ashbys all day. In the afternoon Captn. Marshal came & spent the Evening.

Thomas Marshall (1730–1802), father of Chief Justice John Marshall, was a burgess for Fauquier County 1761–67, 1769–73, and 1775–76. He was a delegate to the first three Virginia Conventions in 1775, and served as colonel of the Third Virginia Regiment during the Revolution. In the 1780s he moved with his family to Kentucky and represented Fayette County in the Virginia House of Delegates. At the time of this entry, Marshall was living at Rosebank near present-day Markham, Va., about five miles from Robert Ashby's Yew Hill home.

13.   Out a Surveying till Night with sevel. attending.

14.   Out in like manner.

15.   Out again with many People attending.

16.   Ditto—Ditto—Ditto.

17.   Executing Leases to those who had taken Lotts—being at Captn. Ashbys.

GW had cut up his purchase of Carter's land into lots of about 100 acres each and was leasing them on a long-term basis to local farmers for about £4 Virginia currency per lot. On this day GW made at least 11 leases, some of which were for more than one lot. In GW's lease to George Russell, a fairly typical one, Russell was to be charged 30s. for each hand over four that was worked on the lot. Within ten years Russell was to plant and tend "at least Fifty Winter Apple trees at Thirty feet distance every way from each other and One hundred Peach trees at Sixteen feet distance every way from each other" and to build "a Good dwelling house at least Sixteen feet square of framed Work or Loggs Sawed and well hewed and a Barne or Tobacco house of Convenient Size or other houses and Buildings Equal thereto." GW retained the right to "all Mines Minerals and Quaries," as well as most of the timber, and reserved to himself "the Priviledge of hunting and fowling in or upon any part" of Russell's lot (17 Mar. 1769, ViWaC).

18.   Went up to Greenway Court where I dined and stayd all Night. Met Colo. Lewis here.

Greenway Court was not only the residence of Lord Fairfax but also the permanent location of the proprietor's land office. There GW and Fielding Lewis, in their capacity as trustees for the sale of George Carter's estate, paid Fairfax the balance of quitrents owed by the estate since 1746 (receipt from Thomas, Lord Fairfax, to GW and Lewis, 18 Mar. 1769, DNA).

19.   Went with Colo. Lewis to his Plantations where I stayd all day & Night.

20.   Executing in the forenoon Deeds, & settling with those who had purchd. Carters Land upon Opechon. In the afternoon rid to Valentine Crawfd.

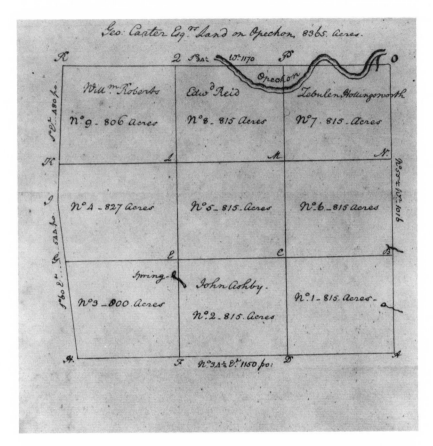

Washington's plat of George Carter's land on Opequon Creek. (Historical Society of Pennsylvania, Gratz Collection)

Opequon Creek, then in Frederick County, now divides Berkeley and Jefferson counties, W.Va. It rises a few miles southeast of Winchester and flows into the Potomac 15 or 16 miles above Harper's Ferry (KERCHEVAL, 305; NORRIS [1], 29).

21.   Went & laid of 4 Lots at the head of Bullskin for several Tenents.

22.   Filling up leases for them at Val Crawfords all day.

23.   Set of homewards. Breakfasted at Mr. Ariss's dind undr. the Ridge & lodgd at Wests.

John Ariss (d. 1799), originally of Westmoreland County, was one of the most successful architects and builders in Maryland and northern Virginia. In

1769 he moved from Richmond County to Frederick (later Berkeley) County. Although he has been credited with participating in work on the Mount Vernon mansion house 1757–59 and 1773–87, no documentary evidence has been found to support such a view (WATERMAN, 243–300, 419). In 1788 he leased 700 acres on GW's Bullskin tract at £60 a year (LEDGER B, 281).

24. Reachd home before dinner. Found Colo. Bassett, Lady & 2 Childn. Betcy & Nancy here also Mr. W[arne]r Washington & Jacky Custis.

Betcy and Nancy are Elizabeth Bassett (b. 1758), who died in childhood, and Anna Maria Bassett (1763–1773), who was the second Bassett daughter so named, the first, born in 1760, having died in infancy.

25. Went a fox hunting with Colo. Bassett & Mr. Bryan Fairfax—who also came here last night. Started & run a fox into a hole after an hours chase. Mr. Fairfax went home after dinner. Dog fox killd.

26. Took an airing with Colo. Bassett on horse back. Mr. R. Alexander came in the Evg.

27. Went a Fox hunting—found and was run out of hearing by some of the Dogs.

28. Hunting again. Found a fox & killd it in an hour and an half. Mr. Magowan & Vale. Crawford came here today.

On 26 Jan. of this year GW wrote to Rev. Jonathan Boucher that Magowan "has been fortunate in a Presentation to a good Parish . . . and is now living therein" (WRITINGS, 2:498–99). This was the parish of St. James (commonly called Herring Creek Parish) which lay between Herring Creek and the West River in Anne Arundel County, Md. Magowan had apparently passed up Frederick Parish, Va., which was much larger in area and probably not as wealthy as St. James.

29. Rid with Colo. Bassett into the Neck. Vale. Crawford went to Colo. Fairfax's.

30. Dined at Colo. Fairfax's along with Colo. Bassett & Lady—returnd in the Eveng.

31. Hunting—found a fox & killd him in a hour. This & the last were both Dog Foxes. Mr. Magowan went to Alexandria.

An Acct. of the Weather—in March

Mar. 1.   No frost but raw & cold. Wind North in the Morning— but No. East afterwards and very cloudy—with Misling Rain at Night.

2.   Not much Rain in the Night but some hard showers today, with the Wind Southwardly in the forepart of the day and No. Wt. afterwds.—then growing clear & cold.

3.   The ground slightly froze. Wind still at No. West—but not cold. Weathr. clear.

4.   Ground again slightly froze. Wind at No. Et., & day lowering. In the Afternoon fine Rain or Mist & wind fresh from the same point. Evening calm but still misty.

5.   Morning clear & Wind Southwardly. Abt. 10 Oclock the Wind came hard from the Westward & contd. all day but not cold.

6.   Ground a little froze. Wind Westwardly but not hard. Pleast. till Evening then raw cold & cloudy. Wind Eastwardly.

7.   Ground slightly froze. Weathr. raw cold cloudy, & in the Afternn. Snowg.; wind Northwd.

8.   Ground coverd two or 3 Inches with Snow but not being cold it thawd fast after the morng. when the Sun broke out.

9.   Ground hard froze—& very raw cold, and cloudy till 12 oclock then more moderate. Wind southwardly and clear.

10.   Exceeding high & cold wind from the No. West all day. Ground hard froze.

11.   Ground excessive hard froze & Morning very cold—wind being fresh from the No. Wt. but the Afternoon more moderate wind falling.

12.   Ground hard froze. Calm Mild & pleasant with passive clouds & sunshine.

13. Ground hard froze but the Weather very mild & pleasant after the Morning.

14. Very pleasant and warm there being but little Wind.

15. Again warm & pleasant with but little Wind.

16. Morning lowering and sometimes raining with high squals of wind.

17. Morning pretty sharp wind having shifted to the No. West in the Night—but the day clear still & pleasant.

18. Lowering with a little rain in the afternn. Wind southwardly and Evening clear.

19. A most delightful morning, & pleast. clear day. Afternoon lowering & windy.

20. A little cool but still clear and pleasant.

21. Clear and very warm the first part of the day. Windy the latter part from the Westward & at Night cool wind at No. West.

22. Cool. Wind still at North West & clear.

23. Clear & pleasant. But little wind & that southwardly.

24. Wind Southwardly, & little of it. Day very warm and clear.

25. Southwardly wind & Warm. Day clear but very smoky as it hath been for sevl. days past.

26. Very warm & clear except smokey. Wind still to the southward.

27. Lowering Morning with rain from 10 Oclock from the No. East all day & Night.

28. Rather cool. Wind at No. West but not hard.

29. Fine warm Morning & Wind afterwards from So. West & cooler.

30.   A little Rain in the Morning, but clear afterwards with the Wind pretty fresh, & somewhat cool from No. Wt.

31.   A fine warm & pleasant day with but little wind and that southwardly.

Remarks & Observations–in Mar[ch]

Mar. 2.   Began to List Corn Ground at the Mill.

6.   Began to List Do. at Muddy hole.

10.   And from that to the 18 laying of Lotts & leasing them in Fauquier & Loudoun Countys on the Land which I bought of Carters Estate.

20.   & from that to the 23d. doing the like on my Land at Bull-skin in Frederick County.

24.   Returnd home from my Journey to Frederick &ca. and found that the Hound Bitch Maiden had taken Dog promiscu-ously. That the Bitch Lady was in Heat & had also been promiscu-ously lined, & therefore I did not shut her up–That Dutchess was shut up, and had been lind twice by Drunkard, but was out one Night in her heat, & supposd to be lind by other Dog's–that Truelove was also in the House–as was Mopsy likewise (who had been lind to Pilot before she was shut up).

26.   The Bitch Musick brought five Puppies one of which being thought not true was drownd immediately. The others being somewhat like the Dog (Rockwood of Mr. Fairfaxs) which got them were saved.

27.   The Hound Bitch Countess brought 7 puppies and was with the Puppies carried away the next day by Alexr.

Mar. 31.   To this time Mopsy had been lind several times by Lawlor as Truelove had been by Drunkard–but as this Bitch got [out] one Night during her Heat it is presumable she was lind by other Dogs especially Pilot, the Master Dog, & one who was seen lying down by her in the Morning.
   Began about the 28th. to Plow behind the Quarter for oats & grass seeds.

[April]

Where & how—my time is—Spent

April 1st. At home all day with Colo. Bassett &ca. and Betcy Washington who came home with us on Thursday last.

GW on this date lost £1 4s. 6d. at cards (LEDGER A, 290).

2. At home all day. In the afternoon Mr. Rozer Mr. Carroll— Mr. Sydebotham & Mr. Magowan came here.

Several Carroll families were living in Maryland at this time. The visitor may have been Charles Carroll (1702–1782) of Annapolis; his son Charles Carroll (1737–1832) of Carrollton in Frederick County, Md., a signer of the Declaration of Independence; Daniel Carroll (1730–1796), of Frederick (later Montgomery) County, Md., later a commissioner of the federal district; or John Carroll (1735–1815), brother of Daniel, later first Roman Catholic bishop in the United States.

William Sydebotham, of Maryland, supplied goods to Maryland troops during the Revolution. After the war he was a claimant against the property of the Loyalist Rev. Jonathan Boucher.

3. Colo. Bassett and family set of homeward as Jacky Custis did to School & the above Gentlemen for Dumfries. Rid to Muddy hole Doeg Run & Mill.

4. After an early Dinner went to Belvoir to pay a visit to Colo. R. Fairfax, returnd at Night.

5. Run the back line of Spencer and Washingtons Patent & came home to Dinner.

The back line of the Spencer-Washington grant was the northern boundary.

6. At home all day. Mr. Magowan returnd from Dumfries.

7. Went a fox hunting in the Morning & catchd a dog fox after running him an hour and treeing twice. After this went to an intended meeting of the Vestry but there was none. When I came home found Mr. Buchanon & Captn. McGachin here—also Captn. Weeden and my Br. Charles.

The vestry did not meet because they lacked a quorum and hence could not legally sign the articles of agreement with Daniel French for constructing the new Pohick Church (Truro Vestry Book, 139–42, DLC).

Captain William McGachin (also McCachen), a sea captain, often supplied GW with goods from London. In 1763 and for some years earlier, he commanded a convict ship, a duty he greatly disliked. GW recommended him to his London merchants, Robert Cary & Co., for the command of one of their ships plying between London and the Potomac, "because a personal acquaintance with Mr. McGachin added to his general good Character enables me to introduce him to you as a Gentleman of known Skill, deligence and Integrety" (GW to Cary & Co., 4 Oct. 1763, DLC:GW).

8. The two first went to Occaquan works & returnd in the Afternoon. At home all day.

9. At home all day with the above Gentlemen & Mr. Tibbles. In the afternoon Captn. Jno. West came here.

10. Captn. McGachin & Mr. Buchanan & Mr. Tibbles went away. We were at home all day.

11. Went a fox hunting & took a fox alive after running him to a Tree. Brot. him home.

12. Chased the above fox an Hour & 45 Minutes when he treed again after which we lost him. Mr. B. Fairfax came this afternoon.

13. Went a Huntg. with him in the Neck & killd a Dog fox after treeing him in 35 Min[utes]. Mr. W[arner] Washington Dind here & both of them stayd all Night. My Br. & Captn. Weeden went away this Morning.

Warner Washington's wife Hannah Fairfax Washington was visiting her brother at Belvoir, where she had given birth the week before to a third daughter, Catharine.

14. Mr. Fairfax & Mr. Washington went away and we set out to go to Captn. McCartys but Patcy being taken with a fit on the road by the Mill we turnd back.

15. Rid to Muddy hole—Doeg run and the Mill.

16. Went to Pohick Church and returnd home to Dinner.

17. Went up to Court & lodgd at Mr. Jno. Wests at Night.

The court met two days in April. GW was present from the beginning today, but he came late the next day, arriving after five items of business were finished (Fairfax County Order Book for 1768–70, 120–27, Vi Microfilm). John West, Jr., and his wife Catherine Colvill West lived near Cameron (GW to West, Dec. 1767, DLC and 4 July 1773, NNebgGW). GW today lost

£2 15s. 6d. at cards and apparently lost £1 1s. more on the following day (LEDGER A, 290).

18.   Went to Court again and come home in the Evening with Colo. Mason—Mr. Auge. Smith Mr. Ross & Mr. Denneson. Found Mr. Stedlar here.

MR. AUGE. SMITH: probably Augustine Smith (1739–1774) of Shooter's Hill plantation in Middlesex County, the eldest son of John Smith of Cabin Point, Westmoreland County (TYLER [2], 95). MR. DENNESON: Since he and Mr. Ross went home together from Mount Vernon (see next entry), this is probably James Dennistone (or Dennistown), a merchant of Colchester. Both Ross and Dennistone signed the nonimportation association in Williamsburg, 22 June 1770, and both men, along with Alexander Henderson, represented Colchester on a committee appointed by the merchants to consider the general state of trade in the colony.

19.   Mr. Wr. Washington came early in the Morng. Mr. Ross & Mr. Denneson went home, & Colo. Mason & myself went to settle the Bounds of our Land.

Mason owned land on the north side of the tract GW had bought from Sampson Darrell (LEDGER A, 61).

20.   Mr. Smith & Mr. Washington went away as did Mr. Stedlar. Colo. Mason & myself again went into the woods a Surveying.

21.   At home with Colo. Mason who went away in the Afternoon.

Mason today signed an agreement promising to sell GW a strip of 100 acres on Little Hunting Creek, adjoining the Darrell tract, for £100 (MASON [2], 1:102; LEDGER A, 61).

22.   Surveying in the Woods all day. Mr. Chichester Mr. Ball Mr. Hale & Miss Sinai McCarty dind here.

MR. BALL: probably Sinah McCarty's first cousin, Burgess Ball (1749–1800), of Lancaster County, who on 2 July 1770 married Richard Chichester's niece, Mary Chichester. MR. HALE: possibly William Heale (many spellings, including Hale), originally of Lancaster County, who was settled in Fauquier County by 1777. Although her name was often spelled "Sinai," Miss McCarty was named after her mother, Sinah Ball McCarty (see HAYDEN, 92, 111–16; HODGES, 274).

23.   Dined at Belvoir. Met Majr. Wagener coming to dine with me. Doctr. Rumney came.

24.   Measuring the Road to Poseys ferry and seeing how a new one coud be laid out. Captn. McCarty dind here.

25. At home all day alone. The above two Gentlemen went away yesterday afternn.

26. At home. Mr. Martin Cockburn & Pierce Baily dind here & went away afterwards.

27. Rid to the Neck Muddy hole & Doeg Run. Captn. McCarty & wife dind here.

28. At home all day. Doctr. Rumney came here in the afternoon.

29. Went up to Alexandria and Mr. Jno. Wests & returnd to Dinner.

John West, Jr., today agreed in writing to sell GW about 200 acres of land lying on the Potomac River next to the Mount Vernon tract for 43s. an acre. This land had been part of John Posey's plantation by virtue of his wife Martha's inheritance from her first husband, George Harrison. She had been given use of it for her lifetime only, and during the past year she had died. According to the terms of Harrison's will, the land then automatically passed to John West, Jr., who as Harrison's nephew was his nearest male descendant (Harrison's will, 21 Nov. 1748, Fairfax County Wills, Book A-1, 260–61, Vi Microfilm). However, West was prevented from deeding the property to GW at this time because of a bitter dispute between West and Posey over the ownership of a thin strip along the Potomac, containing about 6 acres, on which Posey's house and ferry were located. Posey had bought that strip from Thomas Marshall 21 Sept. 1757 for £6 sterling (Fairfax County Deeds, Book D-1, 477–78, Vi Microfilm), but West claimed that it belonged to him, saying that Marshall had no right to sell it to Posey because it was included in the bounds of Harrison's land, which Harrison had bought from William Spencer before Marshall bought Spencer's remaining land in the area. West had recently brought suit to force Posey off the strip, and GW was obliged to await the outcome of that case so that there would be no further confusion over titles or acreages (West's agreement with GW, 29 April 1769, owned by Mr. Sol Feinstone, Washington Crossing, Pa.; West's agreement with GW, 18 Sept. 1770, PHi: Gratz Collection).

30. Set of for Williamsburg with Betcy Dandridge & was forcd into Peytons Ordy. at Aquia where we lodgd.

GW was going to Williamsburg to attend the House of Burgesses, scheduled to convene 8 May. This session promised to be a stormy one because of the deepening crisis in the American colonies over the Townshend Acts, which remained in effect despite American requests for their repeal. Leaders in several colonies north of Virginia had begun to organize nonimportation associations to boycott British goods until Parliament rescinded the offensive duties, and GW, who had heard of those endeavors, was convinced that some kind of nonimportation association was now needed in Virginia. "Addresses to the Throne, and remonstrances to Parliament," he wrote to George Mason on 5 April, "we have already . . . proved the inefficacy of; how far then their attention to our rights & priviledges is to be awakened or alarmed by starving their Trade & manufactures, remains to be tryed" (DLC:GW). GW made this trip to Williamsburg in his chair. (LEDGER A, 191).

An Acct.–of the Weather–in April

Apl. 1st.   Raining all the forenoon with but little Wind & weather warm. In the Afternoon it ceasd but continued cloudy.

2.   Clear, still, warm and very pleasant growing weather.

3.   Clear, Warm and pleasant. Wind southwardly.

4.   Clear & warm. Wind in the same place & fresh.

5.   Cloudy & Lowering. Wind strong from the So. West. At Night very squally with a little Rain when the Wind shifted to No. West & turnd very cold for the Season.

6.   Cold & clear–with a frost to kill the fruit. Wind still at No. West & fresh.

7.   Another frost to freeze the Ground & very cold in the Morning but cloudy & more moderate afterwards.

8.   A harder frost than yesterdays & very cold–Wind fresh from the No. West.

9.   Still cool but not equal to three days past–clear & the wind getting abt. Southwardly.

10.   Warm, clear & pleasant with very little wind.

11.   Warm clear and pleasant with the Wind tho not much of it Southwardly.

12.   But little wind and that from the same Quarter.

13.   Clear & pleasant morning but showery day with thunder Morng. & Evening. In the Afternoon a severe Wind & exceeding

hard rain for about 20 Minutes from the So. West. Afterwards clear & cool wind shiftg. to No. West.

14.　Clear Morning but cool.

15.　Clear & pleasant Morning but raining afternoon. Clear & cool Evening. Wind at No. West.

16.　Clear & somewhat cool. Wind Westwardly and at Night No. West.

17.　Very cold and disagreeable Wind being fresh & raw from the No. West.

18.　Wind at So. Et. in the first part of the day. Raw cold & showery at 2 & 3 Oclock & clear & cold from the No. West afterwards. A large frost this Morning.

19.　Clear and very cold. Wind at No. West and fresh—more moderate at Noon.

20.　Rather warmer this morning but very lowering, with rain abt. 10 Oclock from the No. Et. Abt. 12 clear with the wind at No. West and towards Night very raw & cold.

21.　Wind fresh from the No. West & very raw & cold all day—more moderate at Night.

22.　Wind Southwardly, clear, & much warmer than it hath been for two or three days past.

23.　Morning lowering with Rain, but soon cleard, Wind being fresh from the So. West & warm.

24.　Wind very fresh from the So. West & west with Rain in the forenoon but clear afterwards.

25.　Raining most part of the day with the wind Eastwardly & cold.

26.　Cool in the Morning, wind being at No. West & clear, but mild pleasant & calm in the Afternoon.

27.   Lowering Morning & sometimes Raining with the wind Eastwardly. In the Afternoon slow settled Rain.

28.   Raining of and on all day sometimes pretty fast but always misting. Wind in the same Quartr.

29.   Misty all day with the wind still Eastwardly & fresh.

30.   Wind still Eastwardly & Morning Lowering. Abt. 12 it began to rain & contd. to do so all this afternoon.

Remarks & Observations—in April

Aprl. 3.   Sowed what St. Foin seed I had in the Lucern patch.

4.   Got done threshing at Doeg run Plantation.
Sowed some St. Foine in the Lucerne patch.

11.   The white fish ran plentifully at my sein landing having catchd abt. 300 at one Hawl.

14.   Began to Plant corn at Muddy hole.

15.   Began to Plant Do. at the Mill.
Sowed Oats in the Inclosure behind the Quarter.

18.   Sowed Clover and Burnet Seeds on Do.
Sent Negroe George into the Neck.

BURNET: *Sanguisorba minor,* a perennial affording both grain and hay, which GW and other farmers tried in the latter part of the eighteenth century. It had been pretty well discontinued by 1820.

22.   The Herrings run in great abundance.

27.   Finished planting Corn in the Neck.

30.   Finishd Ditto at Muddy hole.

[May]

Where & how—my time is—Spent

May 1.   Set out from Peytons & passing thro Fredericksburg reachd Hubbards Ordy.

This engraving of Williamsburg public buildings, found in the Bodleian Library at Oxford, played a major part in the modern restoration of that town. (Colonial Williamsburg Photograph)

2.   Got to Eltham—after foundg. my Horse.

GW crossed the Pamunkey at Sweet Hall as he had during the previous year, but since his last trip the name of the ferry there had changed from Claiborne's to Ruffin's. Robert Ruffin, a wealthy planter formerly of Dinwiddie County, had recently acquired Sweet Hall and the ferry from Claiborne and had moved there with his wife Mary, daughter of John and Mary Clack and widow of Col. John Lightfoot (d. 1751) of Brunswick County (*Va. Gaz.*, P&D, 24 Nov. 1768; P, 23 May 1777; RUFFIN, 252). At Ruffin's on this day GW spent 4s. for ferriages and 15s. to care for a sick horse (LEDGER A, 290).

3.   Went into Williamsburg and dined with the Council & spent the Evening in the Daphne.

The Daphne was a room in the Raleigh Tavern, on Duke of Gloucester Street about half a block from the Capitol. Owned at this time by Anthony Hay (d. 1770), a former cabinetmaker, the Raleigh was a center of social, political, and business activities in Williamsburg. Public auctions were often held in front of it, and many important meetings and fashionable balls took place inside its elegant rooms (RALEIGH TAVERN, 7–10). While GW was at the Raleigh on this date, he bought subscriptions to three Williamsburg purse races from Hay (LEDGER A, 290). "There are races at Williamsburgh twice a year," a visitor to the town about this time observed, "that is, every spring and fall, or autumn. Adjoining to the town is a very excellent course, for either two, three or four mile heats. Their purses are generally raised by subscription, and are gained by the horse that wins two four-mile heats out of three; they amount to an hundred pounds each for the first day's running, and fifty each day after; the races commonly continuing for a week" (SMYTH, 1:17–19).

   GW also amused himself frequently at the card table during this visit to Williamsburg, winning £4 17s. 6d. this day but losing £1 the next (LEDGER A, 290). He did not lodge at the Raleigh but stayed as usual at Mrs. Campbell's place (LEDGER A, 291).

4.   Dined with the Speaker and spent the Evening (that is supped) at Mrs. Campbells.

GW today borrowed £50 from Fielding Lewis to pay Peyton Randolph for a "tenth of 100 Tickets taken in Partnership with himself and others in Colo. Byrds Lottery" (LEDGER A, 290).

5.   Dined at the Governors and supped at Mr. Carters.

Robert Carter (1728–1804) of Nomini Hall in Westmoreland County, a grandson of Robert "King" Carter, had become a member of the council in 1758 and now lived in a handsome town house next to the Governor's Palace. He returned to live at Nomini Hall in 1771 but remained on the council until the Revolution (MORTON, 42–45).

6.   Dined at Mrs. Campbells & spent the Eveng. there without supping.

Robert Carter, of Nomini Hall in Westmoreland County. (Virginia Historical Society)

7. Dined at Ayscoughs and supped there also.

8. Dined at Anthony Hays and Supped at Mrs. Campbells.

The Raleigh Tavern had been named in honor of Sir Walter Raleigh many years earlier by one of Hay's predecessors, and it was known as the Raleigh throughout the rest of its existence. However, GW and others often referred to the tavern by the name of its current proprietor.

The House of Burgesses sat today as scheduled. Governor Botetourt gave a brief address and committees were appointed. GW was placed on the committee of propositions and grievances and the committee of privileges and elections (H.B.J., 1766–69, 187–92). Later this day he lost £1 at cards but won £1 5s. the next (LEDGER A, 290).

9. Dined at the Palace, & spent the Evening in my own Room.

The burgesses on this day began the routine business of considering various petitions and claims from citizens.

10. Dined at Mrs. Campbells and spent the Evening at Hay's.

GW paid £1 today for two pairs of snap earrings George Mason had asked him to buy (LEDGER A, 290).

11. Again dined at Mrs. Campbells, and spent the Evening at Hays.

12. Dined with Mr. Wythe and Supped at Hays.

A nineteenth-century painting of George Wythe, copied from a John Trumbull portrait. (Independence National Historical Park Collection)

George Wythe, now clerk of the House of Burgesses and a prominent Williamsburg lawyer, lived in a brick mansion on the Palace green.

13. Dined at Mrs. Campbells and went over to Gloucester to Colo. W. Lewis's afterwards.

Col. Warner Lewis (b. 1720), son of Col. John and Frances Fielding Lewis, lived at Warner Hall in Gloucester County. He was the elder brother of Fielding Lewis, husband of GW's sister Betty (SORLEY, 67–68).

Today being Friday, the burgesses adjourned for the weekend after attending to a few items of routine business.

14. At Colo. Lewis's all day.

GW won £1 at cards on this date (LEDGER A, 290).

15. Returnd to Williamsburg by nine oclock in the Morng. after Breakfasting in York Town. Dined at Mrs. Campbells & supped at Hays.

The burgesses resumed their session at the usual hour of 11:00 A.M. GW and several other members were today added to the committee on religion, which handled matters relating to the organization of parishes (H.B.J., 1766–69, 211).

16. Rid over my dower Land in York, to shew that, and the Mill, to the Gentlemen appointed by the Genl. Court to value & report thereon. Came in to Breakfast. Dined at the Speakers and spent the Evening at Hays.

GW had been trying for at least the last two years to rent out the dower property in York County, because it was too far from Mount Vernon for him to inspect as often as he thought he should (*Va. Gaz.*, P&D, 2 April 1767). "Middling Land under a Mans own eye," he later remarked, "is more profitable than rich Land at a distance" (GW to John Parke Custis, 24 July 1776, ViHi). He had now decided to rent the property to Jacky Custis and thus consolidate all the Custis lands in York County under his name, if a place could be found near Mount Vernon to which the dower slaves on the York plantations could be moved and if the General Court, to which GW was responsible for the administration of Jacky's estate, approved the transaction (GW to John Posey, 11 June 1769, DLC:GW; receipt from Edmund Pendleton, 23 Nov. 1769, ViHi: Custis Papers). Both conditions were fulfilled by 1771 when GW began to charge Jacky's account £150 a year for the use of the "Land and Mill in York County as settled with the Genl. Court" (CUSTIS ACCOUNT BOOK). Claiborne's plantation in King William County was rented to Jacky in 1778 (GW to James Hill, 27 Oct. 1778, DLC:GW).

The burgesses on this date sat as a committee of the whole to consider various British treason acts being cited in London as legal grounds for bringing leaders of colonial protests against Parliament's taxes to England for trial. After a debate, four resolutions were put before the house and were promptly passed. Known as the Virginia Resolves, they declared that the burgesses, with the consent of the governor and the council, had the sole right to impose taxes on the inhabitants of Virginia; that Virginians had a right to petition the king for redress of grievances; that Virginians could be tried for treason and other crimes only by established procedures in the established courts within the colony; and that an address should be sent to the king beseeching him "as the Father of all his people . . . to quiet the Minds of his loyal Subjects of this Colony, and to avert from them, those Dangers and Miseries which will ensue, from seizing and carrying beyond the Sea, any Persons residing in America, suspected of any Crime whatsoever, to be tried in any other Manner, than by the ancient and long established Course of Proceeding." Before adjournment, the resolves were ordered to be sent to the assemblies of the other colonies, and a committee was appointed to write the petition to the king (H.B.J., 1766–69, 214–15).

17.   Dined at the Treasurers and was upon a Committee at Hays till 10 oclock.

The address to the king was presented to the burgesses today and accepted without dissent. The house then turned to other business, but about noon Speaker Randolph received a message from Governor Botetourt commanding the burgesses to come immediately to the council chamber. When they were assembled there, Botetourt spoke: "Mr. Speaker, and Gentlemen of the House of Burgesses, I have heard of your Resolves, and augur ill of their Effect. You have made it my Duty to dissolve you; and you are dissolved accordingly" (H.B.J., 1766–69, 215–18). With that statement this session of the house came to an abrupt end, but most of the dissolved burgesses, including GW, promptly reassembled a few doors down the street at Hay's Raleigh Tavern, meeting unofficially in the Apollo Room to consider "their distressed Situation." Peyton Randolph was elected moderator of the group, and a committee was appointed to prepare a plan for a Virginia nonimportation association (H.B.J., 1766–69, xxxix–xl).

18.   Dined at Mrs. Dawsons & went to Bed by 8 Oclock.

Another meeting of the dissolved burgesses was held in the Apollo Room today beginning at 10:00 A.M. The committee appointed on the previous day presented a nonimportation plan, and after being "read, seriously considered, and approved," it was signed by 88 "of the principal Gentlemen of the Colony," including GW. The subscribers promised that "by their own Example, as all other legal Ways and Means in their Power," they would "promote and encourage Industry and Frugality, and discourage all Manner of Luxury and Extravagence." No member of the association was henceforth to import directly or indirectly any article taxed by Parliament for the purpose of raising a revenue in America (except inexpensive paper) or any untaxed article appearing on a long detailed list of European agricultural and manufactured goods. Forbidden items that had been previously ordered could be received, but after 1 Sept. 1769, none in the colony, regardless of date of importation, was to be bought. These agreements were to remain in effect until one month after the repeal of the Townshend Acts or until the members of the association decided to dissolve it, but in the latter case the prohibition against taxed articles would remain in effect until repeal of the taxes (H.B.J., 1766–69, xl–xliii).

GW today bought a copy of John Dickinson's recent pamphlet, *Letters from a Farmer in Pennsylvania to the Inhabitants of the British Colonies.* He also purchased a pair of gloves, medicines, and coffee and paid his bill at Hay's: £2 12s. 9d., including 20s. "arisg. from the Associaters meetg. there" (LEDGER A, 290).

19.   Dined again at Mrs. Dawson's and went to the Queens Birth Night at the Palace.

Today "being the QUEEN's birthday, the flag was displayed on the Capitol; and in the evening . . . the Governour gave a splendid ball and entertainment at the Palace, to a very numerous and polite company of Ladies and Gentlemen" (*Va. Gaz.*, P&D, 25 May 1769).

20.   Left Williamsburg on my return home. Dined at Colo. Bassetts & stayd the rest of the day there.

GW paid two accounts before leaving town: £6 15s. to Mrs. Campbell for his board and lodging and £2 6s. to the barber George Lafong for dressing his hair. He also lent £5 in cash to a friend, Robert Rutherford, burgess from Frederick County in the past session (LEDGER A, 291). At Eltham he paid Mrs. Bassett £3 2s. 3d. for a piece of chintz, a hairpin, and a hair comb (LEDGER A, 291).

21.   Crossd over to my own Plantation. Dined at Todds & lodgd at Port Royal.

22.   Reachd home after going as far as Colo. Harrisons with a view of crossing thro Maryland & being disappointed was obl[iged] to come up the Virginia side. Found Mrs. Bushrod Mrs. W. Washington & their families here—also Mr. Boucher Mr. Addison, Mr. Magowan and Doctr. Rumney—Jacky Custis.

Mildred Washington Bushrod (c.1720–1785), of Gloucester County, a cousin of GW, was the sister of Warner Washington, Sr., and the widow of John Bushrod (d. 1760) of Westmoreland County. She had been his second wife, and he her second husband, but she had no children by either of her two marriages, John Bushrod's daughters Hannah and Elizabeth having been born to his first wife, Jenny Corbin Bushrod (KENNER, 177–78; GW to Ruthey Jones, 25 Sept. 1783, DLC:GW). After John Bushrod died, Mildred apparently returned to Gloucester County, where she was listed on the tax roll for 1770 as owning 1,280 acres of land and a sedan chair (GLOUCESTER, 1:92). Her family on this visit may be children of her other brother, Henry Washington of Middlesex County, who at his death in 1763 had left a son, Thacker, and three underage daughters, Elizabeth, Catherine, and Ann (WAYLAND [1], 325).

MR. ADDISON: probably Rev. Henry Addison (1717–1789), who in 1751 married Rachel Dulany (d. 1774), eldest daughter of Daniel Dulany the elder. The Addison and Dulany families of Maryland were at this time allied in a bitter struggle to oust the rector of Saint Anne's Parish, the parish serving the town of Annapolis. For a new rector they were looking to Addison to bring in Jonathan Boucher, who was willing to open a school in Annapolis for the sons of the Addison and Dulany families (BOUCHER [1], 50–57; LAND, 280–82).

23. Mr. Addison and Mr. Boucher went away. At home myself all day.

24. At home all day. Mr. Magowan went down to Dumfries.

25. Rid to Muddy hole, Doeg Run and Mill & returnd to Dinner.

26. Rid into the Neck and from there went up to a Race at Cameron.

27. Went in to Alexandria to a Barbecue and stayed all Night.

GW on this date won 8s. playing cards (LEDGER A, 291).

28. Returnd home early in the Morning & went to Pohick Church returning to Dinner.

29. At home all day.

30. Rid to Muddy hole about 11 Oclock and returnd to Dinner.

31. Set of with Mrs. Washington & Patcy Mr. W. Washington & wife Mrs. Bushrod & Miss Washington & Mr. Magowan for Towlston in order to stand for Mr. B. Fairfax's 3d. Son which I did together with my Wife, Mr. W[arne]r Washington & his Lady.

MR. B. FAIRFAX'S 3D. SON: Ferdinando Fairfax (1769–1820), who is here becoming a godson of GW, married Elizabeth Cary, was the heir of George William Fairfax, and was a principal mourner at GW's funeral.

An Acct.–of the Weather–in May

May 1. Threatning Morning but clear and pleasant about 10 with little wind and that westwardly.

2. Clear and tolerably warm in the forenoon, but very cold in the Evening the Wind getting to No. Wt. and North.

3.   Cool and clear with the Wind Northwardly. Evening more moderate.

4.   Clear and pleasant but rather cool.

5.   Clear. Wind Southwardly – and warm.

6.   Threatning Morning, & black clouds. Abt. 12 or one clock it began to rain & contd. to do so of & on moderately till 4 & then cleard.

7.   Warm & pleasant with little or no Wind.

8.   Warm clear and pleasant. Wind Southwardly.

9.   Lowering in the Morning but clear afterwards & somewhat cooler than yesterday.

10.   Warm and Sultry. Wind Southwardly & clear.

11.   Wind fresh & warm from the So. West till the afternn. then cool & shifting to the Eastward.

12.   Morning lowering & cool – with rain abt. one & 2 oclock. Clear again abt. 4 with a pleast. afternoon.

13.   Clear & pleast. Morning – as it continued to be all day. Evening cool.

14.   Wind fresh from the southwest with a little thunder & some Rain.

15.   Warm forenoon with a fine Shower abt. two or 3 Oclock & pleast. afterwards.

16.   Brisk southwardly Wind. Warm & lowering.

17.   Wind southwardly and very warm. About five in the Afternoon a pleasant shower & still Warm after it.

18.   Very Warm. Wind Southwardly. Fast & flying Clouds.

19.   Warm with frequent Showers, and thunder and lightning. Wind southwardly.

20.   Wind Northwardly & cool—with thunder and lightning in the Night & high E. Wind.

21.   Wind at No. West and cold—with flying clouds.

22.   Cool Morning with the Wind Northwardly but warmer afterwards and wind at So. West.

23.   Clear and rather cool notwithstandg. the Wind was at So. West and fresh.

24.   Wind Westwardly with several showers of Rain. In the Evening the Wind shifted No. Wt.

25.   Very cool Morning. Wind still at No. Wt. and clear.

26.   Cool in the Morning but warm afterwards & clear. Wind Westwardly.

27.   Lowering with the Wind at So. West & Warm—in the Afternoon a little sprinkling.

28.   Cooler. Wind Westwardly—and lowering. In the Afternoon and Night fine Rain but cool. Wind Eastwardly.

29.   Misty and Cloudy all day with Showers in the Afternoon. Wind still Eastwardly.

30.   Cool & clear. Wind being at No. West.

31.   Very cool and Wind Eastwardly. Weather lowering and like for Rain.

Remarks & Occurances in May

22.   Returnd home from Williamsburg and found my Wheat much better in general; than ever it was at this Season before— being Ranker, better spread over the ground & broader in the Blade than usual.
    It was also observable that in general the head was shot out, and in many places in Blossom.

27.   Finishd breaking up my Corn Ground at the Mill.

29.   Mopsy the Hound Bitch and Truelove another Hound brought 12 Puppies—that is Mopsy had five and the other seven.

30.   Finishd breaking up my Corn ground in the Neck with my Plows.

[June]

Where & how—my time is—Spent

June 1.   Set of from Towlston with the Compy. that went up yesterday on our return home and reachd Mt. Vernon abt. 6 oclock.

2.   Went to Alexandria to Mr. Saml. Johnsons Funeral Sermon & returned to Dinr.

Samuel Johnston (Johnson) had been living on part of the Clifton's Neck land that GW bought in 1760. He remained as a tenant, paying GW 1,013 pounds of tobacco annually for his lot, which was probably at least 100 acres. In 1762 Johnston leased two more lots in Clifton's Neck from GW at the same rental fee. Johnston also ran a ferry from his land to the Maryland shore. His son, Samuel Jr., worked for GW in his wheat and tobacco crops from 1762 to 1764. Johnston was survived by his widow, Hannah, seven children (at least four of whom were married), and two grandchildren (LEDGER A, 77, 132, 134, 200; KING [4], 27).

3.   Mr. Warnr. Washington & family—Mrs. Bushrod and hers—& Mr. Magowan all went away this day. I rid to Muddy hole Doeg run and the Mill.

4.   At home all day—alone.

5.   Dined at Belvoir—Mrs. Washington and Patcy Custis going with me.

6.   At home all day—Mrs. Fairfax, Colo. Fairfax & Mr. Wormely the elder ding. here & returning in the afternoon.

Ralph Wormeley (1715–1790), one of the wealthiest planters in the colony, lived at his family's old home, Rosegill, on the south bank of the Rappahannock River near Urbanna. He served as burgess from Middlesex County 1742–64 and later became comptroller of the Rappahannock River Naval District. He was twice married: in 1736 to Sally Berkeley, daughter of Edmund Berkeley of Middlesex County, and after her death (c.1741), to Jane, probably daughter of James Bowles of St. Mary's County, Md.

Ralph Wormeley of Rosegill. (Virginia Historical Society)

7.   Rid into the Neck and to Muddy hole & returnd to Dinner.

8.   Went with Mrs. Washington & Patcy Custis on a visit to Mr. Wm. Digges & returnd in the Afternoon.

9.   Rid to Captn. Posey's—from thence to the Mill & then home.

John Posey had recently gone to Maryland, where he married Elizabeth Adair of Chestertown. He had not yet brought his bride home to Rover's Delight, but GW today saw the sad state of affairs that would greet the newly married couple there. Almost everything not mortgaged to GW had been attached by the Fairfax County sheriff to be sold for payment of various debts, and, according to Posey's son Hanson, the slaves would be without bread in a few days and the horses had nothing to eat at all. Furthermore, several merchants had brought suit against Posey and GW in the county court to force a sale of the mortgaged property. No action had been taken on the suit to date, but clearly matters had, as GW wrote to Posey two days later, "come to a Crisis." He must either find money to pay all his debts before the end of the year or sell his lands and slaves (11 June 1769, DLC:GW).

10.   At home all day.

11.   Went to Pohick Church. Dined at Captn. McCarty's. Stood for Mr. Chichesters Child & came home in the Aftern.

The second son of Richard and Sarah McCarty Chichester, born 27 Feb. 1769, is here being christened Daniel McCarty Chichester in his grandfather's home.

12.   Rid to Muddy hole Doeg Run, and the Mill. Doctr. Rumney (& Mr. Stedlar, who came yesterday afternoon) Mr. Robt. Scott & Mr. Hy. Peake Dind here. Also Sally Carlyle.

Robert Scott was a Scottish merchant of Dumfries.

13.   Went into the Neck.

14.   Rid to Muddy hole, Doeg Run, and Mill & from thence went to Belvoir to pay my respects to Lord Fairfax. Dind there & returnd in the Afternoon. S. Carlyle wt. Ho[me].

15.   Rid to Muddy hole Doeg run and Mill & returnd to Dinner.

16.   At home all day. Mr. Robt. Alexander & his Brothr. Geo. Dind here and went away in the Afternoon.

17th.   Rid to Muddy hole, Doeg Run, & Mill Plantation.

18.   At home all day—alone.

19.   Went up to Court & returnd in the Evening.

The June court lasted until 24 June. GW and his fellow justice Alexander Henderson arrived today immediately after the first item of business was finished (Fairfax County Order Book for 1768–72, 143–92, Vi Microfilm).

In Alexandria today GW settled with Pierce Baily for this year's taxes. His personal bill was £1 10s. cash for the public tax on his chariot and chair, £2 2s. cash for miscellaneous fees, and 4,754 pounds of tobacco for the county and parish levies: 534 pounds to Fairfax County for 89 tithables at 6 pounds each, 1,140 pounds to Fairfax Parish for 19 tithables at 60 pounds each, and 3,080 to Truro Parish for 70 tithables at 44 pounds each (LEDGER A, 291, 293).

20.   Went up to Court again & returnd in the Evening with Colo. Mason, Mr. Scott and Mr. Bryan Fairfax.

GW was again a little late for court, being recorded present with John Carlyle shortly after it began (Fairfax County Order Book for 1768–70, 153, Vi Microfilm).

21.   Mr. Fairfax went away in the Morning to Court. The other Gentln. stayd all day.

GW remained at Mount Vernon with his company.

22.   Colo. Mason & Mr. Scott went away & I to Court again.

GW arrived after the court's second item of business for the day (Fairfax County Order Book for 1768–70, 168, Vi Microfilm).

23.   Went to Court again and returnd in the afternoon.

GW, Col. John West, and Charles Broadwater were recorded present about a fifth of the way through today's court proceedings (Fairfax County Order Book for 1768–70, 180, Vi Microfilm).

24.   Rid to Muddy hole, Doeg Run, & Mill & returnd to Dinner. Lord Fairfax, the two Colo. Fairfax's & Mr. Digges dind here & returnd.

25.   I dined at Belvoir & returnd in the Eveng.

26.   At home all day—Measuring salt from a Bermudian.

A BERMUDIAN: GW is here receiving salt from a Bermudian vessel, which likely came from Turks Islands in the British West Indies.

27.   Rid into the Neck, and to Muddy hole.

28.   Rid to the Harvest Field at Doeg Run & returnd to Dinner.

29.   Went to the same place again, & Returnd also to Dinner. In the Afternoon Doctr. Rumney came on a visit to Betty.

30.   Went into the Neck where my Harvest People had movd to and returnd to Dinner. Doctr. Rumney went away after Breakfast.

Acct. of the Weather—in June

June 1st.   Still cloudy and like for Rain with the Wind Eastwardly and cold.

2.   Clear, and cool in the Morning—but warmer afterwards. Wind Northwardly.

3.   Clear, and not so cool as yesterday. Midday warm—Wind being at So. Wt.

4.   Clear and pleasant, being neither cold nor Warm. Wind abt. So. West.

5.   Wind fresh from the So. West and warm. The forenoon clear —afternoon having appearances of Rain with rumbg. of Thunder.

6.   Wind very fresh from the So. West with but little Clouds & in general warm.

7.   But little wind & that being Southwardly made the weather Warm & almost Sultry.

8.   Wind in the same place and Weather Warm. In the Afternoon the Wind being fresh and a cloud rising to the So. West we had a fine shower in the Night with some thunder & much lightning.

9.   Warm & fine growing weather, but little wind in the forepart of the day & that Southwardly—fresher in the afternoon.

10.   Wind fresh from the So. West with Clouds a little sprinkle & some thunder. About sun set the wind shifted to the No. Wt.

11.   Clear morning, with lowering afternoon. Wind Southwardly.

12.   Warm and lowering—also Smoky. Wind southwardly & but little of it.

13.   The Wind shifting to the Northward in the Night it became cool in the morning; but at Midday it grew a little warm although the wind hung to the Northwd. all day and was perfectly clear.

14.   Clear and Temperate. But little Wind and that Eastwardly—but varying.

15.   Close still and warm. But little wind & that Southwardly.

16th.   Very warm & some slight appearances of Rain—with little or no Wind till the Eveng. then pretty fresh from the Southward.

17.   Very warm again with little or no Wind in the forenoon but tolerably fresh. Southwardly Wind afterwards.

18.   Wind getting to Northwest and blowg. fresh all day the Air grew cool & was clear.

19.   There being but little wind and that southwardly it grew very warm again.

20.   Very Hot with very little wind & that to the Southward.

21.   Again Hot with the Wind in the same Quarter.

22.   There being flying showers abt. in the Night & Morning tho not hard the Wind shifted to the Northward & grew cool or Rather to the Eastward.

23.   Warm wind getting to the Southward again.

24.   Very warm with great appearan⟨ces⟩ of rain, but none fell here. Still & calm.

25.   Also very warm with the same shows but no rain fell here. Still & calm.

26.   Small breeze from the southward but very hot and sultry notwithstanding w[ith] appearances of Rain.

27.   Very hot and Sultry; indeed extreamly so. A small breeze from the Southwd.

28.   Sun very hot, but the Heat corrected in some degree by a southerly Breeze. In the afternoon frequent Showers of Rain—but little of it here—with pretty smart Wind from the So. West.

29.   Wind getting to the Northward, this day was something more temperate & yet warm. In the Night abt. 11 Oclock a fine Rain.

30.   A shower in the Morng. with Thunder & a Rainbow in the West. In the Eveng. one or two other showers wt. some Thun[der].

Remarks & Occurances in June

June 2d.   Finishd breaking up my Corn gd. with the Plows at Muddy hole.

3d.   Finishd going over the field abt. the Overseers House at the Mill with the Hoes.

6. Went over my plowed Corn at Doeg Run a 2d. time with the Plows.

7. Rid into the Neck, and went all ovr. my Wheat there, which in general I think very good; and at this time free from any appearance of Rust. I think it is observable that the Wheat on the River side appeard to be better head than the other tho not superior in look in any other respect to many other parts of the field.

8. Got over the little field at the Mill with the Hoes, commonly calld the Clover patch.

9. Finish plowing the Field round the Overseers House at the Mill a 2d. time.
This day I went through all my Wheat at the Mill, & find it very likely and promising, & entirely free from any appearance of Rust—the head beginning to expand by the plumping of the grain.

10. Got over my Corn Ground at Doeg Run Quarter a second time with the Plows and began it a third time with the Harrows.
Also got over all the old ground Corn at the same place with the Hoes.

12. Went over all my Wheat at Muddy hole and at Doeg Run & found it at both places good and promising, and entirely clear from every appearance of Rust.
I also found that the Straw at the lower joints was turnd, & turning yellow—that the blade was putting on a yellowish Hue— and that the head was in general grey—& turning yellowish the grain being mostly plump and the departments strutting with the Ripening Corn.

13. Went through my Wheat in the Neck and found it also clear of the Rust, & in much the same state of that of Muddy hole and Doeg run as described yesterday.
This day I put on board my Schooner from the Neck 500 Bushels of Indian Corn for Mr. Ross.

Hector Ross bought 100 barrels of corn from GW at 10s. a barrel, a total of £50 to which £4 3s. 4d. was added for freight (LEDGER A, 276).

17. Finishd going over my Corn at Muddy hole with the Hoes. Also went over my Corn at the Mill this day with the Hoes.

22. Went over my Corn at the Mill the second time with the Plows that is finishd doing so—and began with the Harrows in the field about the Ovr. House.

24. Finishd going over my Corn in the Neck with the Hoes as also with the Plows the second time.

Worked over all the Swamps (North of the Meadow) at Doeg Run with the Hoes.

Jonathan Palmer who came to the House that was provided for him last Night began Working with my People this day.

On this day GW debited Jonathan Palmer, his newly hired master carpenter, "2 Barrels of Herrings delivered per your order to the Waggoner that brought his [Palmer's] family down" (LEDGER A, 294). The house, although not recorded by GW in their contract, was provided rent-free.

27. James Cleveland spaed the three hound Bitches Musick, Tipsey, & Maiden as also two hound puppies which came from Musick & Rockwood.

Note—the Bitch Tipsey was going into heat but had not been lind.

Began in the Afternoon to cut my wheat at Doeg Run Quarter with Jonathan Palmer and 6 other Cradlers.

James Cleveland was employed by GW as the overseer of the River Farm on Clifton's Neck from 1765 to 1775, when he was put in charge of an expedition of workers to GW's lands on the Ohio.

28. Elijah Houghton joind the above at the same place. The whole made but a bad days work. They complaind of the Straw cutting very hard.

Note. The wheat this year appeard different from what it did last year the Straw being quite changd (even the Knots and joints nearly so) when the Grain was not hard. On the Contrary last year—the grain was tolerably hard whilst part of the Straw retaind a good deal of green.

Elijah Houghton was retained by GW as a harvester and paid at the rate of 5s. per day, with an allowance of three Spanish dollars for travel. LEDGER A, 292, shows that on 13 July 1769 he was paid £3 13s.

29. Eliab Roberts, William Acres, Joseph Wilson & Azel Martin set into work today—& I think workd but indifferently. The Wheat on the other side the Run was not cut down. Michael Davy Schomberg & Ned Holt were left with Morris's People to finish it.

Eliab Roberts, William Acres, Joseph Wilson, and Azel Martin were retained by GW as harvesters at the rate of 5s. per day, with an allowance of three Spanish dollars each for travel. The men were paid £4 13s., £3 16s. 4d., £1 15s., and £4 13s., respectively, for their work (LEDGER A, 292). Besides these men and Elijah Houghton, GW also retained Thomas Williams, Thomas Pursel (Pursley), John Pursel, and "Young Palmer," probably a son of Jonathan Palmer (LEDGER A, 292). Michael, Davy, and Schomberg were GW's slaves. Michael was a carpenter and tradesman; Davy, a mulatto, was a servant at the home house plantation 1762–64, a field hand on the Mill plantation 1765–69, and subsequently served for many years as overseer of various Mount Vernon farms; Schomberg was a field hand on River Farm. Ned Holt, who appears in GW's tithable list for 1761 as being at the home plantation, was probably one of GW's slaves.

30.   The Rest of the Cradlers & hands went into the Neck & began there abt. 10 Oclock—Making a poor days Work—having cut only that piece of New Ground containing 14 Acres next the widow Sheridines.

Mrs. Barberry (Barbara?) Sheridine, whose husband John had recently died, continued to live on the land in Clifton's Neck which her father-in-law was renting from GW. Several years later she married Samuel Haley, and the couple remained there until the Revolution.

[July]

Where & how—my time is—Spent

July 1st.   Went into the Neck to my Harvest People & returnd to Dinner.

2.   At home all day—the Captn. of the Burmudian dining here.

THE CAPTN. OF THE BURMUDIAN: Captain Burch, from whom GW bought 562 barrels of salt, a cotton line, and 40 yards of nautical rope, totaling £35 7s. 6d. (LEDGER A, 291).

3.   Rid round to my Harvest field in the Neck with Mrs. Washington, Patcy & Mill[y] Posey. Returnd to Dinner.

4.   Went over into the Neck again & returnd to Dinner with the Captn. of the Burmudian.

5.   Went into the Field in the Neck and returnd to Dinner. The Captn. dind here agn.

6.   Went into my Harvest field in the Neck. On my return to Dinner found Mr. Chichester, his wife and Nancy McCarty here, who stayd all Night.

Anne McCarty, called "Nancy" by GW, was a daughter of Capt. Daniel McCarty and thus a younger sister of Mrs. Chichester.

7.   The above Company going away after Breakfast I went over into the Neck & returnd to Dinner.

8.   Rid to Muddy hole in the Afternoon where We began to Cut Wheat.

9.   At home all day.

10.   Rid to Muddy hole in the forenoon. After dinner rid to Captn. Posey's where Mr. Jno. West was Surveying—and then to my wheat field again. Sally Carlyle came in the Afternoon.

John West, Jr., and Philip Alexander, attorney for John Posey, were today surveying the strip where Posey's house and ferry were located in preparation for a hearing of West's suit to evict Posey from the property (the dated survey is at ViMtV). Posey had by now returned home from Maryland but was unwilling yet to face the reality of his heavy debts, boasting to the assembled company at Rover's Delight today that his new wife had brought him much wealth, including "300 half Joes." GW knew that Posey was bluffing, having heard that his wife had not and would not convey any of her estate to him (GW to Posey, 26 July 1769, DLC:GW).

11.   Rid to Muddy hole and returnd to Dinner. Found Mr. & Mrs. Ramsay & Mr. Stedlar here.

12.   Mr. & Mrs. Ramsay & Mrs. Washington rid with me to Muddy hole & retd. to Dr.

Mrs. William Ramsay is Ann McCarty Ramsay, daughter of Maj. Dennis McCarty (d. 1743), of Cedar Grove, and Sarah Ball McCarty. Through her mother, Mrs. Ramsay was distantly related to GW.

13.   Mr. & Mrs. Ramsay & Sally Carlyle went away. I rid to the Mill where I was cutting of Wheat & returnd to Dinner when I found Mr. Frans. Thornton & my Br. Charles and his son—with whom rid out after Dinnr.

There were several Francis Thorntons. This is probably the one who died about 1795, the oldest son of Col. Francis Thornton of Spotsylvania County. His sister Mildred was Charles Washington's wife. The son of Charles Washington who appears here is probably George Augustine Washington (1763–

1793), who was about six years old at this time. A younger son, Samuel, would have been rather small to travel with his father.

14.   Rid out in the fore and afternoon with my Brothr. & Mr. Thornton—to the Wheat field.

15.   At home all day. Mr. Thornton & my Brothr. & son set of homewards after Dinner.

16.   At Home all day. In the Morning Mr. Vale. Crawford came here—and in the afternoon Colo. Fairfax & Lady.

17.   Went up to Alexandria to Court with Colo. Fairfax & re-turnd in the Evening with him & Mr. Magowan.

The July court met three days. Today GW, George Mason, and Daniel McCarty were recorded as present about two-thirds of the way through the proceedings (Fairfax County Order Book for 1768–70, 192–210, Vi Micro-film).

18.   Colo. Fairfax and Lady went home & I to Court again. Re-turnd in the Evg. with Colo. Richd. Lee.

GW arrived at court shortly after it began today (Fairfax County Order Book for 1768–70, 199, Vi Microfilm). Richard Lee (1726–1795), son of Henry and Mary Bland Lee and an elder brother of Col. Henry Lee of Leesylvania, lived at Lee Hall in Westmoreland County, near present-day Hague, Va. Known as Squire Lee, he was a Westmoreland burgess 1754–74, naval officer of the South Potomac district, and a member of the Ohio Company. He today paid GW 16s. for a spinning wheel (LEDGER A, 292).

19.   Again went up to Court and returnd in the Afternoon.

20.   At home all day. Majr. Waggener came here to Dinner & stay'd all Night.

21.   At home all day. Majr. Wagener & Mr. Magowan went away after Breakfast.

22.   At home all day.

23.   Went to Pohick Church and returnd to Dinner. Mr. Magowan w. us.

24.   Went to an intended Vestry at the cross Roads—but disap-pointed of one by Mr. Henderson's refusg. to Act.

The vestry meeting was to be held at the Crossroads in order to decide on a site "to fix the new Church upon convenient to the said Cross Roads" and to lay out a churchyard (Truro Vestry Book, 138, DLC). GW and his associates had been able to muster only six of the seven vestrymen who supported the Crossroads location. When Alexander Henderson, apparently one of the five vestrymen who had been resisting the new location, realized his presence made a quorum, he prevented the meeting from coming to order by "refusing to act."

25.   At home all day writing Letters & Invoices for England.

GW today ordered goods for Mount Vernon and the Custis plantations from Robert Cary & Co. and Capel & Osgood Hanbury. In his letter to Cary & Co., he requested that if any items on the invoices, except paper, "are Tax'd by Act of Parliament for the purpose of Raising a Revenue in America, it is my express desire and request, that they may not be sent, as I have very heartily enterd into an Association . . . not to Import any Article which now is or hereafter shall be Taxed for this purpose untill the said Act or Acts are repeal'd. I am therefore particular in mentioning this matter as I am fully determined to adhere religiously to it, and may perhaps have wrote for some things unwittingly which may be under these Circumstances" (DLC:GW).

26.   Rid to my Meadow at the Mill & to Doeg Run after Dinner.

27.   Went up in the afternoon to Alexa. with Mrs. Washington & Patcy Custis. Mr. Magowan returnd to Maryland.

Jacky Custis, who had been at Mount Vernon during the past few days for a short vacation from school, apparently returned to Boucher's today, taking with him £1 5s. pocket money and £42 1s. 11d. to pay his schooling and boarding expenses for a year (Jonathan Boucher to GW, 20 July 1769, DLC:GW; LEDGER A, 292).

28.   Rid into the Neck and to Muddy hole.

29.   At home all day posting my Books.

30.   At Home all day preparing for my journey to the Springs.

31.   Set out with Mrs. Washington & Patcy Custis for the Frederick Springs. Dind at Wm. Car Lains, & lodgd at Mr. Chs. Wests.

The family was going to Warm Springs in order to test the efficacy of the waters in relieving Patsy's epileptic fits (GW to John Armstrong, 18 Aug. 1769, PHi: Gratz Collection). GW had intended to leave on 27 July but had been delayed by other matters (GW to Jonathan Boucher, 13 July 1769, FORD [3], 12).
    William Carr Lane and his brother James Lane (sometimes called James Jr.) owned the Newgate (sometimes called the Eagle) Tavern, one of the largest taverns in the Northern Neck at this time. It was on the Colchester

road at Newgate, about 12 miles below Charles West's ordinary, and was kept at this time by Robert Sanford and his wife Kerrenhappuck (MCDONALD, 472–73, 482–84).

Acct. of the Weather–in July

July 1st.   The Rains wch. lately fell, & the wind getting North-wardly coold the air & made it tolerably pleasant.

2.   Clear, warm, and still, their being very little wind & that southwardly.

3.   Very warm, & clear with but little Wind and that South-wardly.

4.   Very sultry, with a breeze of Wind from the southward. Clouds & a little rain to the westward (with some Thunder) but none here.

5.   Hot and sultry in the Morning but cool afterwards. In the afternoon a little Rain from the Westward–but not much.

6.   The wind being pretty fresh from the No. Wt. the day was cool & pleasant.

7.   Wind continuing from the same Quarter. This day was also tolerably pleasant.

8. Calm but not hot. Afternoon Cloudy with much apps. of Rain–wind being Ea⟨st.⟩

9.   Wind being Eastwardly, about ½ after Six it set into Raining and continued to rain slowly till 9 or 10 constantly & in light fine showers afterwards all day.

10.   Light thin showers at times till between 2 and 3 Oclock when it broke away.

11.   Clear cool and pleasant–Wind being Northwardly.

12.   Wind being in the same place–the day was also clear & pleast.

13.   Clear and not warm although the wind had got southwardly.

14.   Wind fresh from the Southwest with appearances and some drops of Rain in the Evening.

15.   Very warm and close with gt. appearances of Rain and frequent showers to the Westward but very little here.

16.   Warm with some Appearances of Clouds—but no Rain. Wind abt. S.W.

17.   Close & Sultry in the forenoon with frequent light showers in the Afternoon & cooler.

18.   Cool, clear & pleasant after the Morning which was Misty.

19.   Wind being Northwardly the day was cool and pleasant—also clear.

20.   About Noon it raind 10 or 15 Minutes pretty smartly and then cleard. Wind being pretty fresh from So. Wt.

21.   Thunder in the Morning with the Appearance of a Settled Rain it beging. & contg. moderately for half an hour or more & then cleard. Wind still contg. at So. Wt.

22.   Wind fresh from the southwest and pleasant. Few Clouds but hazy.

23.   Close and Sultry with Rain in the Night.

24.   Warm with a shower about 3 oclock in the Afternoon.

25.   Clear and pleasant.

26.   Ditto—Ditto—Wind Southly.

27.   Clear and pleast. Wind variable.

28.   Clear and warm. Wind Southwardly.

29.   Wind at southwest. Cloudy Morning. Rainy Midday, but clear Afternoon and warm.

30.   Clear, Still, & warm Morning. About 3 oclock a shower of Rain for a few Minutes with high wind from the So. Wt. and pleasant afterwards.

31.   Clear and Cool—the Wind being fresh from the Northwest.

Remarks & Occurrences—in July

July 1st.   Thoms. Williams, and Thomas Pursley set into Cradling today. The Grain being wet, there was no tying it up till about 10 Oclock—nor did we attempt to stack or House any till the afternoon & then old Palmer & others thought the straw & grain rather too Green.

Thomas Williams and Thomas Pursel (Pursley) were retained by GW as harvesters at the rate of 5s. per day, with an allowance of three Spanish dollars each for travel. LEDGER A, 292, shows that they were paid £3 4s. 8d. and £4 5s., respectively, for their work.

2.   Sunday.

3.   Finishd stacking what was left out on Saturday—also finishd cuttg. and getting to the stacks all the Wheat that was in the half Cut on the River by Dinner and in the afternoon went in to the half of the other Cut adjoing. and got about half of it cut down and Stack'd.

4.   Finishd Cutting, getting in, and Stacking this half by Dinner, and finding our progress very slow & that the Cradlers were too many for the other workers, we reduced them to Ten after Dinner, after which about one half of the other half of the Second Cut was got in, and securd the work all going on well together but then the wheat was thinner which enabled the Rakers and carryers to keep up better.

A Dog coming here which I suspected to be Mad, I shot him. Several of the Hounds running upon him may have got bit. Note the consequences.

5.   Finishd the other half of the Cut between Eleven and 12 (that is Cutting Binding and stacking) and went into the half of the 3d. Cut by the gate just at 12 Oclock with all hands.

6.   Finishd the half cut by the Gate before breakfast & the rest of the other half afterwards, just getting into the last Cut before sunset.

8.   Finishd the whole field about one oclock. And began about five Oclock to cut in Muddy hole field.

12.   Finishd cutting and stacking Muddy hole wheat and dischargd Elijah Houghton—Thomas Williams—and William Acres.

13.   Went to cutting the Wheat at the Mill with the Residue.

15.   Finishd at Do. by Breakfast time and went from hence to Doeg run Plantation & Cut the small field in this side the Run before Dinner. Note—from the Remarks and observations made this year in Harvesting my Wheat, it appeard evident that 10 and sometimes 9 Cradlers (according as the Wheat was thick or thin) were full suff. to keep the rest of my hands employd—and it likewise appeard that it was evidently to my advantage to employ my own hands to Cradle the Wheat rather than to hire white men to do it—and to get Rakers and binders if it be necessary to hire any at all, as these may be got for 2 shillg. or half a Crown a day whereas the Wages of the White Cradlers are exorbitantly high— but if Wheat of different kinds are sowed so as to prevent the Harvest coming on at once it is my opinion that hirelings of all kinds may be dispensed with. Two Rakers in the generality of the Wheat is sufficient to Rake & bind after a Cradle—and the rest of the hands can manage (after the Water Carriers & Cooks are taken out) to get the Wheat into convent. places & attend the Stackers.

Two, and sometimes three Stackers will Stack as fast as it is cut & I am of opinion that two brisk hands is sufft. for this purpose.

From experience it has been found advantageous, to put the Cradlers and their attendants into at least 3 Gangs. The Stops & delays by this means are not so frequent & the Work much better attended to as every Mans Work is distinguishable and the whole Cradles not always stopping for every little disorder that happens to each respective one as is the case when they cut altogether.

17.   Began my Hay Harvest at Doeg Run Plantation.

21.   Began to Sow Wheat at Muddy hole Plantation.

22.   Began to Sow Ditto at Doeg Run Quarter.

28.   The young Hound Bitch Chaunter was lined by Lord Fairfax's Rockwood (who appears to have the Mange) twice this day.
Got over my Corn in the Neck with the Plows the 3d. time.

29.   Chaunter again lined by Rockwood. The black bitch Countess appeard to be going proud, was shut up in order to go to the same Dog.

30.   Chaunter lined again—by Rockwood.

[August]

Where & how—my time is—spent—

Augt. 1st.   Set out from Chs. Wests. Dined at Snickers and got to Mr. W[arne]r Washington's abt. 5 Oclock.

Edward Snickers (d. 1791) settled at a site near Buck Marsh Run in Frederick (now Clarke) County, where he later built his home, Springfield. Snickers' Gap in the Blue Ridge Mountains was named after him. Warner Washington was living in Frederick (now Clarke) County, probably on the 3,000-acre plot he purchased in 1770 from his brother-in-law, George William Fairfax. On this land was built Warner's home, Fairfield, a few miles northwest of Snickers's ordinary.

2.   Remaind there all day. Mr. Washington returnd from Winchester in the Afternoon.

3.   At Mr. Washington's all this day also.

4.   Still at Mr. Washington's. Mr. Thurston & Lady dining there. Note I was detained this day & yesterday by the Waggon's which had my Goods in for the springs loosing 2 Hs.

After stopping at Mount Vernon in mid-February of 1768, Thurston had attended the March meeting of the Frederick Parish vestry, Frederick County, where he offered to take the vacant rectorship. The vestry, having given Walter Magowan nine months to take orders, asked Thurston to come back in November. In May 1768 Thurston bought more than 1,000 acres of land in Frederick (now Clarke) County, located between Snickers' Gap and Warner Washington's home, Fairfield. Thurston returned to the Frederick Parish vestry in Nov. 1768, accepted an offer of the rectorship, and resigned his post in Petsworth Parish, Gloucester County, the following month. His "Lady" was Ann Alexander Thurston, his second wife, whom he had married in 1766.

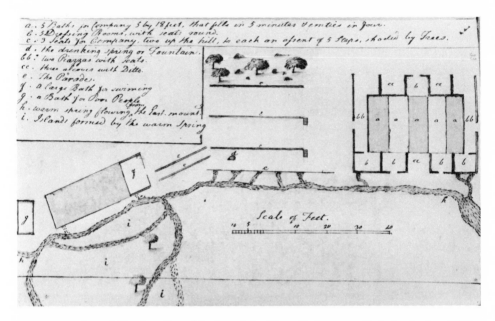

a . 5 Baths for Company 5 by 18 feet, that fills in 5 minutes & emties in four.
b . 5 Dressing Rooms, with seats round.
c . 3 Seats for Company, two up the hill, to each an ascent of 5 steps, shaded by Trees.
d . the drinking spring or Fountain.
bb : two Piazzas with seats.
cc . three alcoves with Ditto.
e . The Parade.
f . a large Bath for swiming
g . a Bath for Poor People
h . warm spring flowing from the East mount
i . Islands formed by the warm Spring

Samuel Vaughan drew this plan of the Warm Springs, now Berkeley Springs, W.Va., in his journal for 1787. (Collection of the descendants of Samuel Vaughan)

5.   Prosecuted our Journey to the springs (by Jacob Hites). Bated at Opeekon and lodged at Joshua Hedges.

Jacob Hite, son of Jost Hite, was a resident of Frederick County. In 1772 he became a justice of the peace of newly formed Berkeley County. Hite married Frances Madison Beale, aunt of President James Madison, and moved with his family to South Carolina in 1773, where most were killed by Indians during the Revolution.

6.   Arrivd at the Springs about One Oclock & dind w. Colo. F[airfa]x.

7.   Rid out into the Country to seek a good Pasture for my Horses & engagd to send them to one John Higgens's.

8.   Sent my Horses to the above place with the Coachman.

9.   Mr. Barcley dined with us – & Mr. Maze.

John Barclay was an Anglican clergyman who came to Virginia by 1756 and was for a brief time in charge of Cumberland Parish, Lunenburg County. Some time before 12 Oct. 1760 he was appointed to All Hallows Parish, Anne Arundel County, Md., and in 1763 to St. Luke's Parish, Queen Anne County, Md. In 1761 Barclay was named one of the commissioners to run the line between Maryland and Pennsylvania. On 4 May 1768, he married Rachel Goldsborough, daughter of Nicholas and Sarah Goldsborough of Maryland (RIGHTMYER, 158–59).

Robert Mease (or Maze) was an Alexandria merchant and a partner in the mercantile firm of McCrea & Mease.

10. Mr. Barcley dined with us again as did Mr. Power and Mr. Geo. Thornton.

George Thornton, of Spotsylvania County, one of Charles Washington's brothers-in-law, married Mary Alexander in 1773. A prominent businessman in Fredericksburg for many years, he was a partner about 1772–74 with William Triplett of King George County in two stores, one in Fredericksburg and one in nearby Falmouth. After 1777 he was a partner with other gentlemen in a Fredericksburg brewery (CROZIER [2], 330, 344, 381). Appointed a major in the Spotsylvania County militia 16 Nov. 1780, he died soon afterwards, reportedly "from drinking cold water on a forced march" (WILSON, 66).

11. Lord Fairfax & Colo. Geo. Fairfax dined with us.

12. Mr. Barclay dined with us this day also.

13. We dined with Lord Fairfax.

14. Colo. Loyd, Mr. Cadwallader & Lady, Mrs. Dalton & Daughter & Miss Terrett dind with us.

Col. Edward Lloyd III (d. 1770) was of a prominent Maryland family and one of a long line of Edward Lloyds of Wye House, Talbot County, Md. He was married in 1739 to Anne Rousby of Patuxent, Md. He had been a member of the Maryland General Assembly, a member of the council, and receiver general of the province. He was in ill health at the time of this visit and died a few months later. His daughter Elizabeth had been married the previous year to John Cadwalader (1742–1786), of Philadelphia.

Mrs. Dalton is the wife of Capt. John Dalton of Alexandria and the daughter of Thomas Shaw (d. 1777). Miss Terret is probably a daughter of William Henry Terret (d. 1758), of Fairfax County, an original member of the Fairfax County court in 1742 and clerk of the Truro Parish vestry 1745–55.

15. Had my Horses brought in to carry Colo. Loyd as far as Hedges on his return home & rid with him as far as Sleepy Creek. Returnd to Dinner & had Mr. Barclay & a Mr. Brown to dine with me.

16.   Horses returnd from carrying Colo. Loyd. Mr. Barclay—Mr. Goldsbury Mr. Hardwick, Mr. Jno. Lewis & Mr. Wn. Washington Junr. dined here.

MR. GOLDSBURY: probably one of the brothers of John Barclay's wife, Rachel Goldsborough Barclay. Her three brothers were Nicholas, Thomas, and Foster Goldsborough (HANSON, 294–96).

John Lewis (1747–1825), only son of Fielding Lewis by his first wife, Catherine Washington Lewis, lived in Fredericksburg until 1811, when he removed to Kentucky. He was married five times (see SORLEY, 131–32).

17.   Mr. Jno. Lewis & W. Washington dind here. We drank Tea with My Lord.

18.   Mr. Barclay, Mr. Wodrow & Mr. Wood dined here. My Lord the two Colo. Fx's & others drank Tea here.

MR. WODROW: probably either Alexander or Andrew Woodrow. Alexander Woodrow served as provisioner of the garrison at Ford Cumberland during the French and Indian War and voted for GW in the Frederick County burgesses election of 1758. In 1774 he served on the committee of safety of King George County. Andrew Woodrow, perhaps a younger brother or son of Alexander, was clerk of the King George County committee of safety in 1775 and served in the Revolution as major and lieutenant colonel of the Virginia militia 1779–81 and as brigadier quartermaster of the Hampshire County militia. He was clerk of the Hampshire County court from c.1787 to c.1793 and represented the county at the Virginia Constitutional Convention in 1788.

James Wood (died c.1777) was Orange County surveyor in 1738 and served as clerk of the Frederick County court 1743–60. The father of later Gov. James Wood (1750–1813), he was a founder of Winchester in 1758, a Frederick Parish vestryman 1764–74, and a Frederick County burgess 1766–76. He signed the Virginia nonimportation agreement of this year and 1770.

19.   Rid with Mrs. Washington & others to the Cacapehon Mountain—to see the prospect from thence. Mr. Barclay, Mr. Thruston & Mr. Power dined with us.

20.   Went to Church in the fore and Afternoon. Mr. Jno. Lewis dind here. Lord Fairfax the two Colo. Fairfaxs & others drank Tea here.

21.   Mr. Maze & Lady, Mr. Sebastian, Mr. Barclay, Mr. Allison dind here. Lord Fairfax &ca. drank Tea here.

Rev. Benjamin Sebastian (c.1745–1834) was rector of Frederick Parish in Frederick County, 1766–67 and of St. Stephen's Parish in Northumberland County, 1767–77. He removed to Maryland and then to Kentucky, where he practiced law and served as a judge during the 1790s (GOODWIN, 305). Allison is probably John Allison, a merchant of Alexandria.

22. Mr. Jno. Lewis dined here.

23. Dined alone – Patcy unwell.

Patsy had "found little benefit" from taking the waters, but the Washingtons had decided to continue the experiment for another week or two in order to be sure there was no help for her here. The springs at this time were crowded with people from all walks of life seeking to restore their health. The waters, GW wrote to a friend, "are applied . . . in all cases, altho there be a moral certainty of their hurting in some. Many poor, miserable objects are now attending here, which I hope will receive the desired benefit, as I dare say they are deprivd of the means of obtaining any other relief, from their Indigent Circumstances" (GW to John Armstrong, 18 Aug. 1769, PHi: Gratz Collection).

24. Rid to Cacapeon with Lord Fairfax, the 2 Colo. Fairfaxs, Mr. Kimble Mrs. Washington & Patcy Custis.

MR. KIMBLE: possibly Peter Kemble (1704–1789), president of the royal council of New Jersey.

25. Dined here Mr. Jno. Lewis and Mr. Flint.

Mr. Flint may be John, John Jr., or Thomas Flint of Frederick County, Md. John Flint was registrar of Prince George's Parish, and Thomas Flint kept a school in Frederick County. A Pennsylvania traveler recorded having been to "Flints on Potomak abot. 12 Miles above Fort Frederick, civil people" (KENNY, 200). This location was at the mouth of the Monocacy River and midway between Mount Vernon and the Pennsylvania line.

26. Dined alone.

27. Dined with Lord Fairfax & drank Tea there also.

28. Lord Fairfax, Colo. R. Fairfax, Mr. Allan, Mr. Meldrum & Colo. Stephen dined here.

Rev. William Meldrum, licensed by the bishop of London to preach in Virginia in 1756, served as rector of Frederick Parish in Frederick County for a time before 1765.

29. Dined alone.

30. Old Mr. Flint dined with us, otherwise we were alone.

31. Mr. Johnston, Mr. Wodrow, Captn. Dalton, his Daughter & Miss Terret Dined here.

August 1769

Acct. of the Weather–in August

Augt. 1st.   Very cool Morning, & not an unpleasant day.

2.   Cool Morning & Evening again but midling warm Midday.

3.   Clear with more warmth – but not hot.

4.   Tolerably warm with the Mornings & Evenings still cool.

5.   Warm morning & hot day with a thunder shower – to the Westward.

6.   Warm again, with appearances of Rain but none fell.

7.   Warm, but a brisk breeze about Noon.

8.   Again Warm with a breeze as usual at & before noon.

9.   Warm with appearances of Rain in the afternoon, but none fell.

10.   Exceeding hot and Sultry, but the Heat corrected a little by the Breeze at Noon.

11.   Lowering Morning with a thunder shower in the Afternoon & exceedg. Hott.

12.   Again very warm – but a breeze as usual & noon wch. however sometimes dies away.

13.   Very Warm with the accustomed breeze down the Vale of the Mountains.

14.   Very warm forenoon with a shower or two in the Afternoon with thunder & sharpe Lightning.

15.   Cool forenoon – the Wind being northwardly & fresh – but warm afternoon the wind dying away.

16.   Wind Northwardly & fresh. Clouds in the Evening but no Rain here.

17.   Wind Eastwardly fresh & Cool especially in the Evening & night.

18.   Morning Cool, but Midday warm notwithstanding the Wind blew fresh.

19.   Morning tolerably pleasant, but very warm Evening. Wind fresh.

20.   Morning Warm. Abt. Noon a shower with rumbling thunder. The afternoon wet.

21.   Tolerably cool & pleasant. Wind northwardly. Night Cool.

22.   Cool and pleasant. Night rather cold.

23.   Clear, cool, and pleasant. Wind northwardly.

24.   Clear & tolerably warm with but little wind.

25.   A fine Shower from the Westward about One oclock with slighter ones afterwards.

26.   Morning lowering but clear & cool afterwards.

27.   Clear and cool especially in the Evening & morning.

28.   Cool morning but Warm Midday & Cloudy afternoon.

29.   Cloudy Morning with a Shower of Rain. Clear & warm afterwards.

30.   Clear but warm wind being southwardly.

31.   Clear and warm with but little Wind and that Southwardly.

[September]

Where & how—my time is—Spent

Septr. 1st.   Mrs. Washington, Patcy & myself dined at Mr. Maze's.

2.   Dined at home. Vale. Crawford dined with us.

3.   Went to Church in the fore & afternoon and dined with Lord Fairfax.

4.   Rid to the Pasture where my Horses were from thence to Mr. Flints & to the Pensylvania line & returnd to Dinnr. with Mr. Allan.

5.   Dined at home alone except Mr. Flint.

6.   Colo. Robt. Fairfax dined here.

7.   Dined alone. Vale. Crawfords Waggon came up for my Goods in the Evening.

8.   Day too unlikely to set out, therefore waited. Dined alone.

9.   Set out on my return home about 8 Oclock but broke the Chariot & made it 11. before we got a Mile. Reachd Joshua Hedges.

10.   Got to Mr. Warner Washingtons—I calling by Vale. Crawfords & Mrs. Stephenson's.

Onora Stephenson (née Grimes, d. 1776) was the mother of William and Valentine Crawford and the widow of Richard Stephenson (d. 1765), by whom she had five sons, Richard, James, John, Hugh, and Marcus.

11.   Continued my Journey and reached Chas. Wests Ordinary after baiting under the Ridge at the blacksmiths shop.

12.   Breakfasted at Wm. Carr Lanes & arrived at home about 3 Oclock in the Afternoon.

13.   Rid to Muddy hole Doeg Run and Mill Plantations.

14.   Went to Alexandria to the Election of Burgesses for Fairfax & was chosen together with Colo. West without a Poll, their being no opposition.

This election was called in consequence of Governor Botetourt's dissolution of the last House of Burgesses in May 1769. When there was no opposition in a burgess election (which was seldom) the sheriff took the vote "by view," although it is not clear whether GW was reelected by voice vote or by a show of hands.

15.   Returnd home. Mr. Grayson & Mr. Robt. Harrison came down in the afternoon.

Robert Hanson Harrison (1745–1790), originally of Charles County, Md., was an Alexandria lawyer. He was a signer of the Fairfax County nonimportation association in 1770. He served as GW's private secretary with the rank of lieutenant colonel 1775–81 and was chief justice of the Maryland General Court 1781.

16.   Mr. Robt. Alexander came before Sun Rise this Morning & we all went a fox huntg. Started one & run him into a hollow tree, in an hour & 20 minutes. Chase him in the afternn. & killd in an h[our and] ½.

17.   At home all day. Mr. Harrison went away in the morning before breakfast. So did Mr. Alexander, and Mr. Grayson went away in the Afternoon.

GW today recorded winning 3s. 9d. at cards (LEDGER A, 296).

18.   Went to court at Alexandria and returnd home in the Evening.

The court was in session 18–20 Sept. (Fairfax County Order Book for 1768–70, 224–40, Vi Microfilm).

19.   Went to Court again today. Stayd all Night & Went to see slight of hand performd.

20.   Returnd home early this morning by a Messenger from Mrs. Washington. Mr. George Alexander dined here & went away in the afternoon.

21.   Captn. Posey calld here in the morng. & we went to a Vestry. Upon my return found Mr. B. Fairfax & Mr. P. Wagener.

The meeting was again scheduled to be held at the Crossroads, and the "Cross-Roads majority" of seven, which was also the minimum needed for a quorum, finally appeared in full strength. These seven, in the name of the vestry, chose the spot for building the Pohick Church which stands today. At the same time they signed the building contract with Daniel French, giving him 36 months to complete the church, which was to be 66 feet long and 45 feet wide, with 28-foot-high walls (SLAUGHTER [1], 73).

22.   Went a huntg. & killd a bitch fox in abt. an hour. Returnd home with an Ague upon me. Mr. Montgomery came to dinner.

Thomas Montgomerie was a prominent merchant in Dumfries. The purpose of his visit today was apparently to discuss the troubled affairs of Mrs. Margaret Savage, the elderly wife of Dr. William Savage, formerly of Dumfries. Mrs. Savage's first husband, Rev. Charles Green, had established a trusteeship for her, and after his death in 1765, GW and George William Fairfax became her trustees, giving the Fairfax County court a bond to guarantee that they would pay her an annuity out of the estate's proceeds (will of Green, 26 April 1763, Fairfax County Wills, Book B-1, 398–99, Vi Microfilm; GW and George W. Fairfax to William Savage, 25 April 1767, DLC: GW). Sometime before 25 April 1767, she married Dr. Savage, who subsequently took control of Green's estate and assumed responsibility for paying his wife's annuity, giving a bond for that purpose to GW and Bryan Fairfax, who were to be her trustees henceforth. By the terms of the doctor's bond, Mrs. Savage was to receive £100 at the beginning of each year (GW to William Savage, 28 June 1768, DLC:GW). However, since 1767, neither of the annuities that had come due had been paid, and during the latter half of 1768, Dr. Savage had taken his wife to Ireland to live, leaving his affairs in Virginia to the care of Thomas Montgomerie (GW to William Ellzey, 3 Sept. 1769, DLC:GW; *Va. Gaz.*, R, 13 Oct. 1768). At Mount Vernon on this or the following day, GW and Bryan Fairfax, still holding Savage's bond, probably tried to convince Montgomerie to pay the annuities or at least one of them, but they had no success, for although Mrs. Savage had repeatedly told both GW and Fairfax in private that she wanted her money, the doctor insisted that she was willing to give up her annuities and had apparently given instructions not to pay them (GW to Margaret Savage, 28 June 1768, and Thomas Montgomerie to GW, 5 Oct. 1769, DLC:GW). The dispute, being complicated by Mrs. Savage's vacillation in the matter and her absence from the colony, would continue in and out of court for several years.

23. Went a huntg. again with the Compy. aforesaid & suppose we killd a fox but coud not find it. Returnd with my Ague again. Mr. Wagener went ho[me].

24. Mr. Fairfax & Mr. Montgomery both went away after breakfast.

25. Rid to Muddy hole Doeg Run & Mill.

26. Rid into the Neck. Found Mr. Stedlar here upon my Return. Mr. Geo. Alexander dined & lodgd here.

27. Rid to Muddy hole, Doeg run and Mill. Mr. Alexr. went away this morng. & Colo. Fairfax & Lady & Sally & Nancy Carlyle dind here.

GW today paid Stedlar £8 12s. for teaching Jacky Custis music for eight months and £10 15s. for teaching Patsy ten months (LEDGER A, 296).

28. Mr. Stedlar went away. I rid to Alexandria to see how my House went on. Returnd to Dinr.

GW had paid £48 10s. in 1764 for two lots on Pitt Street in Alexandria: No. 112 at the corner of Prince Street and No. 118 at the corner of Cameron Street (LEDGER A, 180; plan of Alexandria, MOORE [1], 22–23). The lot at the corner of Prince Street would remain vacant for most of GW's lifetime, but during the spring of this year he had engaged to have a small town house built on the other one. Construction of the house, which would continue until sometime in 1771, was primarily the responsibility of two Alexandria men: Edward Rigdon (d. 1772), a joiner, who was paid £30 19s. 2d., and Richard Lake—variously spelled Leak and Leake— (d. 1775), who was paid a total of £59 16s. 1½d. (LEDGER A, 278, 323, 333; Fairfax County Wills, Book C-1, 136–37, 225, Vi Microfilm). Lake had been granted a license to keep an ordinary in Alexandria during the previous fall but apparently did not remain long in that business, as his license was not renewed (Fairfax County Order Book for 1768–70, 66, Vi Microfilm).

29. Miss Sally Carlyle went away. I rid to Muddy hole Doeg Run and Mill.

30. Went a Hunting. Catchd a Rakoon but never found a Fox. One Doctr. Harris of Goochland dined here.

Several Virginia doctors of this name served in the Revolution. Samuel Harris was an army surgeon; Simeon Harris was surgeon of the 4th Virginia Regiment; and Simon Harris was a navy surgeon who served on the *Revenge* (GWATHMEY).

Acct. of the Weather–in Septembr.

Septr. 1. Cloudy forenoon, but clear afterwards & warm. Wind Southwardly.

2. Rain last Night and constant Rain all day & warm.

3. Clear and Cool. Wind fresh from the Northwest.

4. Cool Morning, but warm midday and clear—with but little Wind.

5. Clear and warm with but little wind & that appearing to be Southwardly.

6. Cloudy Morning and Rainy day with very little wind & not cold.

7. Raining more or less till abt. 5 Oclock in the afternoon when the Sun appeard.

8. Cloudy & sometimes Misting with exceeding high wind from North & No. Et.

9. Morning cool — but clear and pleasant afterwards.

10. Frosty Morning & cool, but warm & clear afterwards.

11. Frost again, but clear, pleasant & rather warm afterwards.

12. Clear and pleasant with the Wind pretty brisk from the Southwards.

13. Clear and pleasant with but little wind & that Northwardly.

14. Clear warm and still.

15. Also clear and Warm with but little Wind and that Southwardly.

16. Clear and tolerably warm. Wind fresh from the So. Et.

17. Clear and pleasant. Wind Northwardly.

18. Wind still Northwardly tho but little of it. Day lowering & the Evening very Cloudy.

19. A pretty heavy Rain fell in the Night. The day clear, still & pleasant.

20. Showers this Morning with the Wind brisk from the So. West in the forenoon & at North West towds. night.

21. Wind Northwardly and day for the most part Cloudy & threatning but no Rain.

22. Clear with the Wind pretty fresh from the Eastward.

23. Clear, Calm and pleasant.

24. Clear and pleasant. Wind Northwardly but not cold nor hard.

25. Clear, pleasant and still.

26.   Clear and pleasant with but little wind.

27.   Also clear, still and pleasant.

28.   Much as yesterday with a light breeze from the Southward.

29.   A Breeze from So. West in the Morning with some appearance of Rain—but clear & calm in the afternoon.

30.   Light showers between day break and Sun Rising—with thin Mists afterwards till Ten Oclock. Wind in the Morning about No. Et. and in the afternoon So. Et. but at no time fresh.

Remarks & Occurences—in Sepr.

Septr. 1st.   Finished Sowing Wheat at my Mill Plantation in all Bushels   75.

4.   Finished Sowing Wheat at Muddy hole with   96

11.   Began to get Fodder at the Mill.

12.   Sowed all the Corn ground at Doeg Run with Wheat except some of the Swamps which were left for Barley   65½
    Began to get Fodder at Muddy hole.

14.   Finished sowing Corn Gd. Wheat in the Neck.

15.   Began to get Fodder there.

27.   Finished sowing the Fallowed Gd. in the Neck with Bushels   151
                      which makes in all sowed there   387½
    Finished getting Fodder at the Mill.

29.   Finished getting Ditto at Muddy hole.

30.   Finished getting Do. at Doeg Run.

Note. The Fallowed Ground above mentioned contain abt. 40 Acres & lay in that part of the 211 Acre Field next to Abednego Adams about 30 Acres of which was old Ground the Rest New.

This Land recd. its first Plowing in the month of Septr. & that part of it which the Corn Rows run through receivd no other Plowing. All the Wheat was Sowed—which was then plowed in and afterwards Harrowed. The other Part was cross Plowed, then sowed and Plowed in, and the end of the Field next to Abednego Adams Harrowed in the following manner—to wit—five Ridges, on Lands of eight feet each, harrowed, five others not harrowed —then 5 Harrowed & five not so for a good way. This was done to see which method was best that is whether the Wheat woud thrive better in the one way than the other & whether the Land was not preservd more by Harrowing than lying in Furrows.

This land of Abednego Adams is probably land willed to his wife Mary Peake Adams by her father in 1761. After her death, Adams married Hannah Moss, of Fairfax County, and settled at Mount Gilead in Loudoun County.

[October]

Where & how—my time—is Spent

Octr. 1.   Dined at Belvoir with Mrs. Washington and Patcy Custis. Returnd in the Evening.

2.   Colo. Carlyle and two Daughters—Captn. Brady and Captn. Posey dined here.

CAPTN. BRADY: possibly William Brady, captain of the Berkeley County militia, later captain in Stephenson's Rifles and captain of the 11th Virginia Regiment in the Continental line. Brady resigned in 1778 and was awarded 4,000 acres of land.

Posey had been drinking heavily in recent weeks and had often been absent from his home, but he came to Mount Vernon today, as GW reported to Robert Hanson Harrison on 7 Oct., "perfectly Sober and proposed of his own voluntary motion to sell his Estate finding it in vain to struggle on longer against the Terms of Debt that oppresses him." The sale was to begin on 23 Oct. (DLC:GW).

3.   Rid to Muddy hole, Doeg Run, and Mill.

4.   Rid to Alexandria to see how my Carpenters went on with my Ho. Returnd to Dinr.

5.   Went after Blew Wings with Humphrey Peake. Killd 3 & returnd by Muddy hole.

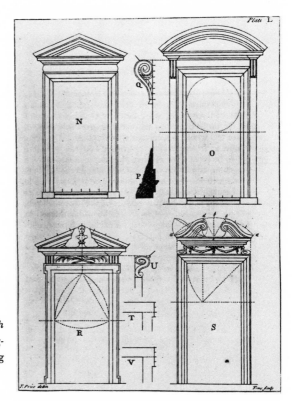

Page from Francis Price's *The British Carpenter,* London, 1768, showing suggested window treatments. (Sterling Memorial Library, Yale University)

6.   Went a hunting but found nothing after which Rid to Muddy hole, D. Run & Mill.

7.   At home all day.

8.   Likewise at home all day. In the afternoon Mr. Robt. Alexander came.

9.   Went a fox hunting & finding a Deer the Dogs ran it to the Water but we never see it. Mr. Alexr. went home.

10.   Went to Captn. Poseys to run the Lines of the Land he bought of Mr. Marshall. Dined there.

This land was the small strip on the Potomac involved in John West, Jr.'s suit against Posey. GW's survey of this day, made "at the particular request of Captn. Posey," differed slightly from the one West and Alexander had made earlier (the dated survey is at ViMtV).

11. At home all day.

12. Rid to Muddy hole Doeg Run and Mill. Captn. Posey dined here ⟨afterw⟩ard.

13. Captn. Marshall came over here & dined & I rid with him round his Land.

Thomas Hanson Marshall owned 480½ acres that bordered the Mount Vernon tract on the west, lying on both sides of the road that ran from Gum Spring to Dogue Creek. GW had long wished to acquire that land, but Marshall, who was in no great want of money, had been reluctant to let it go unless he could make an exchange for land adjoining his Maryland plantation (Marshall to GW, 21 June 1760, DLC:GW; GW to Lund Washington, 15 Aug. 1778, DLC:GW; GW to Lund Washington, 18 Dec. 1778, NjP: de Coppet Collection). Consequently, GW persuaded his fellow fox hunter Robert Alexander to promise to sell him, at £2 Maryland currency an acre, 300 to 400 acres of a tract next to Marshall's plantation that Alexander's wife, Mariamne Stoddert Alexander, had inherited. It was the offer of Mrs. Alexander's land that today brought Marshall to Mount Vernon, where he verbally agreed to give GW that part of his land lying south of the Gum Spring road in return for an equal acreage from the Alexander tract, provided that he could obtain immediate use of the Alexander land (LEDGER A, 96; Marshall to GW, 18 June 1769 and 8 Mar. 1770, DLC:GW).

14. Went a Fox hunting. Started a Dog Fox by old Palmers & run it back of Mr. Clifton & there catched it. Went afterwards into the Neck. Mr. Matthew Campbell dined here.

15. At home all day alone. My Brother Charles came at Night.

16. Went up to Court and returnd at Night.

The court met 16–19 and 24 Oct. (Fairfax County Order Book for 1768–70, 240–47, Vi Microfilm).

17. Went to Court again and returnd. Mr. Fairfax & Mr. Magowan came here.

GW was present when the court began today but soon excused himself from the bench because the suit that various merchants had brought against Posey and him was to be heard, despite the fact that Posey had already volunteered to sell his mortgaged property for the benefit of GW and his other creditors. The justices ordered that 23 Oct. should be the date of sale and authorized GW to hold the sale by himself if necessary (Fairfax County Order Book for 1768–70, 243–45, Vi Microfilm).

18. Went a Fox huntg. with Mr. Fairfax & Mr. Magowan. Found & killd a Dog Fox.

19.   Rid to Muddy hole Doeg Run, & Mill after Mr. Fairfax went away.

20.   At Home all day.

21.   Rid to Muddy hole Doeg Run and Mill. Mr. Magowan went to Colchester.

22.   At home all day—alone.

23.   Went to Poseys Sale. Returnd at Night with Colo. Mason Mr. Ross, Mr. Sebastian Mr. Harrison Mr. Magowan & Colo. Masons Son George.

According to the court's order for the sale, GW was to be the first creditor paid out of the proceeds, with the residue going to the merchants who had brought suit to force the sale. However, GW was not to receive everything that Posey owed him, because the court's order covered only three main portions of the debt: the loans for which GW had mortgages, £820 Virginia currency plus interest of £153 11s. 7d. Virginia; Posey's bond to George Mason for which GW as his security was responsible, £200 sterling plus interest of £20 12s. 7d. sterling; and GW's cost in the merchants' suit, £1 17s. Virginia for lawyers' fees. In a new statement of Posey's account, GW wrote off about £70 Virginia in miscellaneous debts and charged him only with the items in the court's order. That balance was completely discharged during the three days of the sale. GW took £571 16s. Virginia in "sundries" that he bought at the sale for himself, £140 13s. 10d. Virginia in cash, and the remainder in bonds and credits from various gentlemen. GW's "sundries" included the 200 acres of land that Posey had purchased from Charles Washington in 1759, but the strip of land on which Posey's house and ferry were located was not sold to anyone because of John West, Jr.'s suit (Fairfax County Order Book for 1768–70, 243–45, Vi Microfilm; LEDGER A, 256).

24.   Went to the Sale again. Mr. Harrison Mr. Sebastian & Mr. Magowan came home with me also Robt. Alexander. Found Doctr. Rumney here.

At the sale today GW paid George Mason £100 for the 100 acres of land Mason had previously agreed to sell him (LEDGER A, 61). Mason had sent GW the deed for this tract ten days earlier, and it was registered in the Fairfax County court 22 Nov. 1769, being proved by Robert Hanson Harrison, William Carlin, and Humphrey Peake (Mason to GW, 14 Oct. 1769, NN: Washington Collection; Fairfax County Order Book for 1768–70, 256, Vi Microfilm).

25.   Went to the Sale again. Mr. Harrison & Mr. Magowan returnd home with me.

On this and the following day GW paid Robert Alexander a total of £418 14s. Maryland currency for his wife's land: £218 14s. in cash and £200 sent to

Fielding Lewis on Alexander's account. Lund Washington gave Alexander £81 6s. more on 20 Nov., making the total price of the land £500 (LEDGER A, 96).

26.   At home all day, Mr. Harrison went away in the Afternoon.

27.   Rid to Muddy hole Doeg Run and Mill also to my New Purchase of Poseys Land. Mr. Stedlar went away.

28.   At home all day. Mr. Magowan went home.

29.   At home all day. Captn. McCarty came in the Afternoon.

30.   Set out on my Journey to Williamsburg & reached Colo. Henry Lees to a Late Dinner.

Governor Botetourt had summoned the burgesses to a new session beginning 7 Nov. On this trip GW took Mrs. Washington and Patsy with him, traveling in a handsome green chariot trimmed with gold that had arrived from England some time during the past 12 months (invoice of goods shipped to GW, Sept. 1768, DLC:GW).

31.   Set out from thence abt. Nine Oclock and reachd no further than Peyton's Ordy. on Aquia being stopd by Rain.

Acct. of the Weather—in October

Octr. 1.   Clear, Wind being fresh from the No. West till the Evening.

2.   Wind fresh from the Southwest all day—and clear.

3.   Wind Northwardly and cold in the forenoon, but mild afterwards.

4.   Still & clear till Evening then Cloudy with drops of Rain.

5.   Clear & perfectly calm till Evening, then a little Wind from the No. West.

6.   Cool Morning with the Wind fresh from the Northwest. Evening more moderate wind getting southwardly.

7.   Wind southwardly with apps. of Rain. A large circle rd. the Moon.

8.   Cloudy with the Wind southwardly the forenoon & East-wardly afterwards.

9.   Rain in the Night—but not much, & Misting all the forenoon with the Wd. at Et. then shifting to the southward & clearg.

10.   Wind Eastwardly but not fresh. Warm—with a little, fine Rain in the Afternoon.

11.   Misty and foggy all day with sometimes fine Rain.

12.   Wind very fresh from the So. West & very warm with flying Clouds.

13.   Wind tolerably fresh & cool from the No. West with Clouds also.

14.   Wind Eastwardly & very Cloudy in the Afternoon, it set in to raining & continued to do so most part of the Night. Warmer than yesterday.

15.   Wind at No. West again but not hard. Clear & pleasant.

16.   Pleast. Morning, but Wind got very suddenly & very hard from the No. West & also very cold.

17.   A very hard & killing frost last night. Ice ½ Inch thick this Morng. Wind at No. West in the fore part of the day but South-wardly afterwards and raw.

18.   Wind southwardly & fresh. Day tolerably pleasant.

19.   Wind Eastwardly & very cloudy.

20.   Raining in the Night and Misty all day. Wind still East-wardly.

21.   Clear warm & pleasant. Wind Southwardly.

22.   The Weather clear & pleasant with but little Wind and that Southwardly.

23.   Pleast. Morning but the Wind hard from the No. West all day & cold. Weather clear.

24.   Cold, the Wind being exceeding fresh from the No. West & cold & cl.

25.   Clear & tolerably pleasant Wind being moderate & So. Westwardly.

26.   Clear & very pleasant wind southwardly & warm.

27.   Much such a day as the former there being but little Wind & that Southwardly.

28.   Warm and pleasant. Little or no Wind & clear day but lowg. Eveng.

29.   Clear & pleasant with but little wind & that southwardly.

30.   Cloudy Morning and drisling afternoon. Wind Eastwardly.

31.   Cloudy & misty Morning and rainy afternoon. Wind still Eastwdly.

Remarks & Occurs. in Octr.

Octr. 4.   Finished getting Fodder in the Neck.

12.   Finished Hoeing over my Swamps at Doeg Run & preparing them for Barley.

20.   Sowed (at the rate of about two Bushels to the Acre) some large Salt on a piece of fallowed gd. in the Neck that was old & much worn.

Note, the manner in which I did this, was as follows—the Ground being plowed into 8 feet Lands; I sowed two of them and left two, sowed two, and left two alternately sticking Stakes at the Head of the Lands that were Sowed with Salt. This Salt was Sowed on a piece of Flat Ground that has been very much worn and was harrowed after the Wheat had been plowed in.

[November]

Where & how—my time is—Spent

Novr. 1.   Came from Peyton's to Colo. Lewis's after breakfasting at my Mother's.

2.   At Fredericksburg all day.

3.   About one Oclock set out and reachd Parker's Ordy.

Jacky Custis met the family in Fredericksburg, having come from Boucher's school by prior arrangement to join in the trip to Williamsburg (GW to Jonathan Boucher, 3 Oct. 1769, MoSW: Meissner Collection; GW to Boucher, 14 Oct. 1769, NN: Washington Collection).

4.   Set out from thence after Breakfast. Dined at Todds Bridge & lodgd at King Wm. Court House.

5.   Breakfasted at the Causey & Dind at Eltham & lodgd there.

GW's expenses today included 16s. at Ruffin's ferry and 3s. 1½d. for "Seeing Tyger" (LEDGER A, 296). This animal may have been a North American cougar which American colonists often called red tiger.

6.   Came to Williamsburg. Dind at Mr. Carters with Lord Botetout Govr. Eden &ca. and suppd at Mrs. Vobes with Colo. Fitzhugh.

Mrs. Washington and Patsy remained at Eltham today, while Jacky accompanied GW to town, where they lodged at Mrs. Campbell's place (LEDGER A, 296, 299).

Sir Robert Eden (1741–1784), proprietary governor of Maryland 1769–76, was, according to his later friend Jonathan Boucher, "a handsome, lively, and sensible man. . . . He had been in the Army, and had contracted such habits of expense and dissipation as were fatal to his fortunes, and at length to life. Yet with all his follies and foibles, which were indeed abundant, he had such a warmth and affectionateness of heart, that it was impossible not to love him" (BOUCHER [1], 67). Eden's military experience included service with the Coldstream Guards in Germany during the Seven Years' War. In 1765 he had married Caroline Calvert, sister of the current proprietor of Maryland, Frederick Calvert, sixth Baron Baltimore (1732–1771), from whom Eden had received his appointment as governor.

Jane Vobe (died c.1789) operated a well-furnished tavern on Waller Street near the theater, and according to a traveler who had stopped there four years earlier, it was a place "where all the best people resorted" (FRENCH TRAVELLER, 741). Mrs. Vobe was in business as early as May 1757, when GW first patronized her tavern, and she remained at this location until 1771 (LEDGER A, 35).

Col. Fitzhugh is probably Henry Fitzhugh (1723–1783) of Stafford County. He was a son of William Fitzhugh of Bedford and married Sarah Battaile, daughter of Capt. Nicholas Battaile, in 1746. Fitzhugh was a colonel in the Stafford County militia and furnished supplies to the American army during the Revolution.

7.   Dined at the Governors & supped at Anthony Hayes.

The burgesses convened today. A moderate tone was set for this session by Governor Botetourt's opening remarks to the house. Parliament, he assured the burgesses, would soon repeal all taxes for raising a revenue in America except the one on tea, and he pledged his own strong support for this action. The burgesses were not fully appeased by his speech, continuing to object to the tea tax, and no steps were taken to dissolve or modify the association. But Botetourt was personally popular with the burgesses, and they chose not to make an issue of the remaining tax at this time. The session would be a long one devoted to the colony's normal business. GW was today appointed to the same three committees on which he had served during the last session: religion, privileges and elections, and propositions and grievances (H.B.J., 1766–69, 225–30).

8.   Dined at the Speakers & supped at Mrs. Campbells.

9.   Dined at Mrs. Dawsons and supped at Mrs. Campbells.

10.   Dined at the Treasurers and supped at Mrs. Campbells.

GW today paid 5s. to have his watch repaired and gave Jacky £2 in cash for pocket money. Another £1 10s. were lost at the card table (LEDGER A, 296).

11.   Clear & pleast. Dined at Mrs. Dawsons and went up to Eltham.

Today being Saturday, the burgesses adjourned, after transacting the lengthy business of the day, until 11:00 A.M. Monday morning (H.B.J., 1766–69, 247–53).

12.   Stayd at Eltham all day.

13.   Came to Town abt. 11. Oclock. Dined & supp'd at Mrs. Campbells.

Jacky stayed at Eltham with his mother and sister.

14.   Dined and Supped at Mrs. Campbells.

GW on this date paid 2s. 6d. to a tailor and lost 7s. 6d. at cards. "Coffee &ca. at Mrs. Campbells" cost him 2s. (LEDGER A, 296).

November 1769

At Eltham, Patsy was today visited by Dr. John de Sequeyra (1712–1795) of Williamsburg, who prescribed some medicine for her (receipt from Sequeyra, 16 Dec. 1769, ViHi: Custis Papers). Sequeyra (also Siquiyra, Siqueyra, or Sequayra), scion of a distinguished Sephardi Jewish family of physicians in England, was born in London, received his M.D. degree in 1739 from the University of Leyden, and settled in Virginia in 1745. He was one of the attending physicians during Lord Botetourt's last illness and in 1773 became the first visiting physician to the new hospital for the insane in Williamsburg, the first such public hospital in the American colonies (GILL, 95; ROTH, 14:1179).

15. Dined at Mr. Wythes and supped at Anthony Hays.

16. Dined at Mrs. Campbells at or after 5 Oclock, and spent the Evening there without supping.

17. Dined at Mrs. Campbells after 4 & spent the Evening there without supping—Having 1 Bowl of P. & Toddy.

18. Had a Mutton Chop at Mrs. Campbells with Colo. Bassetts abt. One Clock & then came up to Eltham.

The burgesses adjourned today until 11:00 A.M. Monday (H.B.J., 1766–69, 268–71).

19. Went to Church & returnd to Eltham to Dinner w. Mr. Dangerfd. & the Parson.

MR. DANGERFD.: probably William Daingerfield, who at this time was a New Kent County militia colonel and justice of the peace and a vestryman for Blisland Parish. In 1770 he moved to the plantation of Belvidera in Spotsylvania County, which had been inherited by his wife, Sarah Taliaferro Daingerfield. The parson for Blisland Parish in New Kent and James City counties was Rev. Price Davies.

20. At Eltham all day—occasiond by Rain.

The burgesses met today as scheduled (H.B.J., 1766–69, 271–75).

21. Came to Town with Mrs. Washington P & Jacky Custis. I dind at Mrs. Campbells. Mrs. W &ca. dined at Mrs. Dawsons. I spent the Eveng. (without suppg.) at Mrs. Campbells.

Patsy and Jacky lodged with GW at Mrs. Campbell's place (CUSTIS ACCOUNT BOOK). Mrs. Washington may have stayed there also since GW apparently had a private room, or she may have been the guest of Mrs. Dawson or some other acquaintance in the city. GW today bought a padlock for 2s. 6d. (LEDGER A, 296).

[195]

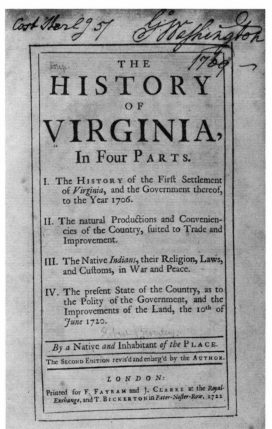

When he bought this book in 1769, the methodical Washington recorded not only the year of purchase but the cost—five shillings sterling. (Boston Athenaeum)

22. Dined at Mrs. Dawsons all of Us. I & J. P. Custis supped at Mrs. Campbells.

23. Dined with Mrs. Washington &ca. at the Speakers by Candlelight & spent the Evg. there also.

GW on this date paid Edmund Pendleton £9 13s. for representing the Custis estate in some legal matters, including asking the General Court whether or not Jacky should rent the dower lands (receipt from Edmund Pendleton, ViHi: Custis Papers).

24. J. P. Custis and I dined with others at the Govrs. I spent the Evening at Hayes.

GW and Thomas Nelson, Jr., of York County were today ordered by the burgesses to prepare "a Bill for laying a Tax upon Dogs." Nelson presented the bill to the house 1 Dec., but it was defeated (H.B.J., 1766–69, 289, 309).

Dr. Sequeyra saw Patsy on 24, 25, 26, and 28 Nov. and 1 Dec. (receipt from John de Sequeyra, 16 Dec. 1769, ViHi: Custis Papers) .

25.   Dined at Mrs. Campbells with Mrs. Washington & JPC[ustis] as also did Colo. & Mrs. Bassett. Spent the Evening in my own Room.

26.   Dined at Colo. Burwells. Mrs. Washington JPC[ustis] & Mrs. Bassett dined at Mrs. Campbells. I spent the Evening in my own Room.

Col. Lewis Burwell (1716–c.1784) of James City County lived at Kingsmill plantation on the James River about four miles southeast of Williamsburg. He was a burgess for James City County 1758–74 and a member of the board of visitors and governors of the College of William and Mary from before 1769 to 1775. Heavily in debt at this time, he was selling much of his property to balance his books, but Kingsmill was not sacrificed until 1781 (MAYS, 1:213, 359; KINGSMILL, 24) .
    The House of Burgesses did not meet today, it being Sunday (H.B.J., 1766–69, 295) .

27.   Dined at Mrs. Dawson's with Mrs. Washington & the Children. Supped with J. P. Custis at Mrs. Campbells.

28.   Dined at Mrs. Campbells by Candlelight. Spent the Evening there without Supping.

29.   Dined at the Treasurers. Mrs. Washington & Mr. & Miss Custis dind at Mrs. Dawson's. I supped at the Treasurers.

30.   Dined at the Presidents & spent the Evening there without Suppg.

Acct. of the Weather—in Novr.

Novr. 1.   Very Cloudy & sometimes Misty with but little Wind & that Eastwardly.

2.   Misty & Raining all day. Wind Eastwardly tho but little of it.

3.   Raing. in the Morning & misty afterwards till 4 Oclock, then clear. Wind Westwardly.

4.   Clear. Wind westwardly.

5.   Clear, Calm, & pleasant.

6.   Lowering with a good deal of Rain Lightning & some thunder in the Night.

7.   Tolerably pleasant, & clear, Wind Northwardly.

8.   Clear and very pleasant with but little wind and that Southwardly.

9.   Very pleast. Morning with the Wind at south. Afternoon Lowering with an Eastwardly wind & a good deal of Rain in the Night.

10.   Clear & pleasant but somewhat cool Wind being Northwardly.

11.   Clear and pleasant Morning but lowering & threatning afternoon.

12.   Rain in the Night. Wind high from the Northwest—but not very cold.

13.   Cool Morning but more moderate afternoon. Wind Southwardly.

14.   Raw & cold Wind at Southwest & like for Snow but turnd to Rain abt. 10 Oclock & cd. to Rain till two.

15.   Wind Westwardly & cold. Ice upon the Waters & ground froze.

16.   Clear and pleasant, tho somewhat cool wind being westwardly & No. Wt.

17.   Clear & not so cool as yesterday tho the wind was in the same Qr.

18.   Morning clear and pleasant but Wind Eastwardly—after which it grew Raw Cold & Cloudy threatning Rain.

19.   Cold & disagreeable. Wind Eastwardly & very fresh. Very Cloudy also.

20. A good deal of Rain in the Night & more or less all day. Wind still East.

21. A great deal of Rain fell last Night. Wind at No. West & After noon clear & cool. Morning Cloudy.

22. Clear & pleasant (but somewhat cool). Little or no Wind.

23. Clear and pleasant with but little Wind till late in the Night, when it shifted to No. Wt. & blew hard & Cold.

24. Wind No. & No. Wt. & very cold but clear.

25. A Remarkable white Frost.

26. Clear forenoon & pleasant with little or no wind. The Afternoon lowering & threatning Rain.

27. Much Rain fell in the Night, & showery all day, with the wind Southwardly & Warm with Lightng. and thunder. Wind shiftg. in the Eveng.

28. Clear and Cold. Wind Northwardly.

29. Clear and Cold. The afternoon lowering & like to Rain.

30. Misting all day but not Cold there being but little Wind.

[December]

Where & how—my time is—Spent

Decr. 1. Dined at Mrs. Campbells with the Speaker, Treasurer & other Company. Mrs. Washington & Childn. Dined at the Attorneys. Myself & J. P. Custis suppd at Mrs. Campbells.

2. Mrs. Washington & children, myself, Colo. Basset, Mrs. Basset & Betcy Bassett all Eat Oysters at Mrs. Campbells abt. One oclock and afterwards went up to Eltham.

The burgesses once more adjourned until 11:00 A.M. Monday. Before the family left town, GW paid Miss P. Davenport £3 3s. 8d. for clothing furnished Patsy and Mrs. Washington. He also paid 3s. for postage and gave Jacky £1 in cash. Mrs. Washington and Patsy had received spending money earlier in the week (H.B.J., 1766–69, 311–12; LEDGER A, 299; receipt from Davenport, 2 Dec. 1769, ViHi: Custis Papers).

3. At Eltham all day.

4. Returnd to Town and dined at Mrs. Campbells. Spent Eveng. there also witht. Supg.

Mrs. Washington and the children remained at Eltham. In town GW bought an ornamental comb for Patsy at John Carter's store on Duke of Gloucester Street (LEDGER A, 299; CUSTIS ACCOUNT BOOK).

5. Dined at Mrs. Campbells & spent the Evening there without supping – in.

GW on this date paid Alexander Craig, a Williamsburg saddler, 9s. 6d. on his own account and 16s. for Jacky (LEDGER A, 299; receipt of Craig, 10 and 30 Nov. 1769, ViHi: Custis Papers). In the House of Burgesses, GW and Richard Henry Lee of Westmoreland County were ordered to prepare "a Bill for clearing and making navigable the River *Potowmack,* from the great Falls . . . up to Fort Cumberland" (H.B.J., 1766–69, 314).

6. Dined at Mr. Cockes & spent the Eveng. there.

7. Dined at Mrs. Campbells & the Evening spent in my Room.

8. Dined at Mrs. Campbells & was engagd. at Charltons abt. Colo. Moore's Lotty. the Evg.

Bernard Moore, of Chelsea in King William County, was forced to raffle all his property in a lottery to pay his debts, part of which were owed to the administrators of Speaker John Robinson's estate (MAYS, 1:144, 182, 205–6). GW was a manager for the lottery.

   In the House of Burgesses today Richard Henry Lee introduced the Potomac navigation bill (H.B.J., 1766–69, 322).

9. Dined at Mrs. Campbells and suppd there with the speaker &ca.

10. Dined at the Speakers & spent the Evening in my own Room.

Today being Sunday, the burgesses did not meet. GW recorded under this date the payment of 7s. 6d. to Benjamin Bucktrout, Williamsburg cabinetmaker and merchant, for repairing a coach house belonging to the printer William Rind (d. 1773). GW may have kept his new chariot there while he was in town (LEDGER A, 299).

11. Dined at Mr. Wythes—and the Eveng. Spent in my own Room.

12. Dined at Mrs. Campbells and Spent the Evening in my own Room.

Dr. Sequeyra visited Patsy today and on 14 Dec., probably at Eltham (receipt of John de Sequeyra, 16 Dec. 1769, ViHi: Custis Papers; CUSTIS ACCOUNT BOOK and LEDGER A, 299). In the House of Burgesses, GW presented a petition on behalf of Daniel McCarty asking the burgesses to dock the entail on 2,000 acres of land McCarty had inherited from his grandfather and to put under entail in place of that land 1,000 acres in Fauquier County he had bought from his son-in-law Richard Chichester. GW and Richard Henry Lee were ordered to prepare a bill for that purpose (H.B.J., 1766–69, 332–33; McCarty to GW, 6 Dec. 1769, DLC:GW).

13. Dined at Mrs. Campbells and went to the Ball at the Capitol.

Today in the House of Burgesses, GW introduced Daniel McCarty's bill, and the Potomac navigation bill was referred for study to a committee composed of GW, Richard Henry Lee, and the burgesses from Frederick and Hampshire counties. The house also approved an address to the king and a memorial to the governor recommending that the colony's western boundary be changed by running a line from "the Western Termination of the North-Carolina line . . . to the River Ohio" (H.B.J., 1766–69, 334–36). The ball was given in the evening by the burgesses for the governor, the council, and the ladies and gentlemen of the town, and the Capitol was illuminated for the occasion. Of the ladies who attended, "near one hundred, appeared in homespun gowns" to show their support of the nonimportation agreement. "It were to be wished," William Rind's *Virginia Gazette* observed the following day, "that all assemblies of American Ladies would exhibit a like example of public virtue and private oeconomy, so amiably united" (R and P&D, 14 Dec. 1769). GW paid £1 toward the subscription for this ball on 16 Dec. (LEDGER A, 299).

14. Dined at Mrs. Campbells & spent part of the Evening in drawing Colo. Moores Lottery.

Richard Henry Lee today reported from the committee on the Potomac navigation bill that the committee had studied the bill and made several amendments to it. The house then approved the amended bill and ordered it to be engrossed for a final vote. However, no such vote was taken during this session, and the bill died for lack of further action (H.B.J., 1766–69, 338).

15. Dined at the Attorney's and went to Southalls in the Evening to draw Colo. Moores Lottery.

James Barrett Southall (b. 1726) was at this time operating a tavern on Duke of Gloucester Street which he had leased from the heirs of its original proprietor, Henry Wetherburn. Located in the block nearest the Capitol, the tavern had become very popular by 1760, when Wetherburn died, and it continued to have an excellent reputation under Southall, who took it over sometime before June 1767. An experienced innkeeper, Southall had been in business elsewhere in Williamsburg as early as 1757, when GW paid him for supper and club. He remained at the Wetherburn Tavern until 1771 (LEDGER A, 35; GIBBS, 196–97, 204–5).

Daniel McCarty's bill was on this day referred to a committee composed of all the burgesses from Westmoreland, Fairfax, Prince William, and Loudoun counties. The committee must have met immediately because before the house adjourned for the day Richard Henry Lee reported the committee had finished its work. The members had found the allegations of the bill to be true and had recommended an amendment to it. The amended bill was then approved by the house and ordered to be engrossed for a final vote (H.B.J., 1766–69, 340–42).

16. Dined at Mrs. Campbells & drawg. Colo. Moores Lottery till 10 Oclock & then compleated it.

GW was today given permission by the House of Burgesses to be absent for a week, and he paid most of his bills in town as if he intended to go home (H.B.J., 1766–69, 343). The barber George Lafong was given £5 9s. 1d. to settle his account against GW, Jacky, and Patsy; James Craig, a Williamsburg jeweler, received £3 for two mourning rings bought for Harrison Manley and 2s. 6d. for repairing Jacky's buttons; Anthony Hay was paid 14s. for three suppers and other expenses at the Raleigh; and Patsy's medical bills were discharged: £10 15s. to Dr. Sequeyra and £2 13s. 3d. to Dr. William Pasteur, probably for medicines from his apothecary shop on Duke of Gloucester Street (LEDGER A, 299; CUSTIS ACCOUNT BOOK). Pasteur, who died in 1791, was the son of a Swiss immigrant. He had been apprenticed to a Williamsburg doctor at an early age and had opened his shop by 1759 (BLANTON, 321–22). GW also paid Pasteur 6s. 4d. on his own account (LEDGER A, 299).

17. Dined at the Palace and went up in the Afternoon to Colo. Bassetts.

The burgesses did not meet today, Sunday. GW paid Mrs. Campbell's account against him, Jacky, and Patsy, a total of £42 12s. 6d. (LEDGER A, 299).

18. Came to Town again abt. 12 Oclock. Dind at Mrs. Campbells, & spent the Evening in my own Room a writing.

GW apparently missed today's meeting of the House of Burgesses, a very brief one (H.B.J., 1766–69, 344–45).

19. Dined at Mrs. Campbells an hour after Candlelight & spent the Eveng. in my own Room.

Daniel McCarty's bill was passed today, and GW was ordered to take it to the council for approval (H.B.J., 1766–69, 347). However, that approval was not forthcoming. The councillors used their prerogative to reject the bill without explanation, and it failed to become law (H.B.J., 1770–72, 55–56). GW apparently attended the two remaining days of this session of the burgesses.

20. Dined at Mrs. Campbells and spt. the Evening in my own Room.

GW today paid 8s. 3d. for "Barber & Washing" (LEDGER A, 299).

21. Dined at Mrs. Campbells & came up to Eltham after the House adjournd.

Governor Botetourt was reluctant to let the burgesses go home at this time, despite the fact that they had sat six days a week for over six weeks. Apparently many matters remained to be considered. "The Inclination of this Assembly," he told them today, "could alone have engaged me to have interrupted the Business of this Session; but as I understand that it is generally desired to adjourn over the Christmas Holidays, and not to meet again till the Month of May, I do direct both Houses to adjourn themselves to the 21st Day of May next" (H.B.J., 1766–69, 355). Before GW left town, he paid Mrs. Campbell £1 10s. 6d. for his expenses at her place since 17 Dec. (LEDGER A, 299).

22. Sett of for home. Dined at Todds Bridge and lodgd at Hubbards.

Jacky Custis had apparently returned to Boucher's school before this date and was not with the family today.

23. Breakfasted at Caroline Ct. House and reachd Fredericksburg abt. 4 Oclock in the Aftern. ding. at Colo. Lewis.

Caroline Court House was about halfway between Todd's Bridge and Fredericksburg, but lay a few miles east of the main road (RICE, 2:176 and pl. 117; *Va. Gaz.*, R, 19 Oct. 1769). GW's expenses there on this day were 8s. 9d. (LEDGER A, 299). The chief tavern at the Court House had been established about 1733 by Samuel Coleman (1704–1748) and was now owned by his son Francis Coleman (d. 1771), a lawyer who served a term as a Caroline burgess 1769–70 (CAMPBELL [1], 410–13; KING [3], 258–59).

24. Went to Prayers, & dined afterwds. at Colo. Lewis. Spent the Evening with Mr. Jones at Julians.

Edward Jones was Mary Ball Washington's overseer at the Ferry Farm. Mrs. Julian kept a tavern on the main street of Fredericksburg until about 1777 (*Va. Gaz.*, P&D, 9 July 1772, and D&H, 15 Aug. 1777).

25. Dined & spent the Evening at Colo. Lewis's.

GW today recorded winning £2 5s. at cards (LEDGER A, 299).

26.   Dined at Colo. Lewis & went over the River and lodgd at my Mothers.

GW today paid 2s. 6d. to a barber and 3s. 9d. for having his chariot repaired (LEDGER A, 299).

27.   Dined and lodgd at Dumfries with Mr. Boucher & J. P. Custis who overtook us on the Road.

Before GW left his mother he gave her £6 in cash (LEDGER A, 299).

28.   Reached home to Dinner with Mr. Boucher & ca.

29.   At Home all day.

30.   Mr. Boucher went away. I Rid to My Mill with [   ] Ball and agreed with [him] to Build here.

GW had decided in the spring to replace his small plantation mill with a merchant mill which could manufacture large quantities of high-grade flour suitable for sale in the colony or for export to lucrative markets abroad (GW to Charles West, 6 June 1769, DLC:GW). By grinding his own wheat he might increase his profit from each year's crop, and if he bought wheat from other farmers and sold flour ground from it, he could make even more money. The new mill was to be built downstream from the old one, near the point where narrow, shallow Dogue Run widened into navigable Dogue Creek, a convenient location for water transportation. But the exact site would not be determined until the terrain in the area had been thoroughly studied.
  The millwright was John Ball of Frederick County, who about this time was sending goods by wagon from the Shenandoah Valley to Falmouth (MALONE, 701). He was also probably the John Ball (1742–1806) who settled on Licking Run, Fauquier County, in 1771 (deed of James and Sarah Duff to John Ball, 2 April 1771, Fauquier County Deeds, Book 4, 158, Vi Microfilm). A son of William Ball (1718–1785) of Lancaster County, this John Ball married Sarah Ellen Payne in 1767 and later became a captain in the Fauquier militia (SNODDY, 308; GWATHMEY, 35). His eldest son, William, may have been the William Ball who was engaged to rebuild GW's mill in 1791 (George Augustine Washington's agreement with William Ball, 16 April 1791, DLC:GW).

31.   At Home all day.

Acct. of the Weather — in Decr.

Decr. 1.   Cloudy & misty the Chief part of the day.

2.   Lowering Forenoon with some Intervals [of] Sun in the Afternoon. Warm. Wind So. Wt.

3. Wind at No. Et. & Raining more or less all day.

4. Lowering & Misty day. But little wind and that at No. Wt.

5. Also lowering & disagreeable Afternoon the Morng. being clear & fine.

6. Cold & Raw. Cloudy afternoon with some Rain.

7. Clear and tolerable pleasant.

8. Clear but cool the Wind at No. West.

9. Clear and Cool the Wind Westwardly.

10. Also clear & cool. Wind in the same quarter.

11. Fine Morning, disagreeable Noon, & Rainy Afternoon. Wind Eastwardly.

12. Wind Southwest—& Misty, Rainy & sometimes Sunshine. Night warm.

13. Wind shifted to No. West in the Morning and blew hard growing amazingly Cold in the Night.

14. Ground exceeding hard froze and day cold (& clear) but not equal to Yesterday Afternoon.

15. Still cold but more moderate than yesterday. The Afternoon lowering & exceeding like for Snow.

16. Clear and more pleasant.

17. Clear & pleasant with but little Wind. Evening Cool.

18. Clear, warm & pleasant in the forenoon. Wind southwardly and Afternoon Lowering. Night Raining.

19. Misting & Raining by turns all day—the Wind being at No. East.

20. Cold Raw and Cloudy Wind what there was of it, Northwardly. Evening more moderate & clearing.

21. Very pleasant, being clear & wind Southwardly.

22. Wind at No. Et. Cloudy & Cold with a little appearance of the Sun.

23. Exceeding cold Morning. Very cloudy with great appearance of Snow. Wind Northwardly.

24. Clear and more moderate but still cool. A very white frost & Wind Northwardly—but little of it.

25. A very white Frost, clear, still, & very pleasant till the Evening then cloudy and boisterous.

26. Clear but cool the Wind blowing fresh from the No. West till the Eveng.

27. A Very white frost but still clear & exceeding pleast. Gd. Hard froze.

28. Ground exceeding hard froze & a very white frost. The day lowerg. & very threatning of Snow. Wind East.

29. Remarkably fine, clear & still.

30. Wind at No. West & fresh & day Cold.

31. Clear, still & remarkably fine and pleasant.

A New Mill and a Journey to the Ohio

1770

[January]

Where & how my time is Spent

Jany. 1.   At home all day alone.

2.   At home all day. Mr. Peake dined here.

3.   At home all day alone.

4.   Went a hunting with Jno. Custis & Lund Washington. Started a Deer & then a Fox but got neither.

5.   Rid to Muddy hole & Doeg Run. Carrd. the Dogs with me but found nothing. Mr. Warnr. Washington & Mr. Thruston came in the Evening.

6.   The two Colo. Fairfaxs and Mrs. Fairfax dind here as did Mr. R. Alexander & the two Gentn. that came the day before. The Belvoir Family returnd after Dinner.

7.   Mr. Washng. & Mr. Thruston went to Belvoir.

GW today paid the Rev. Mr. Thruston £10 for his share of lands on the Ohio to be granted under the Proclamation of 1763 (LEDGER A, 302).

8.   Went a huntg. with Mr. Alexander, J. P. Custis & Ld. W[ashingto]n, killd a fox (a dog one) after 3 hours chase. Mr. Alexr. went away and Wn. & Thruston came in the Aftern.

9.   Went a ducking but got nothing the Creeks and Rivers being froze. Mr. Robt. Adam dined here & returnd.

10.   Mr. W[ashingto]n & Mr. Thruston set of home. I went a hunting in the Neck & visited the Plantn. there. Found & killd a bitch fox after treeing it 3 times, & chasg. it abt. 3 Hr.

11.   At home all day alone.

A large part of Washington's pleasure in fox hunting lay in the breeding of fine hunting dogs. (Mount Vernon Ladies' Association of the Union)

12.   Ditto—Ditto.

13.   Dined at Belvoir with Mrs. Washington Mr. & Miss Custis & returnd afterwds.

14.   At home all day alone.

15.   Went up to Alexandria, expecting Court but there was none.

16.   Rid to the Mill Doeg Run and Muddy hole.

17.   At home all day alone.

18.   Went to the Plantn. in the Neck.

GW today paid a Mr. Awbrey 10s. for prescribing medicines for Patsy Custis (CUSTIS ACCOUNT BOOK) .

19.   At home all day alone.

20.   Went a hunting with Jacky Custis & catchd a Bitch Fox after three hours chace. Founded it on the Ck. by J. Soals.

Joseph Soal, a cobbler, rented a plantation from GW in 1769 and 1770 (LEDGER A, 304) .

21.   At home all day alone.

22.   Rid to Posey's Barn and the Mill.

23.   Went a hunting after breakfast & found a Fox at Muddy hole & killd her (it being a Bitch) after a chace of better than two hours & after treeing her twice the last of which times she fell dead out of the Tree after being therein sevl. minutes apparently we[ll]. Rid to the Mill afterwards. Mr. Semple & Mr. Robt. Adam dind here.

John Semple (d. 1773) was a Scottish speculator who moved from Charles County, Md., to Prince William County, Va., in 1763 and took over the iron furnace and gristmills on Occoquan Creek that John Ballendine had previously operated. About that same time, Semple acquired Keep Triste iron furnace, on the Virginia shore of the Potomac River a short distance above Harpers Ferry, and in May 1765 he bought from Thomas Colvill the tract of land called Merryland lying in nearby Frederick County, Md. (SKAGGS, 63:28 n.15) . He was also an active promoter of a scheme to improve the navigation of the Potomac by forming a company to build locks around the falls and probably discussed the idea with GW on this visit (Semple to GW, 8 Jan. 1770, MnHi) .

24.   At home all day alone.

25.   At home all day alone.

26.   Ditto. Do. Do.

27.   Went a hunting, & after trailing a fox a good while the Dogs Raizd a Deer & run out of the Neck with it & did not (some of them at least) come home till the next day.

28.   At home all day. In the Afternoon Mr. Semple came here.

29.   Dined at Belvoir (with J. P. Custis) & returnd in the Afternoon.

30.   Went a hunting, & having found a Deer by Piney Cover. It run to the head of Accatinck before we coud stop the Dogs. Mr. Peake dined here.

Piney Cover was a densely wooded area along Piney Branch, a small stream flowing southeast into Dogue Run about a mile above GW's present mill. The head of navigation on Accotink Creek was about 2 miles southwest of the mouth of Piney Branch.

31.   At home alone.

Acct. of the Weather in January

Jany. 1st.   Constant Rain the whole day with high & boisterous Wind from the No. Et.

2.   Clear and Cold, wind high from the No. West. River froze over.

3.   Wind in the same Quarter & very fresh remarkably cold & frosty.

4.   But very little Wind, & that Southwardly. Day clear & more moderate but the ground very little thawed.

5.   Clear & pleasant. Wind Southwardly—the Ground notwithstanding close blockd up.

6.   Cloudy Morning, & Rainy Afternoon wind Eastwardly.

7.   Again Cloudy in the Morning & rainy Afternoon. River opened.

8. Clear and Cold. Wind at No. West.

9. Clear & cold Wind Northwardly & fresh River shut up again.

10. Remarkably fine & pleasant being perfectly calm & clear till the Evening then lowering.

11. Raining moderately all day with but little wind and that about So. Wt.

12. Much such a day as yesterday except that what little Wind blew appeard to come [from] the No. East.

13. Cloudy with great appearances of Snow in the forenoon but clear afterwards. Wind at No. West & very cold.

14. Exceeding hard frost River shut up. Wind at No. West and very cold.

15. Exceeding cold tho but little Wind that however at No. West.

16. Very Cold. Wind still at No. West but not hard—yet piercing—clear.

17. Clear & very cold Wind from the same place. Ground not the least thawed.

18. Clear & pleasant in the Morning Cloudy Afternoon & cold. Wind at N. Et.

19. Slightly snowing in the Morning & cloudy afterwards with but little Wind & that Southwardly.

20. Cloudy & still in the morning but a cold Southwesterly wind & wild sky afterwards.

21. Clear & tolerably pleasant Wind being about So. Wt. & yet cool.

22. Clear and tolerably pleasant with variable Wind which abt. Sunset was at No. Et.

23.   Clear and very pleasant Wind being Southwardly & thawing.

24.   Very warm & thawing in the forenoon. Frequent showers in the afternoon & wind shifting from south to North & growing Cold. Ice breaking in the River for the first time since the 14.

25.   Cold and disagreeable with a fine kind of Sleety Snow. Wind Northward⟨ly⟩ & very cloudy.

26.   Raw, cold & cloudy the first part of the day—but clearg. afterwards. Wd. N. W.

27.   Wind Southwardly, pleast. & thawing.

28.   Wind at No. West—tolerably fresh in the Morning but not cold. Still afterwards & pleasant.

29.   Rather lowering, but moderate & pleasant, with but little Wind & that Southwardly. Ice broken again.

30.   Clear and tolerably pleasant but the Wind very high in the Afternoon from the Westward.

31.   Clear and cool again, wind No. West.

[February]

Where & how my time is Spent

Feby. 1.   Went a huntg. (being joind by Mr. Peake Wm. Triplet & Harrison Manley) & after a Chace of near five hours we killd a Fox. Mr. Piper & Mr. Adams came here this afternoon.

2.   Mr. Adam & myself walkd to the Mill & up Doeg Run before Dinner.

Robert Adam, who owned a merchant mill and a bakery near Alexandria, would be a major buyer of flour from GW's new mill.

3.   At home all day, the above Gentlemn. returnd after dinner to Alexandria.

4.   At home all day. Carlin the Taylor came here in the afternoon and stayed all Night.

William Carlin of Alexandria made clothing for GW, Jacky, Patsy, and some of the Mount Vernon house servants 1765–72 (LEDGER A, 217; LEDGER B, 47; GW's account with Carlin 26 Sept. 1772, ViMtV).
   GW today recorded winning £1 5s. at cards (LEDGER A, 302).

5.   At home all day. In the Evening Sally Carlyle & Betty Dalton came here.

6.   Rid to Muddy hole. Sally Carlyle went to Belvoir — Betty Dalton stayd.

7.   Rid to Alexandria to a Meeting of the Trustees. Returnd in the Evening & found Captn. McCarty here.

GW had been appointed a trustee of Alexandria on 16 Dec. 1766, replacing George Johnston of Belvale. However, there is no record in the trustees' minutes of his ever officially attending one of their meetings, even on this day, nor is there any record of his formally resigning the office or being replaced. The business of the trustees today was routine: the draining of marshland, the building of a warehouse, the collection of debts owed to the town, the appointment of a clerk, and the appointment of Jonathan Hall as a trustee in place of John Kirkpatrick (Alexandria town trustees' minutes, 1749–80, 61, 75–76, Vi).
   In Alexandria today GW paid several accounts including one for a pair of shoes for Jacky Custis (LEDGER A, 302).

8.   Captn. McCarty, Doctr. Rumney and Mr. Jno. Ballendine Dined and lodged here.

Ballendine, having been forced by financial difficulties to transfer his Occoquan mills and iron furnace to John Semple, had since 1765 established another commerical complex farther up the Potomac River at Little Falls. At this time it consisted of merchant mills capable of grinding 50,000 bushels of wheat a year, a bakery with three ovens, a landing for large vessels complete with granaries and countinghouses, and a "public house, well finished, with 10 fire places, good cellars, and . . . a fine French cook." In addition, he was currently building another gristmill and a sawmill and had the rights to 40 lots in the town of Philee, which was planned for the area (*Va. Gaz.*, R, 29 Nov. 1770). Financial troubles, however, were again plaguing him. His debts were great, and his many creditors were beginning to press him. Nevertheless, like Semple, he was, and until 1775 would remain, a leading promoter of the Potomac navigation scheme.

9.   Went a hunting — found a fox and lost it. Mr. Ballendine & the Doctr. still here. Captn. McCarty went from the field.

10. Jacky Custis returnd to Mr. Bouchers to School. Mr. Ballendine and myself leveled Doeg Run in ordr. to fix on a Mill seat. Returnd to Dinr. wt. the Doctr.

Jacky's departure had been delayed for several weeks, first by the freezing over of the fords between Mount Vernon and Caroline County, then by the heavy snowfall of 4 Feb. (GW to Jonathan Boucher, 3–10 Feb. 1770, NN). He took 10s. in pocket money with him today and rode on a newly repaired saddle (CUSTIS ACCOUNT BOOK).

11. The Doctr. still here. Mr. Ballendine went away early in the Morng. At home all day.

12. At home all day with the Doctr.

13. At home all day with the Doctr. Mr. Fairfax came in the Afternoon.

14. Went into the Neck with Mr. Fairfax a huntg. but was forcd back by Rain. Doctr. Rumney returnd to Alexandria after breakfast this day.

15. Went a huntg. again with Mr. Fairfax & found a fox at the head of the blind Pocoson which we suppose was killd in an hour but coud not find it. Mr. Peake dind here & Mr. R. Alexr. came after.

The mouth of the blind pocosin was on the Potomac shore below the mansion house, at the southwest corner of the Mount Vernon tract (survey by GW for John Posey, 10 Oct. 1769, ViMtV).

16. Huntg. again—found a bitch fox at Piney branch & killd it in an hour. Mr. Fairfax returnd from there and Mr. Alexr. went away [after] dinner.

17. At home all day alone.

18. Went to Pohick Church and returnd to Dinner.

19. Went to Court at Alexandria and returnd in the Evening.

The February court met 19–24 Feb. (Fairfax County Order Book for 1768–70, 285–331, Vi Microfilm). GW today collected a debt, paid one, and spent 1s. 6d. to have a coffeepot mended (LEDGER A, 302).

20. Went up to Court again and stayd all Night. Lodgd at Captn. Daltons.

21. Came home in the Evening—Mr. Ross with me.

22. Went up to Court again. Mr. Ross returnd to Colchester. Returnd in the Evening and found my Brothers Saml. & John & the latters wife & Daughter Mr. Lawe. Washington & Daughter & the Revd. Mr. Smith here.

John Augustine and Hannah Bushrod Washington had two daughters: Jane Washington (1759–1791) and Mildred Washington (born c.1760). The daughter of Lawrence Washington of Chotank who came with him on this day is apparently Mary Townshend Washington, who married Robert Stith of King George County in 1773 (see main entry for 10 April 1770). The Rev. Mr. Smith is Thomas Smith of Cople Parish, Westmoreland County.

23. At home all day with the above Com[pany].

24. Went out with the hounds but found nothing.

25. At home all day.

26. At home all day.

27. Ditto. Ditto.

28. Went out with Guns returnd about 12 Oclock without killg. of any thing. My Brothers and the Company that came with them still here.

Acct. of the Weather in February

Feby. 1. Clear & tolerably pleasant there being but little Wind, that however was Northwardly & cool.

2. Cloudy with appearances of Snow but clear & pleasant in the Afternoon but little Wind stirring.

3. Cloudy with a slight mixture of fine hail & Rain. But little Wind & that southly.

4. Snowing more or less all day—the snow about 8 Inches deep. Wind Northward.

5. Cool and Clear Wind No. West.

6. Pleasant Wind Southwardly and clear.

7. Clear Morning but lowering afternn. intermixed with Snow. Not very cold.

8. Misty kind of Rain at times with a Southwardly Wind and thawing.

9. Still giving and damp with the Wind Northwardly but not cold. Snow almost gone.

10. Heavy damp Morning, with little or no wind, Evening clear and pleast.

11. Still, Mild and pleasant with Clouds.

12. Wind at No. East and slow rain all day which Increasd in the Evening.

13. Rain in the Morning with the Wind abt. So. West. Cloudy & sometimes misty.

14. Cloudy Morning, and from nine or 10 Oclock, constant Rain till abt. One then appearance of fair weather. Wind Southwardly.

15. Calm, clear, and Warm Morning. About 10 Oclock the Wind came out at No. West and blew pretty fresh but not Cold tho it clouded.

16. Cloudy & cool forenoon, Wind being still at No. West, and sometimes pretty fresh. Afternoon clear.

17. Wind at No. West but neither fresh nor cold. Clear, & the Eveng. very pleast.

18. Clear and exceeding pleasant with the wind at So. and but little of it.

19. Fresh Wind from So. with more or less Rain all day. In the Afternoon late the Weather cleard the wind coming out hard & very cold from the No. West.

20. Hard frost. Wind fresh and cold from the No. West. Indeed it might be said that the Wind was high till the Eveng.

21.   But little Wind. Clear and pleast.

22.   Lowering forenoon & Rainy Afternoon.

23.   Foggy kind of Morning but clear & pleasant afterwards.

24.   Rain in the Night & high Wind from the No. West afterwards & Cold afternoon clear.

25.   Clear & cold in the forenoon wind being at No. West. Lowerg afternoon.

26.   Hard frost. The Wind shifting in the Night to No. West—but the latter part of the day pleast. The Wind getting Southwardly.

27.   Clear forenoon but lowering afternoon with the Wind raising from So. Wt. to No. West & Cool.

28.   Clear and pleasant with but little Wind & that Southwardly.

Remarks & Occurs. in Feby.

Feby. 2d. Agreed with Joseph Goart, to come down and raise Stone out of my Quarry for my Mill at the Rate of Three pounds pr. Month 26 days to the Month and lost time to be made up.

The walls of the new mill were to be built with local sandstone, which the residents of the area called freestone because of its abundance and the ease with which it could be cut and carved (STUDEBAKER, 37). GW's quarry may have been on the banks of the Potomac River west of his mansion house, where a large bed of freestone was located (GW to Daniel Carroll, 16 Dec. 1793, DLC:GW). Goart, whose name GW variously spelled Gort, Goord, Goort, and Gourt, began his work on 6 Mar. (LEDGER A, 314, 333, 340).

3.   Agreed with Mr. Robt. Adam for the Fish catchd at the Fishing Landing I bought of Posey, on the following terms—to wit

He is obligd to take all I catch at that place provided the quantity does not exceed 500 Barls. and will take more than this qty. if he can get Cask to put them in. He is to take them as fast as they are catchd with out giving any interruption to my people; and is to have the use of the Fish House for his Salt, fish, &ca. taking care to have the House clear at least before the next Fishing Season.

In consideration of which he is to pay me Ten pounds for the use of the House, give 3/ a thousd. for the Herrings (Virg. Money) and 8/4 a hundred (Maryland Curry.) for the whitefish.

Mr. Piper and Lund Washington present.

The fishery was on the 200-acre tract of land GW had acquired at Posey's sale the previous October (*Va. Gaz.*, R, 19 Oct. 1769). Taken by seining in the Potomac, the fish were packed with salt in large barrels to be sold to local planters for their slaves or to be shipped abroad, often to the West Indies (Robert Adam to GW, 24 June 1771, DLC:GW). Between 13 April and the end of May, Adam received 473,750 herring and 4,623 shad (whitefish), and on 1 Oct. GW was credited with £102 Virginia currency for his fish and rent of his fish house. For shad he was paid 8s. 4d. Virginia per hundred, a better rate than the 8s. 4d. Maryland per hundred given above (LEDGER A, 310).

[March]

Where & how my time is Spent

Mar. 1.   My Brothers and the Company with them went away about 10 O clock. I went to level the Ground on the other side of Doeg Run. Mr. Magowan & Captn. Wm. Crawford came here this afternoon.

GW was taking elevations west of Dogue Run to determine the best route for a millrace to his new mill. Several months earlier he had been thinking of supplying the new mill with water by having a race dug to it from the pond near his old mill (GW to Charles West, 6 June 1769, DLC:GW). But now he had another plan in mind. The dam near the old mill would be replaced with one farther up Dogue Run, a short distance above the place where it is joined by Piney Branch. From the new Dogue Run dam, a race would be dug southwest to a point on Piney Branch, a few hundred yards above its mouth, where a second dam would be built. Then the race, which would be about two miles in total length, would parallel Dogue Run along the higher ground west of the run down to the new mill, where it would pass through the building into Dogue Creek (VAUGHAN, 56; Warrington Gillingham's map of Mount Vernon, MUIR, between pp. 90 and 91). The idea for this arrangement may have come from John Ball or John Ballendine. Its advantage over GW's first idea was that it would make possible a higher head of water at the mill, because the race would begin at a greater elevation on Dogue Run and would remain near that level by following the higher terrain to the west.

Crawford came today to report on his surveys for GW in western Pennsylvania.

2.   At home all day with the two.

3.   Ditto. Ditto. Ditto.

4.   Mr. Crawford set of for Williamsburg & Mr. Magowan for Colchester the last of whom returnd.

GW lent Crawford £5 for his journey, which the captain repaid upon his return to Mount Vernon later in the month (LEDGER A, 302).

5.   Mr. Magowan went to Dumfries and I to Mr. Rt. Alexanders on a hunting Party where I met Mr. B. Fairfax but first I went over to George Town returng. to Mr. Alexanders at Night.

Established in 1751, Georgetown, Md. (now part of Washington, D.C.), was at this time a small but active trading community at the mouth of Rock Creek, eight miles up the Potomac River from Alexandria. At Georgetown today GW paid John Jost £6 10s. Maryland currency for a rifle and apparently dined at one of the town's two taverns. He also played cards either at Georgetown or at Robert Alexander's house, winning £1 5s. (LEDGER A, 302; RICE, 2:87–88).

6.   Went out a hunting with Mr. Alexander [and] his Brothers. Found two or three Foxes but killd neither.

7.   Went a hunting again. Found a Fox and run it 6 hours & then lost [it]. I returnd home this Evening.

8.   Went to Belvoir with Mr. Magowan, dined and Returnd in the afternoon.

9.   At home all day.

10.   Rid to Muddy hole Doeg Run and the Mill. Mr. Magowan went home.

11.   At home all day alone.

12.   Rid to Muddy hole Doeg Run and the Mill.

13.   Went a huntg. above Darrels Hills & to G. Alexrs. Pocoson. Found a fox by two Dogs in Cliftons Neck but lost it upon joing. the Pack. Returnd abt. 5 Oclock & found Colo. Mason & Mr. Christian here.

Francis Christian, a dancing master from Richmond County who had married Katherine Chinn of Lancaster County in 1750, came this day with Mason to discuss a series of dancing classes to be held during the next few months for the young people of the neighborhood. Some of the classes would meet at Gunston Hall, some at Mount Vernon, and some possibly at other nearby homes (CARTER [3], 2:737; HAYDEN, 76).

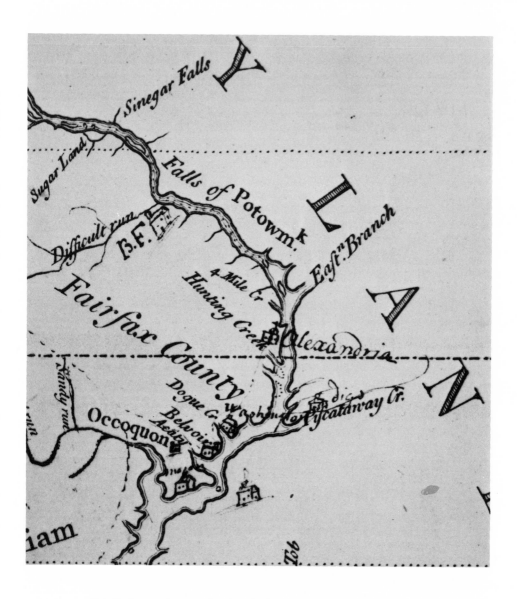

Detail of an early map, showing the Mount Vernon neighborhood. For an accurate map of the area based on recent research, see p. 1:213. (Library of Congress)

14.   At home all day. Colo. Mason & Mr. Christian dined here & returnd afterwards.

15.   At home all day alone.

16.   Went to doeg run and took the hounds with me—found a fox by the Widow Ashfords & soon lost him. Upon my return home found Colo. Lewis my Br[other] Ch[arle]s & Mr. Brooke here. In the Evening Mr. Jno. West & Mr. Stedlar came—also Mr. Whiting.

Elizabeth Ashford (died c.1773) is the widow of John Ashford who sold land on Dogue Run to GW in 1761. Mr. Brooke is probably Richard Brooke (died c.1792), a prominent Spotsylvania County landowner who lived near Fredericksburg, and Mr. Whiting is probably Francis Whiting, of Frederick County (later Berkeley County).

GW lost 6s. 3d. at cards on this day (LEDGER A, 302).

17.   Rid with Mr. West to Mr. Triplets to settle the Lines of Harrisons Patent. Passd by the Mill with Colo. Lewis. Mr. Whiting went home this Mor⟨n⟩ing & Mr. West in the Afternn. from T[riplet]s.

Harrison's patent, a grant of 266 acres made to William Harrison 4 Dec. 1706, lay northwest of Dogue Run between the lands that GW had bought from Pearson and the Ashfords in 1761–62 and Trenn's land, which he had bought in 1764. Part of the patent was now owned by John West Jr.'s mother, Sybil, a daughter of William Harrison, and the remainder by William Triplett (Lord Fairfax's grant to GW, 4 Mar. 1771, Northern Neck Deeds and Grants, Book I, 187, Vi Microfilm; deed of Sybil West to Triplett, 26 Mar. 1777, Fairfax County Deeds, Book M-1, 315–16, Vi Microfilm). The boundaries of the patent were surveyed on this day because GW's proposed new millrace and dams would be near the southeast line and might infringe upon it.

18.   Went to Pohick Church and retur⟨nd⟩ to Dinner. Colo. Lewis &ca. went away this Morning & Jno. Ball the Millright came in the afternoon.

19.   Went to the Mill with Jno. Ball to take the Level of the Run on the otherside. Did not get home till Night.

20.   Went up to Court & returnd in the Evening.

The court was in session 19–23 Mar. GW attended only on this day, arriving late with John West, Jr. (Fairfax County Order Book for 1768–70, 331–55, Vi Microfilm).

21. Joind some dogs that were self hunting & from thence went to the Mill & was levelling all the remainder of the day with Jno. Ball &ca.

22. Rid to the Mill and laid of with the Millwright the foundation for the New Mill House. Upon my return found Captn. Crawford here.

The site selected for the new mill was about one-third of a mile down Dogue Run, on the opposite bank, from the old mill. There, as planned, the tidal waters of the navigable portion of the stream, Dogue Creek, would flow up to the tailrace, enabling flat-bottom boats to deliver grain to the mill's door, from whence it would be "hoisted . . . to the garners above" (advertisement, 1 Feb. 1796, WRITINGS, 34:433–41). The same boats would carry flour down to the mouth of the creek, where a brig or schooner would take the cargo aboard and transport it to the markets at Alexandria, Norfolk, or elsewhere. The site of the new mill was also convenient for land traffic, because the road from Gum Spring to Colchester passed between it and the edge of the creek, being only a few feet from both. The foundations of the building, as laid off on this day, measured roughly 40 by 50 feet (BURSON, blueprint no. 2). When finished, the mill would be 2½ stories high, equipped with a breast wheel 16 feet in diameter and two sets of millstones, one to be used exclusively for merchant work and the other for custom work, that is, grinding local farmers' grain in return for one-eighth of the amount brought in, the legal toll at this time (HENING, 6:58). This custom business would be still another source of income provided by the new mill.

23. At home all day. Captn. Crawford and Mr. Manley here.

On this day GW gave Crawford £8 15s. Pennsylvania currency to buy surveying instruments in Philadelphia and £57 Pennsylvania currency to survey and obtain rights to some tracts of land along the Monongahela and Youghiogheny rivers for him (LEDGER A, 316). Crawford later returned the £57 when doubt arose over whether those lands would be in Pennsylvania after the colony's western boundary was established, but GW continued to be interested in the area for some time (William Crawford to GW, 5 May 1770, DLC:GW). That interest was apparently shared by Harrison Manley, on whose account GW today advanced Crawford £27 Virginia currency plus £10 Virginia currency for Lund Washington and £15 Pennsylvania currency for Samuel Washington (LEDGER A, 115, 313, 315).

24. Surveying the vacancy's of waste Land by Mr. Triplet & straitning the Mill Race.

GW had found there was a small parcel of unclaimed land between Harrison's patent and Dogue Run, and he was now surveying it with the intention of obtaining a grant from Lord Fairfax and thus providing more room along the run to accommodate his new millrace and dams (grant of Lord Fairfax to GW, 4 Mar. 1771, Northern Neck Deeds and Grants, Book I, 187, Vi Microfilm).

25.   At home all day. In the afternoon Messrs. B. Fairfax & Robt. & Philip Alexander came here.

26.   Went a hunting with the above Gentln. & killd a fox after two hours chace. The two Mr. Triplets Peake &ca. were with us. T. Triplet & H. Manley dind he⟨re⟩.

27.   Again went a hunting with the above Compy. but found no Fox. Mr. Geo. Alexander & Mr. Peake dind here with the other Compa.—as Mr. Ramsay did.

28.   Went a huntg. again & killd a fox. All the Compy. went home from the field.

29.   Running some Lines by Mr. Wm. Triplets all day.

30.   At Home. The two Colo. Fairfax's & Mrs. Fairfax dind here & returnd in the afternoon.

31.   At home all day writing.

Acct. of the Weather in March

Mar. 1st.   Wind Northwardly. Cold & Cloudy with Snow every now and then.

2.   Cloudy with a Mixture of Hail Rain & Snow, but not much of it.

3.   Clear and tolerably pleasant, but a little Cool. Wind being rather fresh from the No. West.

4.   Cloudy Morning, then Snow, after that Snow and Rain mixd, and lastly constant Rain.

5.   Snow about 3 Inches deep. Weather clear. Wind Westwardly in the forenoon but calm warm and thawing afterwards.

6.   Clear and pleasant with the wind at South.

7.   Clear & calm in the Morning, with a Northwardly Wind afterwards but pleasant Notwithstanding.

8.   Clear & pleasant with the Wind Southwardly.

9.   Clear and very pleasant with the Wind still Southwardly. In the Afternoon the Wind fresh with appearances of Rain.

10.   Lowering and very smoky all day. Wind very fresh from the Southward in the forenoon but quite calm afterwards.

11.   Raining a little, and misting all the forenoon, which ceased in the Afternoon, but still kept cloudy. Wind variable but for the most part about North.

12.   Cloudy Morning with but little Wind. Clear afternoon with the wind fresh at No. West & Cold.

13.   Ground hard froze—but the morning calm, clear and pleasant. The afternoon raw & cold with the Wind fresh from So. West & very cloudy. In the Night Snow abt. an Inch deep.

14.   Cloudy all day, & sometimes dropg. Rain. Wind being Eastwardly & fresh.

15.   Wind Eastwardly—from thence shifting to North & No. Wt. Constant Snow about abt. Sun rise till 12 or one Oclock then ceasing but cloudy & cold afterwards.

16.   Wind blowing fresh & clear all day from the No. West.

17.   Ground hard froze and Morning Cool. Wind being fresh from the No. West. Afternoon being pleast. & little Wind—also clear.

18.   Clear, warm & pleasant, there being but little Wind.

19.   Cloudy all day—till Evening at least with much appearance of Rain in the Morning, but high Wind at No. West in the afternoon.

20.   Clear & pleasant Morning with the Wind at South but lowering Afternoon & very cloudy Evening.

21.   The Morning was fine, but the Wind and Weather was variable. Afterwards sometimes cloudy & then clear & sometimes calm & then the Wind woud be fresh.

22.   Wind at No. West and very hard. Snowd fast till abt. 9 or 10 Oclock then clear and cold. Wind still high.

23.   Clear, and hard frost. Morning calm and pleasant but high & boisterous wind in the Afternoon from the No. West.

24.   Ground very hard froze. The morning again clear and calm but the Wind hard from the No. West after 9 Oclock.

25.   Clear, calm, warm and pleasant in the Evening. The Wind blew pretty fresh from the Southward.

26.   Very smoky. Calm and some appearance of Rain, but none fell till in the Night & not much then.

27.   Close warm Morning, & Rain (tho not hard) about 10 or 11 Oclock. No. Wind and the Afternoon clear.

28.   Clear & still Morning with some Wind in the Afternoon from the Westward.

29.   Hazy but pleasant notwithstanding. Wind westwardly & fresh.

30.   Clear & pleasant with but little wind.

31.   Clear and pleasant with but little wind and that Southwardly.

Remarks & Occurans. in Mar.

6th.   Joseph Gort a stone Mason came here to raise Stone.
     Began to Enlist Corn Ground at Muddy hole Plantation.
     Began to Enlist Ditto in the Neck that is to lay of the Ground.
     Began the same Work at Doeg Run Plantation.

Goart worked one month and was paid £3 as he and GW had agreed on 2 Feb. (LEDGER A, 314). But, instead of cutting stone in GW's quarry, Goart took it from quarries on George William Fairfax's land, where the stone could be obtained much more easily. Fairfax allowed his quarries to be used as a favor to GW and charged him nothing for that privilege (GW to Fairfax, 27 June 1770, IaST).

26. Countess a hound Bitch after being confind sometime got loose and was lined before it was discovered by my Water dog once and a small foist looking yellow cur twice.

GW had paid £1 16s. for a spaniel on 5 Feb. (LEDGER A, 302).

28. She was lined by Ranger a dog I had from Mr. Fairfax.
   I planted three french Walnuts in the New Garden, & on that side next the work House.

FRENCH WALNUT: *Juglans regia,* now the English walnut but often called the French or Eurasian walnut.

[April]

Where & how my time is Spent

Apl. 1. Went to Pohick Church and returnd home to Dinner.

2. Rid to see Mr. Humphrey Peake who lay ill. Returnd to Dinner.

3. Rid to see Mr. Peake again with Mrs. Washington. Returnd to Dinner.

4. Rid to the Mill—Doeg Run and Muddy hole.

5. Rid into the Neck and called to see Mr. Peake in my way.

6. Went a hunting but found nothing. Returnd to Dinner.

7. Run round the Lines of the Land I bought of the Ashfords. In the Evening Doctr. Craik his Wife and daughter & Mr. Phil Fendall came here.

Dr. James Craik had married Mariamne Ewell (1740–1814), daughter of Charles Ewell of Prince William County, in Nov. 1760. Her mother, Sarah Ball Ewell, was a granddaughter of GW's maternal grandfather, Joseph Ball. The Craiks eventually had nine children, of whom three were daughters: Nancy, Sarah, and Mariamne (HAYDEN, 341–43).
   Philip Richard Fendall (b. 1734) was at this time a merchant and clerk of court in Charles County, Md. (MD. ARCHIVES, 62:280, 462). Son of Benjamin and Elinor Lee Fendall, he had married his cousin Sarah Lettice Lee, daughter of Squire Richard Lee of Blenheim, Charles County, Md. (LEE [1], 108 n.20).

8.   Major Wagener came here to Dinner, & the others went away after.

9.   Major Wagener went away after breakfast. I rid to Muddy hole & from thence to the Mill.

10.   Miss Polly Washington set of home. I rid to the Genl. Muster at Cameron.

Polly Washington must be Mary Townshend Washington, who apparently continued at Mount Vernon after her father and the rest of her party left on 1 Mar. General musters of county militias during this period were held once a year in March or April. Because GW was a county magistrate and held no rank in the Fairfax militia, he was exempt by law from attending its musters (HENING, 7:534, 8:242–45). He probably went to Cameron today to see friends or to conduct some business (LEDGER A, 314).

11.   Rid to Doeg Run Qrs. & returnd to Dinner. Mr. John West came in the Afternoon.

12.   Mr. West & I run and markd the Dividing Line between my Part & that of Spencer's Tract at least began to do it but cd. not finish it.

GW had long been frustrated in attempts to plot accurately the dividing line between the two halves of the Spencer-Washington grant, because about 1741 the northern boundary of the grant had been moved south nearly 200 rods to accommodate other grants (R. O. Brooke's survey, c.1741, CALLAHAN, facing p. 3). Thus, GW did not know whether to run the line as if it were coming from the center of the original northern boundary as stipulated in the 1690 division or from the center of the revised boundary (survey and division by George Brent, 18 Sept. and 23 Dec. 1690, ViMtV). In addition, many of the marking trees mentioned in the old surveys had disappeared or could not be found (survey by GW, 1–2 Oct. 1759, ViMtV). Determined to establish at last the exact western boundary of the Mount Vernon tract, GW had invited John West, Jr., and Thomas Hanson Marshall, the two gentlemen who now owned the portions of the old Spencer tract lying on the line, to join him in making the survey begun today. Marshall declined to come, giving first his own illness and then his wife's as his excuse, probably a legitimate one in the latter case, at least, because Mrs. Marshall died 5 Dec. 1770 (Marshall to GW, 8 and 11 April 1770, DLC:GW; GERALD, 173). None of the Spencer tract now remained in that family's possession, Col. Nicholas Spencer's grandson William having sold it in various parcels 1738–39. Those besides West and Marshall who now owned parts of the tract were Daniel French, Harrison Manley, the Wade sisters, and GW.

13.   We finished to day what we began yesterday & he and Mr. Robt. Adam dined and lodged here.

GW and West probably decided to use Brent's original dividing line, running it as accurately as possible, because West's and Marshall's tracts had been bought from William Spencer before the northern boundary had been changed (deed of Spencer to George Harrison, 25–26 May 1739, Prince William County Deeds, Book D, 94–100, Vi Microfilm; deed of Spencer to Thomas Marshall, 20–21 Nov. 1739, Prince William County Deeds, Book D, 289–94, Vi Microfilm).

14.   Rid to the Mill & fishing Landg. at Poseys. Mr. Stedlar came in the afternoon and Mr. West & Mr. Adam went away in the Morng. before breakfast.

Rid to the Mill & came home by the Fishery at Poseys, found Mr. Stedlar here; & in the Afternoon the Stone Masons came to go about my Mill.

STONE MASONS: See "Remarks" entry for 14 April 1770.

15.   At home all day. Mr. Grayson came here in the Afternoon.

William Grayson had brought suit in Fairfax County court against John Ballendine for recovery of a debt, and the case was to be heard on the following day along with several similar cases involving creditors of Ballendine (Fairfax County Order Book for 1770–72, 4, Vi Microfilm).

16.   Went up to Alexandria to Court & stayed all Night.

The court met 16–17 April. On this day John Ballendine, having been convicted in several cases of debt and being insolvent, was committed to the county jail. After staying there for 20 days, he could, according to law, be released by a warrant from two or more justices, and his creditors could then sue to have his property seized and sold for their benefit (Fairfax County Order Book for 1770–72, 1–15, Vi Microfilm; HENING, 8:329).

17.   Returnd home in the Afternoon with Mr. Josh. Gallaway, & Colo. R. Lee.

In court today Thomas Montgomerie of Dumfries had recorded a letter from Margaret Savage which granted him power of attorney in her affairs (Fairfax County Order Book for 1770–72, 15, Vi Microfilm). Mrs. Savage's husband had apparently coerced or coaxed her into taking this step, which put her trustees, GW and Bryan Fairfax, in the awkward position of having to demand payment of her annuity from Montgomerie as Dr. Savage's agent and then giving the money to him as Mrs. Savage's legal representative. Knowing that Montgomerie had no obligation to send Mrs. Savage her money, GW and Fairfax tried to postpone dealing with him until they could get some clarification of the matter from Mrs. Savage (GW to Bryan Fairfax, 12 Dec. 1770; GW to Margaret Savage, 5 Sept. 1771; and Margaret Savage to GW, 19 Aug. 1772, DLC:GW).

   Joseph Galloway (c.1731–1803) of Philadelphia was a rich and powerful lawyer with scholarly tastes. At this time he was Speaker of the Pennsylvania

Assembly and vice-president of the American Philosophical Society. He also had a great interest in western lands and was a member of the Grand Ohio Company, commonly known as the Walpole Company.

18.   The above Gentlemen went away after breakfast. Patsy Custis, & Milly Posey went to Colo. Mason's to the Dancing School. Mr. Magowan who I found here yesterday stayed. Mr. Ball & one of his People set in to Work today—as did the Mason's to raising stone yesterday.

GW today paid Francis Christian £2 to admit Patsy and Milly to his school (LEDGER A, 314). Christian's dancing classes often lasted several days in each home, and the days were usually long. In a class which he held in Westmoreland County in 1773, "the Scholars" began soon after breakfast by having "their Lesson singly round." Then, "there were several Minuets danced with great ease and propriety; after which the whole company Joined in country-dances." The class continued until 7:30 P.M. with breaks for dinner and candle lighting. Christian was observed to be "punctual, and rigid in his discipline, so strict indeed that he struck two of the young Misses for a fault in the course of their performance" (FITHIAN, 44–45).
   MR. BALL: see "Remarks" for 16 and 18 April 1770.

19.   Mr. Magowan & Mr. Adam dind here. The Mason's began to Dig the foundation of my Mill at 2/6 pr. day. I rid to the Mill & doeg Run.

20.   Rid to see Mr. Peake who was Sick from thence to the Mill & home by Posey's. Mr. Adams dind here.

21.   Rid to where they were digging the foundation of my Mill and home again by the Millwright and the fishery at Poseys.

22.   At home all day. Mr. Adam & Doctr. Rumney dined here and the latter lodged here also & Captn. Posey.

23.   Rid to see Mr. Peake, from thence to Muddy hole & Doeg Run to the Mill & then home by the fishg. Landing. Mr. Adam dined and lodgd here. Captn. Posey also lodgd here.

Although the strip of land on which Posey's house and ferry were located was still involved in the court suit of John West, Jr., GW today agreed to rent it from Posey for £10 a year (LEDGER A, 256). Posey apparently moved to Queenstown on the Eastern Shore of Maryland some time during the next year (John Posey to GW, 25 May 1771, DLC:GW).

24.   Went the same Round as yesterday. Captn. McCarty & Captn. Posey dined here & the Doctr. lodgd here.

25. The Doctr. went away after breakfast and I rid the same round. Colo. Robt. Fairfax calld here in the forenoon but did not stay dinner.

26. Rid my usual rounds before Dinner and the same after dinnr.

27. Went to Belvoir—dined and returnd afterwards.

28. Rid to the Millwrights Mill, & to Mr. Peakes before dinner and to the fishery at Posey, & to the Mill again in the afternoon.

29. At home all day. Doctr. Rumney dined and lodged here & Mr. Matthw. Campbell lodged here.

30. The Doctr. stayed till after dinner and then returnd to Alexandria. I rid to the Mill & my usual rounds before dinner and to the Mill after Dinner.

Acct. of the Weather in April

April 1. Raw & cold Wind at No. Et. with great appearances (sometimes of falling Weather—at other times clear).

2. This Morning the Snow was an Inch or two deep & continued Snowing (fine Snow) all day with the Wind Northwardly & cold but the Snow did not Increase much in depth.

3. Clear and very cold, the Wind blowing hard at No. West notwithstanding wch. the Snow was almost wholely gone before Night.

4. The Ground froze very hard. The Weather clear and exceeding cold. The Wind blowing fresh at No. West.

5. Wind still Westwardly & cool, but not equal to the former days.

6. Warm and pleasant, tho the Wind was still Westwardly and fresh.

7. Cool. Wind blowing fresh at No. West. Weather clear.

8.   Lowering & much like Snow. Wind blowing cold & Raw from the No. & N. Et.

9.   Cold & disagreeable Wind blowing fresh from the No. West again.

10.   Just such a day as yesterday but if anything colder.

11.   Wind still in the same place but not so cold as yesterday.

12.   Wind at So. West and Weather warmer than the preceeding days.

13.   Wind at South, the day very hot & sultry—with thunder, lightning & a Shower of Rain about three oclock.

14.   Cooler than yesterday & lowering with the Wind abt. No. Et. In the Afternoon it began Raining & continued to do so more or less through the Night.

15.   Misty & lowering all day with but little Wind & that from the Southward.

16.   Lowering Morning but clear & Warm afterwards, the Wind being southwardly.

17.   Also warm, notwithstanding the Wind was westwardly & varying to the North and blowing very fresh.

18.   Cold & Raw all day. Wind Eastwardly in the Morning & Southwardly afterwards—much like Rain.

19.   Clear & pleasant weather turning warm again.

20.   Clear & warm in the forenoon—it being still. But cooler in the Afternoon. Wind being tolerably fresh from the Eastward.

21.   Warm and still all the day till the Afternoon, then a floury of wind which soon subsided.

22.   Very warm and still with some appearances of Rain.

23.   Very warm in the forenoon clear and still with severe wind & some Rain from the No. West just at Night.

24.   Wind at No. West & cool compard with the preceeding days.

25.   Wind Northwardly & cool in the M[orning] but warmer in the afternoon. Wind shifting Southwardly.

26.   Something warmer than yesterday but rather cool still. Wind fresh from the Southeast & cloudy in the afternoon.

27.   Wind pretty brisk & cool from the southward. Day cloudy and from abt. 4 Oclock in the Afternoon slow Rain.

28.   Morning Calm, clear and pleast. Afterwards cool & windy from the Northwest.

29.   High Wind from the Northwest all day, & cold.

30.   Wind in the same place and very cold & hard. A smart frost this morning.

Remarks & Occurrances in Apl.

9th.   Finished listing Ground for Corn at Muddy hole.
   The Hound Bitch Singer was lind by Jowler.

11.   The Bitch Truelove was lined twice by Ringwood. She had been frequently shut up with forrister – but it is thought he never lined her.

13.   Forrister was seen lined to Truelove.
   Began my Fishery at Poseys for Mr. Robt. Adam.

14.   She was again lined by Ringwood and Singer I saw lined by Jowler.
   This day I began to draw the Water of my Meadow by breaking the Dam or stop that confind it.
   Hull & the other Stone Mason came here to set about my Mill – but did not began work till the 17th.

GW is having his old millpond drained. John Hull was paid £31 15s. 1d. in September for work done on the new mill, which probably included wages for both stonemasons between April and September. Hull's partner could be Joseph Goart, who continued doing occasional work for GW through the spring of the next year (LEDGER A, 320, 333, 340).

15.   Singer was again lined by Jowler & Truelover by Ringwood.

16.   Mr. Ball the Millwright and one of his People came here to work.

Ball at one time or another had five of his own men working on the mill: Thomas Ball for 38½ days, Richard Talbott for 31 days, John Grinstead for 24½ days, Reason Porter for 19½ days, and Edward Todd for 9 days. The helper who came this day was probably Grinstead, Porter, or Todd. Ball himself worked for 38 days on the mill (LEDGER A, 324).

17.   Hull & his Partner began to raise stone.

18.   Ball and his Apprentice set abt. the shaft for the Mill &ca. Jowler lined Singer & Ringwood Truelove again.

The shaft was the large wooden axle on which the waterwheel was to turn.

19.   The Mason's went to digging the foundation of my Mill at 2/6 pr. day. Jowler lined Singer & Forrister lined truelove.

20.   Jowler again lined Singer.

21.   Richd. Talbot & one other of Ball's hands came here in the Afternoon.

23.   Began to Plant Corn in the Neck—at Muddy hole, and at Doeg Run.
    Mr. Ball, Talbot & Grinnel were levalling the Mill Race. His other hand went for their Tools to Cameron. T. Ball came this Aftern.
    Thomas Bird set to work on the foundation of the Mill at 1/3 pr. day.

GRINNEL: This name does not appear in GW's ledger for this year and may be a garbling of the last name of Ball's helper, John Grinstead. T. BALL: The John Ball who settled in Fauquier County in 1771 had a younger brother Thomas (SNODDY, 308; see main entry for 30 Dec. 1769).
    Thomas Byrd was paid £1 1s. 3d. in May for his work at the mill, and during the summer he received £3 15s. 6d. more for helping to harvest GW's wheat (LEDGER A, 321).

26.   He began to work on my Mill Race at 1/3 pr. Rod & to find himself and Sciagusta a prisoner from the Indians came here, and began to work with my People.

Work on the millrace began near the mill, and during the next year it progressed slowly north toward Piney Branch and the upper part of Dogue

Run. The race was dug several feet into the ground along its two-mile route, except where occasional low-lying areas had to be crossed. In those places earth embankments were raised to keep the water at a constant level, thus preventing any great lowering of the head of water at the mill. The sides of the race were probably supported by timber in both the banked and excavated sections (Lund Washington to GW, 2 Sept. 1778, ViMtV). TO FIND HIMSELF means that Byrd was to supply his own food. "Sciagusta did not work long, as he received but three shillings for his services" (DIARIES, 1:376 n.1; LEDGER A, 314). Other ditchers hired during the next two weeks to work on the millrace would prove to be no more eager to stick to this backbreaking task.

27.   As it Raind from abt. 3 or 4 Oclock in the Afternoon I presume work was stoped by the Millwrights and Masons.

28.   Clevelands Waggon & Team began to Work for me at [   ] pr. day.
   Reason—one of Balls Men did no work by a Boyl under his Arm.

James Cleveland's wagon and team worked ten days at 10s. a day between this date and 9 May. GW had also employed them on 19 and 20 April at 12s. 6d. a day, and on 15 April they had carried two loads for him at 1s. 6d. a load (LEDGER A, 312).

29.   Coxe Rice came to Work at the rate of 30/. pr. Month & Victuals found him.
   Reason Porter went to work again today.

Rice, who may have been hired to help with the mill, was to receive his meals as well as wages for his work, but it is apparent, as he is not mentioned in GW's ledger, that he quit before earning any money.

[May]

Where & how my time is Spent

May 1st.   Rid in the forenoon to where the Millwrights & Masons were at Work—also the Ditchers & the fish Landing at Poseys. In the afternoon rid to the Mill only. Mrs. W. Washington & her youngest Child & Mrs. Bushrod & Katy Washington came in the Eveng.

Mrs. Warner Washington's youngest child at this time was Catharine Washington (b. 1769). KATY WASHINGTON: Catherine Washington, daughter of the deceased Henry Washington of Middlesex County and niece of Mrs. Mildred Bushrod.

2. Mrs. Washington went to Belvoir & Mrs. Bushrod continued here. I rid to the Mill and Ditcher[s] in the forenoon, and afternoon.

3. Went the above rounds before dinner—but did not go out afterwards.

4. Rid to the Masons & Ditchers before dinner.

5. Rid to the Mill Rights—Masons & Ditchers before dinner, & to Doeg Run Qr.

6. At home all day. Colo. Robt. Fairfax Mrs. Fairfax Mrs. W. Washington & the two Miss Carlyles came from Belvoir & dined here. Colo. Fairfax Mrs. Fairfax & Nancy Carlyle returnd after dinr. Mrs. W. & Sally stayed.

7. Rid to the Mill ditchers, &ca. before dinner & to the Mill afterwards.

8. Went the same rounds again and promised the ditchers 18d. a Rod if they woud be brisk and stick to it.
   Miss Betty Ramsay & Milly Hunter also Anthy. Ramsay came here today. The latter returnd after dinner. The others stayed.

For GW's difficulties with the ditchers, see "Remarks" entries for 1–8 May 1770.
   Amelia Hunter, a daughter of the Alexandria physician John Hunter and his wife Elizabeth, married a Mr. Terrett sometime before May 1776 (will of John Hunter, 10 June 1763, Fairfax County Wills, Book B-1, 364–65, Vi Microfilm; will of George Hunter, 17 May 1776, Fairfax County Wills, Book C-1, 257–58, Vi Microfilm). Anthony Ramsay of Alexandria was a lawyer who had been admitted to the bar of the Fairfax County court 19 Feb. 1770 (Fairfax County Order Book for 1768–70, 286, Vi Microfilm). He may have been a son of William Ramsay and thus Betty Ramsay's brother.

9. Mr. Christian danced here—⟨who⟩ (besides his Scholars, and those already mentioned to be here) Mrs. Peake & Niece Mr. Massey—Mr. Piper & Mr. Adams dined here.

Mrs. Humphrey Peake's sister, Sarah Stonestreet, married Richard Edelin of Maryland; the niece is probably a daughter of that marriage, possibly Frances Edelin (see main entry for 28 Dec. 1771).
   Rev. Lee Massey (1732–1814), rector of Truro Parish 1767–77, lived at this time on the Occoquan with his first wife, Mary Johnston Massey, daughter of George and Mary Johnston of Alexandria (will of Mary Johnston, 20 Nov. 1769, Fairfax County Wills, Book C-1, 73, Vi Microfilm; Mason

Family Bible, MASON [2], 1:480–81). After her death he married a Miss Burwell, who soon died also; he then married Elizabeth Bronaugh of Prince William County (MEADE [1], 2:239–40). A lawyer in early life, Massey had been chosen successor to Rev. Charles Green by the Truro vestrymen in Feb. 1766 and had been sent to England for ordination, officially becoming rector the next February (Truro Vestry Book, 110, 119, DLC).

10. Rid to the Mill. Mr. Christian & some of his scholars went away this afternoon. Mrs. W——n & Mrs. B[ushrod] went to B[elvoir].

11. The rest of the Scholars went away after breakfast. Mrs. Washn. & Mr. W. Washington came this Afternoon. Mr. Semple who came last Night went away after Bt. I rid to the Mill &ca. before & after Dinner.

12. At home all day. Mr. Stedlar here. Mr. & Mrs. Washington & Mrs. Bushrod went to Colchester & returnd in the Afternn.

13. Went to Church with all the Compy. here. Dind at Belvoir & returnd in the Afternoon.

14. Rid to Muddy hole to my Ditchers & the Mill. Mr. Washington wife & Child & Mrs. Bushrod &ca. went away.

15. Rid to the Ditchers & Mill before Dinner—at home afterwards.

16. Rid by Muddy hole to the Mill and to the Ditchers & came home by Poseys.

17. Rid to the Mill and Ditchers again.

18. Did the same. Returnd to Dinner with Mr. Ross. Found Mr. Ramsay there. Went in the Afternoon to McCartys Sale of Poseys Effects. He & Mr. Ramsay returnd with me & lodgd.

Daniel McCarty and Bryan Fairfax had given special bail for John Posey in several suits decided against him during Feb. 1770 (Fairfax County Order Book for 1768–70, 234–35, 305–14, Vi Microfilm).

19. Set of for Williamsburg—dind at Dumfries—calld at My Mothers and lodgd at Colo. Lewis's in Fredericksbg.

The burgesses were to begin meeting again on 21 May. Before GW left home, he gave Lund Washington, who was to be in charge of his business at Mount

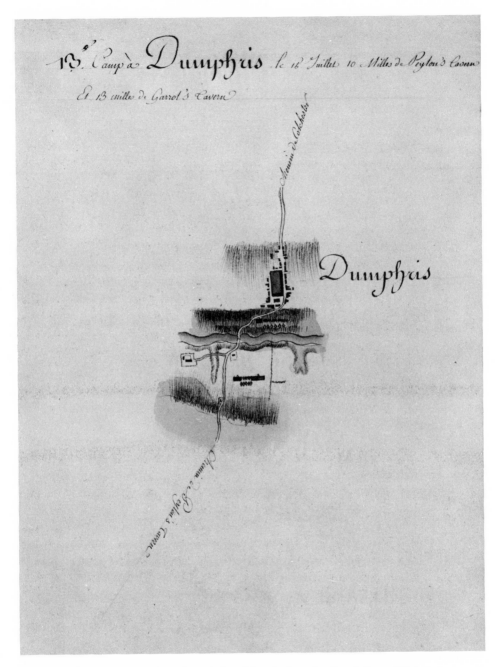

A French officer sketched this plan of Dumfries during the Revolution. (Map Division, Library of Congress)

Vernon while he was gone, £30 in cash to be accounted for (LEDGER A, 313, 314).

20.   Breakfasted at Mr. Bouchers–dind at Coleman's & lodgd at Todds bridge.

Jonathan Boucher had been trying for several years to obtain the rectorate of St. Anne's Parish in Annapolis, Md., which offered a better livelihood than he had in Caroline County. Now, through the influence of Rev. Henry Addison, he was near to achieving that aim. At breakfast on this day, he and GW apparently discussed the matter and agreed that, if the move was made, Jacky would go to Annapolis also and continue his schooling under Boucher there, provided that Mrs. Washington approved. But GW was unwilling to agree with the tutor on another point. Boucher had been recently urging the Washingtons to allow him to take Jacky on an extended tour of Europe be-ginning about 1772. GW did not dispute the educational advantages of such a tour, but he was concerned that its cost would be more than Jacky's estate could afford. Any decision about the trip, he told Boucher, would have to wait until he consulted friends in Williamsburg (Boucher to GW, 9 and 21 May 1770, DLC:GW; GW to Boucher, 2–9 June 1770, NN).

This Coleman tavern was probably at Bowling Green, on the main road from Fredericksburg to Williamsburg, about three miles from Caroline Court House (see main entry for 25 June 1770 and *Va. Gaz.*, R, 19 Oct. 1769). The Bowling Green tavern was owned by John Hoomes (d. 1805), "a very wealthy person" who was now living in Sussex County (RICE, 2:98, 176). He had advertised the tavern for lease during the previous October, and ap-parently a member of the local Coleman family, possibly Francis Coleman of Caroline Court House, had taken it over and had opened it since GW's last trip to Williamsburg, when he had eaten at the Court House (*Va. Gaz.*, R, 19 Oct. 1769). GW and most other travelers through this area preferred to stop at Bowling Green when the tavern there was open, because going to the Court House required a side trip of several miles.

21.   Breakfasted at King Wm. Ct. House & dind & lodgd at Eltham.

GW today spent 3s. at Ruffin's ferry and somewhere on his route bought a pair of shoes costing 6s. for the mulatto manservant, Billy, who accompanied him (LEDGER A, 314).

22.   Reached Williamsburg to Breakfast & dined at the Club at Mrs. Campb[ells] and supped at the Raleigh.

GW lodged at Mrs. Campbell's tavern for his stay in town. The House of Burgesses, which had convened the previous day as scheduled, dealt mostly with private bills during this session and transacted relatively "little business of a public nature" (GW to George W. Fairfax, 27 June 1770, IaST).

23.   Dined at Mrs. Dawson's and spent the Evening in my own Room.

24.   Dined at the Treasurers, & spent the Evening in my own Room.

Between this date and 29 May, GW bought four play tickets for 30s.; clubbed twice at the Raleigh, purchased a vial of red ink costing 1s. 3d., and paid 2s. for postage and coffee (LEDGER A, 314).

25.   Dined at the Palace & attended a Committee of the Association at Hayes. Spent the Eveng. there.

A general meeting of the Virginia nonimportation association had been held in Williamsburg 22 May, and a committee of 20 gentlemen, including GW, had been appointed to revise the agreement that the associators had signed the previous year (*Va. Gaz.*, R, 3 May 1770; CARTER [3], 1:418). Changes were needed, it was generally agreed, because the agreement was causing much confusion and dissatisfaction in the colony and there were many violations of its terms by Virginians. Men in some of the other colonies were complaining that "if some prudent steps are not taken to regulate importation, in a short time Virginia will be remarkable, only, for *resolving*" (*Va. Gaz.*, P&D, 14 June 1770, supp.). However, the members of the committee were deeply divided in opinion about how the nonimportation agreement should be changed. Some members, led by Treasurer Robert Carter Nicholas and Edmund Pendleton, wanted to moderate or abolish it as a gesture of compromise to Parliament for repealing all the disputed taxes except the one on tea. Other members insisted there could be no compromise of principle as long as the tea tax remained, and they favored strengthening the association's agreement with stricter terms and stricter means of enforcement (CARTER [3], 1:418). GW seems to have agreed with this last viewpoint, but he was willing to relax the association in order to obtain a more general adherence to it (GW to Jonathan Boucher, 30 July 1770, IEN; GW to Robert Cary & Co., 20 Aug. 1770, DLC:GW).

26.   Took a Snack at Mrs. Dawson's & went up to Eltham in the Afternn.

The House of Burgesses adjourned after today's meeting until 11:00 A.M. Monday, 28 May (H.B.J., 1770–72, 20).

27.   At Eltham all day.

28.   Returnd to Williamsburg by 9 Oclock. Dined at the Speakers and attended a Committee of the Associn. at Hayes till 11 Oclock.

29.   Dined at Mrs. Dawson's and spent the Evening in my own Room.

30.   Dined at the Club and spent the Eveng. in my own Room.

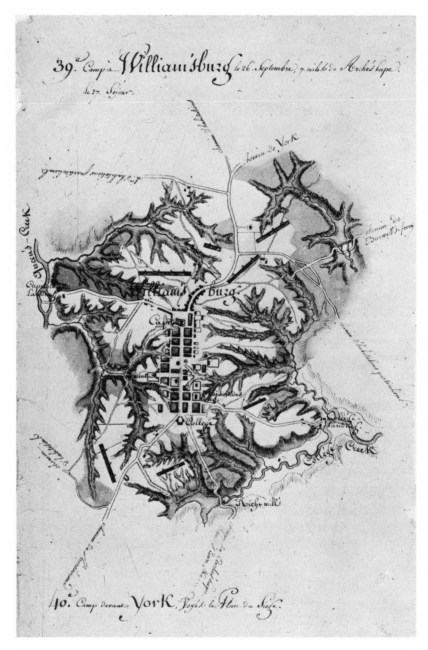

Although drawn a few years later, this map is a good depiction of Williamsburg during Washington's service in the House of Burgesses. (Princeton University Library, Berthier Papers)

May 1770

GW today paid £1 10s. to Col. John Henry (d. 1773), father of Patrick Henry, for a copy of his map of Virginia which had been published the previous February by Thomas Jefferys of London.

31.   Dined at the Attorneys and attended a Committee of the Association at Hayes till One Oclock.

Acct. of the Weather in May

May 1st.   A hard frost which destroyd all the Peaches &ca. from the Water. Wind still at No. Wt. & West but neither so cold nor hard as the two preceeding days.

2.   Calm and tolerably pleasant again altho the Morning was cool.

3.   Wind fresh and cool from the So. West—which shifted to the So. Et. and East, & began to Rain briskly abt. Sunset attended with thunder & Lightg.

4.   Very Cloudy, Misty & sometimes raining. Wind pretty fresh from the Northwest & cool.

5.   Cloudy in the forenoon, & cool. Wind being at No. West— but clear and warm afterwards with but little Wind.

6.   More moderate & pleasant in the forenoon—but cool & windy in the Evening—also Cloudy.

7.   Cool in the Morning but Hot afterwards with appearances of Rain.

8.   Very warm & clear in the forenoon with but little Wind—but a severe Gust of wind & Rain in the Afternn. from the So. West— which moderated abt. dark.

9.   Raining more or less all day with the wind fresh and variable.

10.   Drizzling several times with the Wind westwardly but not so cool as yesterday.

11.   Cloudy & sometimes Misty in the Afternoon. The forenoon clear & wind at No. West but variable.

12.   Cloudy & sometimes Misting in the Morning but clear and pleasant afterwards.

13.   Clear and very warm with but little Wind and that Southwardly.

14.   Very like for Rain in the Morning but cleard afterwards. Wind fresh all day from the East and cool—especially towards Night.

15.   A Lowery cloudy Morning but clear afternoon & tolerably warm.

16.   Much such a day as yesterday, but a good deal warmer.

17.   Misty kind of Morning but clear warm and calm afterwards.

18.   Clear and Warm in the forenoon with but little Wind which howevr. after a little sprinkle came out violent from the No. West & contd. so all the Afternoon.

19.   Clear & cool till abt. Noon. Wind blowg. fresh from No. West—then calm and warm. Eveng. still cool.

20.   Morning & Evening Cool. Mid day warm—there being but little Wd.

21.   Still & Calm forenoon Wind pretty fresh from the Eastward afterwards.

22.   Clear and rather Cool Wind being fresh from the westward.

23.   Clear and still cool for the Season notwithstanding the wind was Southwardly.

24.   Warm with some appears. of Rain of which a little fell in the Night.

25.   Very warm. Wind being Southwardly—a little Rain in the Morning.

26. Wind very fast from the Westwd. all day and towards Evening Cool with appearances of Rain but none fell.

27. Cool and clear all day. Wind being still to the westward.

28. Lowering kind of a Morning but clear afterwards & cool all day.

29. Not as cool as yesterday. Wind variable with appearances of Rain.

30. Wind Eastwardly. Cool and cloudy with Rain towards Night which continued all Night.

31. Raining more or less all day with the wind westwardly.

Remarks & Occurs. in May

May 1st. John Harvey went to Ditchg. on my Mill Race at 1/3 pr. Rod.

Harvey settled 12 Aug. 1770 for £1 in return for his labor for GW (LEDGER A, 288).

2. The Mason's went to laying Stone in the walls of the water Pit (dry Stone). Mr. Flemings ship Carpenter finishd his work here and returnd home havg. been employd 31¼ days. Went to Flatting Sand &ca. round to the mill. Carrd a Load of sand this day.

The water pit was the trough in which the new mill's waterwheel was to turn. DRY STONE: The stones in the pit were fitted together without mortar. The ship carpenter was an indentured servant of Thomas Fleming (d. 1786), shipwright formerly of Annapolis and now of Alexandria. During the past several weeks, Fleming's carpenter had sheathed the bottom of GW's schooner and had made needed repairs (LEDGER A, 135, 314; LEDGER B, 10). FLATTING SAND &CA.: GW had materials needed by the stonemasons brought by flatboat up Dogue Creek to the site of the new mill. The sand was to be mixed with lime and water to form mortar needed to build the exterior walls of the mill.

3. Thomas Emmerson set into ditchg. on my Mill Race on the same terms as above that is 1/3 pr. Rod & finding himself. Finished planting Corn at Muddy hole Plantation.

Thomas Emmison had been hired by Lund Washington in 1764 to work on a mill then being built, apparently under Lund's general supervision, for

William Fitzhugh of Chatham, Stafford County (Lund Washington's account book, 1762–85, MdAN). Lund was probably also responsible for engaging Emmison to help dig GW's millrace, but Emmison, like Coxe Rice, must have done little or no work for GW; he, too, is not mentioned in GW's ledger.

4. Began to flat Stone round—as also to carry wood round for burning Lyme. William Crook began to Work on my Mill Race on the same terms above mentioned.

Freestone from George William Fairfax's quarries and firewood for GW's limekiln are now being brought upstream by the flatboats. GW had oyster shells burned in the kiln to produce lime for making mortar. William Crook was another ditcher who apparently did not stick to his task long enough to justify an entry for payment in GW's ledger.

5. Richard Talbot, one of Mr. Balls hands was absent from work. John Harvey was also absent from his ditching. Finished Planting Corn at Doeg Run Plantation this day—viz the 5th. Richd. Talbot was not at work but went up to Alexandria.

7. Got the Battoe, & the two Boats round to the Mill with stone. William Crook nor Thoms. Emmerson were at work on the Mill Race today.

8. Neither of the above Persons were at work on the Race to-day. But Abel Cellicoe and one of his Sons set into ditching on the Race. Finished Planting of Corn in the Neck this day. Got two Boats load of Lime, Wood & one of Stone to the Mill—but the Battoe was stopd by Wind.

Abel Callico had worked for Lund Washington on Fitzhugh's mill in 1764, but neither he nor his son proved to be of much help in digging GW's mill-race, as they also failed to merit any pay (Lund Washington's account book, 1762–85, 36, MdAN).

9. Dischargd Clevelands Waggon. Ball & his People Went about 12 Oclock to Framing the Mill Work.

10. Mr. Christian went away this afternoon. I rid to the Mill.

11. Eight hands were at work upon dry Mill Race today.

GW had given up hiring ditchers and had set some of his slaves to digging the race.

12. Seven hands were at Work this day upon my Mill Race.

14. Ten or Eleven hands were at Work to day.

15. About 10 hands at Work to day on the Race.

16. Jonathan Palmer and his Family movd to Poseys to live. Abt. 7 hands at Work to day.

17. 10 hands at work to day. The H⟨oist⟩ frame & Mill beam were put up to day. Began also to raise Scaffolds for the Masons this day.

18th. Mr. Ball & his People went into the Woods again to get Scantling to carry on his work there not being sufft. for that purpose.

The scantling was being taken for the new mill from the land Thomas Hanson Marshall had agreed to give GW in exchange for the Maryland property GW had bought from Robert Alexander. This was the most convenient location from which to get the timber. However, because Alexander had not yet given Marshall either use of or title to the land in Maryland, the deal was still pending, and GW was obliged to pay Marshall £5 for the trees cut here. Most of the timber for the mill had been obtained during the previous summer from land belonging indisputably to GW (LEDGER A, 139; GW to Marshall, 16 Mar. 1770, DLC:GW).

19. Set of for Williamsburg to the Assembly.

[June]

Where & how my time is Spent

June 1st. Dined at the Club at Mrs. Campbells (Williamsburg) and attended a Meeting of the Association at the Capitol at 6 Oclock & contd. there till Eleven Oclock.

At this general meeting, it was resolved "THAT a friendly Invitation be given to all Gentlemen Merchants, Traders, and others, to meet the associators, in *Williamsburg*, on *Friday* the 15th Instant, in order to consult and advise touching an ASSOCIATION, and to accede thereto in such Manner as may best answer the Purposes of the same" (*Va. Gaz.*, R, 31 May 1770).

2. Dined at the Club & spent the Evening in my own Room.

GW wrote to Jonathan Boucher on this date, telling him that he had discussed the proposed European tour with several gentlemen in town and they had confirmed his suspicion that the expense would exceed Jacky's income. But he did not close the door on the matter. He would gladly approve the trip, he said, if a way could be found to reduce its cost and to gain the concurrence of the General Court (GW to Boucher, 2–9 June 1770, NN).

Consideration of the tour would drag on inconclusively for several months.
GW on this date paid accounts with a Williamsburg tailor and a blacksmith (LEDGER A, 318).

3.   Dined at the Club and spent the Evening in my own Room.

The burgesses were again adjourned for Sunday (H.B.J., 1770–72, 44).

4.   Dined at the Club and spent the Evening at the Councills Ball at the Capitol.

GW today paid Edmund Pendleton £1 1s. 6d. for a legal opinion on John West, Jr.'s agreement to sell his land adjoining Mount Vernon (LEDGER A, 318). The council's ball was held this evening in honor of the king's birthday. Attending, besides the members of the council, were the governor, the burgesses, and "the magistrates and other principal inhabitants" of Williamsburg (*Va. Gaz.*, P&D, 7 June 1770).

[5.]   Dined at the Club & spent the Evening in my own Room.

6.   Dined at the Club and spent the Evening in my own Room.

7.   Dined with the Council and spent the Evening in my own Room.

8.   Dined at the Club and Spent the Evening in my own Room.

9.   Had a cold Cut at Mrs. Campbells and went up to Eltham in the afternoon.

The burgesses adjourned today until Monday morning, 11 June (H.B.J., 1770–72, 61).

10.   Dined at Eltham and in the Afternoon went to see Mrs. Dandridge & returnd to Eltham again.

11.   Went over to Colo. Thos. Moores Sale & purchasd two Negroes—to Wit Frank & James & returnd to Eltham again at Night.

All of Moore's estate, including 26 slaves and about 1,000 acres of land on the Mattaponi River, was offered for sale at West Point today in order to pay some of his many debts (*Va. Gaz.*, R, 31 May 1770). The Negro Frank cost £31 and James, a boy, cost £55. GW also bought a bay mare at the sale for £8 5s. All sums were credited against Moore's debt to the Custis estate (LEDGER A, 204).

12.   Came to Williamsburg to Breakfast. Dined at the Club and spent the Evening in my own Room.

13. Dined at the Club and spent the Evening in my own Room.

GW on this date received £357 10s. in cash from Joseph Valentine, manager of the Custis plantations (LEDGER A, 318).

14. Dined at the Speakers and went to Bed by 8 Oclock.

15. Dined at the Treasurers and went to a meeting of the Association at which till 11 Oclock then wt. to Bed.

The treasurer of the colony today gave GW £70 on an order from Richard Starke, clerk of the committees of privileges and elections and of propositions and grievances. Starke had given this order to GW 21 Dec. 1769 to pay two years' rent on a house and lots belonging to Jacky Custis, where Starke's mother lived (LEDGER A, 303, 318; GW to Starke, 14 Dec. 1767, DLC:GW). The treasurer also gave GW £4 19s. 6d. on this date as his bounty for making hemp (LEDGER A, 318; see entry for 7 Aug. 1765).

16. Dined at the Club at Mrs. Campbells and went to the Play in the Evening.

GW today paid 6s. 3d. to a blacksmith and spent 15s. 6d. for tickets and other expenses at the play (LEDGER A, 318).

The American Company of Comedians had arrived in town from Philadelphia on 13 June and today opened the theater with *The Beggar's Opera* and "other entertainments" (*Va. Gaz.*, P&D, 14 June 1770). Written by the English playwright John Gay (1685–1732), *The Beggar's Opera* is a burlesque of conventional Italian opera, "a Newgate pastoral, among the whores and thieves there." It was first performed in 1728 and became one of the most popular plays of the century, being included in the repertoire of almost every English acting company (GAY, 1–4).

17. Went to Church in the Forenoon & from thence to Colo. Burwells where I dind & lodgd.

The day being Sunday, the burgesses did not meet (H.B.J., 1770–72, 77). GW probably attended Bruton Parish Church before going to dine at Kingsmill.

18. Came into Williamsburg in the Morning. Dined at the Club and went to the Play in the Afternoon.

In the House of Burgesses today a bill for dividing Frederick Parish was referred to a special committee of six members, one of whom was GW (H.B.J., 1770–72, 78–79). No expenses for the play appear under this date in GW's ledger, but he did record paying the jeweler James Craig £1 10s. for a pair of gold earrings for Patsy Custis and £2 15s. for other merchandise. GW also bought Patsy a tortoiseshell comb costing 3s. 7½d. (LEDGER A, 318; receipt from Craig, ViHi: Custis Papers; CUSTIS ACCOUNT BOOK).

19. Dined at the Club and went to the Play.

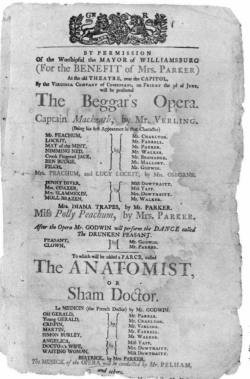

Playbill for a performance of *The Beggar's Opera* in Williamsburg. (Colonial Williamsburg Photograph)

GW on this date spent 7s. 6d. for a play ticket and paid several small accounts in town: 5s. 7d. to Anthony Hay, £2 19s. 6d. to the printer William Rind, and 10s. to the saddler Alexander Craig (LEDGER A, 318).

20.   Dined at the Presidents and went to the Play afterwards.

The House of Burgesses on this date gave permission to GW and two other members to be absent for the remainder of the session (H.B.J., 1770–72, 83). GW spent £1 today for play tickets and discharged two old debts totaling almost £88: one for lottery tickets sold for the benefit of Bernard Moore and the other for shingles bought of John Washington of Suffolk (LEDGER A, 318).

21.   Dined at the Club at Mrs. Campbells at 8 Oclock & went to Bed directly after.

GW today received £60 15s. 6d. from the treasurer of the colony in payment for his burgess's wages and traveling expenses since 30 April 1769 (LEDGER A, 191, 303).

22.   Dined at the Club and went to the Play after meeting the Associates at the Capitol.

On this day a new nonimportation agreement was signed by 164 persons, including GW, and a copy was sent to Governor Botetourt. The new association, GW wrote to George W. Fairfax on 27 June, "is form'd, much upon the old plan, but more relax'd" (IaST). Previously prohibited items now to be allowed included barley, pork, sugar, pewter, trinkets and jewelry, plate and gold, bridles, and cheap hats, shoes, boots, and saddles. Price limitations on several types of cheap cloth were eased somewhat, but horses were added to the list of prohibited imports. To enforce the agreement, the associators in each county were to elect a committee of five men, who would inspect invoices and other papers relating to imports and publish the names of signers who violated the terms (a printed copy of the agreement is in DLC: GW). GW, like many Virginians, was not entirely pleased with this compromise plan, but he was satisfied that "it was the best that the friends to the cause coud obtain . . . and tho too much relaxd from the Spirit, with which a measure of this sort ought to be conducted, yet, will be attended with better effects (I expect) than the last; inasmuch as it will become general, & adopted by the Trade" (GW to Jonathan Boucher, 30 July 1770, IEN).

Joseph Valentine today paid GW £52 10s. in cash (LEDGER A, 318).

23.   Dined at Mrs. Campbells & set off homewards after it— reaching Colo. Bassetts.

In the House of Burgesses today, the report of the committee on the bill to divide Frederick Parish was given by James Mercer of Hampshire County. The house accepted several amendments suggested by the committee and ordered the bill to be engrossed. It was passed on the following day and was approved by the council soon afterwards (H.B.J., 1770–72, 94, 96, 98; HENING, 8:425–28). Before GW left Williamsburg, he paid several more bills, including £2 for play tickets, probably for the previous day's performance; £3 7s. 6d. to his barber George Lafong; £16 13s. 4d. for lodging and food at Mrs. Campbell's tavern; and 14s. to the printers Alexander Purdie and John Dixon (LEDGER A, 318; receipt from Christiana Campbell, NNPM). The House of Burgesses remained in session until 28 June.

24.   Dined at Todds bridge & lodged at Hubbards.

25.   Breakfasted at the Bolling green. Dined at Colo. Lewis's and lodgd at my Mothers.

GW ate breakfast in Coleman's tavern. During the day he paid 8s. to a blacksmith and gave his mother 7s. (LEDGER A, 318).

26.   Breakfasted at my Mothers and dined at home before three Oclock.

27.   Rid to Muddy hole Doeg Run and the Mill before Dinner & to where my People were cuttg. Hay at the upper Meadow.

A miniature of Col. Burwell Bassett by Charles Willson Peale. (Society of the Cincinnati, Anderson House Museum)

28.   Rid into the Neck between breakfast and Dinner. Mr. Addison and Mr. Boucher, who came yesterday in the Afternoon went away today after Breakfast.

Jonathan Boucher had been installed as rector of St. Anne's Parish in Annapolis 12 June, and now, accompanied by his sponsor Rev. Henry Addison, he was returning to Caroline County to settle his affairs there (ST. ANN'S, 10:135; BOUCHER [1], 59–60). Mrs. Washington had by this time given her permission for Jacky to go with him to Annapolis, and GW today paid Boucher £75 on the boy's account (LEDGER A, 318).

29.   Dined at Belvoir. Went on Board the Boston frigate to Drink Tea and returnd in the Afternoon.

The *Boston* was a British man-of-war commanded by Sir Thomas Adams. Sent from England to serve three years on station in American waters, she had arrived at Hampton in early March of this year (*Va. Gaz.*, P&D, 2 Nov. 1769 and 8 Mar. 1770).

30.   Went into the Neck between breakfast and Dinner.

Acct. of the Weather in June

June 1st.   Cloudy & Misty all day. In the Evening a pretty hard shower of Rain.

2.   Clear & exceeding pleasant — being also Warm & growing.

3.   Clear & pleasantly warm. The Wind being at So. West & rather fresh in the Afternoon.

4.   Clear in the forenoon but cloudy & lowering afterwards with the Wind westwardly.

5.   Lowering Morning & sometimes slight Showers—with the Wind about Southwest.

6.   Clear and pleasant with the wind Eastwardly, which occasiond towards Night a lowering sky & Cool Air.

7.   Raining more or less all day & sometimes very hard. Wind Eastwardly but not very cool.

8.   Cloudy & now and then Misty. In the Evening very hard rain. Wind abt. So. West.

9.   Very warm with but little Wind & that southwardly. In the Eveng. a little Rain.

10.   Winds variable in the Afternoon & all Night Rain.

11.   Raining till 10 Oclock with the Wind at So. Et. Afterwards clear with little or no wind.

12.   Clear and Cool. Wind Westwardly.

13.   Wind Southwardly and very warm & sultry—especially in the Afternoon—with appears. of Rain.

14.   Wind Northwardly, & Cool in the Morning—but warm afterwards.

15.   Clear, and tolerably pleasant Afternoon somewhat Cool.

16.   Clear & Pleasant forenoon. Appearances of Rain afterwards but none Fell.

17.   Cloudy forenoon—but clear afterwards and very warm, wind Eastwardly.

18.   Calm and clear till the Afternoon then Showers—but very hot.

19.   Warm and sometimes slight Showers.

20.   Clear and Warmer in the Afternn.

21.   Lowering Morning, but clear day and Warm.

22.   Forenoon clear—Afternoon promising Rain, but none fell. Both very warm.

23.   Very warm with Clouds and a little Rain at Night.

24.   Cool & cloudy with a good deal of Rain about Noon. Wind fresh & variable.

25.   Cool and clear. Wind Northwardly & fresh.

26.   Clear and not very warm. Wind at So. West.

27.   Clear and warm with the Wind Southwardly. Some appearances of Rain but none fell.

28.   Lowering Morning but clear afterwards and Hott.

29.   Clear and very warm. Wind being southwardly and but little of it.

30.   Cooler than yesterday. Wind being fresh from the westward.

Remarks & Occurans. in June

June 25.   Began to cut my Meadow at Doeg Run Quarter.

29.   Finish'd it, & got the Hay all Stack'd.

30.   Got my Mill Walls up to the 2d. Floor of the House—and then quitted it for Harvest.

   Began my Wheat Harvest in the Neck.

This fragment of remarks and occurrences is in the possession of the superintendent of schools, Exeter, N.H.

[July]

Where & how my time is Spent

July 1st. At home—Sir Thomas Adams—the two Colo. Fairfax's & Mr. Waker a Midshipman dined here.

2.   Went into my Wheat field before diner. Mr. Davis a Midshipman dined here.

3.   One of the Bostons Midshipmen breakfasted here. Between breakfast and Dinner I went into my Harvest field.

4.   Went into my Harvest field between breakfast and Dinner.

5.   Sir Thomas Adams and Mr. Glasford his first Lieutt. Breakfasted here. Sir Thos. returnd after it, but Mr. Glasford dined here as did the 2 Lieutt. Mr. Sartell Mr. Johnston of Marines Mr. Norris & Mr. Richmore—two Midshipmen.

6.   At home all day. Mr. Stedlar came to dinner. Mr. Wallace Burser to the Boston came in the Afternoon & purchased & Killed my Bull—the 4 quarters of which weighed 710 lbs. Nett.

MY BULL: see "Remarks" entry for 6 July 1770.

7.   At home all day. In the Afternoon Mr. Edward Smith came.

This visitor may be Edward Smith (1752–1826), a son of John Smith of Cabin Point (TYLER [2], 49, 99–100).

8.   Went to Pohick Church & returnd to Dinner. Mr. Smith went to Colo. Fairfax's & returnd to Dinner & Mr. Stedlar went away after Breakft.

GW had paid Stedlar £21 10s. on the previous day for music lessons given to Jacky and Patsy Custis. Today he let Patsy have £2 2s. pocket money and her friend Milly Posey 7s. 6d. (LEDGER A, 319).

9.   Warm with but little Wind & that Southwardly. Rid to Belvoir to Breakfast in order to take leave of Sir Thos. Adams & Colo. R. Fairfax who was going to the Springs. Returnd by the Mill, Doeg Run & Muddy hole Plantations to Dinr.

10.   Clear and pleasant. In the Afternoon rid to the Harvest field at Muddy hole. On my return found Mr. Montgomerie & Sally Carlyle here.

11.   Mr. Montgomerie went away about 11 Oclock. Mr. Christian & all his scholars except Miss French came here to Dancing—also Miss Bronaugh.

Elizabeth French, daughter of Daniel and Penelope Manley French, was a "celebrated Fortune . . . whom half the world was in pursuit of" for, as her father's only child, she would eventually bring all his land and wealth to the young man who married her (GW to Burwell Bassett, 15 Feb. 1773, NjMoNP). Elizabeth Bronaugh (1738–1805) of Prince William County, a cousin of George Mason, later became Rev. Lee Massey's third wife (HAYDEN, 534).

12.   Rid to my Harvest field at Muddy hole. Upon my return to Dinner found Mrs. Ambler & her daughter here who dind & went away afterwards.

Mary Cary Ambler (1732/33–1781) of Jamestown was a younger sister of Sally Fairfax and the widow of Edward Ambler (1732–1768). Mrs. Ambler and her daughter Sarah (1760–1782) were at this time visiting the Fairfaxes at Belvoir (CARY, 108).

13.   Mr. Christian and all his Scholars except Peggy Massey went away. I rid to the Harvest field at M. Hole.

Peggy Massey was a daughter of Rev. Lee Massey (DLC: Toner Collection).

14.   Rid to my Harvest People at the Mill in the forenoon & in the afternn. likewise with Mrs. W., Peggy Massey & P[atsy].

15.   At home all day alone except Miss Massey being here.

16.   Went to Alexandria to Court and returnd again in the Afternoon.

The court met only on this day in July. Because the governor and his council had issued a new commission of the peace for the Fairfax County court on 13 June, GW and the other justices present today took their oaths of office again as they were required to do (Fairfax County Order Book for 1770–72, 48–49, Vi Microfilm; VA. EXEC. JLS., 6:348). Commissions were reissued from time to time in order to add the names of new justices and eliminate those of the inactive or deceased.

   While GW was in town today he settled his tax account with William Adams, sub-sheriff for Fairfax Parish, and Augustus Darrell, sub-sheriff for Truro Parish. This year he paid 658 pounds of tobacco to the colony for 94 tithables at 7 pounds each, 846 pounds to Fairfax County for the same number of tithables at 9 pounds each, 1,000 pounds to Fairfax Parish for 20 tithables at 50 pounds each, and 4,662 pounds to Truro Parish for 74 tithables at 63 pounds each, or a total of 7,166 pounds of tobacco for his personal taxes this year. He also paid £1 10s. cash for the public tax on his chariot and chair and £2 16s. cash for miscellaneous fees (LEDGER A, 293, 319).

17.   At home all day. Major Wagener dined here, & went away in the Afternn.

18.   Rid to Harvest People at Doeg Run & returnd to Dinner.

19.   At home all day. Alone—except P[eggy] M[assey].

20.   Was riding out to the Mill &ca. met an Augusta Man with Horses with whom I returnd & purchasd four.

In GW's ledger entry for this date, he records purchasing horses from two men: David McCrae, two horses for £21 4s., and Samuel McChesney, two horses for £13 10s. (LEDGER A, 319). McChesney was a trader in Augusta County about this time (*Va. Gaz.*, Pi, 9 Feb. 1775).

21.   At home alone.

22.   At home all day alone except that Miss Massey, still here & Mr. Semple came just after we had dind & went away after dinner was got for him.

23.   Miss Massey went away, and in the Evening Mr. Boucher, Majr. Taylor and Jackey Custis came here.

Boucher was now moving from Caroline County to Annapolis, where Jacky, as had been agreed, was going also to continue his studies under Boucher's direction. Major Taylor may be James Taylor (1732–1814), Caroline County sheriff and militia officer (GRINNAN, 366–67; VA. EXEC. JLS., 6:331; CAMPBELL [1], 369–70).

24.   Colo. Fairfax & Lady and Mrs. Ambler dined here—with the Gentlemen that came yesterday & went away after.

25.   Mr. Boucher & Major Taylor went away after Breakfast. Mr. Alexander (Robt.) who lodged here Last Night and went over to give Notice to his Tenant of Mr. Marshalls want of part of his Tenement dined here and went home afterwards.

Alexander's notice was a legal warning to the planter who was renting Mrs. Alexander's Maryland land that before the end of the year he would have to vacate the portion that GW had bought to exchange with Thomas Hanson Marshall. Marshall may have begun to use the property in 1772 (GW to Lund Washington, 18 Dec. 1778, DLC:GW). Nevertheless, the exchange still could not be concluded because Alexander would not give Marshall a deed, claiming that his wife refused to consent to the transaction of her own free will as required by law. GW admonished Alexander for not prevailing on her "to do an act of justice, in fulfilling his Bargains and complying with his wishes," but the matter remained unresolved until 1779, when Lund

Washington, acting on GW's behalf, bought all Marshall's approximately 480½ acres of land adjoining Mount Vernon for £5,304 in the inflated Virginia currency of the war years (GW to Alexander, 20 Mar. 1777, DLC:GW; deed from GW to Lund Washington, 25 Feb. 1785, Fairfax County Deeds, Book P-1, 415–17, Vi Microfilm). The £500 that GW had given Alexander for the Maryland land was charged to Alexander's account with interest and was finally repaid in 1789 by Col. William Lyle of Alexandria, who had assumed the debt (LEDGER B, 41, 361).

26. Jackey Custis went away after Breakfast to Annapolis to School.

Jacky took £2 13s. pocket money with him (LEDGER A, 319).

27. Went with Mrs. Washington and Patcy Custis to Belvoir to Dinner and returned in the Afternoon.

28. Went up to Alexandria with the Association Papers. Dined at Mr. Ramsays calld at Mr. Jno. Wests and returnd home in the Evening.

GW was apparently taking printed copies of the nonimportation agreement to Alexandria to be circulated and signed. At least 333 signatures were eventually obtained, and sometime before 11 Oct. an association committee was elected for the county. Its members were GW, George Mason, John West, Peter Wagener, and John Dalton (*Va. Gaz.*, R, 11 Oct. 1770; six signed copies of the agreement are in DLC:GW, and one is in DLC: U.S. Broadsides).

29. Captn. Ingles, and his Master, Mr. Bruce and Mr. John West dind here. All of whom returnd afterwards.

CAPTN. INGLES: probably Samuel Inglis, a Norfolk merchant who dealt in flour, wheat, corn, hemp, and West Indian goods (*Va. Gaz.*, P&D, 24 Jan. 1771, 7 July 1774, and P, 26 May 1775). There was a Captain Inglis of the British navy serving in American waters at this time as commander of the armed schooner *Sultana*, but he apparently visited Virginia only in the falls of 1769 and 1770 (*Va. Gaz.*, P&D, 2 Nov. 1769, 18 Oct. 1770; R, 29 Nov. 1770). Several Captain Bruces skippered merchant vessels in the colonial trade before the Revolution, including the impetuous James Bruce, captain of one of the ships involved in the Boston Tea Party of 1773 (ship list for Hampton, P.R.O., C.O.5/1350, ff. 9–10; *Va. Gaz.*, P&D, 15 Sept. 1768, 31 Jan. 1771, and D&H, 11 Oct. 1776; LABAREE [2], 137).

30. After an Early Dinner (which Mr. Peake took with us), we set of for Fredericksburg that is Mrs. Washington, P. Custis & myself. Reachd Mr. Lawson's.

GW had asked the original officers of the Virginia Regiment to meet him at Fredericksburg 1 Aug. to discuss matters relating to bounty lands in the Ohio Valley that Gov. Robert Dinwiddie had promised members of the regiment in 1754 in order to encourage enlistment during the French and Indian War (*Va. Gaz.*, P&D, 21 June 1770; Proclamation, 19 Feb. 1754, P.R.O., C.O.5/ 1348, 334–36). Surveying and distribution of the lands had been delayed first by war and then by the Royal Proclamation of 1763, which prohibited settlement west of the Appalachian Mountains. However, much of the territory was opened by treaties signed with the Indians at Hard Labour and Fort Stanwix in 1768. In Dec. 1769 GW brought the Virginia soldiers' claims to the attention of the current Virginia governor, Lord Botetourt (8 Dec. 1769, DLC:GW), and in the same month presented the governor and the council a petition "in behalf of himself and the Officers and Soldiers who first imbarked in the service of this Colony . . . praying that the Two Hundred Thousand Acres of land which was given to them by Governor Dinwiddie's Proclamation . . . may be allotted to them, in one or more Surveys, on the Monongahela and its waters from the long narrows to or above a place commonly called the great Canhawa [Kanawha]" (VA. EXEC. JLS., 6:337).

The council agreed to the petition, specifying that the grant should be limited to veterans who had entered the service before the battle at Great Meadows in July 1754 and that the 200,000 acres should be "taken up in one or more Surveys, not exceeding twenty, on the great Canhawa and the other places particularized in their Petition so as not to interfere with prior Settlements or surveys actually and legally made." It was also suggested that GW should arrange for a surveyor and insert a notice in the *Virginia Gazette* requiring eligible officers and soldiers to present their claims to him (VA. EXEC. JLS., 6:338). GW advertised for the claims in Purdie and Dixon's newspaper 21 Dec. 1769 and in Rind's newspaper every week from 28 Dec. 1769 to 26 Apr. 1770 (LEDGER A, 322). However, he decided that before beginning the expensive and troublesome business of surveying, he must assemble the officers "to consert measures how we shall proceed" (Andrew Lewis to GW, 1 Mar. 1770, ViU). The meeting at Fredericksburg was the result of that decision.

31.   Got to my Mothers to Dinner and staid there all Night.

Patsy Custis became gravely ill today, suffering not only from "her old complaint" of epilepsy, but also "ague and fever" (GW to Jonathan Boucher, 15 Aug. 1771, excerpt, American Art Assoc. Catalogue, 21–22 Jan. 1926, item 294). Dr. Hugh Mercer of Fredericksburg was promptly summoned to Ferry Farm, where he bled the patient and gave her medicines. Patsy remained under his care until the family returned home nine days later (receipt from Mercer, 8 Aug. 1770, ViHi: Custis Papers). The grip that epilepsy now had on Patsy is documented by a record of her seizures that GW kept 29 June–22 Sept. 1770 on the margins of the printed calendar pages in his almanac. Of the 86 days included in that period, Patsy had "fits" on 26, often two a day. For 31 July GW entered the notation "1 very bad Do.," indicating the exceptional severity of this day's attack.

Acct. of the Weather in July

July 1st.   Lowering Morning and wind at East. Abt. 12 Oclock it began to Rain & continued to do so till after 3 Oclock.

2.   Cloudy Morning but afterwards clear & warm. Then thunder but no Rain.

3.   Clear & very Cool – the Wind being at No. West & fresh.

4.   Also clear but not so Cool as Yesterday. Wind in the same place but not fresh.

5.   Cloudy & lowering all day – but no Rain. Wind Southwardly.

6.   Cloudy & misty all day with some pretty smart showers of Rain. Wind still to the Southward.

7.   Raining more or less till 3 Oclock then clear. With but little Wind.

8.   Clear and pleasant with but little wind and that Southwardly.

9.   Clear and Warm – with but little wind and that Southwardly.

10.   Clear and tolerably pleasant not being warm. Wind Southwardly.

11.   Clear & warm – especially in the afternoon. There being but little wind & that Southwardly.

12.   Warm with thunder at the forenoon & moderate Rain (a good deal of it) in the Afternoon with hard thunder.

13.   Still warm with appearances of Rain but none fell.

14.   Clear and Warm the Wind being Southwardly.

15.   Warm, and clear notwithstanding the Wind blew fresh from the Eastward.

16.   Clear and Warm. Wind Southwardly.

17.   Rather lowering all day with appearances of Rain – but none fell – tho it thunderd a little in the Afternoon.

18.   Hot and Sultry with but little [wind] and that Southwardly.

19. Very hot and Sultry with but little wind.

20. Exceeding hot and Sultry with a southerly Breeze.

21 Also very hot with a black Cloud to the westward and great appearance [of rain] – but none fell here.

22. Clear and Warm in the forenoon with a Black Cloud to the Westward but no Rain here.

23. Again appearances of Rain to the Westward with only a sprinkle here.

24. Clear and Warm all day with but little Wind.

25. Light showers in the afternoon and sevl. of them but not sufft. to wet the Ground.

26. Sevl. very fine Showers but rather heavy in the Afternoon from the Southwest. With wind.

27. Clear and warm with but little Wind – that Northwardly.

28. Very warm. Wind Southwardly in the Afternoon Thunder, lightning and Rain.

29. Clear and Warm. Wind Southwardly again.

30. Exceedingly warm – especially in the Afternoon there being but little wind & that Southwardly.

31. Again very warm & still – especially in the Evening and Night.

Remarks & Occuran. in July

July 2. Prosecuting my wheat Harvest which I began on Saturday last in the Neck.

5. Stately A Hound Bitch was lind by Jowler.

6.   She was again lined by the same Dog. I killed and sold my English Bull to the Boston's Crew at 20/. p. Ct. His 4 Quarters weighd 711 lbs. Nett.

The *Boston*'s purser paid GW £7 2s. in cash for the bull. GW had bought an English bull, probably this one, in Dec. 1765 for £3 (LEDGER A, 222, 318).

10.   About Ten Oclock finished Cutting and Securing my Wheat in the Neck and about Eleven began the field at Muddy hole.

13.   Finished cutting and Securing my Wheat at Muddy hole.

14.   Began my Harvest at the Mill but did not quite finish the field on the other side by the New Mill.

17.   Finished my Harvest at the Mill about 10 or 11 Oclock and began to cut the Wheat at Doeg Run Abt. 12 Oclock.

20.   Compleated my Wheat Harvest altogether & exceeding bad I am apprehensive it will turn out—owing I am of opinion to the frequent Rains in the Month of June. The Heads contain but few grains—the Grain but little flower being for the most part perishd and Milldewed. The frequent Rains had by beating down the straw been the occasion of much loss in the Field both by shattering and unclean cutting & to compleat all I was too late in beginning my Harvest by 3 or 4 day as it ought where a Harvest is to continue 3 Weeks to be begun always before it is ripe as the loss in the shrinkage of Green Wheat is not equal to that of its shattering & various other Accidents when it is over-ripe & the straw falling.

23.   Began to Cut my Meadw. at the Mill.

31st.   Finished Do. Also laid the 2d. Floor of my Mill.

[August]

Where & how my time is Spent

Augt. 1.   Dined at my Mother's. Went over to Fredericksburg afterwards & returnd in the Evening back again.

2.   Met the Officers of the first Virga. Troops at Captn. Weedens where we dined & did not finish till abt. Sun set. Mrs. Washington & Patcy dind at Colo. Lewis's where we lodgd.

Meeting a day later than scheduled, the officers and representatives of officers who were present accepted William Crawford as surveyor for the veterans' bounty lands and resolved that GW should make a journey to the Ohio Valley with Crawford and Dr. James Craik to locate the best areas for the surveys. It was also agreed that the costs involved would be divided proportionately among the officers according to their original ranks, the field officers paying the most and the subalterns the least. GW was empowered to begin collecting the money immediately (minutes of the officers of the Virginia Regiment, 5 Mar. 1771, DLC:GW; LEDGER A, 322).

3.   Dined at my Brother Charles's—spent the Evening there & lodgd at Colo. Lew⟨is⟩.

Charles Washington was now a leading citizen of Fredericksburg, being both a vestryman of St. George's Parish and a Spotsylvania County justice. He owned at least 759 acres of land in the county outside Fredericksburg, and in Aug. 1761 he had bought lots numbered 87 and 88 in town for £80 from Warner Lewis of Gloucester County (deed of Charles and Mildred Washington to Thomas Strachan, 20 April 1780, and deed of Lewis to Charles Washington, 3 Aug. 1761, CROZIER [2], 222, 353). Located on Fauquier Street between Princess Ann and Caroline streets, those lots include the site of the Rising Sun Tavern, which according to popular tradition Charles Washington built and operated (WAYLAND [1], 153–55).

GW today paid James Hunter of King George County £10 5s. for "Mill spindles Gudgeons &ca." to be used in his new mill. This sum was apparently the balance due for the parts, because about six weeks earlier GW had sent Hunter £15 on account of the mill (LEDGER A, 318, 319).

4.   Dined at the Barbicue with a great deal of other Company and stayd there till Sunset.

5.   Went to Church (in Fredg.) and dind with Colo. Lewis.

St. George's Church, built in 1732, had as its minister at this time James Marye, Jr. (1731–1780), who had succeeded his father as parish rector in 1767 (MEADE [1], 68–69).

6.   Dined with Mr. James Mercer.

James Mercer (1735–1793), a younger brother of Lt. Col. George Mercer but no relation of Hugh Mercer, was a prominent Fredericksburg lawyer. Educated at the College of William and Mary, he had been a commander of Fort Loudoun at Winchester, Va., with rank of captain during the French and Indian War and served 1762–76 as a burgess from Hampshire County, where he owned land (GARNETT [1], 90). During 1769 he had bought five lots in Fredericksburg: two from GW, and three, including the ones on which his house and his study stood, from Fielding Lewis (deed of Lewis to Mercer,

4 Sept. 1769, and deed of GW to Mercer, 13 Oct. 1769, CROZIER [2], 268–70).
James Mercer had probably attended the meeting at Weedon's tavern on
2 Aug., because although he had not been a member of the original Virginia
Regiment, he was now handling the affairs of his brother George, who had
joined the regiment in 1754 and was now living in England.

7. Dined at Colo. Lewis's—Colo. Dangerfield & Lady & Miss
Boucher comg. there to see us.

COLO. DANGERFIELD & LADY: possibly Col. William and Sarah Taliaferro
Daingerfield, of Belvidera, just south of Fredericksburg. But more likely they
are Col. William's first cousin, also a Col. William, and his wife, Mary Willis
Daingerfield (d. 1781), of Coventry in Spotsylvania County. It was this
William who served with GW in the Virginia Regiment (see entry for 3 May
1762). Mary Willis Daingerfield was a granddaughter of GW's uncle by
marriage, Col. Henry Willis. The Daingerfields' daughter Catherine later
married George Lewis, son of Fielding and Betty Lewis. Miss Jane Boucher
(1742–1794) lived with her older brother, Rev. Jonathan Boucher.
   While the Washingtons were in Fredericksburg they purchased clothing
and other items. Today GW bought silk and earrings for Patsy, paid George
Weedon £6 for a tent and a marquee, and had a watch repaired for 5s. He
also visited a barber and clubbed at Weedon's tavern in the evening
(LEDGER A, 319).

8. Dined at Colo. Lewis's.

GW apparently clubbed at Weedon's again this evening and played cards,
winning 5s. (LEDGER A, 320).

9. Breakfasted at my Mothers—dined at Dumfries & came home
by Night.

10. Rid to Muddy hole—Doeg Run and the Mill.

11. Rid into the Neck.

12. Rid to Belvoir after Dinner to see Sir Thos. Adams who was
sick there.

Adams's frigate, the *Boston,* returned to Hampton Roads without him, while
he tried to recover his health at Belvoir. He rejoined the vessel in early
September and sailed her soon afterwards to Halifax, Nova Scotia, where he
died in October (*Va. Gaz.,* P&D, 6 Sept. and 18 Oct. 1770, and R, 1 Nov.
1770).

13. Rid to Muddy hole Doeg Run and the Mill.

14. At home all day writing Invoices and Letters.

GW was again preparing invoices to be sent to Robert Cary & Co. in London. In his covering letter dated 20 Aug. 1770, he complained about the cost and quality of goods he had received from the company and about the prices paid for tobacco from the Custis plantations. He also noted that some of the items on his enclosed invoices were currently prohibited by the Virginia association and were to be sent only if the Townshend Acts were totally repealed before his goods were shipped, "as it will not be in my power to receive any Articles contrary to our Non-Importation Agreement, to which I have Subscribd, & shall religiously adhere to, if it was, as I coud wish it to be, ten times as strict" (DLC:GW).

15. Rid to the Mill–by the Ferry and returnd to Dinner. Miss Betty Dalton came here.

16. Rid to the Mill and to the Ditchers.

17. At home all day.

18. Rid to the Mill–Ditchers–Doeg run and Muddy hole.

19. Went to Pohick Church. Calld in our way at Belvoir to take leave of Sir Thos. Returnd to Dinner.

20. Went up to Alexandria to Court. Returnd in the Evening with Jacky Custis & Mr. Magowan.

The August court was in session 20–23 Aug. (Fairfax County Order Book for 1770–72, 49–77, Vi Microfilm).

Jacky came from Annapolis to attend dancing lessons that Christian was to give during the next few days at a neighbor's house. On his way home he had visited Magowan on the West River, and his former tutor had then accompanied him to Mount Vernon (GW to Jonathan Boucher, 15 Aug. 1770, excerpt, American Art Assoc. Catalogue, 21–22 Jan. 1926, item 294; Jonathan Boucher to GW, 18 Aug. 1770, DLC:GW).

21. Went up to Court again and returnd in the Afternoon. Found Mr. Beal here along with Mr. Magowan.

Many members of the Beall family were living at this time in Prince George's and Frederick counties, Md. (BRUMBAUGH, 1–89, 177–257). The Mr. Beall who was at Mount Vernon today was probably Samuel Beall, Jr. (1740–1825), of Frederick County (see main entry for 27 Aug. 1770; MASON [2], 1:xxxiv; BEALL, 79–82).

22. Mr. Beal went away after Breakfast. I continued at home all day.

23. I went up to Alexandria calling by Mr. Jno. Wests going & coming. Returnd again at Night—with Mr. B. Fairfax.

GW was again going to court, arriving there near the end of this day's proceedings (Fairfax County Order Book for 1770–72, 76, Vi Microfilm).

24. Went out a huntg. with Mr. Fairfax. Killd a young fox without running him and returnd to Dinner. Doctr. Rumney dind here & lodged.

25. Mr. Fairfax—Doctr. Rumney—Mr. Magowan and Jacky Custis all went away after Breakfast. I rid into the Neck and to Muddy hole.

Jacky was returning to school in Annapolis.

26. At home all day alone.

27. Went by my Mill & Doeg Run to Colchesters—there to settle a dispute betwen. Doctr. Ross & Company & Mr. Semple.

In Feb. 1763 Dr. David Ross of Bladensburg, Md., became a partner with Richard Henderson of Bladensburg and Samuel Beall, Jr., and Joseph Chapline (d. 1769), both of Frederick County, Md., in a company that built and operated the Antietam (or Frederick) ironworks on the Potomac River near the mouth of Antietam Creek (SINGEWALD, 144–45). By 1770 John Semple was selling pig iron from his Keep Triste furnace to the forge at the Antietam works, and those sales may have led to this dispute with Dr. Ross and his company (proposal of John Semple on Potomac navigation, c.1770, MnHi). But the quarrel probably concerned rights to ore deposits or land, possibly the Merryland tract Semple had bought from Thomas Colvill in 1765 (GW to John Rumney, 24 Jan. 1788, DLC:GW). GW was assisted in arbitrating the dispute by George Mason; Robert Mundell, a merchant from Port Tobacco, Md.; and Hector Ross of Colchester, who was no relation to Dr. Ross. After meeting for six days the arbitrators were unable to resolve the matter and adjourned until 24 Jan. 1771.

28. At Colchester all day—upon the same business.

29. Still at Colchester upon this Affair Colo. Lewis My Sister & Brothr. Chas. passd this in their way to Mount Vernon.

On this date GW paid Dr. Ross £38 1s. 9½d. Maryland currency for about 3,000 pounds of iron (LEDGER A, 320).

30. Still at Colchester upon the business before mentioned.

31. At the same place and on the same business.

Acct. of the Weather in August

Augt. 1.　Clear with the Wind very fresh from the So. West but very warm notwithstanding.

2.　Again very warm with a brisk westwardly breeze.

3.　More moderate — the Wind being Northwardly — cloudy with some thunder but no Rain.

4.　Warm again but no appearance of Rain tho the wind was favourable for it.

5.　Very warm but clear and little wind — that southwardly.

6.　Clear and Warm — with but little [　　].

7.　Clear in the Morning but very cloudy and like for Rain afterwards — tho little or none fell. Wind Eastwardly.

8.　Cool and Clear. Wind fresh from the Northwest.

9.　Clear and cool wind still continuing Northwardly.

10.　Something warmer with but little wind.

11.　Warm again — with some slight appearances of Rain.

12.　Warm and still with Clouds.

13.　Wind abt. So. West afterwards Shifting Eastwardly & blewg. fresh.

14.　Cloudy all day. In the afternoon a hard shower of Rain for a few Minutes.

15.　Cloudy all day with a good deal of Rain about but little or none fell here.

16.　Some Rain again [in] the Night with hard winds.

17.　Showery in the Morning and abt. in Places all day but little here.

18.   Very Cloudy all day at least the forepart of it but clear afterwards. Ground by this got thoroughly wet.

19.   Showers again with the Wind fresh from the southward.

20.   Very warm all Day. In the Night a good deal of Rain and a sudden change in the Air.

21.   Very Cool and Cloudy. Wind being Northwardly & Eastwardly.

22.   Cloudy & very cool all day. Being a close & constant Rain. Wind Eastwardly.

23.   Warmer, Wind being Southwardly. Morning Misty & cloudy all day.

24.   Misty Morning, and sometimes slight showers in the forenoon but clear & warm afternoon.

25.   Cloudy generally through the day with the Wind pretty brisk from the Southwest especialy in the Morning.

26.   Clear and Warm wind being still to the Southward.

27.   Very Hot & even Sultry in the Evening with Clouds to the westward & some Rain.

28.   Still warm but not so hot as yesterday. Raining most part of the Night.

29.   Raining in the Morning but clear & cool afterwards.

30.   Very cool. Wind being at No. West.

31.   A Slight frost in the Morning but clear and cool all day.

Remarks & Occurances Augt.

Augt. 1.   Began to Sow Wheat at Muddy hole–the Ground Grassy & in bad order.
   Began to Sow Ditto at Doeg Run Quarter where the Ground was exceeding foul, Grassy, & hard.

8.   Began to sow Wheat in the Neck in that Cut upon the Creek above Carneys Gut. The Ground here was tolerably clear and in Good Order the Grass and Weeds being Choped over.

Carney's Gut, named for GW's former tenant John Carney, is on the east side of Little Hunting Creek a short distance above the creek's mouth (see illus., p. 3).

10 & 11th.   I rid over all my Corn Ground as well that in the Neck as those at Muddy hole & Doeg Run, and was surprizd to see how much it had fired; especially in Land that was any thing Stiff and poor. It was observable also, that in most of these places there appeard no shoots upon the Stalks and upon the whole the prospect [was] exceedingly shocking. It is further to be observd, that the Corn, in flat stiff places was fired even where it had not been lately workd but more so where it was. Why Corn in so short a droughth shoud fire so badly is difficult to Acct. for Unless it is owning to the great and frequent Rains which fell all the first part of the year and at the same time that it made the Corn Luxurient & exceeding tender baked the Ground hard & prevented the frequent and constant working of it that it ought to have had.

Nothing appears [more] clearly from the experience of this year than that a wet June is very injurious to both Corn and Wheat. The former is run too much into stalk by it—made tender & unable to stand the droughts which follow after & besides this is generally overcome with grass and Weeds. The Latter (that is Wheat) by being injurd in the blossom produces poor perished grain & but little of it—the head being subject to the spot & other defects.

My Corn this year has not been so well cultivated as it ought wch. partly has been owing to two causes—first the exceeding wet weather all the Month of June prevented my Plows from working constantly where the Land was level and next my force of Horses was rather inadequate to the Task & I think more than 35 or 40 Acres of Corn Land (where it is any thing stiff) ought not to be allotted to a plow and two middling good Horses. Finishd Sowg. the Cut upon the Creek above Carneys Gut. Finished the Remainder of that Cut on the other side the Gut.

17.   Finished the Cut at Doeg Run abt. John Gists Houses.

25.   I examined my Corn fields & perceivd that the late Rains had made a great alteration for the better. Many stalks were

putting out entire New Shoots with young and tender Silk—but as the Tassels of most of all the Corn (especially in that field in the Neck) was entirely dry. The question is whether the Corn for want of the Farina will ever fill. This is a matter worthy of attention & should be observd accordingly.

29.   The Rain that Fell last Night made the Ground too wet for plowing.

[September]

Where & how my time is Spent

Septr. 1st.   Returnd from the Arbitration at Colchester. In the Evening my Brothr. Saml. & his wife & children came hither from Fredericksburg in their way to Frederick.

Samuel Washington, the brother of George Washington. (Dr. and Mrs. John A. Washington)

Charles Washington. From an un-known original reproduced in Charles H. Callahan, *Washington the Man and the Mason*, Washington, D.C., 1913. (University of Virginia Library)

Samuel Washington moved his family about this time to Harewood in Frederick County, where he lived until his death in 1781 (see "Remarks" entry for 6 Oct. 1770). His present wife was his fourth, Anne Steptoe Washington, daughter of Col. James Steptoe of Westmoreland County and widow of Willoughby Allerton (d. 1759), also of Westmoreland. The children who came today were probably Thornton Washington (c.1760–1787), Samuel's son by his second wife Mildred Thornton Washington, and Ferdinand Washington (1767–1788), his eldest surviving son by Anne Steptoe Washington, but there may have been others (WAYLAND [1], 143).

2.   At home all day with the Company before Mentioned. Mr. Adam's Miller came here & went to see my Mill.

3.   Went in the Evening a fishing with my Brothers Saml. & Charles.

4.   Rid to My Mill and back to Dinner.

5.   At Home all day playing Cards.

6.   Rid to the Mill with Colo. Lewis &ca. returnd to Dinner.

7.   Went a fishing into the Mouth of Doegs Creek.

8.   A Fishing along towards Sheridine Point. Dined upon the Point.

Sheridine Point (now called Sheridan Point) is on the Potomac about a mile above the mouth of Little Hunting Creek. Part of GW's Clifton's Neck property, it was apparently so named because it was part of the plantation that John Sheridine, Sr., was renting from GW. The point was at this time the site of a fishing landing.

9.   Colo. Lewis, my Sister & Brother Charles went away. At Home all day.

10.   My Brothr. Saml. & self rid to the Mill & Back to Dinner.

11.   Rid to the Mill and Ditchers again.

12.   Rid to the Mill & Ditchers. Mr. Christian & his Scholars came here to Dancing.

Jacky Custis had again come home from Annapolis for dancing lessons (John Parke Custis to GW, 30 Aug. 1770, PHi: Gratz Collection).

13.   Rid to the Mill Ditchers & Morris and Muddy hole—also the Mill in the Afternoon. Mr. Christian went away this afternoon.

George Washington enjoyed fishing with friends, a pastime suggested by this contemporary print. From *The Sportsman's Dictionary*, London, 1735. (Mount Vernon Ladies' Association of the Union)

14.   Rid to the Mill and Ditchers in the forenoon with my Brother. In the Afternoon went a fishing.

15.   Rid to Alexandria with my Brothr. & returnd to Dinner.

16.   At home all day. My Brothr. Sam. and his wife set of in my Chariot for his House in Fredk. Mr. Renney came here this afternoon.

Rev. Robert Renney (d. 1774) served St. Margaret's Church, Westminster Parish, Anne Arundel County, Md., 1767–74 (RIGHTMYER, 209).

17.   Went up to Court, and returnd in the Evening with Mr. Nash & Mr. Peachy.

The court met 17–20 Sept. (Fairfax County Order Book for 1770–72, 78–97, Vi Microfilm). In Alexandria on this day Hector Ross put some of John Ballendine's property up for sale to the highest bidder to settle debts that Ballendine owed him. To be sold were 17 slaves, including 9 skilled craftsmen, and a tract of about 400 acres of land near the Little Falls of the Potomac (*Va. Gaz.*, P&D, 30 Aug. 1770).

MR. NASH: probably one of the several Nashes living in Richmond County at this time, but he could be Col. John Nash, Jr., a prominent citizen of Prince Edward County (RICHMOND COUNTY, 186–87; HENNEMAN, 6:175). MR. PEACHY: probably Col. William Peachey (1729–1802) of Richmond County, but possibly one of his brothers: Samuel Peachey (b. 1732) of Prince William or Essex County; Thomas Griffin Peachey (1734–1810), clerk of Amherst County; or LeRoy Peachey (b. 1736), clerk of Richmond County. William Peachey had been a captain under GW in the Virginia Regiment and was now adjutant general of militia for the colony's Middle District, the area between the James and Rappahannock rivers east of the Blue Ridge (KEMPER, 38–41 n.33; *Va. Gaz.*, P&D, 11 May 1769; R, 15 Feb. 1770; and R, 14 Feb. 1771).

18.   Mr. Renny & Jacky Custis set out for Annapolis. Mr. Nash &ca. went home & I to Court again & returnd in the afternoon.

Jacky had received 17s. pocket money on the previous day (LEDGER A, 320). GW was late in arriving for this day's court session (Fairfax County Order Book for 1770–72, 81, Vi Microfilm).

GW today began to rent from John West, Jr., the undisputed part of the land near Mount Vernon that West had earlier promised to sell him. The rent of this tract of about 200 acres was fixed at £12 10s. a year, and GW was to be allowed to take timber off the land as he pleased. West's earlier agreement to sell all the land to GW at 43s. an acre, after the conclusion of West's suit with Posey, was still in force, and West today specifically reaffirmed his promise to include Posey's small strip in the sale if he should recover it. The case was to be heard before the General Court in Williamsburg this fall (agreement of West with GW, 18 Sept. 1770, PHi: Gratz Collection).

19.   Rid to the Mill & Ditchers & come home to Dinner.

20.   Rid to the Mill & Ditchers again & went by Poseys. Doctr. Rumney came.

21.   Rid to the Mill and Ditchers. Doctr. Rumney went away.

Before Rumney left, GW paid him for services and medicines furnished since February: £6 4s. 6d. on his own account, £5 1s. for Patsy Custis, and £1 for Fielding Lewis (LEDGER A, 320).

22.   Rid to my Mill in the forenoon & afternoon. James McCarmack came here last Night & returnd today.

On this day GW docked Jonathan Palmer £5 for "Six Weeks lost by Sickness and going to Loudoun Court" (LEDGER A, 294). He then renegotiated his contract with Palmer, which was renewed annually through 1773. In June 1774 Palmer returned to help bring in the wheat harvest at a wage of 5s. per day (LEDGER B, 28).

James McCormack (died c.1789) had served under GW in the Virginia Regiment during 1754 and now lived with his wife Mercy, widow of Joshua Hains, on Bullskin Run in Frederick County (VIRKUS, 5:471; TORRENCE, 271).

23.   At Home all day Mr. Campbell and Captn. Sanford dind here.

Capt. Lawrence Sanford, a shipmaster who had been sailing out of Alexandria for the past six years, currently commanded the brig *Swift* of Alexandria owned by Joseph Thompson & Co. (Sanford's deposition, 19 Oct. 1779, NAVAL OFFICE, 294–95; ship lists for South Potomac Naval District, P.R.O., C.O.5/1450, ff. 39–41, and C.O.5/1349, f. 207). He had taken a shipment of fish to the West Indies for GW during the previous year and today was arranging to take some herring jointly owned by GW and Matthew Campbell to Jamaica for sale (GW to Sanford, 26 Sept. 1769, DLC:GW). On 29 Sept. GW instructed Sanford by letter to bring him some West Indian goods on the return voyage: a hogshead of rum, a "Barrel of good Spirits," 200 pounds of coffee, 200 pounds of sugar, and 100 or 200 oranges "if to be had good." Those items were to be paid for out of GW's share of the herring sales, his balance to be rendered in cash (DLC:GW). The *Swift* returned with GW's goods a few months later, but GW received no cash balance, because the cost of his goods, £50 10s. 1d., exceeded his eventual proceeds from the deal, £40 15s. 9d. (Robert McMickan to GW, 7 Dec. 1770, MiU-C: Haskell Collection; Robert McMickan & Co.'s account with GW, 6 Dec. 1770–16 Feb. 1771, ViMtV).

24.   At home all day alone.

25.   Rid to the Mill and Ditchers in the forenoon.

26.   Rid by Posey's and to the Mill & Ditchers again.

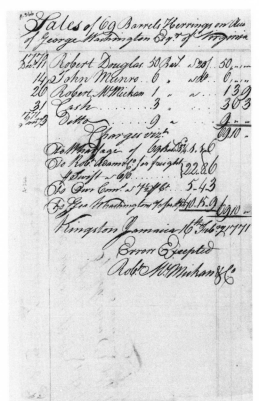

Washington's account with a Jamaican firm that sold sixty-nine barrels of his herring. (Mount Vernon Ladies' Association of the Union)

27.   Rid to the Mill and Ditchers. In the afternoon Doctr. Rumney came here.

28.   Rid to the Mill and Ditchers. Doctr. Rumney here Sick.

29.   At Home all day—Doctr. Rumney still here Sick.

30.   At home all day. Mr. Wr. Washington came in the Evening. Doctr. Rumney still here.

Acct. of the Weather in Septr.

Septr. 1st.   Cool & clear—wind being still Northwardly.

2.   Cool but rather Inclind to be Cloudy Wind being also fresh from the Eastward.

3.   Rain in the forenoon but clear afterwards with but little wind.

4.   Showery with the wind at East.

5.   Clear and tolerably warm and still.

6.   Flying Clouds with the Wind tolerably fresh—but no Rain.

7.   Clear with the Wind tolerably fresh from the North North East.

8.   Still, Calm, Warm, and clear.

9.   Clear and Calm but not so cool as yesterday.

10.   Clear and tolerably Cool Wind being at No. East.

11.   Cloudy with appearances of Rain but none fell.

12.   Rain in the Morning & cloudy afterwards & warm.

13.   Still Cloudy with some Shows for Rain but none fell.

14.   Clear and pleasant with the wind Southwardly.

15.   Clear and warm with but little wind & that Southwardly— warm.

16.   Clear in the forenoon and warm with some appearance of Rain in the afternoon.

17.   Rain in the Fore & afternoon & Cloudy all day.

18.   Clear and cool Wind at No. West.

19.   Clear and very cool. Wind still continuing Northwardly.

20.   Still cool—but warmer than yesterday—a remarkable great Fog & Dew.

21.   Clear & tolerably warm Wind being Southwardly.

22. Showery in the forenoon with the Wind at Southwest. Clear afterwards.

23. Clear and Cool—Wind Northwardly & westwardly.

24. Raining all day with variable Wind.

25. Raing. a little in the Morning and a good deal in the afternoon and very warm.

26. Clear and Cool Wind Northwardly.

27. Also clear and cool wind still Northwardly.

28. Something warmer and Cloudy with appearances of Rain.

29. Misting and every now and then a little Rain. Very cloudy all day and wind at No. East. In the Evening it began to Rain pretty constant—tho not hard.

30. Tolerably clear and Warm with the Wind Southwardly.

Remarks & Occurs. in Septr.

Septr. 4th. Got on the 2d. Floor (or rather the last Floor the walls being at their Height) of my Mill.

The Hound Bitch stately brought 7 Puppies viz 2 dogs & 5 Bitches 1 of the former dead—remaing. 1 dog & 5 Bitches.

13. Sett 3 Negroe Men, to Wit Harry, George & Frank to Work upon my Mill Race.

14. Two more men came to work on it from the Neck—to wit—Neptune and George.

Morris at Doeg Run began to sow his third Cut of Wheat.

20. Finishd Sowing Wheat in the Neck. Also at Muddy hole. This day also Dominicus Gubner a Dutch Smith set into work at the Rate of £32 pr. Ann he to be found when at Work here and to have the Plantn. on which John Crook livd (to settle his Family at) & Work in any thing he pleases rent free.

Before this date GW had employed Gubner as a blacksmith on a daily basis, paying him 3s. a day for each of 19 days that he had previously worked in the shop at Mount Vernon (LEDGER A, 325). Under the terms of the one-year contract signed today, Gubner agreed to do blacksmithing for GW on a regular basis, attending to his business in GW's shop "at all hours & seasons that is customary & proper for a Smith to work at" and making up all time lost "by negligence, Sickness, or any private concerns of his own" (DLC:GW). The plantation on which John Crook had lived was apparently part of the Mount Vernon tract; it was first rented by Crook from GW in 1755, two years before GW began to acquire other lands in the area. Crook ceased to live there after 1767 (LEDGER A, 71, 128, 244). Gubner occupied the plantation and worked for GW until the fall of 1773, his contract being twice renewed with no changes in terms (LEDGER B, 34).

22.   Receivd from Edwd. Snickers the Millstones he was to get for [me] which were thinner by two Inch⟨es⟩ than what were bespoke.

GW paid Snickers £20 for these stones when he stopped at Snickers's ordinary 30 Nov. 1770 (LEDGER A, 329).

[October]

Where & how my time is Spent

Octr. 1.   Rid to my Mill and the Ditchers with Mr. Warnr. Washington. Colo. Fairfax dind here. The Doctr. Rumney still here. Mr. Carr came in the Eveng.

William Carr (d. 1791), a Dumfries merchant, dealt in wheat and flour. He had been a trustee of the town since 1761 and in 1765 served as a commissioner to divide Fairfax Parish from Truro Parish (Carr to GW, 17 Dec. 1770, DLC:GW; HENING, 7:424–28, 8:157–59).

2.   At home all day. John Savage formerly a Lieutt. in the Virga. Service & one Wm. Carnes came here to enter their claim to a share in the 200,000 acres of Land. Wr. Washington & Doctr. Rumney here.

Savage was commissioned a lieutenant in the Virginia Regiment 9 Mar. 1754 and promoted to captain in Sept. 1755 but resigned from the regiment the following spring (VA. TROOPS, 284; GW orders, 17 Sept. 1755, DLC:GW; GW to Robert Dinwiddie, 25 June 1756, DLC:GW). He may be the John Savage (d. 1791) who settled on Knobly Mountain, Hampshire County, about 1778 (SAGE AND JONES, 132; SIMS, 226). Carnes (Carns) was a private in the Virginia Regiment as early as 9 July 1754 (VA. TROOPS, 279).

3.   At home all day. Mr. Washington—Mr. Carr—Savage & Carnes went away after Breakfast. The Doctr. still here.

Dr. James Craik, Washington's former comrade in arms. (Alexandria-Washington Lodge No. 22, A.F. & A.M., Alexandria, Va.)

4. In the afternoon Doctr. Rumney went away & Doctr. Craik came.

5. Set out in Company with Doctr. Craik for the Settlement on Redstone &ca. dind at Mr. Bryan Fairfax's & lodged at Leesburg.

Several factors induced GW to make the arduous journey through western Pennsylvania and the Ohio country in the fall of 1770. Among the most pressing was the question of locating bounty lands on the Kanawha and Ohio rivers for the officers and soldiers of the Virginia Regiment (see main entry for 30 July 1770). GW felt a special sense of urgency about this business because rumors had recently reached Virginia of a newly established land company in England whose proposed claims appeared to overlap those of the Virginia veterans (see "Remarks" entry for 8 Oct. 1770, n.1; GW to Lord Botetourt, 5 Oct. 1770, PPRF). Furthermore, GW noted, "any considerable delay in the prosecution of our Plan would amount to an absolute defeat of the Grant inasmuch as Emigrants are daily Sealing the choice Spots of Land and waiting for the oppertunity . . . of solliciting a legal Title under the advantages of Possession & Improvement—two powerful Plea's in an Infant Country" (GW to Lord Botetourt, 9 Sept. 1770, CLU-C). See also William Nelson to Lord Hillsborough, h.b.j., 1770–72, xxii–xxiii.

GW's own land interests also induced him to make a first hand investigation of conditions in western Pennsylvania. In Sept. 1767 GW had instructed William Crawford, his western land agent, to "look me out a Tract of about 1500, 2000, or more Acres somewhere in your Neighbourhood. . . . Any Person . . . who neglects the present oppertunity of hunting out good Lands & in some measure Marking & distinguishing them for their own (in order to keep others from settling them) will never regain it" (GW to Crawford, 21 Sept. 1767, DLC:GW). Crawford proceeded to have a considerable tract of land surveyed for GW in the area of Chartier's Creek (see main entry for 15 Oct. 1770). "When you come up," he informed GW, "you will see the hole of your tract finisht" (Crawford to GW, 5 May 1770, DLC:GW).

There are two sets of diary entries for those portions of Oct. and Nov. 1770 covering GW's trip to the Ohio country. Both entries for a day should be consulted.

6. Bated at old Codleys. Dind and lodgd at my Brother Sam's.

GW's expenses at Codley's (Caudley's) were £6 (LEDGER A, 329). Codley's was located at Williams' (later Snickers') Gap in the Blue Ridge. It was near the site of present-day Bluemont, some 15 miles from Samuel Washington's home at Harewood.

7. Dind at Rinkers and lodgd at Saml. Pritchards.

Casper (Jasper) Rinker's house was located approximately ten miles from Winchester on the Winchester-Cumberland road. Rinker, a member of a family of early German settlers in the Shenandoah Valley, was given a grant of land, 2 June 1762, in what is now Hampshire County, W.Va., on the basis of a survey by GW (Northern Neck Deeds and Grants, Book K, 443, Vi Microfilm).

Samuel Pritchard resided on the Cacapon River some 40 miles from Samuel Washington's establishment. Pritchard was a resident of Frederick County as early as 1758, when he cast his vote against GW for burgess (*Va. Mag.*, 6:169).

8. Vale. Crawford joind us, & he and I went to Colo. Cresaps leaving the Doctr. at Pritchards with my boy Billy who was taken sick.

Thomas Cresap's establishment was at Shawnee Old Town (now Oldtown, Md.). See entry for 21 Mar. 1748. Billy is GW's mulatto body servant William, whom he had bought in 1768 from Mrs. Mary Lee of Westmoreland County, the widow of Col. John Lee, for £61 15s. (LEDGER A, 261). Billy had assumed the surname Lee, and was also referred to by GW as Will or William. He was to accompany his master throughout the Revolutionary War.

9. Went from Colo. Cresaps to Rumney where in the afternoon the Doctr. & my Servant & Baggage arrivd.

The town of Romney on the South Branch of the Potomac River was established in 1762 (HENING, 7:598–600). Here GW apparently met John Savage again, for he today recorded receiving £6 from Savage as part of his share of the surveying costs for the Virginia Regiment's land (LEDGER A, 329).

10. Bought two Horses & sent one of my Servants (Giles) home with those I rid up. Proceeded on our Journey and lodgd at one Wise (now Turners) Mill.

On this day GW paid £16 for a bay and £13 10s. for a gray (LEDGER A, 329). Wise's Mill was on Patterson's Creek.

In this Jonathan Trumbull portrait, Washington's slave Billy Lee is shown at the right. (Metropolitan Museum of Art, Bequest of Charles Allen Munn, 1924)

11.   Set out about 11 Oclock and arrivd at one Gillams on George Creek 10½ Miles from the North Branch & same diste from F[ort] C[umberland].

GILLAMS: probably Joseph Gillam who lived on a branch of George's Creek, a little more than ten miles from the North Branch of the Potomac River. Fort Cumberland is now Cumberland, Md.

12.   Started from Gillams between Sunrising & Day Break and arrivd at the Great crossing of Yaugha. about Sun set or before.

The Great Crossing of the Youghiogheny is near present-day Addison, Pa. GW spent 16s. there (LEDGER A, 329).

13.   Left this place early in the Morning and arrivd at Captn. Crawfords (known by the name of Stewarts crossing) abt. ½ after four Oclock.

Stewart's Crossing was on the Youghiogheny River below present-day Connellsville, Pa. The site was named for William Stewart, who settled there in 1753 (COOK, 15). Braddock's army had crossed the Youghiogheny at this ford in June 1755 on the way to Fort Duquesne. The area was included in the tract of land on the Youghiogheny surveyed and occupied by William Crawford in 1769 (WHi: Draper Papers, E-11).

14.   At Captn. Crawfords all day.

15.   Rid to see the Land he got for me & my Brother's.

This land, which William and Valentine Crawford had surveyed for the Washingtons in 1769, is in the vicinity of Perryopolis, Pa., in what is now Fayette County, Pa.

16.   At Captn. Crawfords till the Evening—then went to Mr. John Stephenson's.

John Stephenson was William and Valentine Crawford's half brother. After the death of the Crawfords' father, their mother, Onora Grimes Crawford (d. 1776), married Richard Stephenson, by whom she had five sons and one daughter (BUTTERFIELD [1], 93). John Stephenson had served in the French and Indian War and settled in the vicinity of the Great Crossing of the Youghiogheny about 1768. He was involved from time to time in the Crawfords' land activities.

17.   Arrivd at Fort—dining at one Widow Miers at Turtle Creek.

GW had arrived at Fort Pitt. The Widow Myers's tavern was probably at Sycamore and Sixth streets within the boundaries of present-day Pittsburgh. It frequently served as a rallying point for frontier militia and was still op-

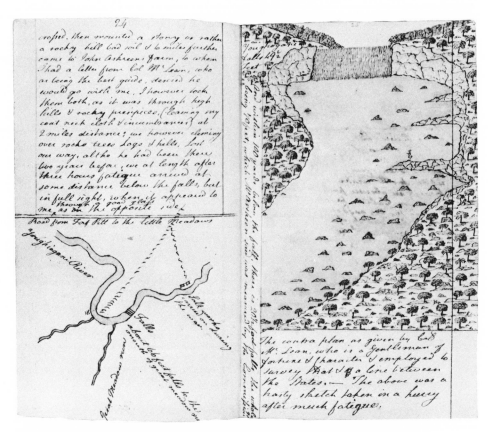

Samuel Vaughan sketched the Youghiogheny River and the falls in 1787. (Collection of the descendants of Samuel Vaughan)

erating in the 1790s. GW spent 3s. 9d. at the tavern (LEDGER A, 329). Turtle Creek enters the Monongahela above the site of Fort Pitt.

18.   Dined in the Fort at the Officers Club.

19.   Dined at Colo. Croghans abt. 4 Miles from Pittsburg & returnd.

George Croghan was living at Croghan Hall near Pittsburgh. He and GW were old acquaintances from the 1754 campaign against the French, in which Croghan had agreed to provision the Virginia troops. At that time GW had been highly critical of his efforts (GW to William Fairfax, 11 Aug. 1754,

DLC:GW). After the French and Indian War, Croghan acquired, on paper at least, an empire of some 250,000 acres of land in New York and 200,000 acres in Pennsylvania. By 1770, however, his pyramid of land speculation was crumbling and his creditors were pressing him for payment. In July 1770 he returned from his New York lands to his establishment near Fort Pitt, hoping to confirm title to his Pennsylvania holdings and sell them before returning to develop his tracts in New York. Exaggerated reports of land sales sent out by his agents had evidently reached GW, since at their meeting in mid-October they discussed the possibility of his purchasing a tract from Croghan. He wrote Croghan, 24 Nov., from Stewart's Crossing on his return from the Ohio, that he would be willing to buy a single tract of 15,000 acres. Since Croghan had had difficulty in securing an uncontested title to the Pennsylvania lands he had acquired from the Indians, GW added cautiously that the acres would be purchased only when legal title could be confirmed (DLC:GW). Croghan was optimistic after GW's visit: "I am likely to sell another Tract to Col. Washington and his Friends—if I do *that*, I expect to have One good Nights Rest before Christmas, which is more than I have had for eight Months past I assure you" (Croghan to Samuel Wharton, Jr., 25 Oct. 1770, PHi: Sarah A. G. Smith Family Papers). However, GW soon began to have serious doubts about the validity of Croghan's title and by late 1771 decided against purchasing the tract (William Crawford to GW, 2 Aug. 1771; GW to Crawford, 6 Dec. 1771, DLC:GW).

20.   Set out for the Big Kanhawa with Dr. Craik Captn. Crawford & others. Incampd abt. 14 Miles off.

21.   Got abt. 32 Miles further and Incampd abt. 3 Miles below little Bever Ck.

Little Beaver Creek empties into the Ohio from the north, about 42 miles from Fort Pitt (POWNALL, 166).

22.   Reachd the Mingo Town abt. 29 Miles by my Computation.

Mingo Town (now Mingo Junction, Ohio) was an Indian village several miles below Steubenville, Ohio. "This was the only Indian village in 1766 on the banks of the Ohio from that place to Fort Pitt; it contained at that time 60 families" (CRAMER, 25n). Mingo Town appears on Thomas Hutchins's 1778 map of the Ohio.

23.   Stayd at this place till One Clock in the Afternoon & padled abt. 12 Miles down the River & Incamped.

24.   We reachd the Mouth of a Creek calld Fox Grape vine Creek (10 Miles up which is a Town of Delawares calld Franks Town) abt. 3 Oclock in the afternoon—distant from our last Camp abt. 26 Miles.

Fox Grape Vine Creek, also called Captina Creek, flows into the Ohio from the west. Frank's Town was a well-known Delaware village about six miles from the Juniata River. Originally called Assunepachla, it was referred to as Frank's Town, for the Pennsylvania trader Frank Stevens, as early as 1734. Apparently it was deserted by the Delawares before Braddock's Defeat in 1755. A Delaware village called Frank's Town on Captina Creek does not appear on early maps but it is possible that the Delawares had established such a settlement in the area. It may have been another name for the Grape Vine Town. "As late as 1772 the Rev. David Jones, a Baptist missionary, on his way to preach to the Ohio Indians, met a Frank Stephens at the mouth of Captina Creek (on the west side of the Ohio River, twenty miles below Wheeling). This man was an Indian, who had received his English name from that of Frank Stevens, the Trader. Possibly he may have been a half-blood son of the trader" (HANNA, 1:259–60).

25.　Incampd in the long reach abt. 30 Miles from our last lodge according to my Computation.

The "long reach" of the Ohio is a section of the river with relatively few curves stretching approximately from Paden City to Raven Rock, W.Va. Its length is 18 to 20 miles.

26.　Incampd at the Mouth of a Creek about 4 Miles above the Mouth of Muskingham distant abt. 32 Miles.

The Muskingum River joins the Ohio River from the Ohio side at Marietta.

27.　Incampd at the Mouth of great Hockhocking distant from our last Incampment abt. 32 Miles.

The Little Hocking enters the Ohio from the west about 19 miles below Marietta. The Great Hockhocking is now the Hocking River. It flows into the Ohio at Hockingport, Ohio, some 26 miles below Marietta.

28.　Meeting with Kiashuta & other Indian Hunters we proceeded only 10 Miles to day, & Incampd below the Mouth of a Ck. on the west the name of wch. I know not.

GW had met Guyasuta during his journey to the French commandant in 1753 (see entry for 30 Nov. 1753, n.49). After joining the French in 1755, Guyasuta had actively engaged in hostilities against the British during the French and Indian War and was a leader in Pontiac's rebellion. After the war he was again friendly to the English and aided the firm of Baynton, Wharton, & Morgan in opening up the Illinois trade. He maintained his allegiance to the British during the Revolution and participated in the attack against Hannastown, Pa., in 1782. After the Revolution he settled in the area of Pittsburgh and died there about 1800.

29.　Went round what is calld the Great Bent & Campd two Miles below it distant from our last Incampment abt. 29 Miles.

The Great Bend of the Ohio is in the region of Meigs County, Ohio.

30. Incampd Early Just by the old Shawna Town distant from our last no more than 15 Miles.

Shawnee Town appears on Lewis Evans's 1766 map of the middle colonies just north of the confluence of the Ohio and the Great Kanawha rivers. It is not the Lower Shawnee Town at the mouth of the Scioto River.

31. Went out a Hunting & met the Canoe at the Mouth of the big Kanhawa distant only 5 Miles makg. the whole distance from Fort Pitt accordg. to my Acct. 266 Miles.

GW's calculations on the distance from Fort Pitt to the mouth of the Great Kanawha at present-day Point Pleasant, W.Va., agree substantially with those of Capt. Harry Gordon, chief engineer of the Northern Department in North America. In Gordon's table of distances it is logged as 266¼ miles (POWNALL, 166).

Acct. of the Weather in October

Octr. 1st.   Wind Southwardly and warm with flying Clouds.

2.   Raining, Hailing, or Snowing the whole day—with the wind Northerly Cold & exceeding disagreeable.

3.   Clear but cold. Wind being very high from the Northwest.

4.   Clear and pleasant. Wind being fresh and very fresh.

5.   Clear, warm & remarkably pleasant with very little or no Wind.

6.   Again clear pleasant and still.

7.   As pleasant as the two preceeding days.

8.   Pleasant forenoon—but the wind Rising. About Noon it Clouded & threatned hard for Rain. Towards Night it raind a little & ceasd but contd. Cloudy.

9.   Exceeding Cloudy & heavy in the forenoon & constant Rain in the Afternoon.

10.   Cloudy with Rain & sunshine alternately.

11.   Wet Morning with flying Clouds afterwards. Towards the Evening the Wind sprung out at No. West.

12.   Rain in the Night with flying Clouds accompanied with a little Rain now and then all day. Cold & Raw.

13.   Clear and pleasant. Wind tolerably fresh from the Westward all day.

14.   Very pleasant but wind fresh in the Afternoon.

15.   Exceeding Cloudy & sometimes droppg. Rain but afterwds. clear.

16.   Frosty Morning—but clear and pleasant afterwards.

17.   Exceeding warm & very pleasant till the Evening then lowering.

18.   Misty & Cloudy in the Evening. The Forepart of the day being very warm.

19.   Misty & Cloudy all day.

20.   Misty—but the Evening clear tho somewhat Cool.

21.   Cloudy & very raw & cold in the forenoon. About Midnight it began to Snow & contd. to do so more or less all the remaing. part of the Night & next day.

22.   Very raw & cold. Cloudy, & some times Snowing & sometimes Raining.

23.   Exceeding Cloudy & like for Snow & sometimes really doing so.

24.   Clear & pleasant Morning but cloudy & cold afterwards.

25.   Rain in the Night but clear & warm till abt. Noon—then Windy & cloudy.

26.   Clear and pleasant all day.

27. A little Gloomy in the Morning but clear, still, & pleast. afterwards.

28. Much such a day as the preceeding one.

29th. Pleasant forenoon & clear but Cloudy and Wet afternoon.

30. Raining in the Night. Raw cold & cloudy forenoon but clear & pleasant afternoon.

31. Remarkably clear & pleasant with but little wind.

Remarks & Occurrs. in October

Octr. 5th.[1] Began a journey to the Ohio in Company with Doctr. Craik his Servant, & two of mine with a lead Horse with Baggage. Dind at Towlston[2] and lodgd at Leesburg distant from Mount Vernon abt. 45 Miles. Here my Portmanteau horse faild in his stomach.

[1] For additional annotation of GW's diary entries for October, see the previous section.

[2] Towlston Grange was Bryan Fairfax's home in Fairfax County.

6. Fed our Horses on the Top of the Ridge at one Codleys & arrivd at my Brother Samls. on Worthingtons Marsh[1] a little after they had dind the distance being about 30 Miles. From hence I dispatchd a Messenger to Colo. Stephens[2] apprising him of my arrival and Intended Journey.

[1] Samuel Worthington, a Quaker, had settled as early as 1730 on a crown grant of some 3,000 acres northwest of present-day Charles Town, W.Va., on Evitt's Marsh or Evitt's Run. Much of the land went to his son Col. Robert Worthington (1730–1799) (WAYLAND [2], 20–21). Lawrence Washington purchased 230 acres of this property from Worthington and in his will (20 June 1752, DLC:GW) bequeathed these acres to his half brothers Samuel, John, and Charles. Samuel located in the area by 1768 and began construction of his home Harewood, some three miles from the site of Charles Town. He probably moved his family to Harewood from Stafford County in 1770, although the house may not have been finished until 1771 (see WAYLAND [1], 132–35).

[2] After the French and Indian War, Adam Stephen settled on a farm in Frederick County, near present-day Martinsburg, W.Va.

7.   My Portmanteau Horse being unable to proceed, I left him at my Brothers & got one of his & proceedd. by Jolliffs [1] & Jasper Rinkers to Saml. Pritchards on Cacapehen; distant according to Acct. 39 Miles; but by my Computation 42 thus reckond 15 to Jolliffs, 14 to Rinkers; & 13 to Pritchards. At Rinkers which appears to be a cleanly House my boy was taken Sick but continued on to Pritchards. Pritchards is also a pretty good House, their being fine Pasturage good fences, & Beds tolerably clean.

[1] William Jolliffe, Sr. (1695–1765), a Quaker and a practicing attorney, moved with his family to the Shenandoah Valley about 1743 and settled in the vicinity of Opequon Creek, north of Winchester. His sons, William, James, Edmund, and John, all lived in Frederick County, in the area of Hopewell Meeting (JOLLIFFE, 66–79).

8.   My Servant being unable to Travel I left him at Pritchards with Doctr. Craik & proceedd. myself with Vale. Crawford to Colo. Cresaps in ordr. to learn from him (being just arrivd from England) the particulars of the Grant said to be lately sold to Walpole [1] & others, for a certain Tract of Country on the Ohio. The distance from Pritchards to Cresaps according to Computation is 26 Miles, thus reckond; to the Fort at Henry Enochs [2] 8 Miles (road exceedg. bad) 12 to Cox's [3] at the Mouth of little Cacapehon and 6 afterwards.

[1] Undoubtedly one of the factors which prompted GW's trip to the Ohio in the fall of 1770 to examine western lands was information concerning a new land scheme being promoted in England. The project had grown out of negotiations between Thomas Walpole, a prominent British politician, and Samuel Wharton, Philadelphia merchant and land speculator. The plan called for the acquisition of an initial grant of 2,400,000 acres from the crown, later increased to some 20,000,000 acres, which would have encompassed much of the area of Kentucky, southwestern Pennsylvania, and the western part of West Virginia. The proposal included a plan to establish a new colony to be called Vandalia. In Dec. 1769 the Grand Ohio Company was formed to further the scheme. At its height the new company included such influential Englishmen as Thomas Pownall, Lord Hertford, Richard Jackson, George Grenville, Anthony Todd, and William Strahan and such prominent Americans as the Whartons, Benjamin Franklin, Sir William Johnson, George Croghan, and William Trent. On 20 July 1770 the Board of Trade sent Virginia Governor Botetourt extensive information on the Walpole petition (P.R.O., C.O.5/1369, ff. 17–18), and on 9 Sept. and 5 Oct. GW wrote to the governor pointing out the conflict between the Walpole associates' claims and the interests of Virginia (CLU-C, PPRF). It had soon become clear that the boundaries of the new grant would overlap the claims of the Mississippi Company (of which GW was a member) and those of the Ohio Company of Virginia and would encroach on the bounty lands claimed by veterans of the

Virginia Regiment and the lands ceded to the "Suffering Traders" by the Six Nations, although some of these claims were recognized by the Walpole associates and concessions made to their holders (see SOSIN, 181–209; ABERNETHY, 40–58; George Mercer to GW, 18 Dec. 1770, DLC:GW). For the reaction in Virginia to the proposed grant, see William Nelson to Lord Hillsborough, 18 Oct. 1770, H.B.J., 1770–72, xxii–xxv.

Thomas Cresap had spent much of 1770 in England and had made a particular inquiry into the affairs of the new company (BAILEY [4], 127). During their meeting on 8 Oct., Cresap gave GW extensive information about the new company including the fact that shares in the enterprise might be available from the members (see George Croghan to Joseph Wharton, Jr., 25 Oct. 1770, PHi: Sarah A. G. Smith Family Papers; GW to George Mercer, 22 Nov. 1771, DLC:GW). That GW was interested at least for a time in acquiring some interest in the Walpole company is indicated by the fact that he wrote to Croghan, 24 Nov. 1770, inquiring the latter's price for his share in the new company (DLC:GW). He made similar inquiries of George Mercer in 1771 (GW to Mercer, 22 Nov. 1771, DLC:GW).

[2] Henry Enoch had received a grant on 22 April 1753 for 388 acres on Cacapon River based on a survey done for him by GW in 1750. He received a further grant of 271½ acres in Hampshire County in 1761 (Northern Neck Deeds and Grants, Book H, 280, Book K, 228, Vi Microfilm). See also KEITH [1]. Enoch's fort, erected after Braddock's Defeat, was built at the forks of the Great Cacapon River, on the road from Winchester in what is now Hampshire County, W.Va. GW had suggested the fort on a list of frontier defenses drawn up in 1756 (DLC:GW).

[3] Cox's fort appears on Thomas Hutchins's 1778 map at the mouth of the Little Cacapon River. It was apparently a supply center during the French and Indian War (KOONTZ, 114–15). GW had surveyed this area for Friend Cox, 25 April 1750 (DLC:GW).

9.   Went up to Rumney in order to buy work Horses, & meet Doctr. Craik and my Baggage. Arrivd there abt. 12 distance 16 Miles. In the Afternoon Doctr. Craik my Servt. (much amended) and the Baggage, arrivd from Pritchards; said to be 28 Miles.

10.   Having purchasd two Horses, and recoverd another which had been gone from me near 3 Years, I dispatchd my boy Giles with my two Riding Horses home, & proceeded on my journey; arriving at one Wises (now Turners) Mill about 22 Miles it being Reckond Seven to the place where Cox's Fort formerly stood; 10 to One Parkers; & five afterwards. The Road from the South Branch to Pattersons C[ree]k is Hilly—down the C[ree]k on which is good Land, Sloppy to Parkers & from Parkers to Turners Hilly again.

11.   The Morning being wet & heavy we did not set of till 11 Oclock & arrivd that Night at one Killams on a branch of Georges

C[ree]k, distant 10½ Measurd Miles from the North Branch of Potomack where we cross at the lower end of my Decd. Brother Auge. Bottom, known by the name of Pendergrasses.[1] This Crossing is two Miles from the aforesaid Mill & the Road bad as it likewise is to Killams, the Country being very Hilly & stony.

From Killams to Fort Cumberland is the same distance that it is to the Crossing above mentiond, & the Road from thence to Jolliffs by the old Town much better.

[1] Pendergrass's Bottom was purchased by Lawrence Washington from Garret Pendergrass, probably when Pendergrass, an early settler and trader in the area, moved to Pennsylvania about 1752. In his will Lawrence left the land to his brother Augustine Washington (20 June 1752, DLC:GW).

12.   We left Killams early in the Morning—breakfasted at the little Meadows 10 Miles of, and lodgd at the great Crossings 20 Miles further, which we found a tolerable good days work.

The Country we traveld over today was very Mountainous & stony, with but very little good Land, & that lying in Spots.

13.   Set out about Sunrise, breakfasted at the Great Meadows 13 Miles of, & reachd Captn. Crawfords about 5 Oclock.

The Lands we travelld over to day till we had crossd the Laurel Hill [1] (except in smal spots) was very Mountainous & indifferent —but when we came down the Hill to the Plantation of Mr. Thos. Gist [2] the L[an]d, appeard charming; that which lay level being as rich & black as any thing coud possibly be. The more Hilly kind, tho of a different complexion must be good, as well from the Crops it produces, as from the beautiful white Oaks that grows thereon. Tho white Oak in generl. indicates poor Land, yet this does not appear to be of that cold kind. The Land from Gists to Crawfords is very broken tho not Mountainous—in Spots exceeding Rich, & in general free from Stone. Crawfords is very fine Land; lying on Yaughyaughgane at a place commonly called Stewards Crossing.

[1] Laurel Hill was a western ridge of the Alleghenies.
[2] Thomas Gist was the son of Christopher Gist. He had accompanied his father to the frontier in the 1750s. After his father's death in 1759, Thomas had taken over his plantation, which he called Monongahela, at the foot of Laurel Hill, in the vicinity of present-day Mount Braddock, Pa.

Sunday 14th.   At Captn. Crawfords all day. Went to see a Coal Mine not far from his house on the Banks of the River. The

Coal seemd to be of the very best kind, burning freely & abundance of it.

Monday 15th.   Went to view some Land which Captn. Crawford had taken up for me near the Yaughyaughgane distant about 12 Miles.[1] This Tract which contains about 1600 Acres Includes some as fine Land as ever I saw—a great deal of Rich Meadow and in general, is leveller than the Country about it. This Tract is well Waterd, and has a valuable Mill Seat (except that the stream is rather too slight, and it is said not constant more than 7 or 8 Months in the Year; but on acct. of the Fall, & other conveniences, no place can exceed it).

In going to this Land I passd through two other Tracts which Captn. Crawford had taken up for my Brothers Saml. and John. That belonging to the former, was not so rich as some I had seen; but very valuable on acct. of its levelness and little Stone, the Soil & Timber being good. That of the latter, had some Bottom Land up on sml. Runs that was very good (tho narrow) the Hills very rich, but the Land in genl. broken. I intended to have visited the Land which Crawford had procurd for Lund Washington this day also, but time falling short I was obligd to Postpone it making it in the Night before I got back to Crawfords where I found Colo. Stephen.

The Lands which I passd over today were generally Hilly, and the growth chiefly white Oak, but very good notwithstanding; & what is extraordinary, & contrary to the property of all other Lands I ever saw before, the Hills are the richest Land, the soil upon the sides and Summits of them, being as black as a Coal, & the Growth Walnut, Cherry, Spice Bushes &ca. The flats are not so rich, & a good deal more mixd with stone.

[1] This area in Fayette County, Pa., was later known as Washington Bottom. In 1774 GW built a mill there in partnership with Gilbert Simpson.

Tuesday 16.   At Captn. Crawfords till the Evening, when I went to Mr. John Stephenson (on my way to Pittsburg) & lodgd. This day was visited by one Mr. Ennis who had traveld down the little Kanhawa (almost) from the head to the Mouth, on which he says the Lands are broken, the bottoms neither very wide nor rich, but covd. with Beach. At the Mouth the Lands are good, & continue so up the River; & about Weeling, & Fishing Ck., is according to his Acct. a body of fine Land. I also saw a Son of Captn. John Hardens who said he had been from the Mouth of little Kanhawa to the big, but his description of the Lands seemed

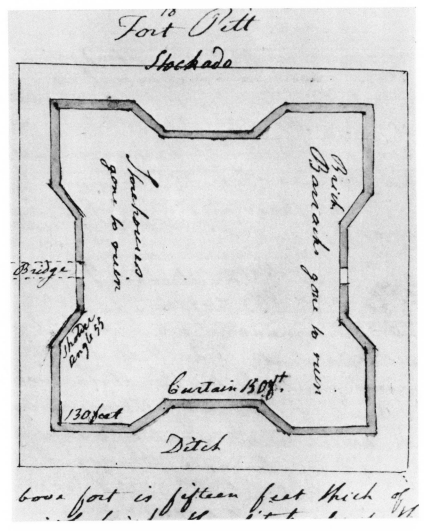

A plan of Fort Pitt, drawn by Samuel Vaughan. (Collection of the descendants of Samuel Vaughan)

to be so vague and indeterminate, that it was[1] much doubted whether he ever was there or not. He says however that at the Mouth of the Big Kanhawa there may be abt. 20 or 25,000 acres of Land had in a Body that is good—that you are not above five or 6 Miles to the Hills, & that the Falls of the Kanhawa are not above 10 Miles up it.

[1] At this point GW wrote: "Go to the end of the Almk." The diary entries are continued on the back pages of the almanac.

Wednesday 17. Doctr. Craik & myself with Captn. Crawford and others arrivd at Fort Pitt, distant from the Crossing 43½ Measurd Miles. In Riding this distance we pass over a great deal of exceeding fine Land (chiefly White Oak) especially from Sweigley Creek [1] to Turtle Creek [2] but the whole broken; resembling (as I think all the lands in this Country does) the Loudoun Land for Hills.

We lodgd in what is calld the Town—distant abt. 300 yards from the Fort at one Mr. Semples [3] who keeps a very good House of Publick Entertainment. These Houses which are built of Logs, & rangd into Streets are on the Monongahela, & I suppose may be abt. 20 in Number and inhabited by Indian Traders &ca.

The Fort is built in the point between the Rivers Alligany & Monongahela, but not so near the pitch of it as Fort Duquesne stood. It is 5 sided & regular, two of which (next the Land) are of Brick; the others Stockade. A Mote incompasses it. The Garrison consists of two Companies of Royal Irish Commanded by one Captn. Edmondson. [4]

[1] Big Sewickley Creek in Westmoreland County, Pa., flows into the Youghiogheny near present-day West Newton, Pa.

[2] Turtle Creek flows into the Monongahela about 12 miles above Pittsburgh.

[3] GW is referring to the tavern kept by Samuel Semple in Baynton, Wharton, & Morgan's former storehouse. The tavern stood at what is now the corner of Water and Ferry streets in Pittsburgh. Apparently GW's total expenditures for the party at Semple's were £26 1s. 10d., which he paid 21 Nov. on his return to Fort Pitt from the Ohio (LEDGER A, 329).

[4] Capt. Charles Edmonstone of the 18th Regiment of Foot (Royal Irish). Edmonstone was still in command at Fort Pitt when British troops withdrew on General Thomas Gage's orders, 20 Nov. 1772 (GAGE PAPERS, 2:638); he supervised the demolition of the fort and the sale of its materials to Pittsburgh civilians (FRONTIER FORTS, 2:123).

Thursday 18th. Dind in the Fort with Colo. Croghan & the Officers of the Garrison. Supped there also meeting with great Civility from the Gentlemen, & engagd to dine with Colo. Croghan the next day at his Seat abt. 4 Miles up the Alligany.

Friday 19th. Recd. a Message from Colo. Croghan, that the White Mingo [1] & other Chiefs of the 6 Nations had something to say to me, & desiring that I woud be at his House abt. 11. (where they were to meet) I went up and receivd a Speech with a String of wampum from the White Mingo to the following effect.

That as I was a Person who some of them remember to have

seen when I was sent on an Embassy to the French,[2] and most of them had heard of; they were come to bid me welcome to this Country, and to desire that the People of Virginia woud consider them as friends & Brothers linked together in one chain—that I wd. inform the Governor, that it was their wish to live in peace and harmy. with the white People, & that tho their had been some unhappy differences between them and the People upon our Frontiers, it was all made up, and they hopd forgotten; and concluded with saying, that, their Brothers of Virginia did not come among them and Trade as the Inhabitants of the other Provences did, from whence they were affraid that we did not look upon them with so friendly an Eye as they coud wish.

To this I answerd (after thanking them for their friendly welcome) that all the Injuries & Affronts that had passd on either side was now totally forgotten, and that I was sure nothing was more wishd and desird by the People of Virginia than to live in the strictest friendship with them. That the Virginians were a People not so much engagd in Trade as the Pensylvanians, &ca., wch. was the Reason of their not being so frequently among them; but that it was possible they might for the time to come have stricter connections with them, and that I woud acquaint the Govr. with their desires.

After dining at Colo. Croghan we returnd to Pittsburg—Colo. Croghan with us, who intended to accompany us part of the Way down the River, having engagd an Indian calld the Pheasant[3] & one Joseph Nicholson[4] an Interpreter to attend us the whole Voyage. Also a young Indn. Warrior.

---

[1] The White Mingo (Conengayote) was a Six Nations chief of some importance in this area. He had been present at the conference at Fort Pitt in April and May 1768 of agents of Pennsylvania, the crown, and the Indians concerning settlers' encroachment on Indian lands. He had apparently settled at "White Mingo's Castle" on the Allegheny across the river from George Croghan's establishment and was living there after 1777. He is said to have married Mary Montour, niece of Andrew Montour, which would have connected him with one of the frontier's most important Indian families (CRAIG, 1:344, 419). He should not be confused with another well-known Seneca also called White Mingo (Kanaghragait or John Cook), who was murdered by a trader on Middle Creek in present-day Snyder County, Pa., in Jan. 1768 (HANNA, 2:56; JOHNSON PAPERS, 12:454).

[2] See GW's diary of his "Journey to the French Commandant," 1753.

[3] The Pheasant had attended the Indian Congress at Fort Stanwix in 1768 with a delegation of 16 warriors. He may have been an Oneida (JOHNSON PAPERS, 12:628). GW paid the Pheasant and the young warrior £ 10 13s. for their services on the trip to the Ohio (LEDGER A, 329).

[4] Joseph Nicholson was well known on the frontier as a trader and inter-

preter. As early as 1766 he was in trade with the Tuscarora (JOHNSON PAPERS, 5:384), and he acted as interpreter on Maj. Gen. Daniel Brodhead's campaign in 1779. In May 1790 he was commissioned to bring the Indian chiefs Cornplanter, Half Town, and New Arrow to Philadelphia to confer with GW, and acted as interpreter during the talks.

Saturday 20th.   We Imbarkd in a large Canoe with sufficient Stores of Provision & Necessaries, & the following Persons (besides Doctr. Craik & myself) to wit—Captn. Crawford Josh. Nicholson Robt. Bell—William Harrison—Chs. Morgan & Danl. Reardon a boy of Captn. Crawfords,[1] & the Indians who went in a Canoe by themselves. From Fort Pitt we sent our Horses & boys back to Captn. Crawford wt. orders to meet us there again the 14th. day of November.

Colo. Croghan, Lieutt. Hamilton[2] and one Mr. Magee[3] set out with us. At two we dind at Mr. Magees & Incampd 10 Miles below, & 4 above the Logs Town. We passd several large Island which appeard to [be] very good, as the bottoms also did on each side of the River alternately; the Hills on one side being opposite to the bottoms on the other which seem generally to be abt. 3 and 4 hundred yards wide, & so vice versa.

[1] Robert Bell had served with the Virginia Regiment in 1754 and was discharged for injuries in Jan. 1755 (H.B.J., 1752–55, 273). In 1775 he was living near present-day McKee's Rocks, near Pittsburgh (see CRESSWELL, 70). William Harrison was William Crawford's son-in-law. He was killed by Indians on the disastrous Sandusky campaign in 1782, which also claimed the life of his father-in-law (WHi: Draper Papers, E-11, 44). Charles Morgan and Daniel Reardon have not been further identified.

[2] Lt. Robert Hamilton of the Fort Pitt garrison was an officer in the 18th Regiment of Foot (Royal Irish).

[3] Alexander McKee (c.1742–1799), son of Capt. Thomas McKee, a Pennsylvania trader, acted as a British Indian agent at Fort Pitt 1755–75 and acquired extensive landholdings in Pennsylvania in the area of McKee's Rocks and in Kentucky (HOBERG). During the American Revolution he remained loyal to the crown, was held prisoner for a time at Pittsburgh, and finally fled to Detroit. He was a vigorous British agent among the Indians throughout the war and helped inflict extensive damage on the Americans on the frontier. After the Revolution he settled at Detroit, holding the post of deputy agent for Indian affairs for the area, and when the Americans occupied Detroit in 1796 he moved his establishment to the mouth of the Thames River in Canada.

Sunday 21.   Left our Incampment abt. 6 Oclock & breakfasted at the Logs Town, where we parted with Colo. Croghan &ca. abt. 9 Oclock. At 11 we came to the Mouth of big Bever Creek,[1] opposite to which is a good Situation for a House, & above it, on the same side (that is the west) there appears to be a body of fine Land. About 5 Miles lower down on the East side comes in Racoon C[ree]k[2] at the Mouth of which, & up it appears to be a body of good Land also. All the Land between this Creek & the Monongahela & for 15 Miles back, is claimd by Colo. Croghan under a purchase from the Indians (and which sale, he says is confirmd by his Majesty). On this Creek where the Branches thereof interlock with the Waters of Shirtees Creek[3] there is, according to Colo. Croghan's Acct. a body of fine Rich level Land. This Tract he wants to sell, & offers it at £5 sterg. pr. hundd. with an exemption of Quitrents for 20 years; after which, to be subject to the payment of 4/2 Sterg. pr. Hundd., provided he can sell it in 10,000 Acre Lots. Note the unsettled state of this Country renders any purchase dangerous.

From Racoon Creek to little Bever Creek[4] appears to me to be little short of 10 Miles, & about 3 Miles below this we Incampd; after hiding a Barrl. of Bisquet in an Island[5] (in Sight) to lighten our Canoe.

[1] Big Beaver Creek (now Beaver River) in Beaver County, Pa., flows into the Ohio from the north about 30 miles below Pittsburgh.

[2] Raccoon Creek enters the Ohio from the south about 32 miles below Pittsburgh and 2 miles below Big Beaver Creek (CRAMER, 78).

[3] Chartier's Creek, Washington and Allegheny counties, Pa., flows northeast into the Ohio about 2½ miles below Pittsburgh. In 1771 GW acquired land in this area on Miller's Run, a branch of Chartier's Creek.

[4] Little Beaver Creek enters the Ohio from the north, 10¾ miles below Raccoon Creek and about 42 miles below Pittsburgh (CRAMER, 78; POWNALL, 166).

[5] Probably Mill Creek Island or Custard's Island.

Monday 22d.   As it began to Snow about Midnight, & continued pretty steadily at it, it was about ½ after Seven before we left our Incampment. At the distance of about 8 Miles we came to the Mouth of Yellow Creek[1] (to the West) opposite to, or rather below which, appears to be a long bottom of very good Land, and the Assent to the Hills apparently gradual. There is another pretty large bottom of very good Land about two or 3 Miles above this. About 11 or 12 Miles from this, & just above what is calld the long Island[2] (which tho so distinguishd is not very remarkable for length breadth or goodness) comes in on the East side the River, a small Creek[3] or Run the name of which I coud not learn; and a Mile or two below the Island, on the West Side, comes in big stony Creek (not larger in appearance than the other) on neither of which does there seem to be any large bottoms or body's of good Land. About 7 Miles from the last Mentiond Creek 28 from our last Incampment, and about 75 from Pittsburg, we came to the Mingo Town Situate on the West side the River a little above the Cross Creeks.[4]

This place contains abt. Twenty Cabbins, & 70 Inhabitants of the Six Nation.

Had we set of early, & kept pritty constantly at it, we might have reachd lower than this place today; as the Water in many places run pretty swift, in general more so than yesterday.

The River from Fort Pitt to the Logs Town has some ugly Rifts & Shoals, which we found somewhat difficult to pass, whether from our inexperience of the Channel, or not, I cannot undertake to say. From the Logs Town to the Mouth of little Bever Creek is much the same kind of Water; that is, Rapid in some places—gliding gently along in others, and quite still in many. The Water from little Bever Creek to the Mingo Town, in general, is swifter than we found it the preceeding day, & without any shallows, there being some one part or other always deep which is a natural consequence as the River in all the distance from Fort Pitt to this Town has not widend any at all nor doth the bottoms appear to be any larger. The Hills which come close to the River opposite to each bottom are steep; & on the side in view, in many places, Rocky & cragged; but said to abound in good land on the Top. These are not a range of Hills but broken, & cut in two as if there were frequent water courses running through (which however we did not perceive to be the case consequently they must be small if any). The River along down abounds in Wild Geese, and severl. kinds of Ducks but in no great quantity.[5] We killd five wild Turkeys today.

Upon our arrival at the Mingo Town we receivd the disagreeable News of two Traders being killd at a Town calld the Grape Vine Town, 38 Miles below this; which causd us to hesitate whether we shoud proceed or not, & wait for further Intelligence.

---

[1] Yellow Creek flows into the Ohio from the west, approximately 57 miles below Pittsburgh (see also HANNA, 2:193).

[2] Probably Brown's Island, 9 miles below Yellow Creek.

[3] This stream may be King Creek, flowing into the Ohio from the east (CLELAND, 250).

[4] Creeks flowing into the Ohio from opposite shores appear at several points on the Ohio and on the early maps are designated as Cross Creeks. The two referred to by GW are about 3¼ miles below present-day Steubenville, Ohio. The creek on the Ohio side is Indian Cross Creek; that on the West Virginia side, Virginia Cross Creek (see CRAMER, 80).

[5] The stretch of the river between Fort Pitt and Mingo Town was similarly described by Capt. Harry Gordon: "The country between these two Places is broken, with many high ridges or hills; the vallies narrow, and the course of the river plunged from many high grounds which compose its banks. When the water is high, you go with moderate rowing from six to seven miles an hour" (POWNALL, 158).

Tuesday 23.   Several imperfect Accts. coming in agreeing that only one Person was killd, & the Indians not supposing it to be done by their people, we resolvd to pursue our passage, till we coud get some more distinct Acct. of this Transaction. Accordingly abt. 2 Oclock we set out with the two Indians which was to accompany us, in our Canoe, and in about 4 Miles came to the Mouth of a Creek calld Seulf Creek,[1] on the East side; at the Mouth of which is a bottom of very good Land, as I am told there likewise is up it.

The Cross Creeks (as they are calld) are not large, that on the West side however is biggest. At the Mingo Town we found, and left 60 odd Warriors of the Six Nations going to the Cherokee Country to proceed to War against the Cuttawba's. About 10 Miles below the Town we came to two other cross Creeks[2] that on the West side largest, but not big; & calld by Nicholson French Creek. About 3 Miles or a little better below this, at the lower point of some Islands[3] which stand contiguous to each other we were told by the Indians with us that three Men[4] from Virginia (by Virginians they mean all the People settled upon Redstone &ca.) had markd the Land from hence all the way to Redstone— that there was a body of exceding fine Land lying about this place and up opposite to the Mingo Town—as also down to the Mouth of Fishing Creek.[5] At this Place we Incampd.

[1] Probably Beech Bottom Run, near Wellsburg, W.Va.

[2] GW is referring to a second set of cross creeks, Indian Short Creek on the Ohio side and Virginia Short Creek on the West Virginia side (CRAMER, 82).

[3] These must be Pike Island and the Twin Islands (see CRAMER, 82).

[4] These men were possibly Silas, Ebenezer, and Jonathan Zane, members of a prominent pioneer family, who had explored this area in 1769 and moved their families to the vicinity of present-day Wheeling, W.Va., about 1770.

[5] Fishing Creek flows into the Ohio River near New Martinsville, W.Va., some 32 miles below Wheeling (CRAMER, 85).

Wednesday 24th.   We left our Incampment before Sunrise, and abt. Six Miles below it, we came to the Mouth of a pretty smart Creek comg. in to the Eastward calld by the Indians Split Island Creek,[1] from its running in against an Island. On this C[ree]k there is the appearance of good Land a distance up it. Six Miles below this again, we came to another Creek on the West side, calld by Nicholson Weeling [2] and abt. a Mile lower down appears to be another small Water coming in on the East side,[3] which I remark, because of the Scarcity of them; & to shew how badly furnishd this Country is with Mill Seats. Two or three Miles below this again, is another Run on the West side; up which is a near way by Land to the Mingo Town; and about 4 Miles lower comes in another on the East at which place is a path leading to the settlement at Redstone. Abt. A Mile & half below this again, comes in the Pipe Creek so calld by the Indians from a Stone which is found here out of which they make Pipes. Opposite to this (that is on the East side), is a bottom of exceeding Rich Land; but as it seems to lye low, I am apprehensive that it is subject to be overflowd. This Bottom ends where the effects of a hurricane appears by the destruction & havock among the Trees.[4]

Two or three Miles below the Pipe Creek is a pretty large Creek on the West side calld by Nicholson Fox Grape Vine by others Captema Creek on which, 8 Miles up it, is the Town calld the Grape Vine Town; & at the Mouth of it, is the place where it was said the Traders livd, & the one was killd. To this place we came abt. 3 Oclock in the Afternoon, & findg. no body there, we agreed to Camp; that Nicholson and one of the Indians might go up to the Town, & enquire into the truth of the report concerning the Murder.

[1] Probably Wheeling Creek and Wheeling Island, site of Wheeling, W.Va.

[2] This creek may be McMahon's Creek, 2 miles below Wheeling (CRAMER, 84).

[3] McMahon Run enters the Ohio near McMechen, W.Va. (CLELAND, 253).

[4] Pipe Creek enters the river from the Ohio side, about 7 miles above Captina Creek in Belmont County, Ohio. GW later acquired this bottomland. In advertising his Ohio lands for sale, 1 Feb. 1796, he described it as "Round Bottom . . . about 15 miles below Wheeling, a little above Captenon, and opposite to Pipe-Creek; bounded by the river in a circular form for 2 miles and 120 poles containing 587 acres" (WRITINGS, 34:438).

Thursday 25th.   About Seven Oclock Nicholson & the Indian returnd; they found no body at the Town but two Old Indian women (the Men being a Hunting). From these they learnt that the Trader was not killd, but drownd in attempting to Ford the Ohio; and that only one boy, belonging to the Trader, was in these parts; the Trader (fathr. to him) being gone for Horses to take home their Skins.

About half an hour after 7 we set out from our Incampment around which, and up the Creek is a body of fine Land. In our Passage down to this, we see innumerable quantities of Turkeys, & many Deer watering, & brousing on the Shore side, some of which we killd. Neither yesterday nor the day before did we pass any Rifts or very rapid water—the River gliding gently along— nor did we perceive any alteration in the general face of the Country, except that the bottoms seemd to be getting a little longer & wider, as the Bends of the River grew larger.

About 5 Miles from the Vine Creek comes in a very large Creek to the Eastward calld by the Indian's Cut Creek,[1] from a Town, or a Tribe of Indians which they say was cut of entirely in a very bloody battle between them and the Six Nations. This Creek empties just at the lower end of an Island,[2] and is 70 or 80 yards wide and I fancy is the Creek commonly calld by the People of Redstone &ca. Weeling.[3] It extends according to the Indians acct. a great way, & Interlocks with the Branches of Split Island Creek; abounding in very fine bottoms, and exceeding good Land. Just below this, on the west side, comes in a sml. Run;[4] & about 5 Miles below it on the West side also another midling large Creek emptys, calld by the Indian broken Timber Creek;[5] so named from the Timber that is destroyd on it by a Hurricane; on the head of this was a Town of the Delawares, which is now left. Two Miles lower down, on the same side, is another Creek smaller than the last & bearing (according to the Indians) the same name.[6] Opposite to these two Creeks (on the East side) appears to be a large bottom of good Land. About 2 Miles below the last mentiond Creek on the East side, & at the end of the bottom aforementioned, comes in a sml. Creek or large Run.[7] Seven Miles from this comes in Muddy Creek[8] on the East Side the River—a pretty large Creek and heads up against, & with, some of the Waters of Monongehela (according to the Indians Acct.) & con- tains some bottoms of very good Land; but in general the Hills are steep, & Country broken about it. At the Mouth of this Creek is the largest Flat I have seen upon the River; the Bottom extend- ing 2 or 3 Miles up the River above it, & a Mile below; tho it does not seem to be of the Richest kind and yet is exceeding good upon the whole, if it be not too low & subject to Freshes.

About half way in the long reach we Incampd, opposite to the beginning of a large bottom on the East side of the River. At this place we through out some lines at Night & found a Cat fish of the size of our largest River cats hookd to it in the Morning, tho it was of the smallest kind here. We found no Rifts in this days pas-

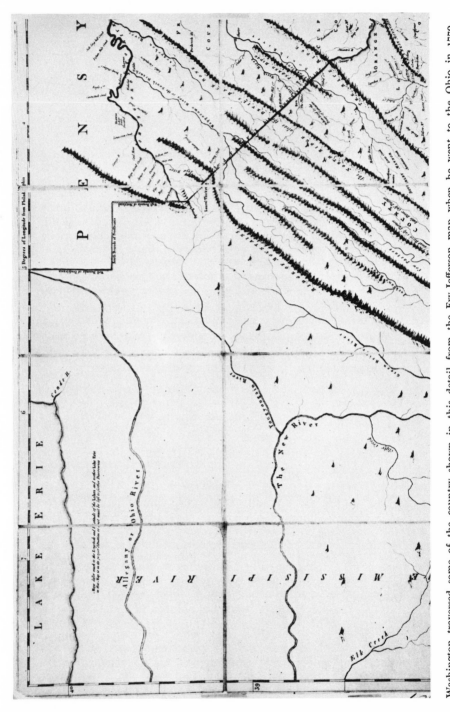

Washington traversed some of the country shown in this detail from the Fry-Jefferson map when he went to the Ohio in 1770.
(Tracy W. McGregor Library, University of Virginia)

sage, but pretty swift Water in some places, & still in others. We found the bottoms increasd in size, both as to length & breadth, & the River more Chokd up with Fallen Trees & the bottom of the River next the shores rather more Muddy but in general stony as it has been all the way down.

[1] Cut Creek is now called Fish Creek, entering the Ohio from the east near present-day Woodlands, Marshall County, W.Va.

[2] Fish Creek Island, Marshall County, W.Va.

[3] GW is mistaken. He had already passed Wheeling Creek and Wheeling Island.

[4] Probably what is now Johnson's Run, which enters the Ohio from the west in Monroe County, Ohio.

[5] Now Bishop Run, Monroe County, Ohio.

[6] Opossum Creek, entering the Ohio from Monroe County, Ohio.

[7] Proctor's Run, Proctor, W.Va.

[8] This stream may be Fishing Creek, entering the Ohio from the east near New Martinsville, W.Va.

Friday 26th.   Left our Incampment at half an hour after 6 Oclock & passd a small run [1] on the West side about 4 Miles lower. At the lower end of the long reach, & for some distance up it, on the East side, is a large bottom, but low, & coverd with beach next the River shore, which is no Indication of good Land. The long reach is a strait course of the river for abt. 18 or 20 Miles which appears the more extraordinary as the Ohio in general, is remarkably crooked. There are several Islands [2] in this reach, some containing an 100 or more Acres of land; but all I apprehend liable to be overflowed.

At the end of this reach we found one Martin & Lindsay two Traders; & from them learnt, that the Person drownd was one Philips attempting in Compa. with Rogers another Indn. Trader, to Swim the River with their Horses at an improper place; Rogers himself narrowly escaping.[3] Five Miles lower down, comes in a large Creek from the Eastward, right against an Island of good land,[4] at least a Mile or two in length. At the mouth of this Creek (the name of wch. I coud not learn except that it was calld by some Bulls Creek from one Bull that hunted on it) is a bottom of good Land, tho rather two much mixd with Beach. Opposite to this Island the Indians showd us a Buffalo Path, the Tracks of which we see.

Five or Six Miles below the last mentiond Creek we came to the three Island [5] (before wch.) we observd a small run on each side coming in. Below these Islands is a large body of flat Land, with a water course running through it on the East Side, and the

Hills back, neither so high, nor steep in appearance as they are up the River. On the other hand, the bottoms do not appear so rich, tho much longer & wider. The bottom last mentioned is upon a strait reach of the River, I suppose 6 or 8 Miles in length; at the lower end of which, on the East side, comes in a pretty large Run from the size of the Mouth. About this, above–below & back, there seems to be a very large Body of flat Land with some little risings in it.

About 12 Miles below the three Islands we Incampd just above the Mouth of a Creek [6] which appears pretty large at the Mouth and just above an Island. All the Lands from a little below the Creek which I have distinguished by the name of Bull Creek, appears to be level, with some small Hillocks intermixd, as far as we coud see into the Country. We met with no Rifts today, but some pretty strong water upon the whole tolerable gentle. The sides of the River was a good deal incommoded with old Trees, wch. impeded our passage a little.

This day provd clear & pleasant, the only day since the 18th. that it did not Rain or Snow or threaten the one or other very hard.

[1] Possibly Grandview Run, near New Matamoras, Ohio (CLELAND, 256).

[2] In this long reach CRAMER, 85, notes five islands: "Peyton's, Williamson, Pursley's, Wilson's and John Williamson's . . . all of which keep to the left."

[3] The identity of these traders is uncertain. MARTIN: may be John Martin, an Englishman who was in trade with the Indians on the Ohio and employed other traders to work for him. A John Martin was a prisoner (c.1764) at the Lower Shawnee Town. LINDSAY: may be John Lindsay, a trader living at Pittsburgh in 1760–61. PHILIPS: possibly Nicholas Phillips, a trader at Pittsburgh in 1760, or Philip Phillips, a Pittsburgh householder in 1761 who was active on the frontier and acted as interpreter for Sir William Johnson at Fort Stanwix in 1768 (HANNA, 1:244, 2:191, 231, 288, 360–61).

[4] Probably Middle Island and Middle Island Creek.

[5] Eureka, Broadback, and Willow islands, commonly called the Three Brothers.

[6] Probably the Little Muskingum, which enters the Ohio from the west just above Devol's Island.

Saturday 27.   Left our Incampment a Quarter before Seven, and after passing the Creek near wch. we lay, & another much the same size & on the same side (West) ; [1] also an Island [2] abt. 2 Miles in length (but not wide) we came to the Mouth of Muskingham,[3] distant from our Incampment abt. 4 Miles. This River is abt. 150 yards wide at the Mouth; a gentle currant & clear stream runs out of it, & is navigable a great way into the Country for Canoes.

From Muskingham to the little Kanhawa [4] is about 13 Miles. This is about as wide at the Mouth as the Muskingham, but the water much deeper. It runs up towards the Inhabitants of Monongahela, and according to the Indians Acct. Forks about 40 or 50 Miles up it; and the Ridge between the two Prongs leads directly to the Settlement.[5] To this Fork, & above, the Water is navigable for Canoes. On the upper side of this River there appears to be a bottom of exceeding rich Land and the Country from hence quite up to the 3 Islands level & in appearance fine. The River (Ohio) running round it in the nature of a horse shoe, forms a Neck of flat Land wch. added to that rung. up the 2d. long reach (aforementiond) cannot contain less than 50,000 Acres in view.

About 6 or 7 Miles below the Mouth of the Canhawa we came to a small Creek on the west side, which the Indns. calld little Hockhocking; but before we did this, we passd another sml. Creek [6] on the same side near the Mouth of the River & a cluster of Islands afterwards. The lands for two or three Miles below the Mouth of the Canhawa on both sides the Ohio, appear broken & indifferent; but opposite to the little hockhocking there is a bottom of exceeding good Land, through wch. there runs a smal water course. I suppose there may be of this bottom & flat Land together, two or three thousand Acres. The lower end of this bottom is opposite to a smal Island wch. I dare say little of it is to be seen when the River is high. About 8 Miles below little Hockhocking we Incampd opposite to the Mouth of the great Hockhocking, which tho so calld is not a large water; tho the Indians say Canoes can go up it 40 or 50 Miles.

Since we left the little Kanhawa the Land neither appear so level nor good. The Bends of the River & Bottoms are longer indeed but not so rich, as in the upper part of the River.

[1] Duck Creek is almost opposite Devol's Island.

[2] Devol's or Meigs' Island, now called Kerr's Island (COOK, 21).

[3] The Muskingum River flows into the Ohio from the west at Marietta, Ohio.

[4] The Little Kanawha flows into the Ohio from the east at Parkersburg, W.Va.

[5] THE SETTLEMENT: that is, the settled area in the vicinities of Fort Pitt and Red Stone.

[6] The small creek is probably Putnam's Run or Davis Run, entering the Ohio from the west. At this time there were five islands in the stretch of river between the Little Kanawha and the Little Hocking rivers, known later as Blennerhassett, Four Acre, Towhead, Newbury, and Mustapha. "It seems evident that Washington passed the head of Blennerhassett without observing the Virginia channel. . . . The 'cluster of Islands' would not have been ob-

served until Washington's party had proceeded down the river to the foot of the large island, when, would have come into view, the 'Four Acre' lying in the Virginia channel, and 'Towhead' just below." Changes in the course of the river have now made both part of Blennerhassett Island (COOK, 22–23). GW later acquired land in this area. On 1 Feb. 1796, he offered for sale "the first large bottom below the mouth of the Little Kenhawa, beginning 3 or 4 miles therefrom, and about 12 or 15 miles below Marietta. Its breadth on the river is 5 miles and 120 poles, and contents 2314 [acres]" (WRITINGS, 34:438).

Sunday 28th.   Left our Incampment about 7 Oclock. Two Miles below, a sml. run comes in on the East side [1] thro a piece of Land that has a very good appearance, the Bottom beginning above our Incampment, & continuing in appearance wide for 4 Miles down, to a place where there comes in a smal Run [2] & to the Hills. And to where we found Kiashuta and his Hunting Party Incampd.

Here we were under a necessity of paying our Compliments, As this person was one of the Six Nation Chiefs, & the head of them upon this River. In the Person of Kiashuta I found an old acquaintance. He being one of the Indians that went with me to the French in 1753. He expressd a satisfaction in seeing me and treated us with great kindness, giving us a Quarter of very fine Buffalo. He insisted upon our spending that Night with him, and in order to retard us as little as possible movd his Camp down the River about 3 Miles just below the Mouth of a Creek the name of which I could not learn (it not being large). [3] At this place we all Incampd. After much Councelling the overnight they all came to my fire the next Morning, with great formality; when Kiashuta rehearsing what had passd between me & the Sachems at Colo. Croghan's, thankd me for saying that Peace & friendship was the wish of the People of Virginia (with them) & for recommending it to the Traders to deal with them upon a fair & equitable footing; and then again expressd their desire of having a Trade opend with Virginia, & that the Governor thereof might not only be made acquainted therewith, but of their friendly disposition towards the white People. This I promisd to do.

[1] Lee's Creek, Wood County, W.Va.
[2] Pond Creek, Wood County, W.Va.
[3] Probably Shade River, Meigs County, Ohio.

Monday 29th.   The tedious ceremony which the Indians observe in their Councellings & speeches, detained us till 9 Oclock. Opposite to the Creek just below wch. we Incampd, is a pretty long bottom,[1] & I believe tolerable wide; but abt. 8 or 9 Miles below the aforemend. Creek, & just below a pavement of Rocks on the west side, comes in a Creek [2] with fallen Timber at the Mouth, on which the Indians say there is wide bottom's, & good Land. The River bottom's above for some distance is very good, & continues for near half a Mile below the Creek. The pavement of Rocks are only to be seen at low water. Abt. a mile, or a little better below the Mouth of the Creek there is another pavement of Rocks on the East side in a kind of Sedgey Ground. On this Creek many Buffaloes use[d to be] according to the Indians Acct. Six Miles below this comes in a small Creek [3] on the west side at the end of a small naked Island, and just above another pavement of Rocks. This Creek comes thro a Bottom of fine Land, & opposite to it (on the East side the River) appears to be large bottom of very fine Land also. At this place begins what they call the great Bent. 5 Miles below this again, on the East side, comes in (abt. 200 yds. above a little stream or Gut) another Creek; which is just below an Island,[4] on the upper point of which are some dead standing trees, & a parcel of white bodied Sycamores. In the Mouth of this Creek lyes a Scycamore blown down by the wind. From hence an East line may be Run 3 or 4 Miles; thence a North Line till it strikes the River, which I apprehend woud Include about 3 or 4000 Acres of exceeding valuable Land. At the Mouth of this C[ree]k which is 3 or 4 Miles above two Islands (at the lower end of the last, is a rapid,[5] & the Point of the Bend) is the Wariors Path to the Cherokee Country. For two Miles & an half below this the River Runs a No. Et. Course, & finished what they call the Great Bent. Two Miles & an half below this again we Incampd.

[1] The Long Bottom is in Meigs County, Ohio.

[2] Big Sandy Creek enters the Ohio at Ravenswood, W.Va. GW later acquired 2,448 acres of bottomland in this area (WRITINGS, 34:438).

[3] Probably Oldtown Creek, which flows into the Ohio from the west.

[4] George's Island in the Ohio just above Big and Little Mills creeks, which enter the river from the east.

[5] Letart's Rapids, Mason County, W.Va. The islands were unnamed but are numbered 44 and 45 in CRAMER, 94. Pownall noted that "the Water is so rapid that they are obliged to haul the Canoes with Ropes in coming up for near a Furlong along the South East Side" (POWNALL, 139).

Tuesday 30th.   We set out at 50 Minutes passd Seven—the Weather being Windy & Cloudy (after a Night of Rain). In about 2 Miles we came to the head of a bottom (in the shape of a horse Shoe) which I judge to be about 6 Miles r[oun]d; the beginning of the bottom appeard to be very good Land, but the lower part (from the Growth) did not seem so friendly. An East course from the lower end woud strike the River again above, about the Beging. of the bottom.

The upper part of the bottom we Incampd in was an exceeding good one, but the lower part rather thin Land & coverd with Beach. In it is some clear Meadow Land and a Pond or Lake. This bottom begins just below the Rapid at the point of the Great Bent, from whence a N. N. Wt. Course woud answer to run a parrallel to the next turn of the River.

The River from this place narrows very considerably, & for 5 or 6 Miles or more, is scarcely more than 150 or 200 yards over. The Water yesterday, except the Rapid at the Great Bent, & some swift places about the Islands was quite Dead, & as easily passd one way as the other; the Land in general appeard level & good. About 10 Miles below our Incampment & a little lower down than the bottom describd to lye in the shape of a horse Shoe comes in a small Creek on the West side,[1] and opposite to this on the East begins a body of flat Land which the Indians tell us runs quite across the Fork to the Falls[2] in the Kanhawa, and must at least be 3 days walk across. If so the Flat Land containd therein must be very considerable. A Mile or two below this we Landed, and after getting a little distance from the River we came (without any rising) to a pretty lively kind of Land grown up with Hicky. & Oaks of different kinds, intermixd with Walnut &ca. here & there. We also found many shallow Ponds, the sides of which abounding in grass, invited innumerable quantities of wild fowl among which I saw a Couple of Birds in size between a Swan & Goose; & in colour somewhat between the two; being darker than the young Swan and of a more sutty Colour. The Cry of these was as unusual as the Bird itself, as I never heard any noize resembling it before.[3] Abt. 5 Miles below this we Incampd. in a bottom of Good Land which holds tolerably flat & rich for some distance out.

[1] Probably Leading Creek, entering the Ohio from the east, 18 miles below Letart's Rapids.

[2] The Falls of the Great Kanawha are approximately 2 miles below the junction of the Gauley and New rivers. Hutchins notes, "After going 10 miles up *Kanhawa* the land is hilly, and the water a little rapid for 50 or 60 miles further to the *Falls*, yet Batteaus or Barges may be easily rowed thither. These Falls were formerly thought *impassable;* but late discoveries have proved, that a waggon road may be made through the mountain" (HUTCHINS, 22).

[3] Perhaps the great northern diver, or common loon, although GW's description would also fit the great blue heron or the American bittern.

Wednesday 31st.   I sent the Canoe along down to the Junction
of the two Rivers abt. 5 Miles that is the Kanhawa with the Ohio
and set out upon a hunting Party to view the Land.[1] We steerd
nearly East for about 8 or 9 Miles then bore Southwardly, & westwardly, till we came to our camp at the confluence of the Rivers.
The Land from the Rivers appeard but indifferent, & very
broken; whether these ridges might not be those that divide the
Waters of the Ohio from the Kanhawa is not certain, but I believe they are. If so the Lands may yet be good. If not, that which
lyes of the River bottoms is good for little.

[1] Roy Bird Cook suggests that this "apparently involved a journey to the
headwaters of Oldtown Creek, West Virginia, over the divide to Crooked
Creek and down that stream to the site of Point Pleasant. It marked the
southernmost point ever reached by Washington in the Ohio Valley; four
miles above the site of the French settlement at Gallipolis, Ohio, and forty
miles above the site of Huntington, West Virginia" (COOK, 25).

[November]

November 1st.   A little before eight Oclock we set of with our
Canoe up the River to discover what kind of Lands lay upon the
Kanhawa.[1] The Land on both sides this River just at the Mouth is
very fine; but on the East side when you get towards the Hills
(which I judge to be about 6 or 700 yards from the River) it appears to be wet, & better adapted for Meadow than tillage. This
bottom continues up the East side for about 2 Miles, & by going
up the Ohio a good Tract might be got of bottom Land Including
the old Shawna Town, which is about 3 Miles up the Ohio just
above the Mouth of a C[ree]k—where the aforementiond bottom
ends on the East side the Kanhawa. An[othe]r begins on the W.
which extends up it at least 50 Miles by the Indns. Acct. and of
great width (to be ascertaind, as we come down) in many places
very rich, in others somewhat wet & pondy; fit for Meadow; but
upon the whole exceeding valuable, as the Land after you get out
of the Rich bottom is very good for Grain tho not rich. We judgd
we went up this River about 10 Miles today. On the East side appear to be some good bottoms but small—neither long nor wide,
& the Hills back of them rather steep & poor.

[1] The Great Kanawha.

Novr. 2d.   We proceeded up the River with the Canoe about 4
Miles more, & then incampd & went a Hunting; killd 5 Buffaloes &

wounded some others—three deer &ca. This Country abounds in Buffalo & wild game of all kinds; as also in all kinds of wild fowl, the⟨re⟩ being in the Bottoms a great many small grassy Ponds or Lakes which are full of Swans, Geese, & Ducks of different kinds.

Some of our People went up the River 4 or 5 Miles higher & found the same kind of bottom on the West side, & we were told by the Indians that it continued to the Falls which they judgd to be 50 or 60 Miles higher up. This Bottom next the Water (in most places) is very rich. As you approach to the Hills you come (in many) to a thin white Oak Land, & poor. The Hills as far as we coud judge were from half a Mile to a Mile from the River; poor & steep in the parts we see, with Pine growing on them. Whether they are generally so, or not, we cannot tell but I fear they are.

Saturday 3d.   We set of down the River on our return home-wards, and Incampd at the Mouth; at the Beginning of the Bottom above the Junction of the Rivers, and at the Mouth of a branch on the Eastside, I markd two Maples, an Elm, & Hoop-wood Tree as A Cornr. of the Soldiers L[an]d (if we can get it) intending to take all the bottom from hence to the Rapids in the Great Bent into one Survey.[1] I also markd at the Mouth of another Gut lower down on the West side (at the lower end of the long bottom) an Ash and hoopwood for the Beginning of another of the Soldiers Survey to extend up so as to Include all the Bottom (in a body) on the West side.

In coming from our last Incampment up the Kanhawa I en-deavourd to take the courses & distances of the River by a Pocket Compass, & guessing; which I make thus. N. by W. 2 Mile—NNW 1½ Do. NW ½ Do. to the Mouth of a pretty smart Creek to the Eastward—No. Wt. 2 Do. to another Creek of the same size on the same side—West ½ a Mile—WNW ½ a Mile—N. Wt. 1 Do. WNW 2 Do. W by N 2 Do.—NW 1½ Do. WNW ½ Do. to the Mouth.

[1] Some 80 square miles of this land was eventually surveyed and granted to officers of the Virginia Regiment other than GW (see COOK, 27).

Sunday 4.   The Ohio from the Mou⟨th⟩ of the Kanhawa runs thus—North 2 Miles—NNW 1¼ to the Mouth of a Creek & old Shawne Town N 6 W 1½ Miles—NEt. 1 Do.—NE by Et. 1½ NNEt. 4 Do. ENE ¾ of a Mile to the Mouth of a C[ree]k on the west side,[1] & to the Hills, wch. the Indians say is always a fire to which the Bottom from the Mouth of the Kanhawa continues & then ends. After passing these Hills (which may run on the River near a Mile) there appears to be another pretty good Bottom on the East side. At this place we met a Canoe going to the Illinoies with Sheep and at this place also, that is at the end of the Bottom from the Kanhawa, just as we came to the Hills, we met with a Sycamore abt. 60 yards from the River of a most extraordinary size it measuring (3 feet from the Gd.) 45 feet round, lacking two Inches & not 50 yards from it was another 31.4 round (3 feet from the Gd. also).

The 2d. Bottom hinted at the other side (that is the one lying above the Bottom that reaches from the Kanhawa) is that taken notice of the 30th. Ulto. to lye in the shape of a Horse Shoe, & must from its situation, & quantity of level Ground be very valuable, if the Land is but tolerably good.

After passing this bottom & abt. a Mile of Hills we enterd into the 3d. Bottom and Incampd. This bottom reaches within about half a Mile of the Rapid at the point of the Great Bent.[2]

[1] Opposite the mouth of Campaign Creek, Gallia County, Ohio.

[2] Roy Bird Cook suggests this camp was "about the mouth of Broad Creek, above New Haven, West Virginia" (COOK, 27).

Monday 5th.   I set of the Canoe with our Baggage & walkd across the Neck on foot with Captn. Crawford distant according to our Walking about 8 Miles as we kept a strait course under the Foot of the Hills which run about So. Et. & was two hours & an half walking of it.[1]

This is a good Neck of Land the Soil being generally good; & in places very rich. Their is a large proportion of Meadow Ground, and the Land as high, dry, & Level as one coud wish. The growth in most places is beach intermixd with walnut &ca. but more especially with Poplar (of which there are numbers very large). The Land towards the upper end is black Oak, & very good. Upon the whole a valuable Tract might be had here, & I judge the quantity to be about 4000 Acres.

After passing this Bottom & the Rapid, as also some Hills wch. just pretty close to the River, we came to that Bottom before remarkd the 29th. Ulto.; which being well describd, there needs no further remark except that the Bottom within view appears to be exceeding rich; but as I was not out upon it, I cannot tell how it

is back from the River. A little above this Bottom we Incampd—
the afternoon being rainy & Night wet.

[1] GW and Crawford had now crossed to the Ohio shore. GW later acquired
4,395 acres on the opposite side of the river in the area of the Great Bend
(WRITINGS, 34:438). This land is in the vicinity of Millswood, W.Va.

Tuesday 6th.   We left our Incampment a little after daylight, &
in about 5 Miles we came to Kiashutes Hunting Camp which was
now removd to the Mouth of that Creek noted Octr. 29 for having
fallen Timber at the Mouth of it, in a bottom of good land. Between the Bottom last describd & this bottom, there is nothing but
Hills on the East side except a little flat of a 100 Acres or so, between. This Bottom thro which the Creek comes may be about
4 or 5 Miles in length & tolerably wide. Grown up pretty much
with Beach tho the Soil is good.

By the kindness, and Idle ceremony of the Indians, I was detaind at Kiashutas Camp all the remaing. part of this day; and
having a good deal of conversation with him on the Subject of
Land. He informd me, that, it was further from the mouth of
the Great Kanhawa to the Fall of that River than it was between
the two Kanhawas—that the Bottom on the West side (which begins near the Mouth of the Kanhawa) continues all the way to
the Falls without the Interposition of Hills, and widens as it goes,
especially from a pretty large Creek that comes in abt. 10 or 15
Miles higher up than where we were—that in the Fork there is a
body of go⟨od⟩ [1] Land and at some pretty consider⟨able⟩ distance
above this, the River forks again at an Island, & there begins the
Reed or Cain to grow—that the Bottoms on the East side of the
River are also very good, but broken with Hills and that the
River is easily passd with Canoes to the Falls wch. cannot be less
than 100 M⟨iles⟩ but further it is not possible to go with them and
that there is but one ridge f⟨rom⟩ thence to the Settlements upon
the River above, that it is possible for a Man to travel; the Country betw⟨een⟩ being so much broken with steep Hills & precipices.

He further informd (which ⟨   ⟩ seemed to be corroborated
by all ⟨   ⟩ with whom I conversd) that the ⟨   ⟩ back of
the Short broken Hills th⟨   ⟩ but down upon the Rivers are
⟨   ⟩ uneven, & not rich, except the ⟨   ⟩ upon Creeks, till
you come towards ⟨   ⟩ heads of the Creeks; then the
La⟨   ⟩ grows leveller, and the soil rich ⟨   ⟩.

[1] Entries in the diary from this point to Nov. 17 have been badly mutilated.
The entries are not complete enough to identify landmarks with certainty.

Wednesday 7th.   We set out ⟨   ⟩ ½ an hour after Seven and
af⟨   ⟩sing the Botton through which ⟨   ⟩ Creek with the
fallen Timber at the Mouth Runs & which I believe is calld Buffalo Creek, we came to a range of Hills for a Mile or more in
length upon the River (East side) then comes in the Bottom,
opposite to wch. the Creek below wch. we lodgd at with the Indians the 28th. Ulto. empties. This also appears to be a bottom
of 4 or 5 Miles in length, and tolerable good from the River.
When we ⟨   ⟩ pass this Bottom the Hills (rather ⟨   ⟩aller
& flatter than usual) comes ⟨   ⟩se to the River (East side for
4 or ⟨   m⟩iles) then begins another Bottom ⟨   ⟩ above,
or opposite to a small ⟨   ⟩nd; but before we came to this
⟨   m⟩ile, or two, we passd a good smart ⟨   ⟩ on the East
side. This Bottom ⟨   ⟩ opposite to Great Hockhocking
⟨   ⟩ above which, & opposite to Dela⟨ware⟩ Hunting Party,
we Incampd.

⟨Thur⟩sday 8th.   We left our Incamp⟨ment⟩ as soon as we coud
clearly dis⟨tingu⟩ish the rocks; and after pas⟨   ⟩ Bottom
which neither ap⟨   ⟩ to be long, wide, nor very ⟨   ⟩
came to a Second Bottom noticd the 27th. Ulto. opposite to a
Creek on the west side called by the Indian's little hockhocking,
but may easily be distinguishd by having a lar⟨ge⟩ Stone just at
its Mouth (the upper side) . This bottom is about 7 in length and
appears to be very wide, and go⟨od⟩ and must be very valuable if
it ⟨is⟩ not liable to be overflowd, some pa⟨rt⟩ of it appearing low.
The lower part of this bottom (as was obser⟨ved⟩ the 27th. Ulto.)
is opposite to a smal barren Island with only a few bu⟨shes⟩ on it
—the upper part of it begin⟨   ⟩ at much such another place
o⟨   ⟩ side (and part of a pretty long ⟨   ⟩ and at a drain
or small run Th⟨at   ⟩ comes out of the Hills. This is
⟨   ⟩ in a Mile or two of the Mouth ⟨   ⟩ Kanhawa, & the
next Bottom ⟨   ⟩ except a little narrow slipe ⟨   ⟩ at the
foot of the Hills below the ⟨   ⟩.
   At the Mouth of the Ka⟨nawha⟩ Captn. Crawford, one of the
In⟨dians⟩ and myself, left the Canoe, in⟨ten⟩ding to meet it again
at the ⟨   ⟩ of Muskingham about 13 M⟨iles⟩ above, but the
Indian by ⟨   ⟩ brought us to the River ⟨   ⟩ Miles below
it. In this excursion we passd over various kinds of Lands some
tolerable good white Oak Ground level, & meadowey—some ⟨v⟩ery
Hilly, & broken with Stone; and ⟨s⟩ome black Oak, thinly timberd
but ⟨g⟩ood for Farming and others abt. ⟨   ⟩ Mile before we
came to the River ⟨w⟩hich was at a place where there ⟨wa⟩s no

bottom) exceeding good, full 〈   〉el enough, & well timberd
with 〈   〉 & black Oak; but in all the Gd. 〈   〉 passd over
today, & I suppose 〈   〉 coud not have walkd less than
〈   〉 Miles there was no Water. This 〈   〉art of the Land
where I thoug〈   〉 Octr. 27) 50,000 Acres might 〈   〉t;
but it does not answer my 〈expe〉ctations. However, by falling
〈   〉 the River too low, I apprehend 〈   〉 the worst of
it; as we were 〈   〉 the Ridges that divide the Wa〈   〉t
Ohio from the Kanhawa; & 〈   〉 up, towards the 3 Islands, has
〈   〉 appearance. 〈   〉st below the Mouth of Mus〈   〉
Incampd.

Friday 9th.   The Night proving very Rainy, & Morning wet we
did 〈not〉 set out till ½ after 10 Oclock, & Incampd by the 3 Islands. Seeing a Bear upon the shore we landed, and followd it
abo〈ut〉 half a Mile from the River wch. gave us an opportunity
of s〈eeing〉 a little of the Land, which was hilly but rich.

Saturday 10th.   After a Nig〈ht〉 of incessant Thunder & Lig〈ht〉-
ning, attended with heavy 〈con〉stant Rain till 11 Oclock
th〈   〉 day, we set of about Twelve 〈   〉 (the Rain
then ceasing) and 〈   〉 to the lower end of the long distant
about 12 Miles—〈   〉 little stream, imperceptab〈le   〉
the view in our passage do 〈   〉 now pouring in her mite,
〈   〉 River raising very fast 〈   〉 grows so muddy as
to ren〈der   〉 Water irksome to drink

〈Su〉nday 11th.   The last Night provd 〈a〉 Night of incessant Rain
attended 〈w〉ith thunder and lightning. The 〈ri〉ver by this Morning had raisd abt. 〈   〉 feet perpendicular and was 〈lev〉elling
fast. The Rain seeming 〈to a〉bate a little and the wind spring〈ing〉
up in our favour we were 〈te〉mpted to set of; but were deceivd
〈   〉 both; for the Wind soon ceasd, & 〈the〉 Rain continued
without inter〈rup〉tion till about 4 Oclock when 〈it〉 moderated.
However tho we 〈did〉 not sit of till Eleven, We got 〈to the〉 head
of the long reach abt. 〈   〉les the River continuing to 〈   〉
fast, & much choakd with 〈   〉 wood.

〈Mo〉nday 12th.   There fell a little 〈   〉 in the Night tho
nothing to 〈   〉 of. Abt. Sun rise we left our 〈Incam〉pment
to encounter a very 〈   s〉tream which by this time had
〈   〉 2 feet perpendicular & running 〈   〉t velocity. After
contending 〈   w〉hole day we were not able to get more
than about 〈   〉 Miles. The water still rising, and the Currt.

if possible running ⟨w⟩ith more violence, we came to a res⟨olu⟩-
tion of ordering our Horses (whi⟨ch⟩ by appointment were to be
at P⟨itts⟩burg the 14th. Inst.) to meet us at Mingo Town accordingly.

Tuesday 13th.   We dispatchd ⟨   ⟩ young Indian express to
Val⟨   ⟩ Crawford, who had the charge o⟨f⟩ them to proceed
on ⟨   ⟩ that place, where we purp⟨osed⟩ if possible, to get the
Canoe ⟨it⟩ being about 50 Miles below ⟨   ⟩ In pursuance of
this resolu⟨tion⟩ we Imbark'd again, and with ⟨diffi⟩culty got about
5 Miles furth⟨er⟩ to the Mouth of the Upperm⟨ost⟩ broken timber
Creek. In ⟨   ⟩ of last Night the River rose ⟨   ⟩ perpendicular, and in the w⟨   ⟩ with what it rose in the day
⟨   ⟩ must be now 4 or 5 & twenty fee⟨t⟩ its usual height, & not
a great ⟨   ⟩ below its banks—in low pl⟨aces⟩ them.

This day about 3 In the After⟨noo⟩n we met two Battoes & a
large Ca⟨noe⟩ going (at a very fast rate) to ⟨   ⟩ Illinois with
Provisions for the ⟨G⟩arrison at Fort Chartres.[1]

[1] Fort Chartres is in the Illinois country on the east side of the Mississippi
River some 50 miles below the site of Saint Louis. Originally a French fort, it
had been acquired by the British in 1763. Visiting the fort in 1766, Capt.
Harry Gordon found it "well imagined and finished. It has four bastions of
stone masonry, designed defensible against musquetry. The barracks are also
of masonry, commodious and elegant. The fort is large enough to contain 400
men, but may be defended by one third of that number against Indians"
(POWNALL, 163–64). It was abandoned by the British in 1772 "as it was rendered untenable by the constant washings of the River Missisippi in high
floods" (HUTCHINS, 37).

Wednesday 14th.   The River began ⟨   ⟩e at a stand between
Sunset & dark Night, & contind. for some ⟨   ⟩ so; falling only
2 feet by Sun ⟨   ⟩. About an hour by sun we ⟨   ⟩ our
Incampment and reachd a ⟨   ⟩ above the Captening, (or Fox
grape vine Creek) about 11 Miles; not finding ⟨the w⟩ater quite
so strong as yesterday, ⟨lev⟩eling with a little assistance from
⟨   ⟩ind. About 2 or 3 Miles below ⟨Capte⟩ning I got out (on
the West side) ⟨   ⟩kd through a Neck of as good ⟨   ⟩ as
ever I saw, between that & ⟨   ⟩k; the Land on the Hill sides
⟨   ⟩s rich as the bottoms; than ⟨   ⟩ nothing can exceed.
The bottom ⟨   ⟩ the Mouth of Captening appears ⟨   ⟩
equal goodness with the one below ⟨   ⟩.

⟨Thu⟩rsday 15th.   The Canoe set of ⟨   ⟩ rise, as I did to view
that ⟨   ⟩ opposite to the Mouth of Pike Creek. In ⟨passing

⟩ Neck I found the lower pa⟨rt⟩ N⟨ot⟩ very rich ⟨upon⟩ the Ri⟨ver   ⟩ very ⟨   ⟩ towards the Hills, with ⟨   ⟩ Land well Timberd; and not ⟨   ⟩ only in places—the Mid⟨   ⟩ back of the Rich bottom ⟨   ⟩ black & white Oak Land f⟨   ⟩ming, or any purpose w⟨   ⟩ & intermixd with Meadow.

The upper end is as rich ⟨   ⟩ quite to the Hills (which ⟨   ⟩ as ever I saw, but subjec⟨t   ⟩ to freshes. Of this Bottom ⟨   ⟩ Timberd Land adjoining, I⟨   ⟩ may be 12 or 1500 Acres go ⟨   ⟩ in this manner. Begin⟨   ⟩ the Hills juts down to the ⟨   ⟩ ½ a Mile above Pipe Creek ⟨   ⟩ west) & a Mile or more to ⟨   ⟩ of another C[ree]k on the East, ⟨   ⟩ Bottom above the Capten⟨ing   ⟩ East side the River, & just ⟨   ⟩ destruction of Timber Oc⟨   ⟩ Hurricane of Wind—fro⟨   ⟩ This bottom there is a r⟨un   ⟩ abt. a Mile—then comes in ⟨   ⟩ mentiond (which I coud g⟨   ⟩ on which & up the River ⟨   ⟩ there appears to be a ⟨   ⟩ rich at ⟨   ⟩e is a run ⟨   ⟩—the b⟨ott⟩om ⟨   ⟩ is pretty long but narrow ⟨   ⟩ Creek (on the West side) calld ⟨   ⟩ Nicholson the 24th. Ulto., r⟨   ⟩ the River having fallen at ⟨   ⟩t ⟨   ⟩.

⟨Friday⟩ 16th.   Directing the Canoe ⟨   ⟩ me at the Mouth of the ⟨   ⟩ by the Indians split Island ⟨   ⟩ which I have since found ⟨   ⟩e one distinguished by the ⟨   ⟩t of Redstone &ca. by the ⟨   ⟩eling; I set out with Capt⟨n⟩. ⟨   ⟩n foot, to take a view ⟨   ⟩ a little distance from the ⟨   ⟩ doing this we asscended Hills ⟨   ⟩ to be almost impassable, ⟨   ⟩ the River with stone & ⟨   ⟩ Timber. Back of these ⟨   gro⟩und is very uneven, & ex⟨   ⟩n⟨   ⟩ spots, not very good; ⟨   ⟩ly well Timbered—as far ⟨   ⟩ see into the Country the ⟨   ⟩ his kind. Coming on ⟨   ⟩ split Island Creek) some ⟨   ⟩ on the Mouth, we had ⟨   opportu⟩nity of observing from ⟨   ⟩, which are very high the course of the Creek which Mea⟨n⟩ders through a bottom of fine land especially at the Forks where there appears to be a large body of it. The vail (through which this Creek runs) as far as we coud see up it, appears to be wide, & the Soil of the Hills which confines it good, tho very steep in some places. On this Creek, which heads up a little to the Southward of Redstone Settlement, there is, according to the Indians Acct., & all the accts. I coud get, a great deal of fine land. The Body of flat Land at the Forks is but a very little way from the River in a direct line & may contain I guess a thousand Acres or more. Below the Mouth of this Creek there is a bottom of pretty good Land but not large and about 5 Miles above at the Mouth of a small run which comes in at the lower point of a Island (& which by mistake I calld, Octr. 23d. Fishing Creek) there is a bottom of as fine land as can possibly be but not large containing not more than two or 300 Acres. At the head of this Bottom & a little below the 2d. cross Creeks we Incampd dista⟨nt⟩ from our last 13 or fourteen Miles.

Here it was for the 2d. time that the Indian with me spoke of a fine piece of Land and beautiful place for a House & in order to give me a more lively Idea of it, chalk out the situation upon his Deerskin. It lyes upon Bull Creek, at least 30 Miles from the Mouth, but not more than 5 from the Mouth of Muddy Creek, in an ESE direction. The spot he recommends for a House lyes very high commanding a prospect of a great deal of level Land below on the Creek—the Ground about it very rich & a fine spring in the middle of it about which many Buffaloes use & have made great Roads. Bull Creek according to his Acct. runs parrallel with the long reach in the Ohio—not above 6 or 7 Miles from it, having fine bottoms which widen as it extends into the Country & towards the head of it is large bodies of level rich Land.

Saturday 17th.   By this Morning the River had fallen (in the whole) 2 or 3 & twenty feet, & was still lowering. Abt. 8 Oclock we set out, & passing the lower cross Creeks we came to a pretty long, & tolerable wide & good bottom on the East side the River; then comes in the Hills; just above which, is Buffalo Creek[1] (a Creek I neither see nor remarkd in going down) upon which, and above it, between that & the cross Creeks near the Mingo Town (distant 3 or 4 Miles) is a Bottom of exceeding fine Land but not very large unless it extends up the Creek.

About 3 Oclock we came to the Town without seeing our Horses the Indian (which was sent express for them) having passd through only the morning before (being detained by the Creeks which were too high to ford, without going high up them). Here we resolvd to wait their arrival which was expected tomor⟨row⟩ & here then will end our Water Voyage along a River the general course of which from Bever Creek to the Kanhawa is about S. Wt. (as near as I coud determine); but in its winding thro a narrow Vale, extreamely serpentine; forming on both sides the River alternately, Necks of very good (so⟨me⟩ exceeding fine) Bottoms; lying for the most part in the shape of a half Moon, & of various sizes. There is very little difference in the genl. width

[315]

of the River from Fort Pitt to the Kanhawa; but in the depth I believe the odds is considerably in favour of the lower parts; as we found no shallows below the Mingo Town, except in one or two places where the River was broad; & there, I do not know but there might have been a deep Channel in some part of it. Every here and there are Islands some larger, & some smaller, which operating in the nature of Locks or Stops, occasion pretty still water above but for the most part strong & rapid water alongside of them. However there is none of these so swift but that a Vessel may be Rowd or set up with Poles. When the River is in its Natural State, large Canoes that will carry 5 or 6000 weight & more, may be workd against stream by 4 hands 20 & 25 Miles a day; & down, a good deal more. The Indians who are very dexterous (even there women) in the Management of Canoes, have there Hunting Camps & Cabins all along the River for the convenience of Transporting their Skins by Water to Market. In the Fall, so soon as the Hunting Season comes on, they set out with their Familys for this purpose; & in Hunting will move there Camps from place to place till by the Spring they get 2 or 300, or more Miles from there Towns; Then Bever catch it in there way up which frequently brings them into the Month of May, when the Women are employd in Plantg. — the Men at Market, & in Idleness, till the Fall again; when they pursue the same course again. During the Summer Months they live a poor & perishing life.

The Indians who live upon the Ohio (the upper parts of it at least) are composd of Shawnas, Delawares, & some of the Mingos, who getting but little part of the Consideration that was given for the Lands Eastward of the Ohio, view the Settlement of the People upon this River with an uneasy & jealous Eye, & do not scruple to say that they must be compensated for their Right if the People settle thereon, notwithstanding the Cession of the Six Nations thereto. On the other hand, the People from Virginia & elsewhere, are exploring and Marking all the Lands that are valuable not only on Redstone & other Waters of Monongahela but along down the Ohio as low as the little Kanhawa; & by next Summer I suppose will get to the great Kanhawa, at least; how difficult it may be to contend with these People afterwards is easy to be judgd of from every days experience of Lands actually settled, supposing these to be made; then which nothing is more probable if the Indians permit them, from the disposition of the People at present. A few Settlements in the midst of some of the large Bottoms, woud render it impractacable to get any large qty. of Land Together; as the Hills all the way down the River (as low as I went) come pretty close and are steep & broken incapable of Settlements tho some of them are rich and only fit to support the Bottoms with Timber and Wood.

The Land back of the Bottoms as far as I have been able to judge, either from my own observations or from information, is nearly the same, that is exceeding une⟨ven⟩ & Hilly; & I do presume that there is no body's of Flat rich Land to be found till one gets far enough from the River to head the little runs & drains that comes through the Hills; & to the Sources (or near it) of the Creeks & there Branches. This it seems is the case of the Lands upon Monogahela and yaughe. & I fancy holds good upon this River till you get into the Flat Lands (or near them) below the Falls.

The Bottom Land differs a good deal in quality. That highest up the River in general is richest; tho the Bottoms are neither so wide or long, as those below. Walnut, H. Loc⟨ust⟩ Cherry, & some other Woods, that grow Snarly, & neither Tall nor large, but coverd with Grape Vines (with the Fruit of which this Country at this Instant abounds) are the growth of the Richest Bottoms, but on the other hand these Bottoms appear to me to be the lowest & most subject to Floods. Sugar Tree and Ash, mixd with Walnut &ca. compose the growth of the next richest low grounds and Beach Poplar Oaks &ca. the last. The Soil of this is also good but inferior to either of the other kinds & beach Bottoms are excepted against on Acct. of the difficulty of clearing them there Roots spreading over a large Surface of Ground & being hard to kill.

[1] Buffalo Creek enters the Ohio some 8 miles below Mingo Town, where the travelers were to meet their horses. See HANNA, 2:196.

Sunday, 18th.   Agreed with two Delaware Indians to carry up our Canoe to Fort Pitt for the doing of which I was to pay 6 Dollars & give them a Quart Tinn Can.

Monday 19th.   The Delawares set of with the Canoe and our Horses not arriving, the day appeard exceeding long & tedious. Upon conversing with Nicholson I found he had been two or three times to Fort Chartres at the Illinois, and got from him the following Acct. of the Lands between this & that; & upon the Shawna River; [1] on which he had been a Hunting.

The Lands down the Ohio grow more & more level as you approach the Falls, and about 150 Miles below them, the Country appears quite Flat, & exceeding rich. On the Shawna River (which comes into the Ohio 400 Miles below the Falls [2] & about

1100 from Pittsburg) up which he had hunted 300 & more Miles
the Lands are exceeding Level, rich, fine, but a good deal intermixed with Cain or Reed, which mig⟨ht⟩ render them difficult to
clear; that game of all kinds was to be found here in the greatest
abundance, especially Buffalo—that from Fort Chartres to Pitts
burg by Land, is co⟨m⟩puted 800 Miles; & in travelling th⟨ro⟩ the
Country from that place he f⟨ound⟩ the Soil very rich—the Ground
exceeding level to O. Post [3] (a French s⟨ettle⟩ment) & from Opost
to the Lower Sha⟨w⟩na Town on Scioto equally flat—that he passd
through large Planes 30 Miles in length without a Tree except
little Islands of Wood—th⟨at⟩ in these Planes thousands & 10,000⟨s⟩
of Buffalo may be seen feeding. That the distance from Fort
Cha⟨rtres⟩ to Opost is about 240 Miles & the Country not very
well Waterd—from Opost to the lower Shawna Town about 300
more abounding in good springs & Rivulets—that the remainder
of the way to Fort Pitt is Hilly, & the Hills larger as you approach
the Fort tho the L[an]d in general is also good.

At Fort Pitt I got the distances from place to place down the
Ohio as taken ⟨by⟩ one Mr. Hutchings [4] & which are as follows—
wt. some corrections of mine.

From Fort Pitt to		Miles
Logs Town	W	18½
Big Bever Creek	W	29¼
Racoon Creek	GW E	34
Little Bever Creek	W	44
Yellow Creek	W	52
Big Stony Creek	GW W	66
Mingo Town	W	73
Cross Creeks		74
Buffalo Creek or Sculp C[ree]k	GW E	78
Second cross Creeks	GW	84
Weeling or split Island C[ree]k	GW E	94
Sculp Creek	GW W	100
Path to Redstone	GW E	108
Pipe Creek	GW W	110
Captening	GW W	113
Cut Creek	GW E	118
Broken Timber Creek	GW W	123
2d. Broken Timber C[ree]k	GW W	125
Muddy Creek	GW E	134
Beging. of the long reach		137

		Miles
End of Ditto		155
Bull Creek	GW E	160
A Pretty large C[ree]k on the West		178
Muskingham	W	182
Little Kanhawa	E	195
Little Hockhocking	W	202
Hockhocking	W	210
Creek with fallen Timber at the Mouth	E	230
A sm[al]l Creek on the West & beging. of Great Bent	E	236
Another Sm[al]l C[ree]k on the East just above a Gut	E	241
Rapid at the point of the Great Bent		245
Big Kanhawa	E	272
The distance by Hutchings is		266¼
Big Guyendot [5]	E	308
Big Sandy Creek	E	321
Scioto River [6]	W	366
Big Buffalo Lick [7] – A Mile Eastward of the River	W	390
Large Island divided by a gravelly Creek		410½
Little Mineamie River [8]	W	492¼
Licking Creek	E	500¼
Great Mineamie River [9]	W	527½
Where the Elephants Bones were found [10]	E	560¼
Kentucke River [11]	E	604½
The Falls		682
To where the low Country begins		837¾
Beging. of the 5 Islands		875¼
Large River on the East side		902¼
Verry large Islands in the middle of the River		960¼
Ouabache River [12]		999½
Big Rock, & Cave on the Westside [13]		1042¼
Shawano River [14]		1094
Cherokee River [15]		1107
Fort Massiac [16]		1118¾
Mouth of Ohio [17]		1164
	In all	1164

The Distances from For Pitt to the Mouth of the Great Kanhawa are set down agreeable to my own Computation, but from
thence to the Mouth of River Ohio are strictly according to
Hutchingss. Acct.—which Acct. I take to be erroneous inasmuch
as it appears that the Miles in the upper part of the River are very
long, & those towards the Canhawa short, which I attribute to his
setting of in a falling fresh & running slower as they proceeded
on.

The Letters E and W signifie wch. side of the River the respective Waters come in on, that is, whether on the East or West side.

[1] The Cumberland River, flowing through Tennessee and Kentucky.

[2] The Falls of the Ohio at Louisville, Ky., were formed by a limestone ledge
reaching across the river, which dropped some 26 feet over a distance of 3
miles.

[3] Ouabache or Wabash Post, later Vincennes, Ind.

[4] Thomas Hutchins (1730–1789), a native of Monmouth County, N.J.,
served in the Pennsylvania provincial forces during the French and Indian
War. During his military service he acquired a knowledge of engineering and
surveying. Around 1762 he was commissioned an ensign in the British army
and as assistant engineer took part in the 1764 Bouquet expedition against
the Shawnee and Delaware. In 1766 he accompanied George Croghan, Capt.
Harry Gordon, and trader George Morgan on a trip through the Ohio and
Mississippi valleys (see BOND, 12–13; GORDON). In 1781 he was appointed ge-
ographer to the United States, and after the war he served as a commissioner
to run the boundary between Virginia and Pennsylvania. He supervised the
survey of the western lands ceded to the United States under the Ordinance
of 1785. His major works were *A Topographical Description of Virginia,
Pennsylvania, Maryland and North Carolina* (London, 1778) and *An Historical Narrative and Topographical Description of Louisiana and West-Florida*
(Philadelphia, 1784). For an account of Hutchins's career, see TREGLE, v-xliv.

It is uncertain what version of Hutchins's computations of distance upon
the Ohio GW used. The *Topographical Description of Virginia, Pennsylvania, Maryland and North Carolina* was not published until 1778 and in any
event the distances given by Hutchins in that work vary considerably from
GW's version (see HUTCHINS, appendix). Nor do the distances compare with
those given in the appendix to a work commonly attributed to Hutchins: *An
Historical Account of the Expedition against the Ohio Indians in the Year
MDCCLXIV under the Command of Henry Bouquet, Esq.* (Philadelphia,
1765, reprinted London, 1766), 68. It is possible that GW may have seen
copies of Hutchins's reports, submitted periodically to Gen. Thomas Gage
(see, for example, GAGE PAPERS, 1:309–10, 347). It seems likely that GW may
have had access to one of the versions of the table of distances appended to
the widely circulated journal kept by Capt. Harry Gordon on his trip to the
west in 1766. Gordon was accompanied by Hutchins, and Hutchins may well
have compiled the table. The entries for points beyond the Great Kanawha
agree substantially with the table appended to Gordon's journal (see
POWNALL, 166; GORDON, 488–89).

[5] From this point GW's table substantially agrees with that appended to the

Gordon journal, but several fractions of miles are dropped from the last entries.

[6] The Scioto River flows into the Ohio near Portsmouth, Ohio. The Lower Shawnee Town was opposite the mouth of the Scioto.

[7] Big Buffalo Lick is not noted by Hutchins. GW is possibly referring to Salt Lick Creek, flowing into the Ohio near this point, but more likely he confused the creek with Licking River, entering the Ohio opposite Cincinnati. It was then called the Great Salt Lick and was "remarkable for fine Land. Plenty of Buffaloes, Salt Springs, White Clay, and Limestone" (POWNALL, 145). Christopher Gist noted in his 1750 trip to the Ohio that "Upon the N side of Licking Creek about 6 M from the Mouth, are several Salt Licks, or Ponds, formed by little Streams or Dreins of Water, clear but of a blueish Colour, & salt Taste the Traders and Indians boil their Meat in this Water, which (if proper Care be not taken) will sometimes make it too salt to eat" (GIST, 42).

[8] Little Miami River flows into the Ohio at East Cincinnati.

[9] Great Miami River enters the Ohio in the extreme southwestern part of Ohio.

[10] Big Bone Lick, Boone County, Ky., was so called from the large quantity of fossilized mammoth bones found by early explorers in the area. Christopher Gist visited the area in 1750–51 and sent back one of the teeth to the Ohio Company. He was informed that "about seven Years ago these Teeth and Bones of three large Beasts (one of which was somewhat smaller than the other two) were found in a salt Lick or Spring upon a small Creek which runs into the S Side of the Ohio, about 15 M below the Mouth of the great Miamee River . . . . The Rib Bones of the largest of these Beasts were eleven Feet long, and the Skull Bone six feet wide, across the Forehead, & the other Bones in Proportion" (GIST, 57). See also HUTCHINS, 11.

[11] The Kentucky River flows into the Ohio at Carrollton, Ky.

[12] The Wabash River joins the Ohio at the southwest corner of Indiana.

[13] This may be a reference to Cave-in-Rock on the Illinois shore of the Ohio River, later infamous as a headquarters for river pirates (see BALDWIN, 119–24).

[14] Cumberland River.

[15] Now called the Tennessee River.

[16] Fort Massac, originally Fort Ascension, was built by the French in 1757 and abandoned in 1764. It was "120 miles below the mouth of the Wabash, and eleven miles below the mouth of the Cherokee River" (POWNALL, 161–62).

[17] The Ohio River joins the Mississippi at Cairo, Ill.

Remark & Occurs. in Novr.

Novr. 20th.   About One Oclock our Horses arrivd, having been prevented getting to Fort Pitt by the freshes. At Two we set out & got about 10 Miles. The Indians travelling along with us.

Tuesday 21st.   Reach'd Fort Pitt in the Afternoon, distant from our last Incampment about 25 Miles & as near as I can guess 35 from the Mingo Town.

The Land between The Mingo Town & Pittsburg is of different kinds. For 4 or 5 Miles after leaving the first mentiond place we passd over Steep Hilly ground, hurt with stone; coverd with White Oak; & a thin shallow Soil. This was succeeded by a lively White Oak Land, less broken; & this again by Rich Land the growth of which was chiefly white & red Oak, Mixd; which lasted with some Intervals of indifferent Ridges all the way to Pittsburg.

It was very observable that as we left the River; the Land grew better, which is a confirmation of the Accts. I had before receivd, that the good Bodies of Land lay upon the heads of the Runs & Creeks but in all my Travels through this Country, I have seen no large body of level Land. On the Branches of Racoon Creek there appears to be good Meadow Ground and on Shirtees Creek (over both which we passd) the Lands Looks well. The Country between the Mingo Town and Fort Pitt appears to be well supplied with Springs.

Thursday 22.   Stayd at Pittsburg all day. Invited the Officers & some other Gentlemen to dinner with me at Samples—among which was one Doctr. Connelly (nephew to Colo. Croghan) [1] a very sensible Intelligent Man who had travelld over a good deal of this western Country both by Land & Water & confirms Nicho⟨l⟩sons Acct. of the good Land on the Shawana River up which he had been near 400 Miles.

This Country (I mean on the Shawana River) according to Doctr. Connellys acct. must be exceeding desirable on many Accts. The Climate is exceeding fine—the Soil remarkably good. The Lands well Waterd with good streams & full level enough for any kind of Cultivation. Besides these advantages from Nature, it has others not less Important to a new settlement particularly Game which is so plenty as not only to render the Transportation of Provisions there (bread only excepted) altogether unnecessary but to enrich the Adventurers with the Peltry for which there is a constant & good Market.

Doctr. Connelly is so much delighted with the Lands, & Climate on this River; that he seems to wish for nothing more than to induce 100 families to go there to live that he might be among them. A New & most desirable Government might be established here to be bounded (according to his Acct.) by the Ohio Northward & westward. The Ridge that divides the Waters of the

Tenesee or Cherokee River Southward & Westward & a Line to be Run from the Falls of Ohio, or above so as to cross the Shawana River above the Fork of it.

Docter Connelly gives much the same Acct. of the Land between Fort Chartres in the Illinois Country, and Post St. Vincent (O Post) that Nicholson does, except in the Article of Water, wch. the Doctr. says is bad, & in the Summer Scarce. There being little else than stagnate Water to be met with.

¹ John Connolly, a native of Lancaster, Pa., and at this time a resident of Pittsburgh, had become well known on the frontier during the 1760s as a trader and speculator. GW may have been mistaken in stating he was George Croghan's nephew; his relationship to Croghan has been variously described (see HANNA, 2:71; WAINWRIGHT, 287). In 1774, probably under Croghan's auspices, he claimed the Pittsburgh area for Virginia and proceeded to set up a county government, a plan interrupted by Indian hostilities culminating in Dunmore's War. During the Revolution, Connolly was an active Loyalist.

Friday 23d.   After settling with the Indians ¹ & People that attended me down the River & defray the Sundry Expences accruing at Pittsburg, I set of on my return home and after dining at the Widow Mierss. on Turtle Creek reachd Mr. John Stephenson (two or three hours in the Night).

¹ GW paid the Indians £10 13s. (LEDGER A, 329).

Saturday 24th.   When we came to Stewards Crossing at Crawfords, the River was too high to Ford and his Canoe gone a Drift. However after waiting there 2 or three hours a Canoe was got in which we passd and Swam our Horses. The remainder of this day I spent at Captn. Crawfords it either Raining or Snowing hard all day.

Sunday 25th.   I Set out early in order to see Lund Washington's Land, but the Ground & trees being coverd with Snow, I was able to form but an indistinct opinion of it—tho upon the whole it appeard to be a good Tract of Land and as Level as common indeed more so. From this I went to Mr. Thos. Gists, and Dind, & then proceeded on to the Great crossing at Hoglands ¹ where I arrivd about Eight Oclock.

¹ John Hogeland (DLC: Toner Collection).

Munday 26th.   Reachd Killams on George's Creek where we met several Families going over the Mountains to live—some witht. having any places provided.

The Snow upon the Alligany Mountains was near knee deep.

Tuesday 27th.   We got to Colo. Cresaps at the Old Town after calling at Fort Cumberland & breakfasting with one Mr. Innis at the New store opposite.[1] 25 Miles.

[1] This was presumably James Innes. THE NEW STORE: operated by the Ohio Company (DIARIES, 1:449 n.3).

Wednesday 28th.   The Old Town Gut was so high as to Wet us in crossing it, and when we came to Coxs., the River was Impassable; we were obligd therefore to cross in a Canoe & swim our Horses. At Henry Enochs at the Fork of Cacapehon we dind, & lodgd at Rinkers. The distances thus computed—from the old Town to Coxs. 8 Miles—from thence to Cacapehon 12 and 18 Afterwards in all 38 Miles. The last 18 I do not think long ones.

Thursday 29th.   Set out early & reachd my Brothers by one Oclock (about 22 or 3 Miles). Doctr. Craik having Business by Winchester went that way to meet at Snickers tomorrow by 10 Oclock.

Friday 30th.   According to Appointment the Doctr. and I met & after Breakfasting at Snickers proceeded on to Wests[1] where we arrivd at or about Sunset.

[1] West's ordinary was located at the junction of the Colchester and Carolina roads in Loudoun County near present-day Aldie. By 1765 Charles West had taken over management of the inn from his father, William West (see HARRISON [1], 495).

[November]

Where & how my time is Spent

1.   Went up the Great Kanhawa abt. 10 Miles with the People that were with me.

2.   Hunting the most part of the day. The Canoe went up abt. 5 Miles further.

3.   Returnd down the River again and Incampd at the Mouth.

4.   Proceeded up the Ohio on our return to Fort Pitt. Incampd abt. 9 Miles below the rapid at the Grt. Bent.

5.   Walk'd across a Neck of Land to the Rapid and Incampd about ⟨   ⟩ Miles above it.

6.   In about 5 Miles we came to Kiashutas Camp & there Halted.

7.   Reachd the Mouth of Hockhocking—distant abt. 20 Miles.

8.   Came within a Mile of the Mouth of Muskingham 27 Miles.

9.   Got to the 3 Islands in the 2d. long reach about 17 Miles.

10.   Arrivd at the lower end of the long reach abt. 12 Miles—not setting of till 12 Oclock.

11.   Came about 16 Miles after hard working the greatest part of the day.

12.   Only got about 5 Miles the Currt. being very strong against us.

13.   Reachd the uppermost broken Timber Creek distant about 7 Miles contending with a violent Currt. the whole day.

14.   Came to the Captening or Fox Grape Vine Creek distant about 10 Miles.

15.   Reachd Weeling (on the West) where there had been an Indian Town & where some of the Shawnes are going to settle in the Spring distant from our last Incampment 12 Miles.

16.   Got within 13 Miles of the lower cross Creeks—13 Miles.

17.   Reachd the Mingo Town about 13 Miles more.

18.   At this place all day waiting for Horses which did not arrive.

19.   At the same place, & in the same Situation as yesterday.

20.   Our Horses arriving about One Oclock at 2 we set out for Fort Pitt & got about 10 Miles.

21.   Reachd Fort Pitt in the Afternoon & lodgd at Samples.

22.   Invited the Officers of the Fort and other Gentlemen to dine with me at Samples.

23.   Left Fort Pitt and reachd Mr. John Stephensons.

24.   Got to Captn. Crawfords—the Rivr. Youghyaughgane being very high.

25.   Reachd Hoglands at the great Crossing.

26.   Came to Killams on Georges Creek.

27.   Got to the Old Town to Colo. Cresaps distant from Killams about 25 Miles.

28.   Reachd Jasper Rinkers about 38 Miles from Cresaps & 30 from Cox's—not long ones.

29.   Came to my Brothers (distant about 25 Miles) to Dinner.

30.   Reachd Charles Wests 35 Miles from my Brother's.

Acct. of the Weather in Novr.

Novr. 1.   Calm, cool, & Cloudy, with great appearances of falling weather.

2.   Windy & clear in the forenoon afterwards Rain & Hail—then clear again.

3.   Clear & Windy—first from the So. Wt. then No. Wt.

4.   Clear and pleasant with but little Wind & that Northwardly.

5.   Lowering Morning & rainy afternoon.

6.   Cloudy forenoon but clear afterwards with the Wind high from the No. West.

7.   Clear & moderate Wind from the West.

8.   A lowering threatning Morning but more favourable afternoon & rain at Night.

9. A Good deal of rain fell in the Night & till 10 Oclock this Morng. after which it contind. drisling more or less all day till abt. Sunset then set in to a close hard Rain.

10. About 1 Oclock it began to thunder & Lighten & contind. to do so incessantly till abt. 8 Oclock with constant hard Rain which lasted till about 11 and then ceasd but contd. cloudy & very warm the remaining part of the day.

11. Abt. 9 Oclock last Night it began to Rain again, & contd. to do so the whole Night, sometimes as if pourd out of Buckets; attended with thunder and lightning.

12. Sometimes Cloudy & sometimes threatning hard for Snow.

13. Clear with the Wind fresh & cool from the No. West.

14. Clear with a little wind from the South & very white frost.

15. Very large frost again with little or no wind & clear.

16. Another white frost and calm and clear after it.

17. White frost with Southerly Wind & clear.

18. A Frost as white as Snow but clear & calm.

19. Another white frost but clear calm and exceeding pleasant.

20. Pleasant forenoon but lowering afterwards.

21. Very cloudy all the Forenoon, & Raining moderately afterwards.

22. Raining moderately all day with the Wind at Northwest.

23. Flying Clouds and windy but nothing falling.

24. First Raining, then Snowing all day.

25. Very Windy all day, & snowing the first part of it. Cold.

26. Very clear, and Cold.

27. Lowering Morning, & Snowy Afternoon.

28. Morning threatning but clear afterwards with the Wind fresh from the Northward.

29. Clear & Cold in the forepart of the day but tolerably pleasant afterwards.

30. Clear and Pleasant after the morning which was cold.

[December]

Where & how my time is Spent.

Decr. 1st. Reachd home from Wests after an absence of 9 Weeks and one Day.

2. At home all day alone.

3. Rid to the Mill in the forenoon, and returnd to Dinner.

4. Rid by Posey's to the Mill, and to the Ditchers. Mr. Boucher and Jacky Custis came here in the Afternoon.

Boucher had not given up the idea of taking Jacky to Europe. At this time he was urging the Washingtons to prepare the boy for travel by having him inoculated for smallpox in Baltimore, where Dr. Henry Stevenson ran a popular inoculation clinic, free of legal restrictions that the burgesses had recently imposed on inoculators in Virginia (Jonathan Boucher to GW, 1 Oct. 1770, DLC: GW; H.B.J., 1770–72, 100). Although the question of Jacky's tour was now no closer to being finally resolved than it had been in the spring, GW favored the inoculation, thinking that Jacky should be protected against smallpox whether he went abroad or not (GW to Boucher, 13 May 1770, WRITINGS, 3:12–15). But Mrs. Washington, while agreeing that the benefits were very desirable, feared exposing her son to the inoculating process, which, as practiced during this period, brought on a fatal case of the disease in 1 of every 50 to 60 inoculations (GW to Boucher, 20 April 1771, CSmH; KING [1], 321). Consequently the decision on this matter, like the one on the tour, was postponed.

5. Mr. Boucher went away again to Maryland. I rid to the Mill.

6. Rid by Muddy hole & Doeg Run to the Mill & returnd by Posey's.

7.   Rid to the Mill and returnd to Dinner.

8.   Went a hunting but found nothing. From the Woods I went to my Mill & so home to Dinner. Doc⟨tor⟩ Ross Dind here & went away after.

9.   Went to Pohick Church and returnd to Dinner.

10.   Went up to the little Falls to Balendines Sale. Returnd in the Evening.

John Ballendine was today attempting to satisfy all his creditors by leasing his enterprises at the falls and selling much of his other property, including about 100 hogsheads of tobacco, a large amount of wheat and corn, 50 head of sheep, one set each of blacksmith's and cooper's tools, some household furniture, 1,049 acres of land in Prince William County, and 91 acres in Fauquier County. However, he did not succeed in selling everything on this day, nor did all his creditors appear at the falls today to settle their accounts as he had requested, and a second sale and meeting of the creditors had to be called for 16 May 1771 (*Va. Gaz.*, R, 29 Nov. 1770 and 2 May 1771).

11.   Rid to my Mill and Ditchers before Dinner.

12.   At home all day. Mr. Semple Dined here, & went away afterwar⟨ds.⟩ Doctr. Rumney came in the Afternoon and stayd all Night.

13.   Doctr. Rumney went away after breakfast and the two Mrs. Fairfax's & Miss Nelly Marbray dind here. Mrs. Geo. Fairfax returnd afterds.

NELLY MARBRAY: possibly a member of the Marbury family of Prince George's County, Md. (MACKENZIE [1], 2:488–89).

14.   Mrs. B. Fairfax & Miss Marbray went away after Breakfast & Mr. Peake dind here.

15.   I rid to the Mill and Ditchers by Poseys.

16.   Dined at Belvoir with Jacky Custis & returnd afterwards.

17.   Jacky Custis went to Annapolis & I to Court. Returnd in the afternoon.

Jacky was not eager to return to school. "His mind," GW warned Jonathan Boucher, is "a good deal released from Study, & more than ever turnd to Dogs Horses and Guns" (16 Dec. 1770, NNC). The court met 17–19 Dec. (Fairfax County Order Book for 1770–72, 157–68, Vi Microfilm).

This view of the water end of a mill house illustrates a metal fish serving as a weather vane (5), the millstones (9), and the waterwheel (10). From Oliver Evans, *The Young Mill-Wright and Miller's Guide,* Philadelphia, 1795. (Beinecke Rare Book and Manuscript Library, Yale University)

18.   Rid to my Mill and to the Ditchers in the Fore and Afternoon.

GW today completed a land transaction with Valinda Wade, paying her £175
for her share of the Wade family property on Dogue Run, which she and her
two sisters, Sarah and Eleanor, had inherited. During the past few years
Sarah had died unmarried, and Eleanor, who had married John Barry of
Fairfax County, had recently died also, leaving a son William as her only
heir. Because the 193-acre tract had never been divided among the sisters, it
became, following the deaths of Sarah and Eleanor, the joint property of
Valinda and her underage nephew, whose business affairs were handled by his
father. With this day's purchase, GW obtained Valinda's right to divide the
land with young Barry on an equal basis (deeds of Valinda Wade to GW,
17 Dec. 1770, NjMoNP, and 18 Dec. 1770, CSmH). The property was important to GW not only because it lay near the rest of his land, but because
it was involved in a question of riparian rights on Dogue Run. The millrace
that GW was currently having dug would, when finished, deliver much water
with increased force to the new mill as planned, but it would do so at the
cost of diverting water from Dogue Run between the dam and the mill, the
stretch on which the Wade-Barry property lay. According to common law, a
property owner who suffered damages from having his water diverted without
his permission could sue the responsible person every year the water was
diverted. Thomas Hanson Marshall, who also owned land on the run in the
affected area, apparently would not be able to claim such damages, because
his land was uninhabited and mostly woodland, but the owners of the Wade-
Barry tract, which was inhabited and farmed, would have grounds to sue GW
(Robert H. Harrison to GW, 5 April 1770, DLC:GW).

GW's purchase today from Valinda Wade solved only part of this problem.
He still had to come to terms with William Barry's father either by purchasing the other half of the land or making some agreement about the riparian rights. However, John Barry was determined to drive a hard bargain and
had refused thus far to cooperate with GW in settling the matter (George W.
Fairfax to GW, 12 Mar. 1770, DLC:GW). The dispute would continue for
several months.

19.   Went to Colchester on an Arbitration between McCraes
Exrs. and John Graham—no business done.

Allan Macrae of Dumfries had died in 1766, and the executors of his will
were Thomas Lawson, of the Neabsco iron furnace in Prince William County,
and Capt. John Lee (1709–1789), who lived on Chopawamsic Creek in Stafford County (*Va. Gaz.,* P&D, 11 Dec. 1766). John Graham (1711–1787), clerk
of the Prince William County court, lived on the south side of Quantico
Creek near Dumfries. He came to Virginia from Scotland about 1740 and acquired much land in Prince William County, including the tract on which
Dumfries was established in 1749 (W.P.A. [1], 94). The dispute between Graham and Macrae's executors probably concerned debts he owed Macrae's
estate; in Mar. 1771 he entrusted three slaves, some livestock and household
furniture, and 200 acres of land adjoining Dumfries to two local merchants
to be sold for the benefit of his creditors (*Va. Gaz.,* R, 28 Mar. 1771). The
arbitrators of the dispute, in addition to GW, were George Mason of Fairfax

County and Thomas Ludwell Lee of Stafford County. They met again on 12 Feb. 1771.

20.   Returnd home.

21.   Rid to the Mill in the fore and Afternoon.

22.   Rid to the Mill & Mill Race in the fore and Afternoon.

Jacky Custis had been indulged with a further reprieve from studying and apparently was now at Mount Vernon again; on this date GW recorded giving the boy £2 6s. 3d. "to buy Sundries at Fred[ericksbur]g" (LEDGER A, 329). Jacky was probably sent to that town to spend the holidays visiting friends and relatives and engaging "in his favorite amusement of Hunting." He returned to Annapolis about 2 Jan. with a professed "determination of applying close to his Studies" (GW to Jonathan Boucher, 2 Jan. 1771, WRITINGS, 3:36–37).

23.   Rid to the Mill before Dinner. At home afterwards alone.

24.   Rid to the Mill again in the fore and afternoon.

25.   Went to Pohick Church and returnd to Dinner.

26.   At Home all day alone.

27.   Went a fox Hunting and killd a fox in Company with the two Mr. Triplets and Mr. Peake who dined here.

28.   At the Mill in the Forenoon and Afternoon.

29.   Went a fox hunting in Company with the two Mr. Triplets & Mr. Peake, found no Fox. Upon my return home found Mr. & Mrs. Cockburn here.

30.   Mr. & Mrs. Cockburn went away. My Miller & his wife and Mr. Ball dind here.

GW's miller was William Roberts, a Pennsylvanian who had signed articles of agreement with Lund Washington 13 Oct. 1770 engaging himself to run the new mill at Mount Vernon for £80 a year plus the privilege of feeding a cow and raising domestic fowl at GW's expense (DLC:GW). Roberts was highly skilled in the business of grinding grain, a delicate art requiring great judgment in fixing the speed and interval of the millstones to produce good-quality flour with minimum waste. He was also, like John Ball, a capable millwright who could keep the mill in proper working order, and when he was not grinding grain, he could work in the nearby cooper's shop making barrels needed for flour and other products. Aided by an apprentice miller whom he had brought with him, Roberts worked diligently and honestly for GW for several years, but an addiction to liquor eventually proved to be his undoing (GW to Robert Lewis & Sons, 6 Sept. 1783, and 12 April 1785, DLC:GW).

31.   I rid to My Mill in the forenoon and Afternoon. Nancy Peake came here.

GW gave Nancy £10 as a loan for her father, Humphrey Peake, who repaid the sum in June (LEDGER A, 307).

Acct. of the Weather in Decemr.

Decr. 1st.   Cold & Raw in the forenoon & constant Snow in the Afternoon.

2.   Clear, & tolerably pleasant, except being Cool. Wind at No. West.

3.   Clear & cool, Wind at No. West, & Ground hard froze As it has been for several days.

4.   Clear and Cool, Wind being Northwardly in the forenoon & Southwardly afterwards.

5.   Lowering & like for Snow in the forenoon – but clearer afterwards.

6.   Warm Morning but Cold & blustering Afternoon. Wind No. West.

7.   Tolerably pleasant wind Southerly.

8.   Calm and pleasant Morning but windy & cool afterwards.

9.   Pleasant day and clear with but little Wind.

10.   Very pleasant. Calm, clear & warm.

11.   Lowery Morning and dripping Afternoon.

12.   Drisling all the forenoon. In the Afternoon Rain.

13. Clear Morning & pleasant, but Cloudy & blustering afterwards from the No. Wt.

14. Clear and not windy—nor so cold as Yesterday.

15. Calm and Pleasant forenoon—a little lowering in the afternn.

16. Quite Calm, clear, and exceeding pleasant.

17. Very pleasant Morning, but Cloudy & blustering afterwards.

18. Pleasant again tho a little Cool & frosty.

19. Calm, clear, and Pleasant.

20. Very pleasant, being clear and Calm.

21. Lowering Morning with a little Rain—but clear afterwards & windy.

22. High wind all day from the North West—but not very cold.

23. Clear & pleasant Morning but windy afterwards & a little Cloudy.

24. Cloudy & like for Rain but none fell.

25. Snowing in the Morning, but clear afterwards and Cool. Snow about an Inch deep.

26. Clear and pleasant with but little Wind.

27. Frosty Morning but clear and pleasant afterwards.

28. Clear and pleasant with but little Wind.

29. Very pleasant and quite Calm but somewhat lowering.

30. Exceeding pleast. calm and clear.

31. Also clear and Pleasant.

December 1770

[Remarks and Occurences in December]

Saturday 1st. Reachd home being absent from it Nine weeks and one day.

11th. Agreed with Christr. Shade to drive my Waggon by the year for the doing of which I am to find him in Bed, Board, & Washing, and to pay him Eighteen pounds a year.

Shade was employed by GW as his wagoner until the end of 1774 (LEDGER A, 331; LEDGER B, 39).

19. Finishd digging & levelling the Mill Race from Piney Branch.

The Piney Branch dam had also been completed, and water could now be diverted from the branch into the race.

22. Began to Grind Sand in my Mill the Water being let in upon the Fore Bay.

Dry sand was being ground between the new millstones "to smooth down the sharp points" on their faces. When the faces were fully finished and fitted together, they would be furrowed and dressed for grinding grain (CRAIK [1], 298–99). The forebay was a deep reservoir at the end of the millrace, from which water was taken to run the waterwheel.

27. Shut up Singer after She had been first lined by one or two Cur Dogs. Jowler being put in with her lind her several times; and his Puppies if to be distinguished saved.

29. Truelove another Hound Bitch Shut up with Ringwood & by him alone lined.

Repository Symbols

Bibliography

Index

Repository Symbols

CLU-C	University of California, Los Angeles, William Andrews Clark Memorial Library
CSmH	Henry Huntington Library, San Marino, Calif.
DLC	Library of Congress
DLC:GW	George Washington Papers, Library of Congress
DNA	National Archives
IaST	Scottish Rite Temple, Des Moines, Iowa
IEN	Northwestern University, Evanston, Ill.
MdAN	U.S. Naval Academy, Annapolis, Md.
MiU-C	Clements Library, University of Michigan, Ann Arbor
MnHi	Minnesota Historical Society, Saint Paul
MoSW	Washington University, St. Louis, Mo.
NjMoNP	Washington Headquarters Library, Morristown, N.J.
NjP	Princeton University
NN	New York Public Library
NNC	Columbia University
NNebgGW	Washington's Headquarters, Jonathan Hasbrouck House, Newburgh, N.Y.
NNPM	Pierpont Morgan Library, New York
PHi	Historical Society of Pennsylvania, Philadelphia
PPRF	Rosenbach Foundation, Philadelphia
P.R.O.	Public Record Office, London
Vi	Virginia State Library, Richmond
ViHi	Virginia Historical Society, Richmond
ViMtV	Mount Vernon Ladies' Association of the Union
ViU	University of Virginia, Charlottesville
ViWaC	Fauquier County Circuit Court, Warrenton, Va.
WHi	State Historical Society of Wisconsin, Madison

Bibliography

ABERNETHY   Thomas Perkins Abernethy. *Western Lands and the American Revolution.* New York: Russell & Russell, 1959.

BAILEY [1]   L. H. Bailey. *Manual of Cultivated Plants.* New York: Macmillan Co., 1925.

BAILEY [2]   L. H. Bailey and Ethel Zoe Bailey. *Hortus, a Concise Dictionary of Gardening, General Horticulture, and Cultivated Plants in North America.* New York: Macmillan Co., 1934.

BAILEY [3]   Kenneth P. Bailey. *The Ohio Company of Virginia and the Westward Movement, 1748–1792: A Chapter in the History of the Colonial Frontier.* Glendale, Calif.: Arthur H. Clark Co., 1939.

BAILEY [4]   Kenneth P. Bailey. *Thomas Cresap, Maryland Frontiersman.* Boston: Christopher Publishing House, 1944.

BALDWIN   Leland D. Baldwin. *The Keelboat Age on Western Waters.* Pittsburgh: University of Pittsburgh Press, 1941.

BALLAGH   James Curtis Ballagh, ed. *The Letters of Richard Henry Lee.* 2 vols. New York: Macmillan Co., 1911–14.

BEALL   Fielder Montgomery Magruder Beall. *Colonial Families of the United States Descended from the Immigrants Who Arrived before 1700, Mostly from England and Scotland, and Who Are Now Represented by Citizens of the Following Names, Bell, Beal, Bale, Beale, Beall.* Washington, D.C.: C. H. Potter & Co., 1929.

BLANTON   Wyndham B. Blanton. *Medicine in Virginia in the Eighteenth Century.* Richmond: Garrett & Massie, 1931.

BOND   Beverly W. Bond, Jr., ed. *The Courses of the Ohio River Taken by Lt. T. Hutchins Anno 1766 and Two Accompanying Maps.* Cincinnati: Historical and Philosophical Society of Ohio, 1942.

Bibliography

BOUCHER [1]   Jonathan Boucher. *Reminiscenses of an American Loyalist, 1738–1789, Being the Autobiography of the Revd. Jonathan Boucher, Rector of Annapolis in Maryland and Afterwards Vicar of Epsom, Surrey, England.* Boston and New York: Houghton Mifflin Co., 1925.

BOUCHER [2]   Jonathan Boucher. *A View of the Causes and Consequences of the American Revolution: in Thirteen Discourses, Preached in North America between the Years 1763 and 1775; with an Historical Preface.* London: G. G. & J. Robinson, 1797.

BROWN   Stuart E. Brown, Jr. *Virginia Baron: The Story of Thomas 6th Lord Fairfax.* Berryville, Va.: Chesapeake Book Co., 1965.

BRUMBAUGH   Gaius Marcus Brumbaugh. *Maryland Records: Colonial, Revolutionary, County, and Church from Original Sources.* Vol. 1. Baltimore: Williams & Wilkins Co., 1915.

BURSON   R. E. Burson. "A Report of the Findings of Mr. R. E. Burson on the George Washington Grist Mill, Situated on Dogue Run Creek, Mount Vernon, Va." Mimeographed Report. Richmond: Virginia Division of Parks, 23 March 1932.

BUTTERFIELD [1]   Consul Willshire Butterfield. *The Washington-Crawford Letters, Being the Correspondence between George Washington and William Crawford, from 1767 to 1781, concerning Western Lands.* Cincinnati: Robert Clarke & Co., 1877.

BUTTERFIELD [2]   Lyman H. Butterfield. "Worthington Chauncey Ford, Editor." Massachusetts Historical Society *Proceedings,* 83 (1971), 46–82.

CALLAHAN   Charles H. Callahan. *Washington: The Man and the Mason.* Washington, D.C.: Gibson Bros. Press, 1913.

CAMPBELL [1]   Thomas Elliott Campbell. *Colonial Caroline: A History of Caroline County, Virginia.* Richmond: Dietz Press, 1954.

CAMPBELL [2]   Charles A. Campbell. "Rochambeau's Headquarters in Westchester County, N.Y., 1781." *Magazine of American History,* 4 (1880), 46–48.

CARTER [1]   Clarence E. Carter. *Great Britain and the Illinois Country, 1763–74.* Washington, D.C.: American Historical Association, 1910.

CARTER [2]   Clarence E. Carter. "Documents Relating to the Mississippi Land Company, 1763–69." *American Historical Review,* 16 (1910–11), 311–36.

CARTER [3]   Jack P. Greene, ed. *The Diary of Colonel Landon Carter of Sabine Hall, 1752–1778.* 2 vols. Charlottesville: University Press of Virginia, 1965.

CARY   Wilson Miles Cary. "Wilson Cary of Ceelys, and His Family." *Virginia Magazine of History and Biography,* 9 (1901), 104–11.

CHAMBERLAYNE   C. G. Chamberlayne, ed. *The Vestry Book and Register of St. Peter's Parish, New Kent and James City Counties, Virginia, 1684–1786.* Richmond: Virginia State Library, 1937.

CHITWOOD   Oliver P. Chitwood. *Justice in Colonial Virginia.* 1905. Reprint, New York: Da Capo Press, 1971.

CLARK [1]   James Alton James, ed. *George Rogers Clark Papers, 1771–1781.* Collections of the Illinois State Historical Library, vol. 8 [Virginia Series, vol. 3]. Springfield: Illinois State Historical Library, 1912.

CLARK [2]   Raymond B. Clark, Jr. "The Abbey, or Ringgold House, at Chestertown, Maryland." *Maryland Historical Magazine,* 46 (1951), 81–92.

CLELAND   Hugh Cleland. *George Washington in the Ohio Valley.* Pittsburgh: University of Pittsburgh Press, 1955.

COOK   Roy Bird Cook. *Washington's Western Lands.* Strasburg, Va.: Shenandoah Publishing House, 1930.

CRAIG   Neville B. Craig, ed. *The Olden Time; a Monthly Publication Devoted to the Preservation of Documents and Other Authentic Information in Relation to the Early Explorations and the Settlement and Improvement of the Country around the Head of the Ohio.* 1848. Reprint, 2 vols., 2d ed., Cincinnati: Robert Clarke & Co., 1876.

CRAIK [1]   David Craik. *The Practical American Mill-wright and Miller: Comprising the Elementary Principles of Mechanics, Mechanism, and Motive Power, Hydraulics, and Hydraulic Motors, Mill Dams, Saw-Mills, Grist-Mills, the Oat-Meal Mill, the Barley Mill, Wool Carding and Cloth Fulling and Dressing, Windmills, Steam Power, etc.* Philadelphia: Henry Carey Baird, Industrial Publisher, 1870.

CRAIK [2]   James Craik. "Boyhood Memories of Dr. James Craik, D.D., L.L.D." *Virginia Magazine of History and Biography,* 46 (1938), 135–45.

CRAMER   Zadok Cramer. *The Navigator: Containing Directions for Navigating the Monongahela, Allegheny, Ohio, and Mississippi Rivers; with an Ample Account of These Much Admired Waters, from the Head of the Former to the Mouth of the Latter; and a Concise Description of Their Towns, Villages, Harbours, Settlements, &c.* 7th ed. Pittsburgh: Cramer, Spear & Eichbaum, 1811.

CRESSWELL   Lincoln MacVeagh, ed. *The Journal of Nicholas Cresswell, 1774–1777.* New York: Dial Press, 1924.

CROZIER [1] William Armstrong Crozier, ed. *Virginia Colonial Militia, 1651–1776.* Baltimore: Southern Book Co., 1954.

CROZIER [2] William Armstrong Crozier, ed. *Spotsylvania County Records, 1721–1800.* Baltimore: Southern Book Co., 1955.

CUSTIS ACCOUNT BOOK GW's Accounts Kept for Martha Parke Custis and John Parke Custis, 1760–1775. Manuscript in Custis Papers, Virginia Historical Society, Richmond.

DIARIES   John C. Fitzpatrick, ed. *The Diaries of George Washington, 1748–1799.* 4 vols. Boston and New York: Houghton Mifflin Co., 1925.

EATON   David W. Eaton. *Historical Atlas of Westmoreland County, Virginia; Patents Showing How Lands Were Patented from the Crown & Proprietors of the Northern Neck of Virginia, Including Some History of the Patentees, Indians, Church & State, Parishes, Ministers, Prominent Men, Surveys, Portraits, Maps, Airplane Views, & Other Data.* Richmond: Dietz Press, 1942.

Bibliography

EUBANK H. Ragland Eubank. *Touring Historyland: The Authentic Guide Book of Historic Northern Neck of Virginia, the Land of George Washington and Robert E. Lee.* Colonial Beach, Va.: Northern Neck Association, 1934.

FARQUHAR Charles Stonehill, ed. *The Complete Works of George Farquhar.* 2 vols. New York: Gordian Press, 1967.

FISHER "Narrative of George Fisher." *William and Mary Quarterly,* 1st ser., 17 (1908–9), 100–139, 147–76.

FITHIAN Hunter Dickinson Farish, ed. *Journal & Letters of Philip Vickers Fithian, 1773–1774: A Plantation Tutor of the Old Dominion.* Williamsburg, Va.: Colonial Williamsburg, Inc., 1943.

FLIPPIN Percy Scott Flippin. *The Royal Government in Virginia.* Columbia University Studies in History, Economics and Public Law, Vol. 84, No. 194. New York: Columbia University Press, 1919.

FORD [1] Worthington Chauncey Ford. "Washington's Map of the Ohio." Massachusetts Historical Society *Proceedings,* 61 (1927–28), 71–79.

FORD [2] Worthington Chauncey Ford, ed. *The Writings of George Washington.* 14 vols. New York: G. P. Putnam's Sons, 1889–93.

FORD [3] Worthington Chauncey Ford, ed. *Letters of Jonathan Boucher to George Washington.* Brooklyn, N.Y.: Historical Printing Club, 1899.

FREEMAN Douglas Southall Freeman. *George Washington.* 7 vols. New York: Charles Scribner's Sons, 1949–57.

FRENCH TRAVELLER "Journal of a French Traveller in the Colonies, 1765, I." *American Historical Review,* 26 (1920–21), 726–47.

FRONTIER FORTS *Report of the Commission to Locate the Site of the Frontier Forts of Pennsylvania.* 2 vols. N.p.: Clarence M. Busch, 1896.

GAGE PAPERS Clarence Edwin Carter, ed. *The Correspondence of General Thomas Gage with the Secretaries of State, and with the War Office and the Treasury.* 1933. Reprint, 2 vols., n.p.: Archon Books, 1969.

GARNETT [1]   James Mercer Garnett. "James Mercer." *William and Mary Quarterly,* 1st ser., 17 (1908–9), 85–99, 204–23.

GARNETT [2]   James Mercer Garnett. *Biographical Sketch of Hon. James Mercer Garnett of Elmwood, Essex County, Virginia with Mercer-Garnett and Mercer Genealogies.* Richmond: Whittet & Shepperson, Printers, 1910.

GAY   John Gay. *The Beggar's Opera.* Ed. Peter Elfed Lewis. Edinburgh: Oliver & Boyd, 1973.

GERALD   Herbert P. Gerald. "Marshall Hall Burying Ground at Marshall Hall, Md." *Maryland Historical Magazine,* 24 (1929), 172–76.

GIBBS   Patricia Ann Gibbs. "Taverns in Tidewater Virginia, 1700–1774." Master's thesis, College of William and Mary, 1968.

GILL   Harold B. Gill, Jr. *The Apothecary in Colonial Virginia.* Williamsburg, Va.: Colonial Williamsburg, Inc., 1972.

GIST   William M. Darlington, ed. *Christopher Gist's Journals with Historical, Geographical, and Ethnological Notes and Biographies of His Contemporaries.* Cleveland: Arthur H. Clark Co., 1893.

GLOUCESTER   Polly Cary Mason, comp. *Records of Colonial Gloucester County, Virginia: A Collection of Abstracts from Original Documents concerning the Lands and People of Colonial Gloucester County.* 2 vols. Newport News, Va.: Mrs. George C. Mason, 1946–48.

GOODWIN   Edward Lewis Goodwin. *The Colonial Church in Virginia.* Milwaukee: Morehouse Publishing Co., 1927.

GOOLRICK   John T. Goolrick. *Fredericksburg and the Cavalier Country, America's Most Historic Section, Its Homes: Its People and Romances.* Richmond: Garrett & Massie, Publishers, 1935.

GORDON   "Journal of Captain Harry Gordon, 1766." *In* Newton D. Mereness, ed. *Travels in the American Colonies.* New York: Macmillan Co., 1916.

GREENE [1]   Jack P. Greene. "The Case of the Pistole Fee." *Virginia Magazine of History and Biography,* 66 (1958), 399–422.

GREENE [2]   Evarts B. Greene and Virginia D. Harrington, eds. *American Population before the Federal Census of 1790.* New York: Columbia University Press, 1932.

GRINNAN   Daniel Grinnan. "James Taylor." *Virginia Magazine of History and Biography,* 34 (1926), 366–67.

GWATHMEY   John Hastings Gwathmey. *Historical Register of Virginians in the Revolution: Soldiers, Sailors, Marines, 1775–1783.* Richmond: Dietz Press, 1938.

HAMILTON [1]   Stanislaus Murray Hamilton, ed. *Letters to Washington and Accompanying Papers.* 5 vols. Boston and New York: Houghton Mifflin Co., 1898–1902.

HAMILTON [2]   Harold C. Syrett, ed. *The Papers of Alexander Hamilton.* New York: Columbia University Press, 1961–.

HANNA   Charles A. Hanna. *The Wilderness Trail, or The Ventures and Adventures of the Pennsylvania Traders on the Allegheny Path.* 2 vols. New York: G. P. Putnam's Sons, 1911.

HANSON   George A. Hanson. *Old Kent: The Eastern Shore of Maryland.* Baltimore: John P. Des Forges, 1876.

HARRISON [1]   Fairfax Harrison. *Landmarks of Old Prince William.* Reprint. Berryville, Va.: Chesapeake Book Co., 1964.

HARRISON [2]   Fairfax Harrison. *The Proprietors of the Northern Neck.* Richmond: Old Dominion Press, 1926.

HAYDEN   Horace Edwin Hayden. *Virginia Genealogies: A Genealogy of the Glassell Family of Scotland and Virginia.* 1891. Reprint, Baltimore: Genealogical Publishing Co., 1973.

H.B.J.   H. R. McIlwaine and John Pendleton Kennedy, eds. *Journals of the House of Burgesses of Virginia.* 13 vols. Richmond: Virginia State Library, 1905–15.

HEADS OF FAMILIES   *Heads of Families at the First Census of the United States Taken in the Year 1790: Virginia.* 1908. Reprint, Baltimore: Genealogical Publishing Co., 1970.

HENING   William Waller Hening, ed. *The Statutes at Large; Being a Collection of All the Laws of*

Bibliography

Virginia from the First Session of the Legislature, in the Year 1619. 13 vols. New York, Philadelphia, Richmond: various publishers, 1819–23.

HENNEMAN   J. B. Henneman. "Trustees of Hampden-Sidney College." *Virginia Magazine of History and Biography,* 6 (1898–99), 174–84, 288–96, 358–64; 7 (1899–1900), 30–38.

HOBERG   Walter R. Hoberg. "Early History of Colonel Alexander McKee." *Pennsylvania Magazine of History and Biography,* 58 (1934), 26–36.

HODGES   Frances Beal Smith Hodges. *The Genealogy of the Beale Family, 1399–1956.* Ann Arbor, Mich.: Edwards Brothers, 1956.

HOOPER   Robert Hooper. *Lexicon-Medicum or Medical Dictionary: Containing an Explanation of the Terms in Anatomy, Botany, Chemistry, Materia Medica, Midwifery, Mineralogy, Pharmacy, Physiology, Practice of Physic, Surgery, and the Various Branches of Natural Philosophy Connected with Medicine; Selected, Arranged, and Compiled from the Best Authors.* New York: J. & J. Harper, 1826.

HUTCHINS   Thomas Hutchins. *A Topographical Description of Virginia, Pennsylvania, Maryland, and North Carolina, Comprehending the Rivers Ohio, Kenhawa, Sioto, Cherokee, Wabash, Illinois, Mississippi, &c. . . .* London: J. Almon, 1778.

ISLE OF WIGHT   "Isle of Wight County Records." *William and Mary Quarterly,* 1st ser., 7 (1899), 205–315.

JETT   Dora C. Jett. *Minor Sketches of Major Folk and Where They Sleep: The Old Masonic Burying Ground, Fredericksburg, Virginia.* Richmond: Old Dominion Press, 1928.

JOHNSON PAPERS   *The Papers of Sir William Johnson.* 14 vols. Albany: University of the State of New York, 1921–65.

JOLLIFFE   William Jolliffe. *Historical, Genealogical, and Biographical Account of the Jolliffe Family of Virginia, 1652 to 1893.* Philadelphia: J. B. Lippincott Co., 1893.

JONES [1]   Hugh Jones. *The Present State of Virginia from Whence Is Inferred a Short View of Maryland and North Carolina.* Ed. Richard L.

Morton. Chapel Hill: University of North Carolina Press, 1956.

JONES [2]   William Jones. *Finger-Ring Lore: Historical, Legendary, & Anecdotal.* London: Chatto & Windus, 1898.

KEITH [1]   Arthur L. Keith. "The Enoch (Enochs) Family." *Tyler's Quarterly Magazine,* 4 (1922–23), 442–45.

KEITH [2]   Charles P. Keith. "Andrew Allen." *Pennsylvania Magazine of History and Biography,* 10 (1886), 361–65.

KEMPER   Charles E. Kemper. "Notes to Council Journals." *Virginia Magazine of History and Biography,* 33 (1925), 25–46.

KENNER   "Kenner Family." *William and Mary Quarterly,* 1st ser., 14 (1906), 173–79.

KENNY   John W. Jordan, ed. "Journal of James Kenny, 1761–1763." *Pennsylvania Magazine of History and Biography,* 37 (1913), 152–201.

KERCHEVAL   Samuel Kercheval. *A History of the Valley of Virginia.* 4th ed. Strasburg, Va.: Shenandoah Publishing House, 1925.

KETCHUM   Richard M. Ketchum. *The World of George Washington.* New York: American Heritage Publishing Co., 1974.

KING [1]   Lester S. King. *The Medical World of the Eighteenth Century.* Chicago: University of Chicago Press, 1958.

KING [2]   George H. S. King. "General George Weedon." *William and Mary Quarterly,* 2d ser., 20 (1940), 237–52.

KING [3]   George H. S. King. "Some Notes on the Coleman Family of Caroline County, Virginia." *Virginia Magazine of History and Biography,* 54 (1946), 258–60.

KING [4]   Junie Estelle Stewart King, comp. *Abstract of Wills and Inventories, Fairfax County, Virginia, 1742–1801.* Beverly Hills, Calif.: privately printed, 1936.

KINGSMILL   "Kingsmill Plantation." *William and Mary Quarterly,* 1st ser., 12 (1903–4), 24.

KOONTZ   Louis K. Koontz. *The Virginia Frontier, 1754–1763.* Baltimore: Johns Hopkins Press, 1925.

LABAREE [1] Leonard W. Labaree, ed. *Royal Instructions to British Colonial Governors, 1670–1776.* 1935. Reprint, 2 vols., New York: Octagon Books, 1967.

LABAREE [2] Benjamin Woods Labaree. *The Boston Tea Party.* New York: Oxford University Press, 1964.

LAND Aubrey C. Land. *The Dulanys of Maryland: A Biographical Study of Daniel Dulany, the Elder (1685–1753) and Daniel Dulany, the Younger (1722–1797).* Baltimore: Maryland Historical Society, 1955.

LEDGER A Manuscript Ledger in George Washington Papers, Library of Congress.

LEDGER B Manuscript Ledger in George Washington Papers, Library of Congress.

LEE [1] Cazenove Gardner Lee, Jr. *Lee Chronicle.* Ed. Dorothy Mills Parker. New York: New York University Press, 1957.

LEE [2] Worthington Chauncey Ford, ed. *Letters of William Lee.* 3 vols. Brooklyn, N.Y.: Historical Printing Club, 1891.

MACAULAY Alexander Macaulay. "Journal of Alexander Macaulay." *William and Mary Quarterly,* 1st ser., 11 (1902–3), 180–91.

MCDONALD Cornelia McDonald. *A Diary with Reminiscences of the War and Refugee Life in the Shenandoah Valley, 1860–1865.* Nashville: Cullom & Ghertner Co., 1935.

MACKENZIE [1] George Norbury Mackenzie, ed. *Colonial Families of the United States of America.* 7 vols. Baltimore: Genealogical Publishing Co., 1966.

MACKENZIE [2] Frederick Mackenzie. *Diary of Frederick Mackenzie, Giving a Daily Narrative of His Military Service as an Officer of the Regiment of Royal Welch Fusiliers during the Years 1775–1781 in Massachusetts, Rhode Island, and New York.* 2 vols. Cambridge, Mass.: Harvard University Press, 1930.

MACMASTER Richard K. MacMaster and David C. Skaggs, eds. "The Letterbooks of Alexander Hamilton, Piscataway Factor." *Maryland Historical Magazine,* 61 (1966), 146–66, 305–28; 62 (1967), 135–69.

Bibliography

MALONE [1]   Miles S. Malone. "Falmouth and the Shenandoah: Trade before the Revolution." *American Historical Review*, 40 (1934–35), 693–703.

MALONE [2]   Dumas Malone. *Jefferson and His Time*. Boston: Little, Brown and Co., 1948–.

MASON [1]   Frances Norton Mason, ed. *John Norton & Sons, Merchants of London and Virginia: Being the Papers from Their Counting House for the Years 1750 to 1795*. New York: Augustus M. Kelley, Publishers, 1968.

MASON [2]   Robert A. Rutland, ed. *The Papers of George Mason, 1725–1792*. 3 vols. Chapel Hill: University of North Carolina Press, 1970.

MAYS   David John Mays. *Edmund Pendleton, 1721–1803: A Biography*. 2 vols. Cambridge, Mass.: Harvard University Press, 1952.

MD. ARCHIVES   *Archives of Maryland*. Baltimore: Maryland Historical Society, 1883–.

MEADE [1]   William Meade. *Old Churches, Ministers, and Families of Virginia*. 2 vols. Philadelphia: J. B. Lippincott Co., 1910.

MEADE [2]   Everard Kidder Meade. "Frederick Parish, Virginia, 1744–1780: Its Churches, Chapels, and Ministers." *Proceedings of the Clarke County Historical Association*, 5 (1945), 18–38.

MOORE [1]   Gay Montague Moore. *Seaport in Virginia: George Washington's Alexandria*. Reprint. Charlottesville: University Press of Virginia, 1972.

MOORE [2]   Frank Moore. *Diary of the American Revolution*. 2 vols. New York: Charles Scribner, 1859.

MORTON   Louis Morton. *Robert Carter of Nomini Hall, a Virginia Tobacco Planter of the Eighteenth Century*. Williamsburg, Va.: Colonial Williamsburg, Inc., 1941.

MUIR   Dorothy Troth Muir. *Potomac Interlude: The Story of Woodlawn Mansion and the Mount Vernon Neighborhood, 1846–1943*. Washington, D.C.: Mount Vernon Print Shop, 1943.

MVAR   Mount Vernon Ladies' Association of the Union *Annual Report*.

Bibliography

NAVAL OFFICE — "Naval Office on the Potomac." *William and Mary Quarterly,* 2d ser., 2 (1922), 292–95.

NICKLIN [1] — J. B. Calvert Nicklin. "The Barnesfield Graveyard." *Virginia Magazine of History and Biography,* 48 (1940), 368–72.

NICKLIN [2] — J. B. Calvert Nicklin. "The Calvert Family." *Maryland Historical Magazine,* 16 (1921), 50–59, 189–204, 313–18, 389–94.

NORRIS [1] — J. E. Norris, ed. *History of the Lower Shenandoah Valley.* Chicago: A. Warner & Co., 1890.

NORRIS [2] — Walter B. Norris. *Annapolis: Its Colonial and Naval History.* New York: Thomas Y. Crowell Co., 1925.

PETSWORTH — C. G. Chamberlayne, ed. *The Vestry Book of Petsworth Parish, Gloucester County, Va., 1677–1793.* Richmond: Virginia State Library, 1933.

POWELL — Mary G. Powell. *The History of Old Alexandria, Virginia, from July 13, 1749, to May 24, 1861.* Richmond: William Byrd Press, 1928.

POWNALL — Thomas Pownall. *A Topographical Description of the Dominions of the United States of America.* Ed. Lois Mulkearn. Pittsburgh: University of Pittsburgh Press, 1949.

RALEIGH TAVERN — *The Raleigh Tavern.* Williamsburg, Va.: Colonial Williamsburg, Inc., 1934.

RANDOLPH — John Randolph. *A Treatise on Gardening by a Citizen of Virginia.* Ed. M. F. Warner. Reprint. Richmond: Appeals Press, 1924.

RANKIN — Hugh F. Rankin. *The Theater in Colonial America.* Chapel Hill: University of North Carolina Press, 1960.

RICE — Howard C. Rice, Jr., and Anne S. K. Brown, eds. *The American Campaigns of Rochambeau's Army, 1780, 1781, 1782, 1783.* 2 vols. Princeton, N.J., and Providence: Princeton University Press and Brown University Press, 1972.

RICHMOND COUNTY — "Marriages, Births and Deaths in Richmond County, Extracts from North Farnham Parish Register Kept in the Clerk's Office at Warsaw." *William and Mary Quarterly,* 1st ser., 13 (1904–5), 129–32, 182–92.

Bibliography

RIGHTMYER   Nelson Waite Rightmyer. *Maryland's Established Church*. Baltimore: Church Historical Society for the Diocese of Maryland, 1956.

ROTH   Cecil Roth et al. *Encyclopedia Judaica*. 16 vols. New York: Macmillan Co., 1971–72.

ROWLAND [1]   Kate Mason Rowland, ed. *The Life of Charles Carroll of Carrollton, 1737–1832, with His Correspondence and Public Papers*. 2 vols. New York: G. P. Putnam's Sons, 1898.

ROWLAND [2]   Kate Mason Rowland, ed. *The Life of George Mason, 1725–1792*. 2 vols. New York: G. P. Putnam's Sons, 1892.

RUFFIN   "Ruffin Family." *William and Mary Quarterly*, 1st ser., 18 (1909–10), 251–58.

SAGE AND JONES   Clara McCormack Sage and Laura Sage Jones. *Early Records, Hampshire County, Virginia, Now West Virginia, Including at the Start Most of Known Va. Aside from Augusta District*. Delavan, Wis.: Delavan Republican, 1939.

SIMS   Edgar B. Sims. *Sims Index to Land Grants in West Virginia*. Charleston, W.Va.: State of West Virginia, 1952.

SINGEWALD   Joseph T. Singewald, Jr. *The Iron Ores of Maryland with an Account of the Iron Industry*. Baltimore: Johns Hopkins Press, 1911.

SKAGGS   David C. Skaggs and Richard K. MacMaster, eds. "Post-Revolutionary Letters of Alexander Hamilton, Piscataway Merchant." *Maryland Historical Magazine*, 63 (1968), 22–54; 65 (1970), 18–35.

SLAUGHTER [1]   Philip Slaughter. *The History of Truro Parish in Virginia*. Philadelphia: G. W. Jacobs & Co., 1908.

SLAUGHTER [2]   Philip Slaughter. *A History of St. Mark's Parish, Culpeper County, Virginia, with Notes of Old Churches and Old Families and Illustrations of the Manners and Customs of the Olden Time*. Baltimore: Innes & Co., 1877.

SMYTH   John Ferdinand Dalziel Smyth. *A Tour in the United States of America; Containing an Account of the Present Situation of That Country; The Population, Agriculture, Commerce, Customs, and Manners of the Inhab-*

Bibliography

itants. . . . 2 vols. London: Printed for G. Robinson, J. Robson, and J. Stewell, 1784.

SNODDY   Mrs. Allen B. Snoddy. "Ball Notes." *Virginia Magazine of History and Biography,* 23 (1915), 308–09.

SORLEY   Merrow Egerton Sorley. *Lewis of Warner Hall: The History of a Family.* Columbia, Mo.: E. W. Stephens Co., 1937.

SOSIN   Jack M. Sosin. *Whitehall and the Wilderness: The Middle West in British Colonial Policy, 1760–1775.* Lincoln: University of Nebraska Press, 1961.

ST. ANN'S   "Vestry Proceedings, St. Ann's Parish, Annapolis, Md." *Maryland Historical Magazine,* 6 (1911), 325–51; 7 (1912), 59–82, 166–83, 268–86, 395–408; 8 (1913), 66–73, 149–68, 270–86, 353–68; 9 (1914), 47–53, 162–69, 280–89, 336–47; 10 (1915), 37–41, 127–43.

STUDEBAKER   Marvin F. Studebaker. "Freestone from Acquia." *Virginia Cavalcade, 9* (1959–60), 35–41.

SYDNOR   Charles S. Sydnor. *American Revolutionaries in the Making.* 1952. Reprint, New York: Collier-Macmillan, Free Press, 1965.

TORRENCE   Clayton Torrence, comp. *Virginia Wills and Administrations, 1632–1800: An Index of Wills Recorded in Local Courts of Virginia, 1632–1800, and of Administrations on Estates Shown by Inventories of the Estates of Intestates Recorded in Will (and Other) Books of Local Courts, 1632–1800.* 1930. Reprint, Baltimore: Genealogical Publishing Co., 1972.

TREGLE   Thomas Hutchins. *An Historical Narrative and Topographical Description of Louisiana, and West-Florida. A Facsimile Reproduction of the 1784 Edition.* Introduction and Index by Joseph G. Tregle, Jr. Gainesville: University of Florida Press, 1968.

TUNNEY   Hubert J. Tunney, ed. "Home's Douglas." *Bulletin of the University of Kansas,* 25 (1924).

TYLER [1]   Lyon G. Tyler. "Original Records of the Phi Beta Kappa Society." *William and Mary Quarterly,* 1st ser., 4 (1895–96), 213–59.

TYLER [2]   Lyon G. Tyler. "The Smiths of Virginia." *William and Mary Quarterly* 1st ser., 4 (1895–96), 46–52, 95–103, 183–87.

VA. EXEC. JLS.   H. R. McIlwaine, Wilmer L. Hall, and Benjamin Hillman, eds. *Executive Journals of the Council of Colonial Virginia.* 6 vols. Richmond: Virginia State Library, 1925–66.

VA. TROOPS   "Virginia Troops in French and Indian Wars." *Virginia Magazine of History and Biography,* 1 (1893–94), 278–87, 378–90.

VAUGHAN   Samuel Vaughan. "Minutes made by S. V. from Stage to Stage on a Tour to Fort Pitt or Pittsbourg in Company with Mr. Michl. Morgan Obrian, from Thence by S. V. Only through Virginia, Maryland, & Pensylvania (18 June to 4 Sept. 1787)." Manuscript diary in the collection of the descendants of Samuel Vaughan.

VIRKUS   Frederick Adams Virkus, ed. *The Compendium of American Genealogy: The Standard Genealogical Encyclopedia of the First Families of America.* 7 vols. Chicago: various publishers, 1925–42.

WAINWRIGHT   Nicholas B. Wainwright. *George Croghan, Wilderness Diplomat.* Chapel Hill: University of North Carolina Press, 1959.

WALKER   Leola O. Walker. "Officials in the City Government of Colonial Williamsburg." *Virginia Magazine of History and Biography,* 75 (1967), 35–51.

WATERMAN   Thomas Tileston Waterman. *The Mansions of Virginia, 1706–1776.* Chapel Hill: University of North Carolina Press, 1946.

WATKINS   C. Malcolm Watkins. *The Cultural History of Marlborough, Virginia.* Washington, D.C.: Smithsonian Institution Press, 1968.

WAYLAND [1]   John Walter Wayland. *The Washingtons and Their Homes.* 1944. Reprint, Berryville, Va.: Virginia Book Co., 1973.

WAYLAND [2]   John Walter Wayland. *Historic Homes of Northern Virginia and the Eastern Panhandle of West Virginia.* Staunton, Va.: McClure Co., 1937.

Bibliography

WEBB [1] Lyon G. Tyler, ed. "The Webb Family." *Tyler's Quarterly Magazine*, 7 (1925–26), 191–98, 269–77.

WEBB [2] Worthington Chauncey Ford, ed. *Correspondence and Journals of Samuel Blachley Webb.* 3 vols. New York: Wickersham Press, 1893.

WILSON George Wilson. "Historical and Genealogical Notes: Gen. Posey-Thornton-Adams, etc." *William and Mary Quarterly*, 1st ser., 6 (1897–98), 65–68.

W.P.A. [1] W.P.A. Writers' Project. *Prince William: The Story of Its People and Its Places.* Manassas, Va.: Bethlehem Good Housekeeping Club, 1941.

W.P.A. [2] W.P.A. Writers' Project. *Maryland: A Guide to the Old Line State.* New York: Oxford University Press, 1940.

WRITINGS John C. Fitzpatrick, ed. *The Writings of George Washington from the Original Manuscript Sources, 1745–1799.* 39 vols. Washington, D.C.: Government Printing Office, 1931–44.

Index

The index in the final volume of the *Diaries* will be complete and extensive. Preliminary indexes, such as the one that follows, consist primarily of references to persons. The abbreviation "id." is used for "identification."

Accotink Creek, 38
Acres, William, 164, 165, 172
Adair, Elizabeth, 158
Adam, Robert, 100, 207, 209, 212, 217, 218, 227, 228, 229, 232, 235, 269
Adams, Abednego, 52, 53, 185-86
Adams, Hannah Moss, 186
Adams, Mary Peake, 52, 186
Adams, Sir Thomas, 250, 253, 262, 263
Adams, William, 254
Addison, Anthony, 123, 126
Addison, Daniel Dulany, 123, 126
Addison, Henry, 123, 126, 153, 154, 238, 250
Addison, Thomas, 123
Addison family, 154
Alexander, Ann ("Nancy"), 126
Alexander, Charles, 69
Alexander, David, 39
Alexander, Frances Brown, 69
Alexander, George Dent, 96, 159, 181, 182, 219, 223
Alexander, George *or* Gerard, 219
Alexander, Gerard (d. 1761), 41, 126
Alexander, John, 44
Alexander, Lucy Thornton, 44
Alexander, Mariamne Stoddert, 188, 189, 255
Alexander, Mary, 175
Alexander, Mary Dent, 126
Alexander, Morgan, 38, 39
Alexander, Philip (1704-1753), 44
Alexander, Philip (d. 1790), 41, 44, 110, 166, 219, 223
Alexander, Robert, 96; fox hunting with GW, 30, 31, 37, 40, 44, 99, 121, 181, 207, 214, 219, 223; at Mount Vernon, 31, 37, 52, 77, 83,

96, 99, 108, 110, 115, 121, 136, 139, 159, 181, 187, 189, 207, 214, 223, 255; at Bryan Fairfax's with GW, 32; hunting dogs, 33, 43, 139; GW visits, 40, 41, 219; location of house, 41; land transactions, 188, 189-90, 245, 255-56; attends Posey's sale, 189
Alexander family, 39
Allan (at Warm Springs), 177, 180
Allerton, Willoughby, 269
Allison, John, 176, 177
Alton, John, 162, 163, 164
Ambler, Edward, 254
Ambler, Mary Cary, 254, 255
Ambler, Sarah, 254
Ariss, John, 135-36
Ashby, Robert, 133, 134
Ashby, Thomas, 133
Ashford, Elizabeth, 221
Ashford, George, 221, 226
Ashford, John, 221, 226
Assunepachla. *See* Frank's Town
Aubrey (sells medicine to GW), 209
Aylett, John, 108
Aylett, William (d. 1744), 63
Aylett, William (1743-c.1781), 108
Ayscough, Anne, 106
Ayscough, Christopher, 106, 150
Ayscough's tavern, 106

Baily, Pierce, 86, 143, 159
Ball, Burgess, 142
Ball, Jesse, 88
Ball, John, 204, 218, 221, 222, 229, 230, 233, 234, 244, 245, 332-33
Ball, Joseph, 226
Ball, Mary Chichester. *See* Chichester, Mary
Ball, Sarah Ellen Payne, 204

[357]

Index

Index